studysync

Table of Contents

studysync®

Reading & Writing Companion

GRADE 10 UNITS

Destiny • Taking a Stand

Technical Difficulties • The Human Connection

studysync

studysync.com

Send all inquiries to:
BookheadEd Learning, LLC
610 Daniel Young Drive
Sonoma, CA 95476

2015 G10

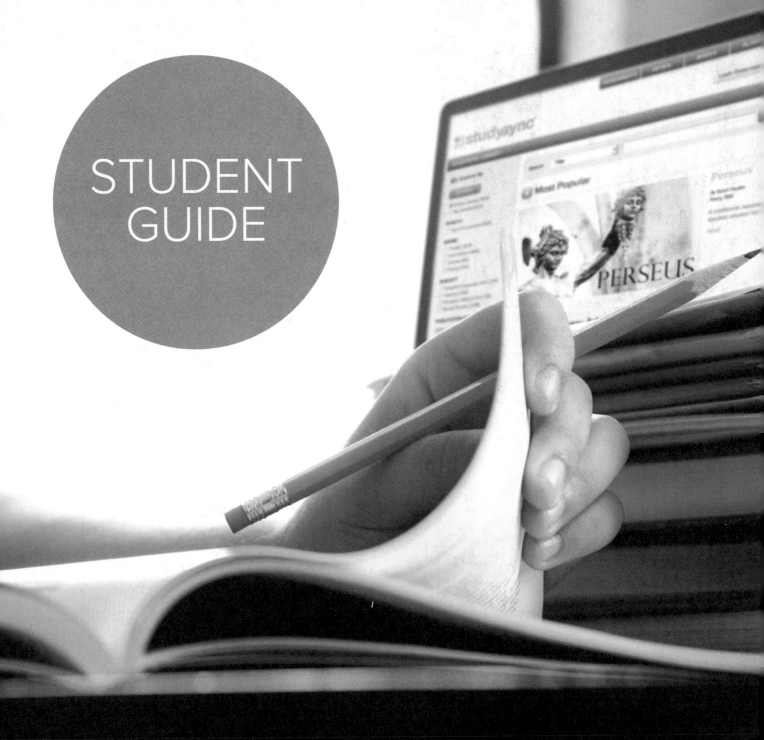

STUDENT GUIDE

GETTING STARTED

Welcome to the StudySync Reading and Writing Companion! In this booklet, you will find a collection of readings based on the theme of the unit you are studying. As you work through the readings, you will be asked to answer questions and perform a variety of tasks designed to help you closely analyze and understand each text selection. Read on for an explanation of

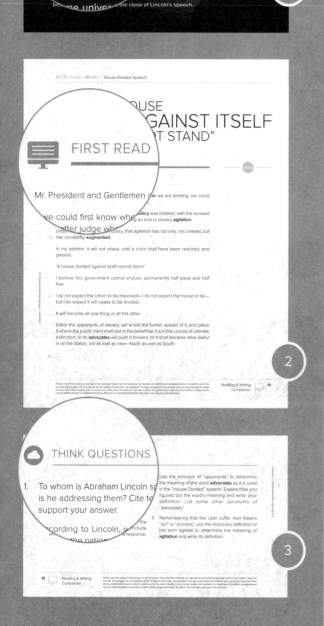

1 INTRODUCTION

An Introduction to each text provides historical context for your reading as well as information about the author. You will also learn about the genre of the excerpt and the year in which it was written.

2 FIRST READ

During your first reading of each excerpt, you should just try to get a general idea of the content and message of the reading. Don't worry if there are parts you don't understand or words that are unfamiliar to you. You'll have an opportunity later to dive deeper into the text.

Many times, while working through the Think Questions after your first read, you will be asked to **annotate** or **make annotations** about what you are reading. This means that you should use the "Notes" column to make comments or jot down any questions you may have about the text. You may also want to note any unfamiliar vocabulary words here.

3 THINK QUESTIONS

These questions will ask you to start thinking critically about the text, asking specific questions about its purpose, and making connections to your prior knowledge and reading experiences. To answer these questions, you should go back to the text and draw upon specific evidence that you find there to support your responses. You will also begin to explore some of the more challenging vocabulary words used in the excerpt.

4 CLOSE READ & FOCUS QUESTIONS

After you have completed the First Read, you will then be asked to go back and read the excerpt more closely and critically. Before you begin your Close Read, you should read through the Focus Questions to get an idea of the concepts you will want to focus on during your second reading. You should work through the Focus Questions by making annotations, highlighting important concepts, and writing notes or questions in the "Notes" column. Depending on instructions from your teacher, you may need to respond online or use a separate piece of paper to start expanding on your thoughts and ideas.

5 WRITING PROMPT

Your study of each excerpt or selection will end with a writing assignment. To complete this assignment, you should use your notes, annotations, and answers to both the Think and Focus Questions. Be sure to read the prompt carefully and address each part of it in your writing assignment.

6 EXTENDED WRITING PROJECT

After you have read and worked through all of the unit text selections, you will move on to a writing project. This project will walk you through steps to plan, draft, revise, edit, and finally publish an essay or other piece of writing about one or more of the texts you have studied in the unit. Student models and graphic organizers will provide guidance and help you organize your thoughts as you plan and write your essay. Throughout the project, you will also study and work on specific writing skills to help you develop different portions of your writing.

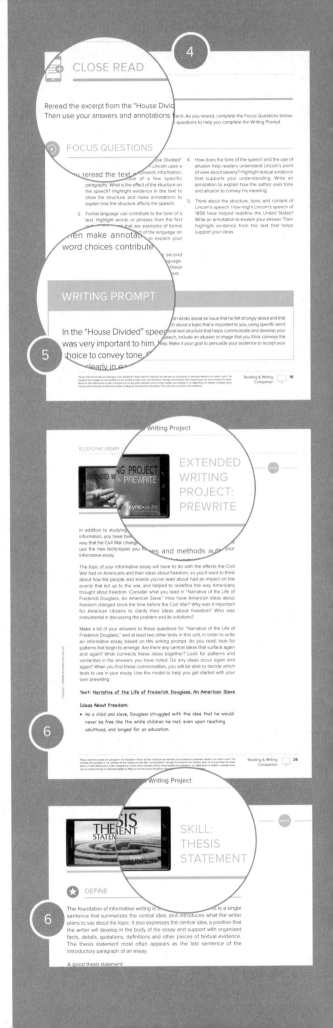

studysync®

Reading & Writing Companion

How much of what happens in our lives do we control?

Destiny

Destiny

 TEXTS

TEXTS

EXTENDED WRITING PROJECT

425

Text Fulfillment through StudySync

THE SPORTS GENE

NON-FICTION
David Epstein
2013

INTRODUCTION

In *The Sports Gene*, author David Epstein takes on the age-old debate of nature v. nurture, investigating how much of an individual's athletic success depends on the fortunate roll of the genetic dice. In this chapter, he finds that the right genes might just mean everything.

"Thomas decided to put his hops where his mouth was."

FIRST READ

Excerpt from Chapter 2: A Tale of Two High Jumpers
(Or: 10,000 Hours Plus or Minus 10,000 Hours)

1   On January 19, 2006, [Donald] Thomas was sitting in the cafeteria at Lindenwood University in Saint Charles, Missouri, boasting about his slam dunking **prowess** with a few guys from the track team. Carlos Mattis, Lindenwood's top high jumper, had enough of Thomas' lip and bet him that he could not clear 6'6" in a high jump competition.

2   Thomas decided to put his hops where his mouth was. He went home and grabbed a pair of sneakers and returned to the Lindenwood field house where a smirking Mattis had already set the bar at 6'6". Mattis stepped back and waited for the big talker to fall to earth. And Thomas did, but the bar did not come with him. To Mattis' amazement, Thomas cleared it easily. So Mattis pushed the bar up to 6'8". Thomas cleared it. Seven feet. Without a semblance of graceful high-jump technique — Thomas hardly arched his back and his legs flailed in the air like the streamers trailing a kite — he cleared it.

3   Mattis rushed Thomas over to the office where head track coach Lane Lohr was organizing his roster for the upcoming Eastern Illinois University Mega Meet and told the coach he had a seven-foot high jumper. "The coach said there's no way I could do that. He didn't believe it," Thomas recalls. "But Carlos was like, 'Yeah, he really did it.' So he asked if I wanted to go to track meet on Saturday." Lohr picked up the phone and pleaded with the meet organizer to permit a late entry.

4   Two days later, in a black tank top and white Nike sneakers and shorts so baggy they blanketed the bar as he passed over it, Thomas cleared 6'8.25" on his first attempt, qualifying for the national championships. Then he cleared 7'0.25" for a new Lindenwood University record. And then, on the seventh high jump attempt of his life, with rigid form akin to a man riding an invisible

deck chair backward through the air, Thomas cleared 7'3.25", a Lantz Indoor Fieldhouse record. That's when Coach Lohr forced him to stop out of concern that he might hurt himself.

5   It would get better. Two months later, Thomas competed at the Commonwealth Games in Australia against some of the best professional jumpers in the world, wearing tennis shoes. He placed fourth in a world-class field, a result that actually confused him because he did not yet understand how tiebreakers work in high jump and thought he was in third place until the results were announced.

     ...

6   In August 2007, with a total of eight months of legitimate high-jump training to his name, Thomas donned his pole vault shoes and the gold and aquamarine of his native Bahamas and traveled to Osaka for the World Championships. In non-Olympic years, the World Championships are the Super Bowl of track and field.

7   Thomas advanced easily to the final, as did Stefan Holm [the reigning Olympic champion]. When the men's high jump finalists were introduced, broadcasters announced a laser-focused Holm as the favorite. Thomas, looking cool in sunglasses beneath the bright lights illuminating the stadium, was described as "very much an unknown quantity."

8   Early in the competition, it appeared that Thomas would fold in his first world spotlight. While the rest of the jumpers took such lengthy approaches that they had to start on the running track, Thomas began on the infield, as if he were using the high jump equivalent of the short tees at a golf course. He stutter-stepped his way to a miss at 7'3" – each jumper gets three attempts at every height – lower than he jumped in that first meet at Eastern Illinois. Meanwhile, Holm was cruising, passing over 7'3", 7'5", 7'6.5", and 7'7.73" without a single miss, as his father watched through a video camera and pumped his fist in the stands.

9   But Thomas began to hit his form, managing to alternate makes and misses. He arrived at 7'8.5" along with a handful of other jumpers, including Holm.

10   For his first attempt, Holm stood with his eyes closed, envisioning himself floating over the bar. He approached, leapt, and barely grazed the bar. As it fell to the ground, he executed a frustrated backflip on the mat. Next, Yaroslav Rybakov, a 6'6" Russian, nudged the bar off the stand. Then came Thomas. He slowed down so drastically as he approached the bar that it seemed impossible that he could clear it. And yet, flailing his legs and with his back nearly straight, he passed 7'8.5" on his first attempt, putting his hand down behind him as if to break his fall because he was still uncomfortable with the

NOTES

sensation of falling backward. He rolled off the mat and **gamboled** across the track in celebration. But Holm was up again.

11   Another miss, just barely. Holm shook his palms in front of him as if **beseeching** the high jump gods. They didn't listen. On his final attempt, Holm clipped the bar with the back of his legs and fell to the mat with his head in his palms.

12   The guy in pole vault shoes who thinks high jump is "kind of boring" was crowned the 2007 world champion. On his winning jump, Thomas raised his center of mass to 8'2". Had he any semblance of the back arch that every other pro jumper does, he would have shattered the world record.

...

13   In 2008, the Japanese television station NHK asked Masaki Ishikawa, then a scientist at the Neuromuscular Research Center at the University of Jyväskylä in Finland, to examine Thomas. Ishikawa noted both Thomas's long legs relative to his height and also that he was gifted with a giant's **Achilles tendon**. Whereas Holm's Achilles was a more normal-sized, incredibly stiff spring, Thomas's, at ten and a quarter inches, was uncharacteristically long for an athlete his height. The longer (and stiffer) the Achilles tendon, the more elastic energy it can store when compressed. All the better to rocket the owner into the air.

14   "The Achilles tendon is very important in jumping, and not just in humans," says Gary Hunter, exercise physiologist at the University of Alabama-Birmingham, and an author of studies on Achilles tendon lengths. "For example, the tendon in the kangaroo is very, very long. That's why they can bounce around more economically than they can walk."

15   Hunter has found that a longer Achilles tendon allows an athlete to get more power from what's called the "stretch shortening cycle," basically **compression** and subsequent decompression of the springlike tendon. The more power that is stored in the spring when it is compressed, the more you get when it is released. (A typical example is a standing vertical jump, in which the jumper bends down quickly, shortening the tendons and muscles, before jumping skyward.) When Hunter puts subjects on a leg-press machine and drops weights down on them, the longer the person's Achilles tendon the faster and harder he was able to fling the weights back in the opposite direction. "That's not exactly the same as a jump," Hunter says, "but it has a lot of similarities. And that's why people jump higher when they have a drop step or a few steps: they use the velocity of the descent toward the ground to compress the tendon, just like a spring."

16   Tendon length is not significantly impacted by training, but rather is a function of the distance between the calf muscle and the heel bone, which are

NOTES

connected by the tendon. And while it appears that an individual can increase tendon stiffness by training, there is also evidence that stiffness is partly influenced by an individual's versions of genes involved in making collagen, a protein in the body that builds ligaments and tendons.

17 Neither Ishikawa nor Hunter would suggest that the sole secret to the jumping success of Holm and Thomas is in their Achilles tendons. But the tendons are one puzzle piece that helps explain how two athletes could arrive at essentially the same place, one after a twenty-year love affair with his craft, and the other with less than a year of serious practice after stumbling into it on a friendly bet. Interestingly, Thomas has not improved one centimeter in the six years since he entered the professional circuit. Thomas debuted on top and has not progressed. He seems to contradict the deliberate practice framework in all directions.

Excerpted from *The Sports Gene* by David Epstein, published by the Penguin Group.

THINK QUESTIONS

1. Refer to one or more details from the text to support your understanding of what made Donald Thomas a successful high jumper—both from ideas that are directly stated and ideas that you have inferred from clues in the text.

2. How does the author structure this excerpt to describe the success and techniques of two very different athletes competing for the same event? Why do you think the author uses this particular structure? Support your response with evidence from the text.

3. What can you tell from this excerpt about the author's purpose in writing *The Sports Gene*? Do you think he is favoring Donald Thomas's approach to the high jump over Stefan Holm's technique, or Holm over Thomas? Or is he not taking sides? Support your response with details from the text.

4. Use context to determine the meaning of the word **prowess** as it is used in *The Sports Gene*. Write your definition of *prowess* here.

5. Use a print or online dictionary or a medical reference book to determine the meaning of **Achilles tendon**. Write your definition of *Achilles tendon* here.

INTO THE WILD

NON-FICTION
Jon Krakauer
1996

INTRODUCTION

After graduating from Emory University, Chris McCandless broke from his past by donating $24,000 dollars from his college fund to Oxfam and adopting the moniker "Alexander Supertramp." In a modern-day Walden experience, he hitchhiked to Alaska, pared his possessions down to a bag of rice, a few books, a camera, and a rifle, and walked off into the wilderness alone. Four months later he was discovered dead, starved or poisoned by his meager diet. Author Jon Krakauer retraced McCandless' steps to piece together the details and provide an understanding of the young ascetic's idealism, courage, and naïveté

"His exact words were 'I think I'm going to disappear for a while.'"

FIRST READ

Excerpt from Chapter Three: Carthage

1   In May 1990, Chris graduated from Emory University in Atlanta, where he'd been a columnist for, and editor of, the student newspaper, *The Emory Wheel,* and had distinguished himself as a history and anthropology major with a 3.72 grade point average. He was offered membership in Phi Beta Kappa but declined, insisting that titles and honors are **irrelevant**.

2   The final two years of his college education had been paid for with a forty-thousand-dollar bequest left by a friend of the family's; more than twenty-four thousand dollars remained at the time of Chris's graduation, money his parents thought he intended to use for law school. "We misread him," his father admits. What Walt, Billie, and Carine didn't know when they flew down to Atlanta to attend Chris's commencement—what nobody knew—was that he would shortly donate all the money in his college fund to OXFAM America, a charity dedicated to fighting hunger.

    ...

3   Chris had purchased the secondhand yellow Datsun when he was a senior in high school. In the years since, he'd been in the habit of taking it on extended solo road trips when classes weren't in session, and during that graduation weekend he casually mentioned to his parents that he intended to spend the up-coming summer on the road as well. His exact words were "I think I'm going to disappear for a while."

4   Neither parent made anything of this announcement at the time, although Walt did gently admonish his son, saying "Hey, make sure you come see us before you go." Chris smiled and sort of nodded, a response that Walt and Billie took as an affirmation that he would visit them in Annandale before the summer was out, and then they said their good-byes.

NOTES

5   Toward the end of June, Chris, still in Atlanta, mailed his parents a copy of his final grade report: A in Apartheid and South African Society and History of Anthropological Thought; A minus in Contemporary African Politics and the Food Crisis in Africa. A brief note was attached:

6   *Here is a copy of my final transcript. Gradewise things went pretty well and I ended up with a high cumulative average.*

7   *Thank you for the pictures, the shaving gear, and the postcard from Paris. It seems that you really enjoyed your trip there. It must have been a lot of fun.*

8   *I gave Lloyd [Chris's closest friend at Emory] his picture, and he was very grateful; he did not have a shot of his diploma getting handed to him.*

9   *Not much else is happening, but it's starting to get real hot and humid down here. Say Hi to everyone for me.*

10 It was the last anyone in Chris's family would ever hear from him.

11 During that final year in Atlanta, Chris had lived off campus in a monkish room furnished with little more than a thin mattress on the floor, milk crates, and a table. He kept it as orderly and spotless as a military barracks. And he didn't have a phone, so Walt and Billie had no way of calling him.

12 By the beginning of August 1990, Chris's parents had heard nothing from their son since they'd received his grades in the mail, so they decided to drive down to Atlanta for a visit. When they arrived at his apartment, it was empty and a FOR RENT sign was taped to the window. The manager said that Chris had moved out at the end of June. Walt and Billie returned home to find that all the letters they'd sent their son that summer had been returned in a bundle. "Chris had instructed the post office to hold them until August 1, apparently so we wouldn't know anything was up," says Billie. "It made us very, very worried."

13 By then Chris was long gone. Five weeks earlier he'd loaded all his belongings into his little car and headed west without an itinerary. The trip was to be an **odyssey** in the fullest sense of the word, an epic journey that would change everything. He had spent the previous four years, as he saw it, preparing to fulfill an absurd and onerous duty: to graduate from college. At long last he was unencumbered, emancipated from the stifling world of his parents and peers, a world of abstraction and security and material excess, a world in which he felt grievously cut off from the raw throb of existence.

14 Driving west out of Atlanta, he intended to invent an utterly new life for himself, one in which he would be free to wallow in unfiltered experience. To symbolize the complete severance from his previous life, he even adopted a new name.

No longer would he answer to Chris McCandless; he was now Alexander Supertramp, master of his own destiny.

Excerpt from Chapter 4: Detrital Wash

15 Detrital Wash extends for some fifty miles from Lake Mead into the mountains north of Kingman; it drains a big chunk of country. Most of the year the wash is as dry as chalk. During the summer months, however, superheated air rises from the scorched earth like bubbles from the bottom of a boiling kettle, rushing heavenward in turbulent convection currents. Frequently the updrafts create cells of muscular, anvil-headed cumulonimbus clouds that can rise thirty thousand feet or more above the Mojave. Two days after McCandless set up camp beside Lake Mead, an unusually robust wall of thunderheads reared up in the afternoon sky, and it began to rain, very hard, over much of the Detrital Valley.

16 McCandless was camped at the edge of the wash, a couple of feet higher than the main channel, so when the bore of brown water came rushing down from the high country, he had just enough time to gather his tent and belongings and save them from being swept away. There was nowhere to move the car, however, as the only route of **egress** was now a foaming, full-blown river. As it turned out, the flash flood didn't have enough power to carry away the vehicle or even to do any lasting damage. But it did get the engine wet, so wet that when McCandless tried to start the car soon thereafter, the engine wouldn't catch, and in his impatience he drained the battery.

17 With the battery dead there was no way to get the Datsun running. If he hoped to get the car back to a paved road, McCandless had no choice but to walkout and notify the authorities of his predicament. If he went to the rangers, however, they would have some irksome questions for him: Why had he ignored posted regulations and driven down the wash in the first place? Was he aware that the vehicle's registration had expired two years before and had not been renewed? Did he know that his drivers license had also expired, and the vehicle was uninsured as well?

18 Truthful responses to these queries were not likely to be well received by the rangers. McCandless could endeavor to explain that he answered to **statutes** of a higher order—that as a latter-day adherent of Henry David Thoreau, he took as gospel the essay "On the Duty of Civil Disobedience" and thus considered it his moral responsibility to **flout** the laws of the state. It was improbable, however, that deputies of the federal government would share his point of view. There would be thickets of red tape to negotiate and fines to pay. His parents would no doubt be contacted. But there was a way to avoid such aggravation: He could simply abandon the Datsun and resume his odyssey on foot. And that's what he decided to do.

19   Instead of feeling distraught over this turn of events, moreover, McCandless was exhilarated: He saw the flash flood as an opportunity to shed unnecessary baggage. He concealed the car as best he could beneath a brown tarp, stripped it of its Virginia plates, and hid them. He buried his Winchester deer-hunting rifle and a few other possessions that he might one day want to recover. Then, in a gesture that would have done both Thoreau and Tolstoy proud, he arranged all his paper currency in a pile on the sand—a pathetic little stack of ones and fives and twenties—and put a match to it. One hundred twenty-three dollars in legal tender was promptly reduced to ash and smoke.

Excerpted from Into the Wild *by Jon Krakauer, published by Doubleday.*

 THINK QUESTIONS

1. Summarize the details in the text that support the author's main idea about what Chris McCandless wanted to do with his life.

2. Explain what the author thinks of Chris McCandless's actions, citing details from the text to support your response.

3. The author claims that Chris McCandless planned to sever himself completely from his earlier life. Cite at least three examples of evidence that this was what McCandless planned.

4. What Remembering that the Latin prefix *ir-* means "not," use the context clues in the first paragraph of the passage to define the word **irrelevant**. Write your definition of *irrelevant* here, and say what context clues helped you guess it.

5. The first use of the word **odyssey** in the passage includes a restatement. Write the restatement, which defines *odyssey*, here.

CLOSE READ

Reread the excerpts from *Into the Wild*. As you reread, complete the Focus Questions below. Then use your answers and annotations from the questions to help you complete the Writing Prompt.

FOCUS QUESTIONS

1. As you reread the text of *Into the Wild*, find the author's central ideas. Highlight the key details that support the idea. What is the author saying about Chris McCandless's actions? What are the author's ideas based on? Highlight evidence in the text and make annotations to explain your answer.

2. In paragraph 1, the author describes a belief Chris McCandless held that hints at his future actions. What is this belief? How do his later actions reflect it? Highlight evidence to support your ideas and make annotations to explain your response.

3. In paragraph 14, the author uses rhetoric that hints at his opinion of Chris McCandless's actions. What specific phrases does the author use? What do they tell you about the author's opinion of McCandless? Highlight your evidence and annotate to explain your ideas.

4. The author includes a letter Chris McCandless wrote to his parents. Why do you think he chose to include this letter? What do you infer about McCandless from the letter? Highlight textual evidence and make annotations to explain your response.

5. Use your understanding of main idea and detail in these chapters to explain the author's point of view toward Chris McCandless. Highlight evidence from the text that will help support your ideas.

6. How much control did Chris McCandless have over his life? Weigh evidence for and against McCandless having control, and come to your own conclusion. Support your answer with textual evidence.

WRITING PROMPT

How does the author use rhetoric to convey his ideas and attitudes in *Into the Wild*? What are those ideas and attitudes? Use your understanding of rhetoric and of author's purpose and point of view to help you infer the answers. Be sure to include plentiful evidence from the text to support your inferences.

INVICTUS

POETRY
William Ernest Henley
1875

INTRODUCTION

William Ernest Henley was a Victorian poet best known for his poem "Invictus." The title of the poem means "unconquered" in Latin, an appropriate title for a poem in which the speaker declares that he is the master of his own destiny. South African freedom fighter Nelson Mandela is among the many who have been inspired by the poem's powerful message.

"My head is bloody, but unbowed."

FIRST READ

1 Out of the night that covers me,
2 Black as the pit from pole to pole,
3 I thank whatever gods may be
4 For my unconquerable soul.

5 In the **fell** clutch of circumstance
6 I have not winced nor cried aloud.
7 Under the **bludgeonings** of chance
8 My head is bloody, but unbowed.

9 Beyond this place of wrath and tears
10 **Looms** but the horror of the **shade,**
11 And yet the menace of the years
12 Finds, and shall find, me unafraid.

13 It matters not how **strait** the gate,
14 How charged with punishments the scroll,
15 I am the master of my fate:
16 I am the captain of my soul.

THINK QUESTIONS

1. What is the author's emotional state—both the circumstances in which he finds himself and how he deals with them? Use ideas that are directly stated and ideas that you have inferred from clues in the text.

2. How does the rhyme scheme add to the meaning and tone of the poem? Support your answer with specific evidence from the text.

3. As you read "Invictus," think about the Big Question. How does the main idea of the poem address the question as to how much control we have over our destiny? Support your answer with evidence from the text.

4. Use context clues and your own prior knowledge to determine the meaning of the word **bludgeonings** in the second stanza. Write your definition of the word and list the context words you used to determine the meaning.

5. Based on the context words *horror* and *menace*, and the descriptive words that indicate darkness and night used in the previous stanzas, what might be another word for a **shade**?

Please note that excerpts and passages in the StudySync® library and this workbook are intended as touchstones to generate interest in an author's work. The excerpts and passages do not substitute for the reading of entire texts, and StudySync® strongly recommends that students seek out and purchase the whole literary or informational work in order to experience it as the author intended. Links to online resellers are available in our digital library. In addition, complete works may be ordered through an authorized reseller by filling out and returning to StudySync® the order form enclosed in this workbook.

Reading & Writing
Companion

23

CLOSE READ

Reread the poem "Invictus". As you reread, complete the Focus Questions below. Then use your answers and annotations from the questions to help you complete the Writing Prompt.

FOCUS QUESTIONS

1. As you reread "Invictus," highlight and annotate the figurative language the author uses to describe the hardships he has endured. What language does he use to describe the difficulties he has experienced? How does that add to your understanding of the poem?

2. Which line most clearly states the author's theme? Summarize the theme in your own words. Do you agree with the author's claim? Why or why not?

3. How does the author of the poem make the theme clear by using images that contrast that theme? Highlight and annotate the lines that give contrast to the poem's overall idea. Do these specific images make the poem more relatable? Why or why not?

4. Highlight and annotate the words that fall into a specific rhyme scheme. At the end of the poem, create an annotation that answers the following questions: If you were to write a poem about the difficulties in your life, would you use the regular rhythm and rhyme? Why or why not? What might the use of rhyme, or the lack thereof, reveal about your experiences?

5. Look at the last lines of stanzas one, two, and three. How are they different from the first three lines in each of those stanzas? What does the beginning and ending of the poem suggest about how much of what happens in our lives we actually control?

WRITING PROMPT

Does the author's final assertion ("I am the master of my fate: / I am the captain of my soul.") ring true? Do you believe that he can guide his future in the direction he wants it to go? Use textual evidence, and a summary of the poem, as well as your personal experience, to write your response.

IF

POETRY
Rudyard Kipling
1899

INTRODUCTION

Born in Bombay, Rudyard Kipling (1865–1936) went back to England for his education, but returned to India in 1882 and began writing for newspapers. Perhaps most famous for his children's classic, *The Jungle Book*, Kipling was awarded the Nobel Prize for literature in 1907 "in consideration of the power of observation, originality of imagination, virility of ideas and remarkable talent for narration." His poem "If" stacks the list of conditions for manhood quite high, but does so with wit and wisdom.

"If you can dream—and not make dreams your master."

FIRST READ

NOTES

1 IF you can keep your head when all about you
2 Are losing theirs and blaming it on you,
3 If you can trust yourself when all men doubt you,
4 But make **allowance** for their doubting too;
5 If you can wait and not be tired by waiting,
6 Or being lied about, don't deal in lies,
7 Or being hated, don't give way to hating,
8 And yet don't look too good, nor talk too wise:

9 If you can dream—and not make dreams your master;
10 If you can think—and not make thoughts your aim;
11 If you can meet with Triumph and Disaster
12 And treat those two **impostors** just the same;
13 If you can bear to hear the truth you've spoken
14 Twisted by **knaves** to make a trap for fools,
15 Or watch the things you gave your life to, broken,
16 And stoop and build 'em up with worn-out tools:

17 If you can make one heap of all your winnings
18 And risk it on one turn of pitch-and-toss,
19 And lose, and start again at your beginnings
20 And never breathe a word about your loss;
21 If you can force your heart and nerve and **sinew**
22 To serve your turn long after they are gone,
23 And so hold on when there is nothing in you
24 Except the Will which says to them: 'Hold on!'

25 If you can talk with crowds and keep your **virtue**,
26 Or walk with Kings—nor lose the common touch,
27 If neither foes nor loving friends can hurt you,
28 If all men count with you, but none too much;

29 If you can fill the unforgiving minute
30 With sixty seconds' worth of distance run,
31 Yours is the Earth and everything that's in it,
32 And—which is more—you'll be a Man, my son!

 THINK QUESTIONS

1. Using text evidence to inform your response, write one or two sentences to summarize the poem.

2. Refer to one or more details from the text to support your understanding of the poem—of what is the author trying to convince his son?

3. Does the author think that doing these things is an easy task? How do you know? Support your response with evidence from the text.

4. Use context to determine the meaning of the word **knaves** as it is used in "If." Write your definition of *knaves* here.

5. Describe two uses of the word **allowance**. What do these two uses have in common?

Please note that excerpts and passages in the StudySync® library and this workbook are intended as touchstones to generate interest in an author's work. The excerpts and passages do not substitute for the reading of entire texts, and StudySync® strongly recommends that students seek out and purchase the whole literary or informational work in order to experience it as the author intended. Links to online resellers are available in our digital library. In addition, complete works may be ordered through an authorized reseller by filling out and returning to StudySync® the order form enclosed in this workbook.

Reading & Writing Companion **27**

CLOSE READ

Reread the poem *If*. As you reread, complete the Focus Questions below. Then use your answers and annotations from the questions to help you complete the Writing Prompt.

FOCUS QUESTIONS

1. As you reread "If," highlight the anaphora. Why do you think repetition is used at those specific places in the poem? Also, consider where the author has chosen to place the anaphora throughout the poem. Why do you think the author chose to vary the placement of the anaphora within the stanzas?

2. How would it change the poem to make the lines shorter or longer? How would the poem be different without the rhyme?

3. In the second stanza, the author urges the reader to fix the broken things in life with "worn-out tools." Why do you think the author chose to use this figurative language?

4. In the last stanza, the author urges his son to fill the "unforgiving minute." Why would the author describe something that seems so small in such a negative way?

5. What does the author imply about how much of our lives we can control through our actions?

WRITING PROMPT

Do you agree or disagree with the poem's theme about what it takes to be a fully realized person? Reread the poem and write about how the form of the poem contributes to its theme.

MACBETH
(ACT I, SCENE III)

DRAMA
William Shakespeare
1606

INTRODUCTION

I n this excerpt from early in Shakespeare's *Macbeth*, Macbeth and his friend Banquo have just finished a bloody battle to put down a rebellion against King Duncan. On their way home, they encounter three witches eager to make predictions about both of their futures. The effect of these prophecies on Macbeth are immediate and will have far-reaching consequences on Shakespeare's great

"If chance will have me king, why, chance may crown me, Without my stir."

 FIRST READ

One Act I, Scene iii

1   A heath near Forres.
2   *[Thunder. Enter three Witches]*

3   FIRST WITCH: Where hast thou been, sister?

4   SECOND WITCH: Killing swine.

5   THIRD WITCH: Sister, where thou?

6   FIRST WITCH: A sailor's wife had chestnuts in her lap,
7   And munch'd, and munch'd, and munch'd:--
8   'Give me,' quoth I:
9   'Aroint thee, witch!' the rump-fed **ronyon** cries.
10 Her husband's to Aleppo gone, master o' the Tiger:
11 But in a sieve I'll thither sail,
12 And, like a rat without a tail,
13 I'll do, I'll do, and I'll do.

14 SECOND WITCH: I'll give thee a wind.

15 FIRST WITCH: Thou'rt kind.

16 THIRD WITCH: And I another.

17 FIRST WITCH: I myself have all the other,
18 And the very ports they blow,
19 All the quarters that they know
20 I' the shipman's card.
21 I will drain him dry as hay:
22 Sleep shall neither night nor day

23 Hang upon his pent-house lid;
24 He shall live a man forbid:
25 Weary se'nnights nine times nine
26 Shall he dwindle, peak and pine:
27 Though his bark cannot be lost,
28 Yet it shall be tempest-tost.
29 Look what I have.

30 SECOND WITCH: Show me, show me.

31 FIRST WITCH: Here I have a pilot's thumb,
32 Wreck'd as homeward he did come.

33 *[Drum within]*

34 THIRD WITCH: A drum, a drum!
35 Macbeth doth come.

36 ALL: The weird sisters, hand in hand,
37 Posters of the sea and land,
38 Thus do go about, about:
39 Thrice to thine and thrice to mine
40 And thrice again, to make up nine.
41 Peace! the charm's wound up.

42 *Enter MACBETH and BANQUO*

43 MACBETH: So foul and fair a day I have not seen.

44 BANQUO: How far is't call'd to Forres? What are these
45 So wither'd and so wild in their attire,
46 That look not like the inhabitants o' the earth,
47 And yet are on't? Live you? or are you aught
48 That man may question? You seem to understand me,
49 By each at once her chappy finger laying
50 Upon her skinny lips: you should be women,
51 And yet your beards forbid me to interpret
52 That you are so.

53 MACBETH: Speak, if you can: what are you?

54 FIRST WITCH: All hail, Macbeth! hail to thee, thane of Glamis!

55 SECOND WITCH: All hail, Macbeth, hail to thee, thane of Cawdor!

56 THIRD WITCH: All hail, Macbeth, thou shalt be king hereafter!

NOTES

57 BANQUO: Good sir, why do you start; and seem to fear

58 Things that do sound so fair? I' the name of truth,

59 Are ye fantastical, or that indeed

60 Which outwardly ye show? My noble partner

61 You greet with present grace and great prediction

62 Of noble having and of royal hope,

63 That he seems **rapt** withal: to me you speak not.

64 If you can look into the seeds of time,

65 And say which grain will grow and which will not,

66 Speak then to me, who neither beg nor fear

67 Your favours nor your hate.

68 FIRST WITCH: Hail!

69 SECOND WITCH: Hail!

70 THIRD WITCH: Hail!

71 FIRST WITCH: Lesser than Macbeth, and greater.

72 SECOND WITCH: Not so happy, yet much happier.

73 THIRD WITCH: Thou shalt get kings, though thou be none:

74 So all hail, Macbeth and Banquo!

75 FIRST WITCH: Banquo and Macbeth, all hail!

76 MACBETH: Stay, you imperfect speakers, tell me more:

77 By Sinel's death I know I am thane of Glamis;

78 But how of Cawdor? the thane of Cawdor lives,

79 A prosperous gentleman; and to be king

80 Stands not within the **prospect** of belief,

81 No more than to be Cawdor. Say from whence

82 You owe this strange intelligence, or why

83 Upon this blasted heath you stop our way

84 With such prophetic greeting? Speak, I charge you.

85 *[Witches vanish]*

86 BANQUO: The earth hath bubbles, as the water has,

87 And these are of them. Whither are they vanish'd?

88 MACBETH: Into the air; and what seem'd corporal melted

89 As breath into the wind. Would they had stay'd!

90 BANQUO: Were such things here as we do speak about?

91 Or have we eaten on the insane root

92 That takes the reason prisoner?

93 MACBETH: Your children shall be kings.

94 BANQUO: You shall be king.

95 MACBETH: And thane of Cawdor too: went it not so?

96 BANQUO: To the selfsame tune and words. Who's here?

97 *[Enter ROSS and ANGUS]*

98 ROSS: The king hath happily received, Macbeth,

99 The news of thy success; and when he reads

100 Thy personal venture in the rebels' fight,

101 His wonders and his praises do contend

102 Which should be thine or his: silenced with that,

103 In viewing o'er the rest o' the selfsame day,

104 He finds thee in the stout Norweyan ranks,

105 Nothing afeard of what thyself didst make,

106 Strange images of death. As thick as hail

107 Came post with post; and every one did bear

108 Thy praises in his kingdom's great defence,

109 And pour'd them down before him.

110 ANGUS: We are sent

111 To give thee from our royal master thanks;

112 Only to herald thee into his sight,

113 Not pay thee.

114 ROSS: And, for an earnest of a greater honour,

115 He bade me, from him, call thee thane of Cawdor:

116 In which addition, hail, most worthy thane!

117 For it is thine.

118 BANQUO: What, can the devil speak true?

119 MACBETH: The thane of Cawdor lives: why do you dress me

120 In borrow'd robes?

121 ANGUS: Who was the thane lives yet;

122 But under heavy judgment bears that life

123 Which he deserves to lose. Whether he was combined

124 With those of Norway, or did line the rebel

125 With hidden help and vantage, or that with both
126 He labour'd in his country's wreck, I know not;
127 But treasons capital, confess'd and proved,
128 Have overthrown him.

129 MACBETH: [*Aside*] Glamis, and thane of Cawdor!
130 The greatest is behind.
131 *To ROSS and ANGUS*
132 Thanks for your **pains**.
133 *To BANQUO*
134 Do you not hope your children shall be kings,
135 When those that gave the thane of Cawdor to me
136 Promised no less to them?

137 BANQUO: That trusted home
138 Might yet enkindle you unto the crown,
139 Besides the thane of Cawdor. But 'tis strange:
140 And oftentimes, to win us to our harm,
141 The instruments of darkness tell us truths,
142 Win us with honest trifles, to betray's
143 In deepest consequence.
144 Cousins, a word, I pray you.

145 MACBETH: [*Aside*] Two truths are told,
146 As happy **prologues** to the swelling act
147 Of the imperial theme.–I thank you, gentlemen.
148 [*Aside*]
149 Cannot be ill, cannot be good: if ill,
150 Why hath it given me earnest of success,
151 Commencing in a truth? I am thane of Cawdor:
152 If good, why do I yield to that suggestion
153 Whose horrid image doth unfix my hair
154 And make my seated heart knock at my ribs,
155 Against the use of nature? Present fears
156 Are less than horrible imaginings:
157 My thought, whose murder yet is but fantastical,
158 Shakes so my single state of man that function
159 Is smother'd in surmise, and nothing is
160 But what is not.

161 BANQUO: Look, how our partner's rapt.

162 MACBETH: [*Aside*]
163 If chance will have me king, why, chance may crown me,
164 Without my stir.

NOTES

165 BANQUO: New horrors come upon him,
166 Like our strange garments, cleave not to their mould
167 But with the aid of use.

168 MACBETH: [*Aside*]
169 Come what come may,
170 Time and the hour runs through the roughest day.

171 BANQUO: Worthy Macbeth, we stay upon your leisure.

172 MACBETH: Give me your favour: my dull brain was wrought
173 With things forgotten. Kind gentlemen, your pains
174 Are register'd where every day I turn
175 The leaf to read them. Let us toward the king.
176 Think upon what hath chanced, and, at more time,
177 The interim having weigh'd it, let us speak
178 Our free hearts each to other.

179 BANQUO: Very gladly.

180 MACBETH; Till then, enough. Come, friends.

181 [*Exeunt*]

THINK QUESTIONS

1. Why do you think Shakespeare uses the prophecy of the witches to set Macbeth's rise to power in motion? Support your answer with evidence from the text.

2. What can you tell about Macbeth and Banquo from the way each reacts to the witches' prophecy? Support your answer with evidence from the text.

3. What does the use of paradox—*foul and fair, cannot be ill, cannot be good*—say about Macbeth's situation?

4. Use context to determine the meaning of the word **pains** as it is used in *Macbeth*. Write your definition of *pains*.

5. Think about the word *rapture* that is related to the word **rapt** used in Macbeth. How does this related word help you infer the meaning of *rapt*? Write your definition of *rapt*.

Please note that excerpts and passages in the StudySync® library and this workbook are intended as touchstones to generate interest in an author's work. The excerpts and passages do not substitute for the reading of entire texts, and StudySync® strongly recommends that students seek out and purchase the whole literary or informational work in order to experience it as the author intended. Links to online resellers are available in our digital library. In addition, complete works may be ordered through an authorized reseller by filling out and returning to StudySync® the order form enclosed in this workbook.

Reading & Writing
Companion

CLOSE READ

Reread the excerpt from *Macbeth*. As you reread, complete the Focus Questions below. Then use your answers and annotations from the questions to help you complete the Writing Prompt.

FOCUS QUESTIONS

1. Highlight the characters mentioned in the scene that do not appear on stage. Annotate the text to explain where you would go to find out who these characters are.

2. The scene with the witches cackling together contains complicated language that is difficult to understand. Highlight the text aids that help you understand what is happening.

3. What text aids help the reader understand that Macbeth sometimes speaks to himself? Highlight the text aids that help you find these areas.

4. What do the witches foreshadow for Macbeth in their conversation with Macbeth and Banquo? How does Macbeth react to the information? Highlight the lines in the text where Macbeth reacts to the foreshadowed information and make annotations to explain your ideas.

5. The witches make a prophecy for Banquo as well as for Macbeth. How does Banquo react to the foreshadowing? Highlight the text evidence to support your answer.

6. As the scene closes, Macbeth worries over what will happen in the future. What does he worry will happen in his rise to power? Highlight the evidence to support your answer.

7. How does foreshadowing play a part in the broader theme of fate and destiny or the theme of the struggle for power and its ability to corrupt individuals? How does the play address the concept of control over one's fate? Add an annotation at the end of the passage with your answer.

WRITING PROMPT

Choose three important passages from Act I, Scene iii and write margin notes to explain what happens in each passage, define vocabulary, identify the meaning of the symbolism or action, and tell its greater relevance to the story of Macbeth.

THE IRAQ WAR BLOG:

AN IRAQI FAMILY'S INSIDE VIEW OF THE
FIRST YEAR OF THE OCCUPATION

NON-FICTION
Faiza Al-Araji, Raed
Jarrar, and Khalid Jarrar
2004

INTRODUCTION

Authored by members of an Iraqi family, *The Iraq War Blog* describes life in Baghdad in the months after coalition forces led by the United States invaded the country and toppled the regime of Saddam Hussein. The war took a heavy toll on residents of the city, who lived under constant fear of missile strikes, nighttime attacks, and, as evidenced by the excerpt here, kidnapping. The family's account of life in Baghdad during the American occupation offers a harrowing look at how they responded to these daily acts of violence.

"...he didn't know there was an angel guarding him, smiling, and standing by his side."

 FIRST READ

Wednesday, April 16, 2003

1   I woke up very tired, as if my body and my feelings were crushed.

2   Yesterday, when I went to the funeral parlor, it was depressing and frustrating. Women wearing black, weeping over a man killed by a stray bullet; talk about neighbors who died last night; talk of the bombing of houses and residential buildings and innocent people killed.

3   At night I couldn't sleep; the sounds of continuous explosions frightened me, so I ran to another room, far away from the street.

4   In the morning, Abu-Selah, the gardener, said that the **occupation** forces were blowing up Iraqi tanks in Rathwania area.

5   I feel that this war has **devastated** my personality and shaken me; that my whole nervous system has become like fragile threads. I feel very weak and exhausted from my grief for people and what has befallen them. For Iraq, for Baghdad—my darling beloved—and what happened to her: plunder, fire, and destruction. And I tell myself, it all happened by the will of God; there is no God but God, and neither strength nor possibilities unless by the power of God.

6   And I remembered the Al-Kahaaf verse from the Holy Qur'an, and the dialogue of Moses (God bless him) and Al-Kuther who said to Moses, "How could you be patient about something you know nothing of?"

7   It is a great disgrace that has befallen us, and everyone makes suggestions and gives speeches, but no one comprehends the truth but God Almighty.

8   *Sunday, February 29, 2004*

9   Today was a hectic day at work. I took care of many customers that were working with **humanitarian** organizations. I respect them very much because they are risking their lives for others. These people remind me that good hasn't been cut away from all humans: there are still those who believe in helping humanity.

10   Then one of my relatives called and her voice just didn't sound right to me. I asked her what was wrong and she told me that her son had been **abducted** this morning while he was on his way to the university. People dragged him out of the car and took him away. He called from his mobile phone and told his father that he was in the trunk of the car. "I've been kidnapped by someone," he said.

11   We hear these stories every day and I expect it to happen to me or my kids. No one has protection. We leave our homes terrified and return the same way. Those relatives of ours own a shop and they have new cars. Those are the two things that attract thieves—especially since they don't live in an expensive neighborhood. I called the boys to tell them I was going to be late, and went directly to our relative's house. I got to the parking area of their building and parked my car. I calmly stepped out and knocked on the door. One of the guests opened it. The house was strangely silent, though full of people.

12   I said, "Al Salamu Alaikum. God willing he'll be back safe." I wasn't sure what to say to someone on an occasion like this. The father thanked me and told me to go inside where the women were. He pointed to the right and I went to the room where the boy's mother, her relatives, and neighbors were sitting. She was pale and her eyes were swollen. I held her to me and said, "Be patient and pray to God that he may be back safe." I sat and listened to her telling the story.

13   "I told him in the morning, 'Don't take the car—I need it today,'" she said. "But he was stubborn and he went off to college. His father had left for work before him, but he came back early and told me that our son had called him and said that some unknown people had abducted him. He was in the trunk of the car and they were taking him to a strange place." He had left the car near the house. The car, of course, had been an old model and that was probably why they didn't take it. Had it been one of those newer cars, they would have taken it with the boy. And now we were sitting and waiting for them to call and give their conditions.

14   There is no ideal way to prevent such things from happening. If the boy leaves alone in his car, they'll abduct him. If he leaves with a driver—related or not— no one can prevent an abduction. We heard of many situations. Every story

NOTES

has different details that leads one to believe that there is no way to prevent it. There are even people who were abducted right in the middle of their personal bodyguards, so I know it's not from a lack of caution.

15 I am convinced that it is a case of God's will—he does what he wants. I recalled a short story Tolstoy had written about a man sleeping in the forest. A bee came along to sting him; it hovered and hovered and an angel chased it away. A bear came along—or something like that, I can't remember exactly—but couldn't hurt the man. Then came thieves who wanted to steal his wallet, and somehow they ended up running away without taking it. Several tragedies occurred, but not a single one harmed him. He woke up, smiled, yawned, and said," What a lovely place this is. And how safe it is!" Of course, he didn't know there was an angel guarding him, smiling, and standing by his side. I still believe in that angel, or I wouldn't be here, and I wouldn't be able to **cope** with the daily difficulties.

16 I got home before dark. I called my relatives late at night. There had been a phone call from the abductors and negotiations. They told them that they would call in the morning to give them the final answer. How will the night pass for his mother, father, and siblings? I stayed up thinking all night and waiting for morning.

Excerpted from *The Iraq War Blog: An Iraqi Family's Inside View of the First Year of the Occupation* by Faiza Al-Araji, Raed Jarrar and Khalid Jarrar, published by Second Chance Publishing.

 THINK QUESTIONS

1. How does the author feel about the occupation of Baghdad? Refer to one or more details from the text to support your answer.

2. Summarize the situation that the author experiences in Baghdad and how she deals with it. Provide specific details from the text that support your summary.

3. In *The Iraq War Blog,* the author connects personal experience to the more general reality of life in Baghdad. Analyze how the author moves from the specific to the general in a passage from the blog.

4. Use context clues to determine the meaning of the word **abducted** as it is used in *The Iraq War Blog*. Write your definition of *abducted*.

5. Noticing that the word **humanitarian** contains the word *human*, use context clues provided in the passage to determine the meaning of *humanitarian*. Write your definition of *humanitarian*.

CLOSE READ

Reread the excerpt from *The Iraq War Blog*. As you reread, complete the Focus Questions below. Then use your answers and annotations from the questions to help you complete the Writing Prompt.

FOCUS QUESTIONS

1. *The Iraq War Blog* is written by someone who is living in Baghdad during the war. The entire passage is told from her point of view. Readers see things through her eyes. In the first blog entry, dated Wednesday, April 16, 2003, the author both describes what is happening and expresses how she feels about it. Highlight the parts from that segment of the text that tell you what the writer is thinking and feeling about the war in Baghdad.

2. In the second blog entry, the author describes what happened to her relatives. Cite evidence from the text that shows that she is sympathetic to what has happened to them. Cite specific parts of the text that show her identification with them.

3. Based on the text and on your previous knowledge about blogs, what can you infer about the author's purpose for writing *The Iraq War Blog*? Cite evidence from the text to support your answer.

4. How would the text be different if it were written by an American journalist who was reporting about the incidents described in the blog?

5. The author writes about her belief that what happens is God's will. Identify parts of the text in which she writes about the limits of what people can do in Baghdad to control what is happening in their lives. From what she has written, what can you infer about what the author thinks about *taqdeer*, or fate?

WRITING PROMPT

How does the point of view expressed in *The Iraq War Blog* help you understand the experience of civilian (non-military) people living in Iraq during the war? What can you infer about the author's belief in fate or destiny? Use specific evidence from the text of the blog entries in your response.

Please note that excerpts and passages in the StudySync® library and this workbook are intended as touchstones to generate interest in an author's work. The excerpts and passages do not substitute for the reading of entire texts, and StudySync® strongly recommends that students seek out and purchase the whole literary or informational work in order to experience it as the author intended. Links to online resellers are available in our digital library. In addition, complete works may be ordered through an authorized reseller by filling out and returning to StudySync® the order form enclosed in this workbook.

Reading & Writing Companion   **41**

OEDIPUS REX

DRAMA
Sophocles
429 BCE

INTRODUCTION

Author of 120 plays, the great Greek tragedian Sophocles first staged *Oedipus Rex* in 429 BCE at the annual festival and competition honoring Dionysus, the god of wine and pleasure. Sophocles won second prize for the play that would later spur Sigmund Freud to coin the term "Oedipus Complex" to denote a boy's latent desire for his mother and jealousy towards his father. In the play, King Oedipus learns that his city is suffering a plague because the murderer of the former king has not been caught. Unaware that he himself is the culprit, Oedipus vows to track down the killer, little knowing how his tragic fate will play out. In this scene, Teiresias, a blind seer, introduces Oedipus to truths he is not ready to accept.

"...what misery to be wise when wisdom profits nothing!"

 ## FIRST READ

1 *[Enter TEIRESIAS, led by a boy.]*

2 OEDIPUS: Teiresias, **seer** who comprehendest all,
3 Lore of the wise and hidden mysteries,
4 High things of heaven and low things of the earth
5 Thou knowest, though thy blinded eyes see naught,
6 What plague infects our city; and we turn
7 To thee, O seer, our one defense and shield.
8 The purport of the answer that the God
9 Returned to us who sought his oracle,
10 The messengers have doubtless told thee—how
11 One course alone could rid us of the pest,
12 To find the murderers of Laius,
13 And slay them or expel them from the land.
14 Therefore begrudging neither **augury**
15 Nor other divination that is thine,
16 O save thyself, thy country, and thy king,
17 Save all from this defilement of blood shed.
18 On thee we rest. This is man's highest end,
19 To others' service all his powers to lend.

20 TEIRESIAS: Alas, alas, what misery to be wise
21 When wisdom profits nothing! This old lore
22 I had forgotten; else I were not here.

23 OEDIPUS: What ails thee? Why this melancholy mood?

24 TEIRESIAS: Let me go home; prevent me not; 'twere best
25 That thou shouldst bear thy burden and I mine.

Reading & Writing
Companion

26 OEDIPUS: For shame! no true-born Theban patriot
27 Would thus withhold the word of prophecy.

28 TEIRESIAS: Thy words, O king, are wide of the mark, and I
29 For fear lest I too trip like thee...

30 OEDIPUS: Oh speak, Withhold not,
31 I adjure thee, if thou know'st,
32 Thy knowledge. We are all thy suppliants.

33 TEIRESIAS: Aye, for ye all are witless, but my voice
34 Will ne'er reveal my miseries—or thine.

35 OEDIPUS: What then, thou knowest, and yet willst not speak!
36 Wouldst thou betray us and destroy the State?

37 TEIRESIAS: I will not vex myself nor thee. Why ask
38 Thus idly what from me thou shalt not learn?

39 OEDIPUS: Monster! thy silence would incense a flint.
40 Will nothing loose thy tongue? Can nothing melt thee,
41 Or shake thy dogged **taciturnity**?

42 TEIRESIAS: Thou blam'st my mood and seest not thine own
43 Wherewith thou art mated; no, thou taxest me.

44 OEDIPUS: And who could stay his choler when he heard
45 How insolently thou dost flout the State?

46 TEIRESIAS: Well, it will come what will, though I be mute.

47 OEDIPUS: Since come it must, thy duty is to tell me.

48 TEIRESIAS: I have no more to say; storm as thou willst,
49 And give the rein to all thy pent-up rage.

50 OEDIPUS: Yea, I am wroth, and will not stint my words,
51 But speak my whole mind. Thou methinks thou art he,
52 Who planned the crime, aye, and performed it too,
53 All save the assassination; and if thou
54 Hadst not been blind, I had been sworn to boot
55 That thou alone didst do the bloody deed.

56 TEIRESIAS: Is it so? Then I charge thee to abide
57 By thine own proclamation; from this day
58 Speak not to these or me. Thou art the man,
59 Thou the accursed polluter of this land.

Copyright © BookheadEd Learning, LLC

NOTES

60 OEDIPUS: Vile slanderer, thou blurtest forth these taunts,
61 And think'st forsooth as seer to go scot free.

62 TEIRESIAS: Yea, I am free, strong in the strength of truth.

63 OEDIPUS: Who was thy teacher? not methinks thy art.

64 TEIRESIAS: Thou, goading me against my will to speak.

65 OEDIPUS: What speech? repeat it and resolve my doubt.

66 TEIRESIAS: Didst miss my sense wouldst thou goad me on?

67 OEDIPUS: I but half caught thy meaning; say it again.

68 TEIRESIAS: I say thou art the murderer of the man
69 Whose murderer thou pursuest.

70 OEDIPUS: Thou shalt rue it
71 Twice to repeat so gross a **calumny**.

72 TEIRESIAS: Must I say more to aggravate thy rage?

73 OEDIPUS: Say all thou wilt; it will be but waste of breath.

74 TEIRESIAS: I say thou livest with thy nearest kin
75 In infamy, unwitting in thy shame.

76 OEDIPUS: Think'st thou for aye unscathed to wag thy tongue?

77 TEIRESIAS: Yea, if the might of truth can aught prevail.

78 OEDIPUS: With other men, but not with thee, for thou
79 In ear, wit, eye, in everything art blind.

80 TEIRESIAS: Poor fool to utter gibes at me which all
81 Here present will cast back on thee ere long.

82 OEDIPUS: Offspring of endless Night, thou hast no power
83 O'er me or any man who sees the sun.

84 TEIRESIAS: No, for thy weird is not to fall by me.
85 I leave to Apollo what concerns the god.

86 OEDIPUS: Is this a plot of Creon, or thine own?

87 TEIRESIAS: Not Creon, thou thyself art thine own bane.

88 OEDIPUS: O wealth and empiry and skill by skill

89 Outwitted in the battlefield of life,

90 What spite and envy follow in your train!

91 See, for this crown the State conferred on me.

92 A gift, a thing I sought not, for this crown

93 The trusty Creon, my familiar friend,

94 Hath lain in wait to oust me and suborned

95 This mountebank, this juggling **charlatan**,

96 This tricksy beggar-priest, for gain alone

97 Keen-eyed, but in his proper art stone-blind.

98 Say, sirrah, hast thou ever proved thyself

99 A prophet? When the riddling Sphinx was here

100 Why hadst thou no deliverance for this folk?

101 And yet the riddle was not to be solved

102 By guess-work but required the prophet's art;

103 Wherein thou wast found lacking; neither birds

104 Nor sign from heaven helped thee, but I came,

105 The simple Oedipus; I stopped her mouth

106 By mother wit, untaught of auguries.

107 This is the man whom thou wouldst undermine,

108 In hope to reign with Creon in my stead.

109 Methinks that thou and thine abettor soon

110 Will rue your plot to drive the scapegoat out.

111 Thank thy grey hairs that thou hast still to learn

112 What chastisement such arrogance deserves.

113 CHORUS: To us it seems that both the seer and thou,

114 O Oedipus, have spoken angry words.

115 This is no time to wrangle but consult

116 How best we may fulfill the oracle.

117 TEIRESIAS: King as thou art, free speech at least is mine

118 To make reply; in this I am thy peer.

119 I own no lord but Loxias; him I serve

120 And ne'er can stand enrolled as Creon's man.

121 Thus then I answer: since thou hast not spared

122 To twit me with my blindness—thou hast eyes,

123 Yet see'st not in what misery thou art fallen,

124 Nor where thou dwellest nor with whom for mate.

125 Dost know thy lineage? Nay, thou know'st it not,

126 And all unwitting art a double foe

127 To thine own kin, the living and the dead;

128 Aye and the dogging curse of mother and sire

129 One day shall drive thee, like a two-edged sword,

130 Beyond our borders, and the eyes that now

NOTES

131 See clear shall henceforward endless night.
132 Ah whither shall thy bitter cry not reach,
133 What crag in all Cithaeron but shall then
134 Reverberate thy wail, when thou hast found
135 With what a hymeneal thou wast borne
136 Home, but to no fair haven, on the gale!
137 Aye, and a flood of ills thou guessest not
138 Shall set thyself and children in one line.
139 Flout then both Creon and my words, for none
140 Of mortals shall be striken worse than thou.

 ## THINK QUESTIONS

1. Based on evidence from the text, how would you describe Oedipus's character?

2. What lesson do you think theatergoers in ancient times took away when they saw this play? Use evidence from the text to support your answer.

3. How does Oedipus react to the news he hears from Teiresias? Answer in a sentence or two.

4. Use context to determine the meaning of the word **charlatan** as it is used in *Oedipus Rex*. Write your definition of *charlatan*.

5. The Latin suffix *-ity* forms a noun denoting the quality or condition of something. Use the context clues provided in the drama to determine the meaning of **taciturnity**. Write your definition of *taciturnity*.

Please note that excerpts and passages in the StudySync® library and this workbook are intended as touchstones to generate interest in an author's work. The excerpts and passages do not substitute for the reading of entire texts, and StudySync® strongly recommends that students seek out and purchase the whole literary or informational work in order to experience it as the author intended. Links to online resellers are available in our digital library. In addition, complete works may be ordered through an authorized reseller by filling out and returning to StudySync® the order form enclosed in this workbook.

Reading & Writing Companion   **47**

CLOSE READ

Reread the excerpt from *Oedipus Rex*. As you reread, complete the Focus Questions below. Then use your answers and annotations from the questions to help you complete the Writing Prompt.

FOCUS QUESTIONS

1. At the beginning of the excerpt, what text evidence helps the reader to understand that wisdom is one of the themes of the story?

2. Use your understanding of the elements of Greek dramas to highlight and annotate text that explains why you think Oedipus is a tragic hero.

3. Highlight evidence from the text to indicate the news that Teiresias is bringing to Oedipus. Then annotate the text to indicate how past events affected Oedipus's misunderstanding of what Teiresias was telling him.

4. What do you think the scene says about the theme of leadership? Reread the selection and highlight text that indicates whether you think Oedipus is a good leader. Explain why Oedipus thinks Teiresias is a charlatan, and discuss why he attacks Teiresias' taciturnity.

5. How much of Oedipus's life does he actually have control over? Highlight textual evidence and make annotations to explain your answer.

WRITING PROMPT

Teiresias says "...what misery to be wise/When wisdom profits nothing!" What does Teiresias mean by this, and why do you think he believes this is so? Do you agree with him? Reread the text and the context of the line. In an essay of at least 300 words, explain your opinion, drawing on examples in both your life and Teiresias's experience.

INTRODUCTION TO
OEDIPUS
THE KING

NON-FICTION
Bernard Knox
1982

INTRODUCTION

Classics expert and critic Bernard Knox wrote insightfully about the plays of Sophocles. Here, Knox explains the pervasive belief in destiny and divine prophecy in ancient Greek society, including the role of the oracle. Knox also argues that the great playwright Sophocles created a dramatic masterpiece by having the tragically-fated Oedipus take heroic and meaningful action.

"Oedipus did have one freedom: he was free to find out or not find out the truth."

FIRST READ

1   This play is universally recognized as the dramatic masterpiece of the Greek theater. Aristotle cites it as the most brilliant example of theatrical plot, the model for all to follow, and all the generations since who have seen it staged—no matter how inadequate the production or how poor the translation—have agreed with his assessment as they found themselves moved to pity and fear by the swift development of its ferociously logical plot. The story of Oedipus, the myth, was of course very old in Sophocles' time and very well known to his audience. It was his use of well-known material that made the play new. He chose to concentrate attention not on the actions of Oedipus which had made his name a byword—his violation of the two most **formidable** taboos observed by almost every human society—but on the moment of his discovery of the truth. And Sophocles engineered this discovery not by divine agency (as Homer did) and not by chance, but through the persistent, courageous action of Oedipus himself. The hero of the play is thus his own destroyer; he is the detective who tracks down and identifies the criminal—who turns out to be himself.

    ...

2   The voice of destiny in the play is the oracle of Apollo. Through his priests at Delphi, Apollo told Laius that he would be killed by his own son, and later told Oedipus that he would kill his father and marry his mother. At the beginning of the play Apollo tells Creon that Thebes will be saved from the plague only when the murderer of Laius is found and expelled. This Delphic oracle, which for modern poets—Yeats, for example—can conjure up mystic romantic visions, was, for Sophocles and his audience, a fact of life, and institution as present and solid, as uncompromising (and sometimes infuriating) as the Vatican is for us. States and individuals alike consulted it as a matter of course about important decisions; Sparta asked Apollo if it should declare war on Athens in 431 B.C. (it was told to go ahead and was promised victory), and at the end of the war young Xenophon asked it whether he should join the

expedition of Cyrus and go up-country into Asia Minor as a mercenary soldier fighting against the Great King. The oracle maintained contacts with peoples and rulers all over the Greek and barbarian worlds; it promoted revolutions, upheld dynasties, guided the foundation of colonies—its wealth and political influence were immense.

3   Its power was based on a widespread, indeed in early times universal, belief in the **efficacy** of divine prophecy. The gods knew everything, including what was going to happen, and so their advice was precious; the most influential dispenser of such advice was Apollo, son of Zeus. His knowledge is celebrated in a famous passage of the Ninth Pythian Ode of Pindar, who wrote in the same century as Sophocles:

> You know the appointed end
> of all things, and all the ways.
> You know how many leaves the earth unfolds in spring,
> how many grains of sand are driven by storm wind and wave
> in the rivers and the sea.
> You see clear the shape of the future
> and what will bring it to pass.

4   In such a faith, private individuals and official representatives of state had for centuries made the journey by land and sea to Apollo's temple in its magnificent setting on a high plateau below Mount Parnassus; in gratitude for the god's advice kings and cities had lavished gifts on the sanctuary and even built treasuries on the site to house their precious offerings.

...

5   The soul of drama, as Aristotle says, is plot—the action that demands and succeeds in engaging our attention so that we are no longer detached spectators but are involved in the progress of the stage events. Its outcome is important for us; in the greatest plots (and the plot of this play by Sophocles is perhaps the greatest) it is for the moment the most important thing in the world. But this engagement of the audience proceeds from an identification with the figures on stage, and this is not possible if we are made to feel that the action of the characters is not free, not effective. We expect to be made to feel that there is a meaningful relation between the hero's action and his suffering, and this is possible only if that action is free, so that he is responsible for the consequences.

...

6   Oedipus did have one freedom: he was free to find out or not find out the truth. This was the element of Sophoclean sleight-of-hand that enabled him to make a drama out of the situation which the philosophers used as the

classic demonstration of man's **subjection** to fate. But it is more than a solution to an apparently **insoluble** dramatic problem; it is the key to the play's tragic theme and the protagonist's heroic stature. One freedom is allowed him: the freedom to search for the truth, the truth about the prophecies, about the gods, about himself. And of this freedom he makes full use. Against the advice and appeals of others, he pushes on, searching for the truth, the whole truth and nothing but the truth. And in this search he shows all those great qualities that we admire in him—courage, intelligence, **perseverance**, the qualities that make human beings great. This freedom to search, and the heroic way in which Oedipus uses it, make the play not a picture of man's utter feebleness caught in the toils of fate, but on the contrary, a heroic example of man's dedication to the search for truth, the truth about himself. This is perhaps the only human freedom, the play seems to say, but there could be none more noble.

Excerpted from *The Three Theban Plays: Antigone; Oedipus the King; Oedipus at Colonus* by Sophocles, Robert Fagles (Translator) and Bernard Knox (Introduction), published by the Penguin Group

 THINK QUESTIONS

1. Refer to one or more details from the text to support your understanding of Knox's point of view about Oedipus's freedom to act—both from ideas that are directly stated and ideas that you have inferred from clues in the text.

2. Write three or four sentences explaining how Knox introduces and develops his ideas, and how the development eventually leads to his central idea. Support your response using evidence from the text.

3. In *Introduction to Oedipus the King,* Bernard Knox describes the importance of prophecy in the ancient Greek world. Choose several examples from the text of how Knox develops this central idea and discuss the rhetoric he uses to advance his point of view.

4. Use context to determine the meaning of the word **efficacy** as it is used in *Introduction to Oedipus the King.* Write your definition of *efficacy.*

5. Remembering that the Latin prefix *in-* means "not," use the context clues in the passage to determine the meaning of **insoluble**. Write your definition of *insoluble.*

CLOSE READ

Reread the excerpt from *Introduction to Oedipus the King*. As you reread, complete the Focus Questions below. Then use your answers and annotations from the questions to help you complete the Writing Prompt.

FOCUS QUESTIONS

1. As you reread the text of *Introduction to Oedipus the King*, remember that the selection is an informational text written by a classics expert and critic. Use the strategies you learned about identifying the author's point of view for an informational text. First, closely examine the words that the author uses. Second, figure out and annotate the connotations—positive, negative, neutral—of key words. Third, highlight the text to find evidence and make inferences about the author's point of view.

2. An author's point of view or purpose in an informational text may include the author's opinions and how they are revealed. What is Knox's opinion of Sophocles' play *Oedipus Rex* expressed in paragraph 1? Highlight evidence to support your ideas and write annotations to explain your choices.

3. The way an author develops ideas also reveals his or her point of view in an informational text. What is the central idea of paragraphs 2 and 3? What evidence does the author provide to support this central idea? Highlight the textual evidence you find and annotate your ideas.

4. In paragraph 4, Knox writes "The soul of drama, as Aristotle writes, is plot...." What dramatic problem does the plot of the Oedipus story present to Sophocles? How does Sophocles solve this problem? What is Knox's point of view about Sophocles' solution? Highlight your evidence and make annotations that will help to support your ideas.

5. According to the final paragraph, how much control does Oedipus actually have over what happens to him? How do his free choices and actions bring his fate about, and how does free choice contribute to his stature as a tragic hero? Highlight your evidence and make annotations to support your ideas.

WRITING PROMPT

How does the point of view of Bernard Knox help you understand why Oedipus is a tragic hero? How do Knox's central ideas and rhetoric support his point of view? Use your understanding of point of view, central ideas, and rhetoric to explain how Sophocles solves the dramatic problem of keeping his audience interested in a story of which the audience already knows the outcome.

Please note that excerpts and passages in the StudySync® library and this workbook are intended as touchstones to generate interest in an author's work. The excerpts and passages do not substitute for the reading of entire texts, and StudySync® strongly recommends that students seek out and purchase the whole literary or informational work in order to experience it as the author intended. Links to online resellers are available in our digital library. In addition, complete works may be ordered through an authorized reseller by filling out and returning to StudySync® the order form enclosed in this workbook.

Reading & Writing Companion   **53**

FATE SLEW HIM, BUT HE DID NOT DROP

POETRY

Emily Dickinson
1865

INTRODUCTION

n "Fate slew Him, but He did not drop," Emily Dickinson uses her characteristic short contrasting phrases and the imagery of a battle royale to portray the epic struggle between fate and free will. The short poem compresses much into little

"He neutralized them all—"

FIRST READ

1 Fate slew Him, but He did not drop—
2 She **felled**—He did not fall—
3 Impaled Him on Her fiercest stakes—
4 He **neutralized** them all—

5 She stung Him—**sapped** His firm Advance—
6 But when Her Worst was done
7 And He—unmoved regarded Her—
8 **Acknowledged** Him a Man.

THINK QUESTIONS

1. How would you describe Fate as presented in this poem? Use text evidence to support your answer.

2. Using evidence from the text, write one or two sentences to summarize the poem.

3. What do you think the poem implies about how much of our destiny we actually control in life? Support your answer with evidence from the text.

4. Use context to determine the meaning of the word **sapped** as it is used in "Fate slew Him, but He did not drop." Write your definition of *sapped*.

5. The base word of **acknowledged** is *knowledge*, and the base word of *knowledge* is *know*. Use the base words and context clues to write a definition of the word *acknowledged*.

Please note that excerpts and passages in the StudySync® library and this workbook are intended as touchstones to generate interest in an author's work. The excerpts and passages do not substitute for the reading of entire texts, and StudySync® strongly recommends that students seek out and purchase the whole literary or informational work in order to experience it as the author intended. Links to online resellers are available in our digital library. In addition, complete works may be ordered through an authorized reseller by filling out and returning to StudySync® the order form enclosed in this workbook.

Reading & Writing Companion

55

CLOSE READ

Reread the poem "Fate slew Him, but He did not drop". As you reread, complete the Focus Questions below. Then use your answers and annotations from the questions to help you complete the Writing Prompt.

FOCUS QUESTIONS

1. Why is "Fate slew Him, but He did not drop—" an example of the ballad form? Highlight elements in the text that show it is a ballad.

2. Dickinson's use of the ballad form gives the characters and action an epic size. Highlight and annotate three examples in the text where the characters and action are portrayed as larger-than-life.

3. Which lines portray Man as heroic?

4. Reread "Fate slew Him, but He did not drop" and look back and reread "If." Then consider the anaphora in that poem. Both use types of repetition. How do these two poems use repetition to amplify their energy? Do you find one to be more successful than the other?

5. What is unexpectedly ironic about the outcome in the poem?

6. Does the speaker seem optimistic or pessimistic about the relationship between human beings and their destiny or fate? How do you know?

WRITING PROMPT

Look at the line "And He—unmoved regarded Her—." How does He act in the face of the trials She (Fate) has put him through? How is Fate's "acknowledgement" of Man ironically informed by his attitude? Give examples of how you see this battle between Fate and Man played out in your life.

LUCK IS NOT CHANCE

POETRY

Emily Dickinson

1875

INTRODUCTION

n "Luck is not chance," Emily Dickinson has a lesson for her readers concerning luck and fortune. Are these rewards heaven-sent, or do they depend on hard work and sacrifice? Dickinson's tone, as in much of her poetry, is ironic and

"Fortune's expensive smile
Is earned—"

FIRST READ

NOTES

1 Luck is not chance—
2 It's **Toil**—
3 **Fortune's** expensive smile
4 Is earned—
5 The Father of the Mine
6 Is that old-fashioned Coin
7 We spurned—

THINK QUESTIONS

1. How do the first two lines of the poem display an ironic reversal?

2. Personification is the use of figurative language to give human characteristics to non-human things. What is one example of personification in this poem? Why is it personification?

3. How do the poem's last three lines sum up the overall theme?

4. Use context to determine the meaning of the word **toil** as it is used in "Luck is not chance."

5. Use context to determine the meaning of the word **fortune** as it is used in "Luck is not chance—."

CLOSE READ

Reread the poem "Luck is not chance". As you reread, complete the Focus Questions below. Then use your answers and annotations from the questions to help you complete the Writing Prompt.

FOCUS QUESTIONS

1. As you reread "Luck is not chance," consider the line "The Father of the Mine." Is this personification or a metaphor?

2. By using nontraditional form, how was Dickinson using the form to speak to a wider audience about what she saw as a downturn in society? Highlight evidence in the text that supports your answer.

3. What is ironic about the poem's theme, or overall message? How does Dickinson reverse your expectations?

4. Highlight the rhyming words *earned* and *spurned*. How does the contrast between these words contribute to the poem's theme?

5. What does the poem suggest about the ability of human beings to assume control of their destiny or fate?

WRITING PROMPT

How does Dickinson use the phrases *The Father of the Mine* and the *old-fashioned Coin* to reverse their usual meaning and argue that work is more important than taking one's chances on luck?

Please note that excerpts and passages in the StudySync® library and this workbook are intended as touchstones to generate interest in an author's work. The excerpts and passages do not substitute for the reading of entire texts, and StudySync® strongly recommends that students seek out and purchase the whole literary or informational work in order to experience it as the author intended. Links to online resellers are available in our digital library. In addition, complete works may be ordered through an authorized reseller by filling out and returning to StudySync® the order form enclosed in this workbook.

Reading & Writing Companion

59

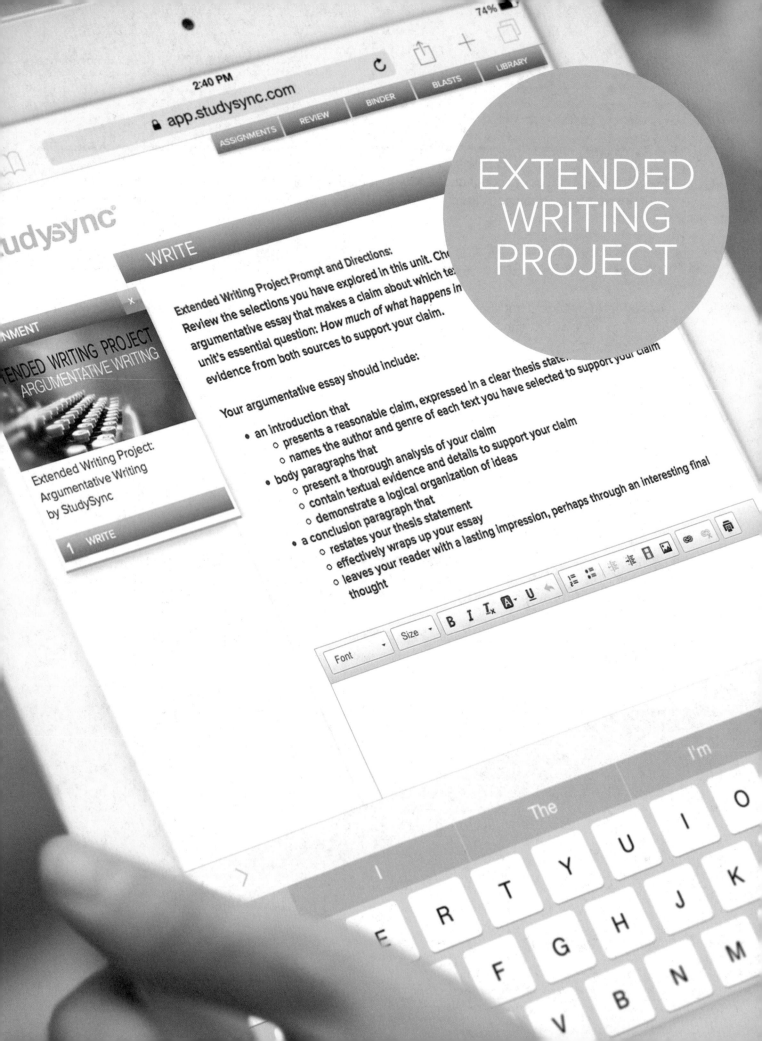

EXTENDED WRITING PROJECT

WRITE

Extended Writing Project Prompt and Directions:
Review the selections you have explored in this unit. Cho[se]
argumentative essay that makes a claim about which te[xt]
unit's essential question: *How much of what happens in[ ]*
evidence from both sources to support your claim.

Your argumentative essay should include:

- an introduction that
  - presents a reasonable claim, expressed in a clear thesis statem[ent]
  - names the author and genre of each text you have selected to support your claim
- body paragraphs that
  - present a thorough analysis of your claim
  - contain textual evidence and details to support your claim
  - demonstrate a logical organization of ideas
- a conclusion paragraph that
  - restates your thesis statement
  - effectively wraps up your essay
  - leaves your reader with a lasting impression, perhaps through an interesting final thought

Extended Writing Project:
Argumentative Writing
by StudySync

1 WRITE

Font   Size

B I Iₓ A U

NOTES

EXTENDED WRITING PROJECT
ARGUMENTATIVE WRITING

ARGUMENTATIVE WRITING

WRITING PROMPT

Review the selections you have explored in this unit. Choose two and write an argumentative essay that makes a claim about which text most convincingly answers the unit's essential question: *How much of what happens in our lives do we control?* Use text evidence from both sources to support your claim.

Your argumentative essay should include:
- an introduction that
  › presents a reasonable claim, expressed in a clear thesis statement
  › names the author and genre of each text you have selected to support your claim

- body paragraphs that
  › present a thorough analysis of your claim
  › contain textual evidence and details to support your claim
  › demonstrate a logical organization of ideas

- a conclusion paragraph that
  › restates your thesis statement
  › effectively wraps up your essay
  › leaves your reader with a lasting impression, perhaps through an interesting final thought

Argumentative writing is a type of nonfiction writing in which a writer establishes a strong position on a topic and develops it with paragraphs that support that position with evidence. The purpose of argumentative writing is to persuade an audience to agree that the writer's claim is sound and true.

Please note that excerpts and passages in the StudySync® library and this workbook are intended as touchstones to generate interest in an author's work. The excerpts and passages do not substitute for the reading of entire texts, and StudySync® strongly recommends that students seek out and purchase the whole literary or informational work in order to experience it as the author intended. Links to online resellers are available in our digital library. In addition, complete works may be ordered through an authorized reseller by filling out and returning to StudySync® the order form enclosed in this workbook.

Reading & Writing Companion   **61**

Argumentative writing can appear in many forms, including essays, speeches, debates, and letters to the editor of a newspaper.

The most important part of a strong argumentative essay is a clear **claim**. A claim is a writer's central argument or thesis. It communicates the main focus of the writing and allows readers to understand exactly what a writer is arguing. The claim should appear in the introductory paragraph, to help readers understand what will come next.

An argumentative essay should stay focused on the main claim and present information in a logical order that is easy for a reader to follow. Transition words help connect ideas and build the argument point by point. Effective argumentative writing includes strong evidence that supports the writer's reasoning and demonstrates the validity of the claim. It also adopts a formal tone that is appropriate to the purpose and style of this type of writing. A strong argumentative conclusion restates the writer's claim, effectively wraps up the argument, and leaves readers with a lasting impression, perhaps through an interesting final thought. The features of argumentative writing include:

- an introduction with a clear thesis statement
- a clear and logical organizational structure
- supporting details, including valid reasoning and textual evidence
- a formal tone
- a concluding restatement of the claim

As you continue with this extended writing project, you will receive more instructions and practice to help you craft each of the elements of argumentative writing in your own essay.

STUDENT MODEL

You will learn skills of the writer's craft as you follow the writing process steps of Prewrite, Plan, Draft, and Revise, before the final step of Edit, Proofread, and Publish. Before you get started on your own argumentative essay, begin by reading this essay that one student wrote in response to the writing prompt. As you read this student model, highlight and annotate the features of argumentative writing that the student included in her essay.

The Key to Success Is in Our Hands

Some people believe that we have the ability to forge our own successful destinies, while others believe that a successful destiny is predetermined by our natural abilities. Who is right? Two authors, David Epstein and Malcolm Gladwell, take two different positions on this subject. The author of *The Sports Gene*, David Epstein, concludes that innate physical ability is an advantage over athletic practice. Malcolm Gladwell, the author of *Outliers: The Story of Success*, argues that preparation is more important than innate talent. With strong evidence and logical reasoning, Gladwell builds a more convincing argument to support the claim that humans forge their own successful destinies through hard work and practice than Epstein does to support his opposing position, and thus Gladwell better answers the question, *How much of what happens in our lives do we control?*

In *The Sports Gene,* David Epstein describes two high jumpers and their approaches to their sport to illustrate that athletic greatness may be the result of biology. Epstein introduces Donald Thomas, a novice high jumper who began to win championships after only eight months of training, with minimal practice. Epstein then transports readers to the 2007 World Championship, where the "cool" and casual Thomas competed against the disciplined and "laser-focused" reigning Olympic champion of the high jump, Stefan Holm (Epstein 31). Epstein relates the dramatic events of the competition, at the end of which Thomas "was crowned the 2007 world champion" and came close to breaking the world record for the high jump (Epstein 32). Epstein describes studies conducted on Thomas at the Neuromuscular Research Center at the University of Jyväskylä in Finland, in which scientist Masaki Ishikawa noted that Thomas "was gifted with a giant's Achilles tendon" (Epstein 32). He then quotes exercise physiologist Gary Hunter as stating, "The Achilles tendon is very important in jumping" (Epstein 32). Epstein concludes that Thomas's Achilles tendon gives him an advantage over Holm, even though Holm had much more practice. According to Epstein, "the tendons are one puzzle piece that helps explain how two athletes could arrive at essentially the same place, one after a twenty-year love affair with his craft, and the other with less than a year of serious practice after stumbling into it on a friendly bet" (Epstein 33). He goes on to point out that "Thomas debuted on top and has not progressed. He seems to contradict the deliberate practice framework in all directions" (Epstein 33). The fact that Epstein's analysis focuses on only one aspect of only one athlete's physiology, as well as his admission that his conclusions are just "one puzzle piece" to explain Thomas's athletic success, which "seems" to contradict the idea that practice leads to greatness, do not

Please note that excerpts and passages in the StudySync® library and this workbook are intended as touchstones to generate interest in an author's work. The excerpts and passages do not substitute for the reading of entire texts, and StudySync® strongly recommends that students seek out and purchase the whole literary or informational work in order to experience it as the author intended. Links to online resellers are available in our digital library. In addition, complete works may be ordered through an authorized reseller by filling out and returning to StudySync® the order form enclosed in this workbook.

provide adequate support for the idea that our destiny for success is predetermined by our genes.

On the other hand, Malcolm Gladwell makes a compelling argument for the idea that destiny is a result of our choices, rather than our genes. In *Outliers: The Story of Success*, Gladwell describes the results of a research study conducted by psychologist K. Anders Ericsson and two colleagues in an attempt to measure innate talent and its relationship to overall success. In one portion of the study, he explains, violinists at the elite Academy of Music in Berlin were divided into three groups and asked to report the number of hours they had practiced violin since their first childhood encounters with the instrument. As Gladwell notes, ". . . by the age of twenty, the elite performers had each totaled ten thousand hours of practice. By contrast, the merely good students had totaled eight thousand hours, and the future music teachers had totaled just over four thousand hours" (Gladwell 39). Gladwell determines, "Their research suggests that once a musician has enough ability to get into a top music school, the thing that distinguishes one performer from another is how hard he or she works. That's it. And what's more, the people at the very top don't work just harder or even much harder than everyone else. They work *much, much harder*" (Gladwell 39). To further support his claim, Gladwell then quotes neurologist Daniel Levitin, who states, "The emerging picture from such studies is that ten thousand hours of practice is required to achieve the level of mastery associated with being a world-class expert—in anything . . . It seems that it takes the brain this long to assimilate all that it needs to know to achieve true mastery" (Gladwell 40). Gladwell further supports his claim by examining expert testimony on the talent of famous composer Wolfgang Amadeus Mozart, who, he explains, "famously started writing music at [age] six" but "didn't produce his greatest work until he had been composing for more than twenty years" (Gladwell 41). This wealth of evidence makes a strong argument for the claim that our destiny for success is within our individual control.

The authors of both texts agree on certain points about the human capacity for success. Epstein writes that "Tendon length is not significantly impacted by training" but that "it appears that an individual can increase tendon stiffness by training," an admission that training does have some connection to athletic ability (Epstein 33). Gladwell also considers the role of biology in achievement. He asks, ". . . is there such a thing as innate talent? The obvious answer is yes"

NOTES

(Gladwell 38). However, Gladwell offers a more developed view of the factors contributing to success: "Achievement is talent plus preparation" (Gladwell 38). In the end, Gladwell makes a strong case for the human ability to achieve more than innate talent has provided us, and he shows that it is hard work that truly shapes our destinies.

Works Cited

Epstein, David. *The Sports Gene: Inside the Science of Extraordinary Athletic Performance.* New York: Current Trade, 2013. Print.

Gladwell, Malcolm. *Outliers: The Story of Success.* New York: Little, Brown and Company, 2011. Print.

 THINK QUESTIONS

1. What is the topic of the prompt?

2. What claim does the writer make in response to the prompt? Where does the writer make this claim?

3. What is one piece of evidence from the text that supports the claim?

4. What technique does the writer use to organize her essay?

5. Based on what you have read, listened to, or researched, how would you answer the question, *How much of what happens in our lives do we actually control?*

Please note that excerpts and passages in the StudySync® library and this workbook are intended as touchstones to generate interest in an author's work. The excerpts and passages do not substitute for the reading of entire texts, and StudySync® strongly recommends that students seek out and purchase the whole literary or informational work in order to experience it as the author intended. Links to online resellers are available in our digital library. In addition, complete works may be ordered through an authorized reseller by filling out and returning to StudySync® the order form enclosed in this workbook.

Reading & Writing Companion   **65**

NOTES

EXTENDED WRITING PROJECT
PREWRITE

PREWRITE

WRITING PROMPT

Review the selections you have explored in this unit. Choose two and write an argumentative essay that makes a claim about which text most convincingly answers the unit's essential question: *How much of what happens in our lives do we control?* Use text evidence from both sources to support your claim.

Your argumentative essay should include:
- an introduction that
  - › presents a reasonable claim, expressed in a clear thesis statement
  - › names the author and genre of each text you have selected to support your claim

- body paragraphs that
  - › present a thorough analysis of your claim
  - › contain textual evidence and details to support your claim
  - › demonstrate a logical organization of ideas

- a conclusion paragraph that
  - › restates your thesis statement
  - › effectively wraps up your essay
  - › leaves your reader with a lasting impression, perhaps through an interesting final thought

In addition to studying techniques authors use to build an argument, you have been reading and exploring texts that examine how much control people have over their own destinies. In the extended writing project, you will use argumentative writing techniques to compose your own argumentative essay that addresses the unit theme.

As you begin to brainstorm for your essay, think back to the selections you have read in this unit. How do these selections examine how much of what happens in our lives is within our control and beyond our control? What claim can you make based on these selections? What reasons can you think of to support your claim? How will your audience and purpose affect the way you develop your ideas?

Then create a prewriting road map such as this one, completed by the author of the student model:

> My Claim: With strong evidence and logical reasoning, Gladwell builds a more convincing argument to support the claim that humans forge their own successful destinies through hard work and practice than Epstein does to support his opposing position, and thus Gladwell better answers the question, *How much of what happens in our lives do we control?*
>
> Selections I Will Cite to Support My Claim:
> *The Sports Gene* by David Epstein
> *Outliers: The Story of Success* by Malcolm Gladwell
>
> Reasons and Evidence That Support My Claim:
>
> • <u>Reason</u>: The expert quotes Epstein uses to support his claim that innate physical ability is an advantage over athletic practice address only one aspect of only one athlete's physiology and its potential impact.
> • <u>Evidence</u>: Scientist Masaki Ishikawa says that Thomas "was gifted with a giant's Achilles tendon" (p. 32); exercise physiologist Gary Hunter says that "The Achilles tendon is very important in jumping." (p. 32)
>
> • <u>Reason</u>: Some of Epstein's reasoning is vague and unconvincing.
> • <u>Evidence</u>: "the tendons are <u>one puzzle piece</u> that helps explain how two athletes could arrive at essentially the same place, one after a twenty-year love affair with his craft, and the other with less than a year of serious practice after stumbling into it on a friendly bet." (p. 33); "Thomas debuted on top and has not progressed. He <u>seems</u> to contradict the deliberate practice framework in all directions." (p. 33)
>
> • <u>Reason</u>: Gladwell's evidence to support his claim that destiny is a result of our choices, rather than our genes, is strong.

Please note that excerpts and passages in the StudySync® library and this workbook are intended as touchstones to generate interest in an author's work. The excerpts and passages do not substitute for the reading of entire texts, and StudySync® strongly recommends that students seek out and purchase the whole literary or informational work in order to experience it as the author intended. Links to online resellers are available in our digital library. In addition, complete works may be ordered through an authorized reseller by filling out and returning to StudySync® the order form enclosed in this workbook.

Reading & Writing
Companion

67

NOTES

- <u>Evidence</u>: "the elite performers had each totaled ten thousand hours of practice. By contrast, the merely good students had totaled eight thousand hours, and the future music teachers had totaled just over four thousand hours" (p. 39); neurologist Daniel Levitin says, "The emerging picture from such studies is that ten thousand hours of practice is required to achieve the level of mastery associated with being a world-class expert—in anything... It seems that it takes the brain this long to assimilate all that it needs to know to achieve true mastery" (p. 40).

- <u>Reason</u>: Gladwell's reasoning to support his claim is balanced and convincing.

- <u>Evidence</u>: Gladwell recognizes that there is such a thing as innate talent, but states that "Achievement is talent plus preparation" (p. 38); "Their research suggests that once a musician has enough ability to get into a top music school, the thing that distinguishes one performer from another is how hard he or she works. That's it. And what's more, the people at the very top don't work just harder or even much harder than everyone else. They work much, *much* harder" (p. 39); Mozart "famously started writing music at six" but "didn't produce his greatest work until he had been composing for more than twenty years" (p. 41)

Considerations for Audience and Purpose: I should use formal language, a formal tone, and strong, persuasive language to help convince my audience that my claim, reasoning, and evidence are sound.

SKILL:
THESIS
STATEMENT

DEFINE

The **thesis statement** is the most important sentence in an argumentative essay because it introduces what the writer is going to explore and attempt to prove in the essay or analysis. The thesis statement expresses the writer's **central or main idea** about that topic, which is the position or claim the writer will develop in the body of the essay. The thesis statement usually appears in the essay's introductory paragraph and is often the introduction's last sentence. The rest of the paragraphs in the essay all support the thesis statement with specific details, facts, evidence, quotations, and examples. The thesis statement should reappear in some form in the essay's concluding paragraph.

IDENTIFICATION AND APPLICATION

A thesis statement:

- makes a clear statement about the central idea or claim of the essay.
- lets the reader know what to expect in the body of the essay.
- responds fully and completely to an essay prompt.
- is presented in the introductory paragraph and restated in the conclusion.
- is a work-in-progress and should be revised and improved, as needed, during the early stages of the writing process.

MODEL

The following is the introductory paragraph from the student model essay "The Key to Success Is in Our Hands":

> Some people believe that we have the ability to forge our own successful destinies, while others believe that a successful destiny is predetermined by our natural abilities. Who is right? Two authors, David Epstein and Malcolm

Gladwell, take two different positions on this subject. The author of *The Sports Gene*, David Epstein, concludes that innate physical ability is an advantage over athletic practice. Malcolm Gladwell, the author of *Outliers: The Story of Success*, argues that preparation is more important than innate talent. **With strong evidence and logical reasoning, Gladwell builds a more convincing argument to support his claim that humans forge their own successful destinies through hard work and practice than Epstein does to support his opposing position, and thus Gladwell better answers the question, *How much of what happens in our lives do we control?***

The thesis statement is shown above in bold. This student's thesis statement responds to the prompt directly and includes the guiding question from the prompt. It also specifically states the writer's central idea about that topic. In this writer's view, Gladwell presents a stronger argument, backed with evidence and logical reasoning, that better answers the question about how much of our lives we control. This position or main claim, which appears at the end of the essay's first paragraph, sets up the rest of the essay on this topic.

 ## PRACTICE

Draft a thesis statement with pen and paper that states your central idea or claim in a clear and engaging way. Be sure that your thesis statement addresses the prompt. When you are done writing, switch papers with a partner to evaluate each other's work. How clearly did the writer state his or her central idea or claim? Does the thesis statement clearly and effectively address the topic posed in the prompt? Does the thesis statement clearly express the focus of the rest of the essay? Offer suggestions, and remember that they are most helpful when they are informative and constructive.

SKILL: ORGANIZE ARGUMENTATIVE WRITING

DEFINE

The purpose of argumentative writing is to make a claim or take a position on a topic, and then to identify, evaluate, and present relevant evidence that supports the position. To do this effectively, writers need to organize and present their claims, topics, ideas, facts, details, and other information in a logical way that makes it easy for readers to follow and understand.

A strong argumentative essay contains an introductory paragraph, several body paragraphs, and a concluding paragraph. The **introductory paragraph** presents the **topic** and the writer's position or central claim in a **thesis statement**. The introduction is then followed by **body paragraphs**, each of which presents detailed evidence and strong reasoning to support some aspect of the essay's thesis. The fifth paragraph is a **conclusion** that provides a unique restatement of the thesis, reviews the evidence presented, and leaves readers with a lasting impression, perhaps through a compelling final thought.

The content of the essay—that is, the type of prompt the writer is responding to and the nature of the textual evidence to be presented for support and analysis—must also be considered in choosing an overall **organizational structure** that suits the topic. For example, in addressing a topic of a historical nature, the writer might decide that a **sequential** or chronological structure might work best, since events can then be discussed in the order they occurred. On the other hand, if the writer is analyzing the similarities and differences between two authors' treatments of a topic, a **comparison and contrast** structure might be the most effective organizational method. Other organizational structures include: **problem and solution** and **cause-and-effect**. It is important to remember that while an essay or a paragraph may exhibit an overall organizational method, it may be necessary to introduce another organizational technique to convey an important point and make a solid argument.

Please note that excerpts and passages in the StudySync® library and this workbook are intended as touchstones to generate interest in an author's work. The excerpts and passages do not substitute for the reading of entire texts, and StudySync® strongly recommends that students seek out and purchase the whole literary or informational work in order to experience it as the author intended. Links to online resellers are available in our digital library. In addition, complete works may be ordered through an authorized reseller by filling out and returning to StudySync® the order form enclosed in this workbook.

Reading & Writing Companion   **71**

IDENTIFICATION AND APPLICATION

- When selecting an organizational structure, writers must consider the purpose of their writing. They often ask themselves questions about the nature of the writing task in which they are engaging. They might ask themselves the following questions:

  › What is the claim or thesis that I am making about the topic?
  › Am I comparing and contrasting different viewpoints held by different authors about the same topic, issue, or conflict?
  › Would it make sense to relay events related to the topic in the order they occurred?
  › What is the problem and what solutions do the authors propose?
  › Do any natural cause and effect relationships emerge in my analysis of the topic?

- Writers often use word choice to create connections between details and hint at the organizational structure being used:

  › Sequential order: *first, next, then, finally, last, initially, ultimately*
  › Cause and effect: *because, accordingly, as a result, in effect, so*
  › Compare and contrast: *like, unlike, also, both, similarly, although, while, but, however*

- Sometimes, within the overall structure, writers may find it necessary to organize individual paragraphs using other structures — for instance, a paragraph that compares and contrasts might benefit from a quick summary of events presented in chronological order. Be careful that such mixed strategies do not muddy the overall organization of the essay.

MODEL

The writer of the student model essay "The Key to Our Success is in Our Hands" understood from the prompt that she would choose two texts from the unit and compare and contrast them to decide which text most convincingly answers the unit's essential question: *How much of what happens in our lives do we control?* Her prewriting helped her decide that she would compare and contrast the texts *The Sports Gene* by David Epstein and *Outliers: The Story of Success* by Malcolm Gladwell.

The writer knows that in her introductory paragraph, she will state her claim and identify the sources she will use to defend her claim. Because the prompt calls for a comparison and contrast of texts from the unit, the writer created a Venn diagram to organize the similarities and differences between the viewpoints of the authors she will address in her essay:

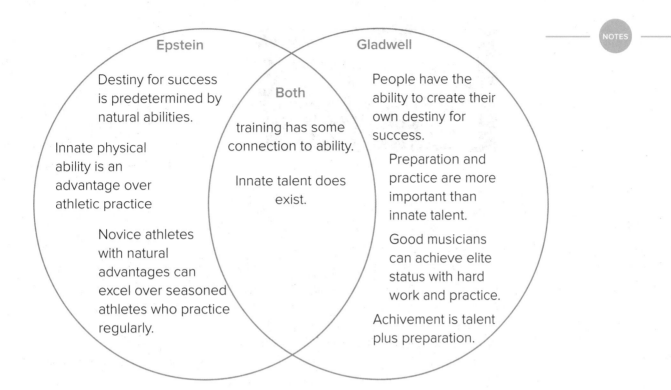

Epstein

Destiny for success is predetermined by natural abilities.

Innate physical ability is an advantage over athletic practice

Novice athletes with natural advantages can excel over seasoned athletes who practice regularly.

Both

training has some connection to ability.

Innate talent does exist.

Gladwell

People have the ability to create their own destiny for success.

Preparation and practice are more important than innate talent.

Good musicians can achieve elite status with hard work and practice.

Achivement is talent plus preparation.

PRACTICE

Using the StudySync Organize Argumentative Writing "Compare and Contrast" Venn diagram handout, fill in the information you gathered in the Prewrite stage of writing your argumentative essay. When you are done writing, switch diagrams with a partner to evaluate each other's work. Did the writer enter different viewpoints of each author or text? Has the writer completed the center of the diagram, to show similarities between the presentation of ideas in each text? Are the ideas appropriate for each section of the diagram? Offer suggestions, and remember that they are most helpful when they are informative and constructive.

SKILL: SUPPORTING DETAILS

DEFINE

Argumentative essays intend to convince readers of an author's position or point of view on a subject. To build an argument, authors introduce **claims**, or arguments, they will support with logical and valid reasoning and relevant evidence from reliable sources. The author's claim is stated in an **argumentative thesis statement**. In order to make a convincing argument, authors must distinguish their claims from **opposing claims,** or **counterclaims**—those that are contrary to the author's position or point of view. Authors then organize the claims, reasons, supporting evidence, and counterclaims into an effective argument.

Before beginning an argumentative essay, writers must search for relevant **supporting details** to reinforce their claims. Writers must evaluate source information to determine its reliability before using it to support a claim. Information that comes from a credible source and is directly related to the writer's main idea provides strong support for a claim. Such relevant information includes facts, statistics, definitions, textual evidence, examples, or quotations that are directly related to the writer's thesis statement, or main idea. Weaker text evidence—that which does not provide strong support for a claim—includes opinions, personal beliefs, emotional appeals, bias, and other information that cannot be proven to be true.

IDENTIFICATION AND APPLICATION

- Supporting evidence helps writers develop and strengthen claims in an argumentative essay.

- All supporting details in an argumentative essay should directly relate to the essay's main claim, or thesis statement.

- Writers often introduce and refute counterclaims to support their own claims.

- A writer's own reasoning can provide support for a claim when it is valid and relevant.

- When planning an argumentative essay, writers should choose details that are appropriate to a particular audience.

 MODEL

The main claim in an argumentative essay forms the argument's thesis statement, and is likely to be found near the beginning. In Chapter Two of Malcolm Gladwell's *Outliers: The Story of Success*, the claim can be found in the last sentence of the first paragraph:

> The question is this: is there such a thing as innate talent? The obvious answer is yes. Not every hockey player born in January ends up playing at the professional level. Only some do—the innately talented ones. Achievement is talent plus preparation. The problem with this view is that **the closer psychologists look at the careers of the gifted, the smaller the role innate talent seems to play and the bigger the role preparation seems to play.**

Gladwell has staked out a position on one side of the debate as to whether success comes from innate ability or from hard work. To support his position, he must supply details. Since the issue is about human psychology, persuasive details could be sought in scientific studies of successful people. Gladwell helpfully provides such details from studies of violinists and pianists at a top music school in Berlin, Germany:

> **Exhibit A in the talent argument is a study done in the early 1990s by the psychologist K. Anders Ericsson and two colleagues at Berlin's elite Academy of Music.** With the help of the Academy's professors, **they divided the school's violinists into three groups.** In the first group were the stars, the students with the potential to become world-class soloists. In the second were those judged to be merely "good." In the third were students who were unlikely to ever play professionally and who intended to be music teachers in the public school system. **All of the violinists were then asked the same question: over the course of your entire career, ever since you first picked up the violin, how many hours have you practiced?**

> Everyone from all three groups started playing at roughly the same age, around five years old. In those first few years, everyone practiced roughly the same amount, about two or three hours a week. But when the students were around the age of eight, real differences started to

Please note that excerpts and passages in the StudySync® library and this workbook are intended as touchstones to generate interest in an author's work. The excerpts and passages do not substitute for the reading of entire texts, and StudySync® strongly recommends that students seek out and purchase the whole literary or informational work in order to experience it as the author intended. Links to online resellers are available in our digital library. In addition, complete works may be ordered through an authorized reseller by filling out and returning to StudySync® the order form enclosed in this workbook.

Reading & Writing Companion   **75**

emerge. The students who would end up the best in their class began to practice more than everyone else.... In fact, **by the age of twenty, the elite performers had each totaled ten thousand hours of practice. By contrast, the merely good students had totaled eight thousand hours, and the future music teachers had totaled just over four thousand hours.**

The counterclaim to Gladwell's position is that success comes from talent, not hard work. Such a counterclaim might use evidence from the life of a musical genius, Wolfgang Amadeus Mozart (1756–1791), who started composing at the age of six. Mozart couldn't have practiced for ten thousand hours by age six, so doesn't his example disprove Gladwell's theory?

However, Gladwell counters the potential counterclaim by incorporating additional research. He quotes a famous music critic and a psychologist who specializes in explaining genius, to show that Mozart really did have the chance to practice for ten thousand hours. The reason, Gladwell claims, is that the music Mozart composed as a child wasn't great—it doesn't count except as practice. Not until he'd practiced for his ten thousand hours, by age 21, did he produce his first masterpiece. Mozart actually "developed late!" This detail isn't based on scientific studies but on another type of high-quality evidence: expert opinion supported by facts. Although it refers to only one musician's life, Gladwell's overall argument is based on statistics from the responses of many musicians.

Look at this graphic organizer, which shows how the details in *Outliers: The Story of Success* support Gladwell's thesis statement:

DETAIL	WHAT POINT DOES THIS DETAIL MAKE?	HOW DOES THIS DETAIL SUPPORT THE THESIS?
In the study done at the Academy of Music in Berlin, psychologists found that music students who were the best in their class practiced much more than the merely good students.	Practice allows people to excel at a trade.	This detail shows that preparation plays a large role in success (perhaps a larger role than innate talent), as proven by experts.

NOTES

Psychologists in this study also failed to discover any "naturals"—students who excelled despite their lack of practice—or "grinds"—students who worked harder than others yet still failed to excel.	Psychologists found a direct correlation between practice and success, yet no correlation between innate talent and success.	This detail shows that preparation plays a larger role in success than innate talent does, as proven by experts.
Neurologist Daniel Levitin states that numerous studies have shown that "ten thousand hours of practice is required to achieve the level of mastery associated with being a world-class expert—in anything."	With the right amount of practice, anyone can master a skill.	This detail shows that practice is directly related to success, as proven by experts.
Psychologist Michael Howe states that Mozart's greatest masterpieces were composed after he had been composing concertos for ten years.	Though Mozart is considered to have possessed innate talent for writing music, he only truly became a master after many years of practice.	This detail shows that even someone with "innate talent" must practice for a long time to achieve true mastery.

 PRACTICE

Complete the StudySync Supporting Details in Argumentative Writing Chart handout with details from your prewriting and from the selections you have chosen to discuss in your argumentative essay. Be sure that your details make relevant points that directly support your thesis statement. When you are done writing, switch completed charts with a partner to evaluate each other's work. How clear are the details on the chart? Are the details relevant and drawn from reliable sources? How well did the writer explain what point each detail makes? Do the details provide strong support for the writer's thesis statement? Offer suggestions for improvement, and remember that they are most helpful when they are informative and constructive.

PLAN

WRITING PROMPT

Review the selections you have explored in this unit. Choose two and write an argumentative essay that makes a claim about which text most convincingly answers the unit's essential question: *How much of what happens in our lives do we control?* Use text evidence from both sources to support your claim.

Your argumentative essay should include:
- an introduction that
  - › presents a reasonable claim, expressed in a clear thesis statement
  - › names the author and genre of each text you have selected to support your claim

- body paragraphs that
  - › present a thorough analysis of your claim
  - › contain textual evidence and details to support your claim
  - › demonstrate a logical organization of ideas

- a conclusion paragraph that
  - › restates your thesis statement
  - › effectively wraps up your essay
  - › leaves your reader with a lasting impression, perhaps through an interesting final thought

As you begin to plan your argumentative essay, use your prewriting to assemble your claim, your sources, and the relevant evidence from those sources you will be using to support your claim. First, create an outline in preparation for writing your extended argumentative essay. At the top, state the claim you will argue. List the main ideas you will address. Underneath

Copyright © BookheadEd Learning, LLC

NOTES

each main idea, list reasons and supporting evidence from the selections you have chosen to support your claim. Check that your outline provides a logical organization for an argumentative essay. If you wish to do additional research to develop your ideas, be sure to keep a record of your sources as you place the information in the outline.

The author of the student model essay, "The Key to Success Is in Our Hands," used an outline to organize her ideas before she started writing her essay. The outline divides evidence from the two articles the student references, in the order in which these details are presented in the articles. Note that all of the evidence cited addresses the original claim. Outlines help writers to eliminate information that is not relevant to the argument.

Look at the outline example and think about how you will outline and organize the information in your own argumentative essay:

Essay Outline:

Essay Claim: With strong evidence and logical reasoning, Gladwell builds a more convincing argument to support the claim that humans forge their own successful destinies through hard work and practice than Epstein does to support his opposing position, and thus Gladwell better answers the question, *How much of what happens in our lives do we control?*

Logical reasoning (to support the claim): Gladwell presents a wealth of evidence that makes a strong argument for the claim that a successful destiny is within our individual control.

1. Claim: Epstein's expert quotes address only one aspect of only one athlete's physiology, and his reasoning is vague and unconvincing.
    a. Epstein's expert quotes, which address only one aspect of only one athlete's physiology and its potential impact (textual evidence):
        i. Scientist Masaki Ishikawa determines that Thomas "was gifted with a giant's Achilles tendon"
        ii. Exercise physiologist Gary Hunter states that "The Achilles tendon is very important in jumping"
        iii. Epstein concludes that Thomas's Achilles tendon gives him an advantage over Holm, even though Holm had much more practice.

    b. Epstein's reasoning is vague and does not support his claim that our destiny for success is predetermined by our genes.
        i. He describes Thomas as "cool" and casual as he competes against the "laser-focused" reigning Olympic champion, Holm.

Please note that excerpts and passages in the StudySync® library and this workbook are intended as touchstones to generate interest in an author's work. The excerpts and passages do not substitute for the reading of entire texts, and StudySync® strongly recommends that students seek out and purchase the whole literary or informational work in order to experience it as the author intended. Links to online resellers are available in our digital library. In addition, complete works may be ordered through an authorized reseller by filling out and returning to StudySync® the order form enclosed in this workbook.

Reading & Writing
Companion

79

ii. Epstein admits that "the tendons are one puzzle piece that helps explain how two athletes could arrive at essentially the same place, one after a twenty-year love affair with his craft, and the other with less than a year of serious practice after stumbling into it on a friendly bet"

    iii. Epstein points out that "Thomas debuted on top and has not progressed. He seems to contradict the deliberate practice framework in all directions"

2. Claim: Malcolm Gladwell makes a compelling argument for the idea that destiny is a result of our choices, rather than our genes.

  a. Gladwell provides solid evidence to support his claim that we can control our destiny for success, to some extent.

    i. Gladwell provides evidence from a study conducted by psychologist K. Anders Ericsson that studied violinists and the relationship between practice hours and innate talent: "the elite performers had each totaled ten thousand hours of practice. By contrast, the merely good students had totaled eight thousand hours, and the future music teachers had totaled just over four thousand hours" (strong text evidence)

    ii. Gladwell quotes neurologist Daniel Levitin: "The emerging picture from such studies is that ten thousand hours of practice is required to achieve the level of mastery associated with being a world-class expert—in anything . . . It seems that it takes the brain this long to assimilate all that it needs to know to achieve true mastery." (supports his claim)

  b. Gladwell's reasoning is sound and supported by the evidence he cites:

    i. "Their research suggests that once a musician has enough ability to get into a top music school, the thing that distinguishes one performer from another is how hard he or she works. That's it. And what's more, the people at the very top don't work just harder or even much harder than everyone else. They work much, *much* harder."

    ii. Gladwell examines expert testimony on Mozart to determine that he "famously started writing music at [age] six" but "didn't produce his greatest work until he had been composing for more than twenty years."

3. Conclusion

  a. The authors of both texts agree on certain points about the human capacity for success.

    i. Epstein admits that "Tendon length is not significantly impacted by training" and that "it appears that an individual can increase tendon stiffness by training" (shows that training does have some connection to athletic ability)

    ii. Gladwell states, "Is there such a thing as innate talent?" Then Gladwell admits, "The obvious answer is yes" (Gladwell 38).

b. Gladwell's view of factors contributing to success is more developed.

    i. "Achievement is talent plus preparation."

Please note that excerpts and passages in the StudySync® library and this workbook are intended as touchstones to generate interest in an author's work. The excerpts and passages do not substitute for the reading of entire texts, and StudySync® strongly recommends that students seek out and purchase the whole literary or informational work in order to experience it as the author intended. Links to online resellers are available in our digital library. In addition, complete works may be ordered through an authorized reseller by filling out and returning to StudySync® the order form enclosed in this workbook.

Reading & Writing Companion   **81**

SKILL:
INTRODUCTIONS

DEFINE

The **introduction** is the opening paragraph or section of an essay or other nonfiction text. To begin an argumentative essay, writers identify the **topic**, or what the essay will be about. For an argumentative essay, the most important part of the introduction is the **thesis statement**, which contains the writer's main claim. An essay introduction should also include a **hook**, a statement or detail that grabs the reader's attention and generates reader interest in the topic.

IDENTIFICATION AND APPLICATION

- To set up the argument and introduce the topic, authors may offer descriptions, anecdotes, and other information to orient the reader.

- A thesis statement often appears as the last sentence of an introduction.

- A thesis statement is not based on an author's opinion of a topic, but is instead a claim made on the basis of reasons and evidence.

- The claim in the thesis statement must be proven in the body of the essay with relevant evidence and clear reasoning.

- The introduction should leave the reader with no doubt about the author's intention.

- The essay introduction should engage the reader and create interest that will encourage the reader to keep reading.

MODEL

To introduce an argument, writers must orient readers to the subject, the claim that will be made, and the kinds of evidence the writer will be using.

The student author of the argumentative essay "The Key to Success Is in Our Hands" has opened her argument with this introductory paragraph:

> **Some people believe that we have the ability to forge our own successful destinies, while others believe that a successful destiny is predetermined by our natural abilities. Who is right?** Two authors, David Epstein and Malcolm Gladwell, take two different positions on this subject. The author of *The Sports Gene*, David Epstein, concludes that innate physical ability is an advantage over athletic practice. Malcolm Gladwell, the author of *Outliers: The Story of Success*, argues that preparation is more important than innate talent. **With strong evidence and logical reasoning, Gladwell builds a more convincing argument to support the claim that humans forge their own successful destinies through hard work and practice than Epstein does to support his opposing position, and thus Gladwell better answers the question, How much of what happens in our lives do we actually control?**

In the very first sentence of the introduction, the student writer establishes the key debate that is at the center of this argumentative essay. The issue is whether "nature or nurture" is responsible for our success. On the one hand are those people who believe in nurture—"we have the ability to forge our own successful destinies . . ." On the other hand are those who believe in nature—that is, "a successful destiny is predetermined by our natural abilities." The student writer then poses the essential question that he or she will focus on in the essay: "Who is right?" Thus, in a concise and precise manner, the writer immediately provides the overall structure that will be used to guide the readers through the two sides of this complex argument. In addition, these two beginning sentences offer a natural hook that is broad and engaging enough to grab the attention of most readers.

In the next three sentences of the introduction, the student writer provides specific details in support of the topic sentence and essential question. The writer does this by naming and describing the positions of the two authors that will be examined and evaluated in the essay: David Epstein's *The Sports Gene* and Malcolm Gladwell's *Outliers: The Story of Success*. Each writer and his position are clearly established, which helps orient the readers as they move through the opposing arguments.

Please note that excerpts and passages in the StudySync® library and this workbook are intended as touchstones to generate interest in an author's work. The excerpts and passages do not substitute for the reading of entire texts, and StudySync® strongly recommends that students seek out and purchase the whole literary or informational work in order to experience it as the author intended. Links to online resellers are available in our digital library. In addition, complete works may be ordered through an authorized reseller by filling out and returning to StudySync® the order form enclosed in this workbook.

Reading & Writing Companion

83

NOTES

In the last sentence of the introductory paragraph, the student writer presents the thesis statement of the essay:

> *With strong evidence and logical reasoning, Gladwell builds a more convincing argument to support the claim that humans forge their own successful destinies through hard work and practice than Epstein does to support his opposing position, and thus Gladwell better answers the question, How much of what happens in our lives do we actually control?*

Note that the writer's thesis statement establishes a claim: Gladwell's argument is more convincing than than Epstein's because of its stronger evidence and reasoning. This thesis statement is not just an opinion offered by the student writer; rather, it is a statement based on reasons and evidence that will be developed in the body of the essay.

 ## PRACTICE

Write an introduction for your argumentative essay that introduces the topic, presents the thesis statement and the sources that will be developed and analyzed in the essay, and includes a hook. When you are finished, trade with a partner and offer each other feedback. How clearly is the topic established? How strong is the claim made in the thesis statement? How effective is the introduction's hook at drawing readers into the essay? Offer each other suggestions for improvement, and remember that they are most helpful when they are constructive.

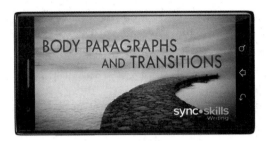

SKILL: BODY
PARAGRAPHS
AND
TRANSITIONS

DEFINE

Body paragraphs are the section of the essay between the introduction and conclusion paragraphs. Body paragraphs reveal a writer's **main points** and **claims**. They also present **evidence**, or information that supports the author's claim. Each body paragraph of an essay typically presents one main point or claim, to avoid confusing the reader. The main point of each body paragraph must support the **thesis statement**, the main claim of the essay.

Each body paragraph of an argumentative essay should contain the following structure:

Topic sentence: The topic sentence is the first sentence of a body paragraph. It should state the main point of the paragraph and support the thesis statement or main claim of the essay.

Evidence #1: A topic sentence is followed by evidence that supports the main point. Evidence can be relevant facts, statistics, definitions, quotations, examples, or other information used to support a claim.

Reasoning #1: Evidence should be followed by reasoning, or an explanation of how that evidence supports the main point. This explanation should also reveal how the evidence supports the overall thesis statement, or main claim of the essay.

Evidence #2: Writers can provide further support for their main points by introducing a second piece of evidence.

Reasoning #2: Again, evidence should be followed by reasoning, or an explanation of how that evidence supports the main point, and overall, the thesis statement.

Concluding sentence: The concluding sentence of a paragraph wraps up the main idea and transitions to the next paragraph.

Please note that excerpts and passages in the StudySync® library and this workbook are intended as touchstones to generate interest in an author's work. The excerpts and passages do not substitute for the reading of entire texts, and StudySync® strongly recommends that students seek out and purchase the whole literary or informational work in order to experience it as the author intended. Links to online resellers are available in our digital library. In addition, complete works may be ordered through an authorized reseller by filling out and returning to StudySync® the order form enclosed in this workbook.

Reading & Writing
Companion

85

NOTES

Transitions are connecting words and phrases that clarify the relationships among ideas in a text. Transitions help writers create an organizational structure and show readers how the information in the essay is connected. Writers use many different types of transitions to connect ideas in the body paragraphs of an argumentative essay:

- **Introductory phrases and clauses**, which begin a sentence and end in a comma, help create connections between ideas. Writers commonly use introductory phrases and clauses such as *Because of these events, As the results showed,* or *According to experts* to introduce evidence and explain how the evidence supports the main point.

- **Cause-and-effect transitions** present a cause-and-effect relationship between ideas. Words such as *since, because, so, therefore, thus, hence,* and *consequently* allow writers to show how one idea leads to another, or to explain how a piece of evidence supports a point.

- **Problem-and-solution transitions** help writers build claims. Writers use transitions such as *so that* and *in order to* to propose solutions and support the claims in an argumentative essay.

- **Illustration transitions** help writers present evidence. Transitions such as *Such as, For example, For instance,* and *To illustrate* connect a writer's main point in the previous sentence to the evidence that will support it.

The most effective argumentative essays will achieve their aim—to persuade a reader to agree with the author's main claim—by containing well-structured body paragraphs that use strong transitions to connect ideas.

IDENTIFICATION AND APPLICATION

- The body paragraphs of an argumentative essay provide the reasons, evidence, and arguments that support the claim made in the thesis statement.
- Writers typically develop one main idea or claim per body paragraph.
- Each body paragraph contains:
  - › a topic sentence to present the main idea of the paragraph
  - › evidence to support the topic sentence
  - › reasoning to explain how the evidence supports the main idea of the paragraph and main claim of the essay

Copyright © BookheadEd Learning, LLC

- A body paragraph may present a counterclaim that is contrary to the thesis statement. The writer then refutes the counterclaim to support the main claim of the essay.

- The conclusion sentence of a body paragraph wraps up the main idea or claim and transitions to the following body paragraph.

- Writers use transition words and phrases to connect and clarify the relationships among ideas in a text.

 ## MODEL

As writers craft an argument, the way they connect claims, reasoning, and evidence will determine the strength of their argument, as well as a reader's ability to follow their logic. The writer of the student model essay "The Key to Success Is in Our Hands" uses a logical structure to present the information that supports her main claim.

Look at the second paragraph of the essay:

> In *The Sports Gene*, **David Epstein describes two high jumpers and their approaches to their sport to illustrate that athletic greatness may be the result of biology. Epstein introduces** Donald Thomas, a novice high jumper who began to win championships after only eight months of training, with minimal practice. **Epstein then transports readers** to the 2007 World Championship, where the "cool" and casual Thomas competed against the disciplined and "laser-focused" reigning Olympic champion of the high jump, Stefan Holm (Epstein 31). **Epstein relates** the dramatic events of the competition, at the end of which Thomas "was crowned the 2007 world champion" and came close to breaking the world record for the high jump (Epstein 32). **Epstein describes** studies conducted on Thomas at the Neuromuscular Research Center at the University of Jyväskylä in Finland, in which scientist Masaki Ishikawa noted that Thomas "was gifted with a giant's Achilles tendon" (Epstein 32). **He then quotes** exercise physiologist Gary Hunter as stating, "The Achilles tendon is very important in jumping" (Epstein 32). **Epstein concludes** that Thomas's Achilles tendon gives him an advantage over Holm, even though Holm had much more practice. **According to Epstein,** "the tendons are one puzzle piece that helps explain how two athletes could arrive at essentially the same place, one after a twenty-year love affair with his craft, and the other with less than a year of serious

NOTES

practice after stumbling into it on a friendly bet" (Epstein 33). **He goes on to point out** that "Thomas debuted on top and has not progressed. He seems to contradict the deliberate practice framework in all directions" (Epstein 33). **The fact that Epstein's analysis focuses on only one aspect of only one athlete's physiology, as well as his admission that his conclusions are just "one puzzle piece" to explain Thomas's athletic success, which "seems" to contradict the idea that practice leads to greatness, do not provide adequate support for the idea that our destiny for success is predetermined by our genes.**

The body paragraph begins with a topic sentence: "In *The Sports Gene*, David Epstein describes two high jumpers and their approaches to their sport to illustrate that athletic greatness may be the result of biology." This topic sentence lets readers know what this paragraph of the essay will be about.

Next the writer discusses the information in the text and provides a wealth of evidence from the text to explain and support the topic sentence. She uses words such as "introduces," "transports," "relates," "describes," "quotes," and "concludes"—as well as phrases such as "According to Epstein" and "He goes on to point out"—to explain the evidence she has drawn from David Epstein's text. This evidence supports the main point she has made in the topic sentence of the paragraph.

The writer then wraps up the ideas in the paragraph with this concluding sentence: "The fact that Epstein's analysis focuses on only one aspect of only one athlete's physiology, as well as his admission that his conclusions are just 'one puzzle piece' to explain Thomas's athletic success, which 'seems' to contradict the idea that practice leads to greatness, do not provide adequate support for the idea that our destiny for success is predetermined by our genes." The concluding sentence support's the writer's thesis statement, which argues that Epstein's text does not as convincingly answer the question, "How much of what happens in our lives do we actually control?" as Gladwell's.

Now look at the first sentence of the next paragraph:

On the other hand, Malcolm Gladwell makes a compelling argument for the idea that destiny is a result of our choices, rather than our genes.

This first sentence of the third paragraph contains the transitional phrase "On the other hand" to set the topic of this paragraph in contrast to the preceding one. This sentence also reveals that the writer will now discuss Malcolm Gladwell's "compelling argument for the idea that destiny is a result of our choices, rather than our genes." This topic sentence clearly supports the writer's thesis statement: "With strong evidence and logical reasoning, Gladwell builds a more convincing argument to support the claim that humans forge their own successful destinies through hard work and practice than Epstein does to support his opposing position, and thus Gladwell better answers the question, *How much of what happens in our lives do we control?* In this third paragraph, the writer will introduce more evidence and reasoning to support the topic sentence of the paragraph and thesis statement of the essay.

 PRACTICE

Write two body paragraphs for your argumentative essay that follow the suggested format. When you are finished, trade with a partner and offer each other feedback. How effective is the topic sentence at stating the main idea of the paragraph? How strong is the evidence used to support the main idea? Does the reasoning for the evidence thoroughly support the main idea? Do the paragraphs contain strong transitions to connect and clarify ideas? Offer each other suggestions and remember that they are most helpful when they are constructive.

SKILL:
CONCLUSIONS

⭐ DEFINE

No argument can be considered "won" without a strong conclusion. The **conclusion** of an argumentative essay effectively brings together the points the writer makes by summarizing or restating the thesis found in the introduction. The thesis contains the claim the writer makes, while the body of the text offers evidence to prove that claim. The conclusion gives the final statement of the argument. For this reason, conclusions should not introduce new information. A conclusion should remind readers of the main points in the argument and reinforce the claim in the thesis statement.

••• IDENTIFICATION AND APPLICATION

- Writers often use phrases and clauses, such as *Because of these events, As the results showed,* or *According to experts,* to help introduce summary items in a conclusion.
- The conclusion of an argumentative essay should contain a restatement of the thesis statement.
- The conclusion of an essay should convince readers that the writer has effectively proven his or her claim.
- An essay conclusion should end in a summary statement that wraps up the ideas in the concluding paragraph.
- A writer may choose to leave the reader with a final thought, to create a lasting impression on the reader.

⟳ MODEL

Read this concluding paragraph from the student model, "The Key to Success Is in Our Hands."

The authors of both texts agree on certain points about the human capacity for success. **Epstein writes that** "Tendon length is not significantly impacted by training" but that "it appears that an individual can increase tendon stiffness by training," an admission that training does have some connection to athletic ability (Epstein 33). **Gladwell also considers** the role of biology in achievement. He asks, ". . . is there such a thing as innate talent? The obvious answer is yes" (Gladwell 38). **However,** Gladwell offers a more developed view of the factors contributing to success: "Achievement is talent plus preparation" (Gladwell 38). **In the end, Gladwell makes a strong case for the human ability to achieve more than innate talent has provided us, and he shows that it is hard work that truly shapes our destinies.**

To frame her conclusion, the writer begins the first sentence by noting both of the authors whose work she cited. She then introduces evidence from both texts to support the statement that "the authors of both texts agree on certain points about the human capacity for success." The transition "However" leads to her final point about the authors: "However, Gladwell offers a more developed view of the factors contributing to success: 'Achievement is talent plus preparation.'" The writer then uses the transitional phrase "In the end" to introduce the final statement of her argument: "Gladwell makes a strong case for the human ability to achieve more than innate talent has provided us, and he shows that it is hard work that truly shapes our destinies." The final restatement of the main claim brings the writer's argument to a solid close.

DRAFT

WRITING PROMPT

Review the selections you have explored in this unit. Choose two and write an argumentative essay that makes a claim about which text most convincingly answers the unit's essential question: *How much of what happens in our lives do we control?* Use text evidence from both sources to support your claim.

Your argumentative essay should include:
- an introduction that
  - › presents a reasonable claim, expressed in a clear thesis statement
  - › names the author and genre of each text you have selected to support your claim

- body paragraphs that
  - › present a thorough analysis of your claim
  - › contain textual evidence and details to support your claim
  - › demonstrate a logical organization of ideas

- a conclusion paragraph that
  - › restates your thesis statement
  - › effectively wraps up your essay
  - › leaves your reader with a lasting impression, perhaps through an interesting final thought

You have already made progress toward writing your own argumentative essay. You have thought about which of two texts most convincingly answers the unit's essential question: *How much of what happens in our lives do we control?* You have decided how to organize your information, and you have gathered supporting details. Now it is time to write a draft.

Use the prewriting and planning you have already done to draft your argumentative essay. Keep in mind all of the skills you have learned up to this point: how your audience and purpose inform your writing style; how to craft a clear and purposeful thesis statement or claim; how to organize your thoughts in order to make the most convincing argument; how to plan where to put the information you have gathered according to the outline of an argumentative essay; how to use supporting details to bolster the main ideas of your body paragraphs; how to write an effective introduction to engage the reader and frame the purpose of your essay as well as an impactful conclusion to summarize your points, restate your thesis, and soundly bring your essay to a close; how to use engaging and smooth transitions throughout your essay to connect all of the ideas and subtopics that support your thesis.

Remember that your draft is not the final essay. While you should maintain an essay format in keeping with argumentative writing, you can use this Draft stage to experiment with different ideas you might have regarding each author's analysis—you can always remove or delete an idea, but an idea unrecorded is gone forever.

When drafting, ask yourself these questions:

- How can I improve my introduction, including my hook, to make it more appealing and encourage my audience to read further?
- What can I do to clarify my thesis statement?
- In what ways do the main points I have provided support the thesis statement?
- Which relevant facts, strong details, and interesting quotations in each body paragraph support the main points?
- Would more precise language or additional details make the text more compelling?
- How thoroughly and effectively have I made my argument that one author's analysis more convincingly answers the essential question than another?
- What final thought do I want to leave with my readers?
- Have I responded to all aspects of the prompt?

Please note that excerpts and passages in the StudySync® library and this workbook are intended as touchstones to generate interest in an author's work. The excerpts and passages do not substitute for the reading of entire texts, and StudySync® strongly recommends that students seek out and purchase the whole literary or informational work in order to experience it as the author intended. Links to online resellers are available in our digital library. In addition, complete works may be ordered through an authorized reseller by filling out and returning to StudySync® the order form enclosed in this workbook.

Reading & Writing
Companion

93

NOTES

EXTENDED WRITING PROJECT
REVISE

REVISE

WRITING PROMPT

Review the selections you have explored in this unit. Choose two and write an argumentative essay that makes a claim about which text most convincingly answers the unit's essential question: *How much of what happens in our lives do we control?* Use text evidence from both sources to support your claim.

Your argumentative essay should include:
- an introduction that
  - › presents a reasonable claim, expressed in a clear thesis statement
  - › names the author and genre of each text you have selected to support your claim

- body paragraphs that
  - › present a thorough analysis of your claim
  - › contain textual evidence and details to support your claim
  - › demonstrate a logical organization of ideas

- a conclusion paragraph that
  - › restates your thesis statement
  - › effectively wraps up your essay
  - › leaves your reader with a lasting impression, perhaps through an interesting final thought

You have written a draft of your argumentative essay. You have also received input from your peers about how to improve it. Now you are going to revise your draft.

Here are some recommendations to help you revise:

- Reread your draft before beginning your revision.
- Review the suggestions made by your peers. Make any adjustments you feel are necessary and warranted.
- Evaluate the strength of your introduction and revise as needed.
- Revise your thesis statement, if needed, to more clearly state your claim.
- Review and adjust the claims and reasoning in the body paragraphs of your essay, to be sure that they are well-organized and support your thesis statement.
- Devise a strong conclusion that summarizes your ideas and restates the thesis.
- Review and revise your transitions, to be sure that they show strong and logical connections between ideas.
- Focus on maintaining a formal style. A formal style suits your purpose, which developing an argument about which of two texts best answers the unit question. It also fits your audience, which is made up of students, teachers, and other readers interested in learning more about your topic.
  - › As you revise, eliminate any slang.
  - › Remove any first-person pronouns such as "I," "me," or "mine" or instances of addressing readers as "you." These are more suitable to a writing style that is informal, personal, and conversational.
- Consult a style manual to check guidelines for formatting and the placement of in-text citations.
- Include a Works Cited page that lists your sources in the proper format.

Please note that excerpts and passages in the StudySync® library and this workbook are intended as touchstones to generate interest in an author's work. The excerpts and passages do not substitute for the reading of entire texts, and StudySync® strongly recommends that students seek out and purchase the whole literary or informational work in order to experience it as the author intended. Links to online resellers are available in our digital library. In addition, complete works may be ordered through an authorized reseller by filling out and returning to StudySync® the order form enclosed in this workbook.

Reading & Writing Companion

95

EDIT,
PROOFREAD
AND PUBLISH

WRITING PROMPT

Review the selections you have explored in this unit. Choose two and write an argumentative essay that makes a claim about which text most convincingly answers the unit's essential question: *How much of what happens in our lives do we control?* Use text evidence from both sources to support your claim.

Your argumentative essay should include:
- an introduction that
    - › presents a reasonable claim, expressed in a clear thesis statement
    - › names the author and genre of each text you have selected to support your claim

- body paragraphs that
    - › present a thorough analysis of your claim
    - › contain textual evidence and details to support your claim
    - › demonstrate a logical organization of ideas

- a conclusion paragraph that
    - › restates your thesis statement
    - › effectively wraps up your essay
    - › leaves your reader with a lasting impression, perhaps through an interesting final thought

You have revised your argumentative essay and received input from your peers on your revision. Now it is time to edit and proofread your essay to produce a final version. Have you addressed all the valuable suggestions from your peers? Ask yourself the following questions:

Copyright © BookheadEd Learning, LLC

NOTES

- Does my essay follow the basic structure of an argumentative essay (introduction, body paragraphs, conclusion)?

- Does my introduction grab the readers' attention in an interesting yet relevant way? Is my thesis statement part of my introduction as well as my conclusion? Does it respond to the prompt clearly and effectively?

- What more can I do to improve my essay's claims, evidence, and organization and thus make my argument more convincing?

- Have I accurately cited my sources both within the body of my essay and in my Works Cited list?

- Do I use appropriate and smooth transitions to connect ideas and details within paragraphs as well as between paragraphs?

- Have I presented my readers with a conclusion that summarizes my purpose and intent as well as coherently restates my thesis?

- Have I incorporated all the valuable suggestions from my peers?

When you are satisfied with your work, move on to proofread it for errors. For example, check that you have used correct punctuation for quotations and citations. Have you used adverbs correctly? Have you correctly used prefixes and suffixes to spell words? Be sure to correct any misspelled words.

Once you have made all your corrections, you are ready to submit and publish your work. You can distribute your writing to family and friends, hang it on a bulletin board, post it on your blog, or submit it to a website or magazine for publication. If you publish online, create links to your sources and citations. That way, readers can follow-up on what they have learned from your essay and read more on their own.

Please note that excerpts and passages in the StudySync® library and this workbook are intended as touchstones to generate interest in an author's work. The excerpts and passages do not substitute for the reading of entire texts, and StudySync® strongly recommends that students seek out and purchase the whole literary or informational work in order to experience it as the author intended. Links to online resellers are available in our digital library. In addition, complete works may be ordered through an authorized reseller by filling out and returning to StudySync® the order form enclosed in this workbook.

Reading & Writing Companion   **97**

studysync®

Reading & Writing Companion

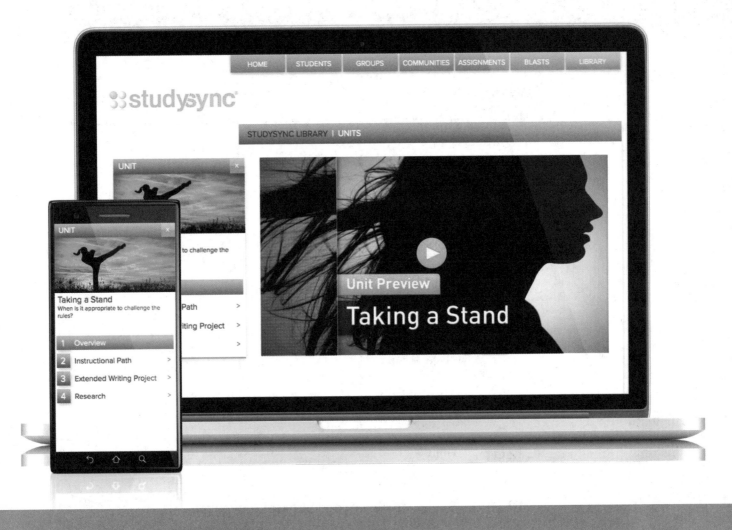

When is it appropriate to challenge the rules?

Taking a Stand

UNIT 2   When is it appropriate to challenge the rules?

Taking a Stand

TEXTS

TEXTS

EXTENDED WRITING PROJECT

425

Text Fulfillment
through
StudySync

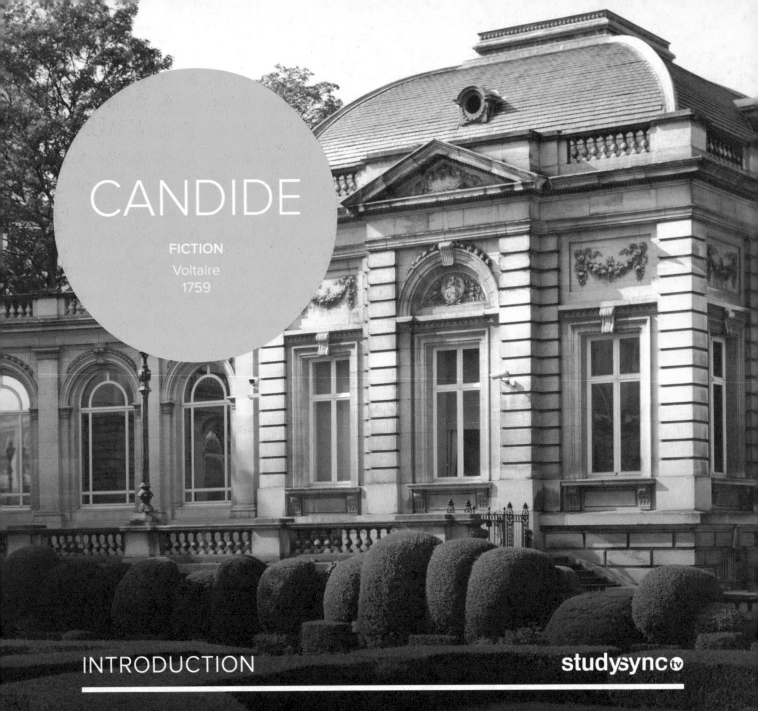

CANDIDE

FICTION
Voltaire
1759

INTRODUCTION

The French philosopher Voltaire first published *Candide* in 1759 during the Age of Enlightenment. Famed for his defenses of civil liberties, Voltaire wrote this work as a satire, a commentary on Liebnizian optimism, a belief that the world is perfect—the best of all possible places. Having experienced such historical events as the Seven Years War and the 1755 Lisbon Earthquake, Voltaire was prompted to write this short novel in which he ridicules religion, theologians, governments, armies, and philosophers through the allegorical story of the naïve Candide. Published to both great success and scandal, this story of innocence and love is taught more than any other work of French literature. In this excerpt from the beginning of the book we are introduced to our good-hearted protagonist

"Candide listened attentively and believed innocently..."

 FIRST READ

Excerpt from Chapter I

HOW CANDIDE WAS BROUGHT UP IN A MAGNIFICENT CASTLE, AND HOW HE WAS EXPELLED THENCE.

1   In a castle of Westphalia, belonging to the Baron of Thunder-ten-Tronckh, lived a youth, whom nature had endowed with the most gentle manners. His countenance was a true picture of his soul. He combined a true judgment with simplicity of spirit, which was the reason, I apprehend, of his being called Candide. The old servants of the family suspected him to have been the son of the Baron's sister, by a good, honest gentleman of the neighborhood, whom that young lady would never marry because he had been able to prove only seventy-one quarterings, the rest of his genealogical tree having been lost through the injuries of time.

2   The Baron was one of the most powerful lords in Westphalia, for his castle had not only a gate, but windows. His great hall, even, was hung with tapestry. All the dogs of his farm-yards formed a pack of hounds at need; his grooms were his huntsmen; and the curate of the village was his grand almoner. They called him "My Lord," and laughed at all his stories.

3   The Baron's lady weighed about three hundred and fifty pounds, and was therefore a person of great consideration, and she did the honours of the house with a dignity that commanded still greater respect. Her daughter Cunégonde was seventeen years of age, fresh-coloured, comely, plump, and desirable. The Baron's son seemed to be in every respect worthy of his father. The Preceptor Pangloss was the oracle of the family, and little Candide heard his lessons with all the good faith of his age and character.

4   Pangloss was professor of metaphysico-theologico-cosmolo-nigology. He proved admirably that there is no effect without a cause, and that, in this best of all possible worlds, the Baron's castle was the most magnificent of castles, and his lady the best of all possible Baronesses.

5   "It is **demonstrable**," said he, "that things cannot be otherwise than as they are; for all being created for an end, all is necessarily for the best end. Observe, that the nose has been formed to bear spectacles—thus we have spectacles. Legs are visibly designed for stockings—and we have stockings. Stones were made to be hewn, and to construct castles—therefore my lord has a magnificent castle; for the greatest baron in the province ought to be the best lodged. Pigs were made to be eaten—therefore we eat pork all the year round. Consequently they who assert that all is well have said a foolish thing, they should have said all is for the best."

6   Candide listened attentively and believed innocently; for he thought Miss Cunégonde extremely beautiful, though he never had the courage to tell her so. He concluded that after the happiness of being born of Baron of Thunder-ten-Tronckh, the second degree of happiness was to be Miss Cunégonde, the third that of seeing her every day, and the fourth that of hearing Master Pangloss, the greatest philosopher of the whole province, and **consequently** of the whole world.

7   One day Cunégonde, while walking near the castle, in a little wood which they called a park, saw between the bushes, Dr. Pangloss giving a lesson in experimental natural philosophy to her mother's chamber-maid, a little brown wench, very pretty and very **docile**. As Miss Cunégonde had a great disposition for the sciences, she breathlessly observed the repeated experiments of which she was a witness; she clearly perceived the force of the Doctor's reasons, the effects, and the causes; she turned back greatly flurried, quite pensive, and filled with the desire to be **learned;** dreaming that she might well be a sufficient reason for young Candide, and he for her.

8   She met Candide on reaching the castle and blushed; Candide blushed also; she wished him good morrow in a faltering tone, and Candide spoke to her without knowing what he said. The next day after dinner, as they went from table, Cunégonde and Candide found themselves behind a screen; Cunégonde let fall her handkerchief, Candide picked it up, she took him innocently by the hand, the youth as innocently kissed the young lady's hand with particular **vivacity** sensibility, and grace; their lips met, their eyes sparkled, their knees trembled, their hands strayed. Baron Thunder-ten-Tronckh passed near the screen and beholding this cause and effect chased Candide

from the castle with great kicks on the backside; Cunégonde fainted away; she was boxed on the ears by the Baroness, as soon as she came to herself; and all was consternation in this most magnificent and most agreeable of all possible castles.

THINK QUESTIONS

1. Candide's name comes from the Latin word *candidus,* meaning "white," to connote purity and innocence. Describe what qualities the main character has that make his name, *Candide,* appropriate. What textual evidence supports your answers?

2. What does Candide admire about the Baron's castle, and why is Candide envious as a result? Cite evidence from the text to support your answer.

3. Why does the Baron throw Candide out of his home? How does this plot event relate to the statement that this is "the best of all possible worlds"?

4. Based on your knowledge of Greek and Latin roots, what do you think someone who studies *metaphisico-theologico-cosmolo-nigology* knows a lot about? Explain how you determined your answer. Why do you think Voltaire created such a subject in this novel?

5. We usually see the word **learned** as a verb, as in "I learned my lesson that day." How can you tell that it is an adjective in this passage?

CLOSE READ

Reread the excerpt from *Candide*. As you reread, complete the Focus Questions below. Then use your answers and annotations from the questions to help you complete the Writing Prompt.

FOCUS QUESTIONS

1. Highlight text in the first paragraph where the narrator reveals the thoughts of the old servants about the Baron's sister and Candide. Why does the narrator include these details? Make annotations to explain what these details suggest about the narrator's point of view.

2. Make annotations about what Candide thinks will make him happiest in the world. What does this show about Candide's character? Highlight text evidence that supports your answer.

3. Highlight the phrase *experimental natural philosophy* in Paragraph 7. Make an annotation to explain this figure of speech and why you think Voltaire used figurative language to describe the situation. Highlight one or two other examples of figurative language and annotate to explain the effect of these on the storytelling.

4. Reread paragraphs 4 and 5. Then highlight textual evidence and make annotations to indicate how Pangloss's phrase *best of all possible worlds* applies to the Baron and his castle. What does this suggest about the character of Pangloss? Why does the Baron keep Pangloss around? Make annotations to explain your answer.

5. Identify the cause and effect mentioned in the last paragraph. What rule has Candide challenged, and does he understand what he has done? Finally, is Candide living in the "best of all possible worlds"? Make annotations to explain your answer. Highlight evidence from the last paragraphs of the excerpt to support your explanation.

WRITING PROMPT

Dr. Pangloss tells Candide that he lives in the "best of all possible worlds," but the narrator offers details that might not support that point of view. Think about how you visualize the world. Do you agree with Pangloss's philosophy? Write a 300-word essay to argue for or against this world view, using details from the text to help you discuss your ideas.

INTRODUCTION
TO ANTIGONE

NON-FICTION
Bernard Knox
1982

INTRODUCTION

In *Antigone*, the Greek playwright Sophocles writes about Oedipus's daughter Antigone and her desire to bury the body of her brother Polynices, who has died fighting in a civil war. In order to fulfill her family duty, Antigone will need to defy the new ruler, Creon, who believes that Polynices was a traitor and has forbidden Antigone and her sister Ismene from honoring him with a burial. The excerpt below from Bernard Knox's introduction to the play provides background on the ancient

"Denial of burial in their homeland to traitors...was not unknown in Greece."

FIRST READ

From: "Antigone"

1 [Creon] represents a viewpoint few Greeks would have challenged: that in times of crisis, the supreme loyalty of the citizen is to the state and its duly **constituted** authorities.

2 It is important to remember this since the natural instinct of all modern readers and playgoers is to sympathize fully with Antigone, the rebel and martyr. This is of course a correct instinct; in the end the gods, through their spokesman, the prophet Tiresias, uphold her claim that divine law does indeed prescribe burial for all dead men. But though she appeals to this law—"the great unwritten, unshakable traditions" (505)—in her magnificent challenge to Creon, she has other motives too. She proclaims again and again, to her sister Ismene as to her opponent Creon, the duty she owes to her brother, to the family relationship. "If I had allowed / my own mother's son to rot, an unburied corpse"—she tells the king, "that would have been an agony!" (520–22). "He is my brother," she tells her sister Ismene, "and—deny it as you will— / your brother too" (55–56). Creon's denial of burial to the corpse of Polynices has assaulted this fierce devotion to blood relationship at a particularly sensitive point, for the funeral rites, especially the emotional lament over the dead, were, in an ancient Greek household, the duty and privilege of the women. (In the villages of Greece today they still are.) Antigone and Ismene are the last surviving women of the house of Oedipus; this is why it seems to Antigone that Creon's decree is aimed particularly at them—"the martial law our good Creon / lays down for you and me" (37–38)—and why she takes it for granted Ismene will help her and turns so **contemptuously** and harshly against her when she refuses.

...

Reading & Writing Companion

3　Antigone appeals not only to the bond of kindred blood but also to the unwritten law, **sanctioned** by the gods, that the dead must be given proper burial—a religious principle. But Creon's position is not anti-religious; in fact he believes that he has religion on his side. The gods, for him, are the gods of the city, which contains and protects their shrines, celebrates their festivals and sacrifices, and prays to them for **deliverance;** Creon finds it unthinkable that these gods should demand the burial of a traitor to the city who came with a foreign army at his back

to burn their temples ringed with pillars,
. . . scorch their hallowed earth
and fling their laws to the winds. (323–25)

4　Once again, there would have been many in the audience who felt the same way. These vivid phrases would have recalled to them the **destruction** of Athens and the desecration of its temples by the Persian invaders in 480; they would have had no second thoughts about denying burial to the corpse of any Athenian who had fought on the Persian side. Denial of burial in their homeland to traitors, real or supposed, was not unknown in Greece.

Excerpted from *The Three Theban Plays: Antigone; Oedipus the King; Oedipus at Colonus* by Sophocles, Robert Fagles (Translator) and Bernard Knox (Introduction), published by the Penguin Group.

 THINK QUESTIONS

1. According to Knox, what is the difference between Creon's role concerning the burial of Polynices' corpse and the role of Antigone in the minds of modern readers and theatergoers? How does this help set up the action of the play? Cite evidence from the text to support your answer.

2. Briefly summarize Antigone's argument that as Polynices' sister she has a right to demand that he be buried. How might this information help develop the plot of the play? Cite evidence from the text to support your answer.

3. According to Knox, why wouldn't Creon and the Greeks of this time have second thoughts about denying burial rights to a traitor? What does this tell you about the culture of the time? Provide a quotation from the text that supports your response.

4. Use context to determine the meaning of the word **contemptuously** as it is used at the end of the second paragraph in "Introduction to *Antigone*." Write an explanation of how you used the clues and then write your definition of *contemptuously*.

5. The word **consecrate** comes from the Latin *consecrare* meaning "sacred," so *consecrate* means "to honor or to make sacred." The Latin prefix *de-* means "apart, away, off, or from." Use your understanding of Latin roots as well as context clues in the passage to determine the meaning of **desecration** in the last paragraph. Write your explanation and your definition of *desecration*.

CLOSE READ

Reread the excerpt from *Introduction to Antigone*. As you reread, complete the Focus Questions below. Then use your answers and annotations from the questions to help you complete the Writing Prompt.

FOCUS QUESTIONS

1. According to Knox, what is the cause of Antigone's anger toward Creon? What are the possible effects of this on herself and those around her? Highlight textual evidence in the excerpt to support your ideas. Make annotations to explain your choices.

2. How does compare-and-contrast text structure of the essay help readers understand the different points of view in the play *Antigone*? Highlight evidence in the text and make annotations to explain your choices.

3. What connections does Knox draw between Antigone's personality, her beliefs, and her actions? How does he develop his claims? Highlight textual evidence and write annotations to explain your idea.

4. Knox states that Antigone believes that Creon's decision not to let Polynices be buried is aimed at her and her sister personally. How does his analysis support his ideas? Highlight your evidence and make annotations that support your understanding.

5. Based on the ways Knox compare and contrasts the points of view in the play *Antigone* in this excerpt, does he think that Antigone has the right to challenge the rule of law set down by Creon? Highlight textual evidence in the paragraph and use the annotation tool to support your answer.

WRITING PROMPT

Use your understanding of key ideas, organizational structure, and point of view to explain how Knox's *Introduction to Antigone* might enhance your reading of the library excerpt from the play, *Antigone*. How does Bernard Knox's analysis of the play and explanation of cultural history help you understand the central conflict of *Antigone*, as well as the characters? Cite textual evidence to support your response.

ANTIGONE

DRAMA
Sophocles
circa 441 BCE

INTRODUCTION

Born around 497 BCE, Sophocles was one of the three great dramatists from Ancient Greece whose plays survived to modern times. *Antigone* is one of his "Theban" plays, three tragedies that focus on the fate of the city-state Thebes during and after the reign of the mythical King Oedipus. In the play, Antigone's two brothers have killed each other in battle. Antigone wants to honor each of them, but her uncle, Creon, the new king, has forbidden it. In this passage,

"Go thine own way; myself will bury him."

 FIRST READ

1 [ANTIGONE *and* ISMENE *before the Palace gates.*]

2 ANTIGONE: Ismene, sister of my blood and heart,
3 See'st thou how Zeus would in our lives fulfill
4 The weird of Oedipus, a world of woes!
5 For what of pain, affliction, outrage, shame,
6 Is lacking in our fortunes, thine and mine?
7 What can its purport be? Didst hear and heed,
8 Or art thou deaf when friends are banned as foes?

9 ISMENE: To me, Antigone, no word of friends
10 Has come, or glad or **grievous,** since we twain
11 Were reft of our two brethren in one day
12 By double fratricide; and since i' the night
13 Our Argive leaguers fled, no later news
14 Has reached me, to inspirit or deject.

15 ANTIGONE: I know 'twas so, and therefore summoned thee
16 Beyond the gates to breathe it in thine ear.

17 ISMENE: What is it? Some dark secret stirs thy breast.

18 ANTIGONE: What but the thought of our two brothers dead,
19 The one by Creon graced with funeral rites,
20 The other disappointed? Eteocles
21 He hath consigned to earth (as fame reports)
22 With obsequies that use and wont ordain,
23 So gracing him among the dead below.
24 But Polyneices, a dishonored corse,
25 (So by report the royal **edict** runs)
26 No man may bury him or make lament—

Reading & Writing
Companion

27 Must leave him tombless and unwept, a feast
28 For kites to scent afar and swoop upon.
29 Such is the edict (if report speak true)
30 Of Creon, our most noble Creon, aimed
31 At thee and me, aye me too; and anon
32 He will be here to **promulgate,** for such
33 As have not heard, his mandate; 'tis in sooth
34 No passing humor, for the edict says
35 Whoe'er transgresses shall be stoned to death.
36 So stands it with us; now 'tis thine to show
37 If thou art worthy of thy blood or **base**.

38 ISMENE: But how, my rash, fond sister, in such case
39 Can I do anything to make or mar?

40 ANTIGONE: Say, wilt thou aid me and abet? Decide.

41 ISMENE: In what bold venture? What is in thy thought?

42 ANTIGONE: Lend me a hand to bear the corpse away.

43 ISMENE: What, bury him despite the interdict?

44 ANTIGONE: My brother, and, though thou deny him, thine.
45 No man shall say that I betrayed a brother.

46 ISMENE: Wilt thou persist, though Creon has forbid?

47 ANTIGONE: What right has he to keep me from my own?

48 ISMENE: Bethink thee, sister, of our father's fate,
49 Abhorred, dishonored, self-convinced of sin,
50 Blinded, himself his executioner.
51 Think of his mother-wife (ill sorted names)
52 Done by a noose herself had twined to death;
53 And last, our hapless brethren in one day,
54 Both in a mutual destiny involved,
55 Self-slaughtered, both the slayer and the slain.
56 Bethink thee, sister, we are left alone;
57 Shall we not perish wretchedest of all,
58 If in defiance of the law we cross
59 A monarch's will? —Weak women, think of that,
60 Not framed by nature to contend with men.
61 Remember this too that the stronger rules;
62 We must obey his orders, these or worse.

Please note that excerpts and passages in the StudySync® library and this workbook are intended as touchstones to generate interest in an author's work. The excerpts and passages do not substitute for the reading of entire texts, and StudySync® strongly recommends that students seek out and purchase the whole literary or informational work in order to experience it as the author intended. Links to online resellers are available in our digital library. In addition, complete works may be ordered through an authorized reseller by filling out and returning to StudySync® the order form enclosed in this workbook.

Reading & Writing
Companion

113

63 Therefore I plead compulsion and entreat
64 The dead to pardon. I perforce obey
65 The powers that be. 'Tis foolishness, I ween,
66 To overstep in aught the golden mean.

67 ANTIGONE: I urge no more; nay, wert thou willing still,
68 I would not welcome such a fellowship.
69 Go thine own way; myself will bury him.
70 How sweet to die in such employ, to rest—
71 Sister and brother linked in love's embrace—
72 A sinless sinner, banned awhile on earth,
73 But by the dead commended; and with them
74 I shall abide for ever. As for thee,
75 Scorn, if thou wilt, the eternal laws of Heaven.

76 ISMENE: I scorn them not, but to defy the State
77 Or break her ordinance I have no skill.

78 ANTIGONE: A **specious** pretext. I will go alone
79 To lap my dearest brother in the grave.

80 ISMENE: My poor, fond sister, how I fear for thee!

81 ANTIGONE: O waste no fears on me; look to thyself.

82 ISMENE: At least let no man know of thine intent,
83 But keep it close and secret, as will I.

84 ANTIGONE: O tell it, sister; I shall hate thee more
85 If thou proclaim it not to all the town.

86 ISMENE: Thou hast a fiery soul for numbing work.

87 ANTIGONE: I pleasure those whom I would liefest please.

88 ISMENE: If thou succeed; but thou art doomed to fail.

89 ANTIGONE: When strength shall fail me, yes, but not before.

90 ISMENE: But, if the venture's hopeless, why essay?

91 ANTIGONE: Sister, forbear, or I shall hate thee soon,
92 And the dead man will hate thee too, with cause.
93 Say I am mad and give my madness rein
94 To wreck itself; the worst that can befall
95 Is but to die an honorable death.

96 ISMENE: Have thine own way then; 'tis a mad endeavor,

97 Yet to thy lovers thou art dear as ever. [*Exeunt*]

 ## THINK QUESTIONS

1. What is the relationship between Antigone and Ismene, and what are they discussing as this excerpt from the play opens? Cite textual evidence to demonstrate your understanding.

2. Who is Creon, and how does Antigone feel about him? Cite textual evidence to demonstrate your understanding.

3. What is Antigone's plan, and what is Ismene's response? Cite textual evidence and explain your understanding.

4. Use context to determine the meaning of the word **edict** as it is used in line 25. Write your explanation of the context clues and then write your definition.

5. Antigone tells her sister, "now 'tis thine to show/ If thou art worthy of thy blood or **base**." The word *or* tells you that *base* is being contrasted with *worthy of thy blood*. Given that, what do you suppose **base** means? Write your ideas.

Please note that excerpts and passages in the StudySync® library and this workbook are intended as touchstones to generate interest in an author's work. The excerpts and passages do not substitute for the reading of entire texts, and StudySync® strongly recommends that students seek out and purchase the whole literary or informational work in order to experience it as the author intended. Links to online resellers are available in our digital library. In addition, complete works may be ordered through an authorized reseller by filling out and returning to StudySync® the order form enclosed in this workbook.

Reading & Writing Companion **115**

CLOSE READ

Reread *Antigone*. As you reread, complete the Focus Questions below. Then use your answers and annotations from the questions to help you complete the Writing Prompt.

FOCUS QUESTIONS

1. What does Creon's treatment of Polyneices tell you about the culture in which Antigone lives? Highlight textual evidence that supports your understanding. Write annotations to explain your ideas.

2. Think about the language Ismene uses to describe Antigone's plans. What does this use of language say about Ismene and her view of the society she lives in? Highlight textual evidence to demonstrate the way Ismene uses language. Write annotations to explain your ideas.

3. Based on this scene from the play, what do you know about Antigone's character? Highlight lines from the text, including what she says herself and what is said about her, to demonstrate your understanding. Write annotations to explain your ideas.

4. How does Antigone's attitude toward her sister change over the course of the scene? What does this shift reveal about both of their characters? Highlight lines or phrases that indicate the changes in attitude. Write annotations to explain your ideas.

5. Why does Antigone believe she is right to challenge Creon's rule? Highlight textual evidence that points out the causes of their cultural clash, and then write annotations to explain your ideas.

WRITING PROMPT

Imagine you are Antigone. What do you want for your brother, what do you want for yourself, and why are you so determined to defy Creon? Examine your motives in a private journal entry of at least 300 words. Make sure your writing reflects the character of Antigone as depicted in Sophocles's play. Refer to the play to collect ideas and to develop an appropriate tone for your journal entry.

FAHRENHEIT 451

FICTION
Ray Bradbury
1953

INTRODUCTION

Guy Montag is a fireman. However, in the world of Ray Bradbury's futuristic novel, *Fahrenheit 451*, firemen do not put out fires; they set them. And what they burn, in this anti-intellectual society, are books—a tradition Montag seems more than willing to uphold. In this excerpt from the beginning of the novel, the fireman is walking home from a day of burning, his senses alert to the sounds and smells of the night. Then he encounters Clarisse, an unusual young woman whose naïve questions unsettle his status quo and challenge the values

"It was a pleasure to burn."

FIRST READ

NOTES

Excerpt from Part 1: "The Hearth and the Salamander"

1   It was a pleasure to burn.

2   It was a special pleasure to see things eaten, to see things blackened and changed. With the brass nozzle in his fists, with this great python spitting its venomous kerosene upon the world, the blood pounded in his head, and his hands were the hands of some amazing conductor playing all the symphonies of blazing and burning to bring down the tatters and charcoal ruins of history. With his symbolic helmet numbered 451 on his **stolid** head, and his eyes all orange flame with the thought of what came next, he flicked the igniter and the house jumped up in a gorging fire that burned the evening sky red and yellow and black. He strode in a swarm of fireflies. He wanted above all, like the old joke, to shove a marshmallow on a stick in the furnace, while the flapping pigeon-winged books died on the porch and lawn of the house. While the books went up in sparkling whirls and blew away on a wind turned dark with burning.

3   Montag grinned the fierce grin of all men singed and driven back by flame.

4   He knew that when he returned to the firehouse, he might wink at himself, a minstrel man, burnt-corked, in the mirror. Later, going to sleep, he would feel the fiery smile still gripped by his face muscles, in the dark. It never went away, that smile, it never ever went away, as long as he remembered.

5   He hung up his black beetle-colored helmet and shined it; he hung his flameproof jacket neatly; he showered **luxuriously,** and then, whistling, hands in pockets, walked across the upper floor of the fire station and fell down the hole. At the last moment, when disaster seemed positive, he pulled his hands from his pockets and broke his fall by grasping the golden pole. He slid to a squeaking halt, the heels one inch from the concrete floor downstairs.

Copyright © BookheadEd Learning, LLC

NOTES

6   He walked out of the fire station and along the midnight street toward the subway where the silent air-propelled train slid soundlessly down its lubricated flue in the earth and let him out with a great puff of warm air onto the cream-tiled escalator rising to the suburb.

7   Whistling, he let the escalator waft him into the still night air. He walked toward the corner, thinking little at all about nothing in particular. Before he reached the corner, however, he slowed as if a wind had sprung up from nowhere, as if someone had called his name.

8   The last few nights he had had the most uncertain feelings about the sidewalk just around the corner here, moving in the starlight toward his house. He had felt that a moment prior to his making the turn, someone had been there.

    ...

9   "Do you mind if I walk back with you? I'm Clarisse McClellan."

10 "Clarisse. Guy Montag. Come along. What are you doing out so late wandering around? How old are you?"

11 They walked in the warm-cool blowing night on the silvered pavement and there was the faintest breath of fresh apricots and strawberries in the air, and he looked around and realized this was quite impossible, so late in the year.

12 There was only the girl walking with him now, her face bright as snow in the moonlight, and he knew she was working his questions around, seeking the best answers she could possibly give.

13 "Well," she said, "I'm seventeen and I'm crazy. My uncle says the two always go together. When people ask your age, he said, always say seventeen and insane. Isn't this a nice time of night to walk? I like to smell things and look at things, and sometimes stay up all night, walking, and watch the sun rise."

14 They walked on again in silence and finally she said, thoughtfully, "You know, I'm not afraid of you at all."

15 He was surprised. "Why should you be?"

16 "So many people are. Afraid of firemen, I mean. But you're just a man, after all . . ."

17 He saw himself in her eyes, suspended in two shining drops of bright water, himself dark and tiny, in fine detail, the lines about his mouth, everything there, as if her eyes were two miraculous bits of violet amber that might capture and hold him intact. Her face, turned to him now, was fragile milk

crystal with a soft and constant light in it. It was not the **hysterical** light of electricity but—what? But the strangely comfortable and rare and gently flattering light of the candle. One time, as a child, in a power failure, his mother had found and lit a last candle and there had been a brief hour of **rediscovery,** of such illumination that space lost its vast dimensions and grew comfortably around them, and they, mother and son, alone, transformed, hoping that the power might not come on again too soon . . .

18   And then Clarisse McClellan said:

19   "Do you mind if I ask? How long've you worked at being a fireman?"

20   "Since I was twenty, ten years ago."

21   "Do you ever read any of the books you burn?"

22   He laughed. "That's against the law!"

23   "Oh. Of course."

24   "It's fine work. Monday burn Millay, Wednesday Whitman, Friday Faulkner, burn 'em to ashes, then burn the ashes. That's our official slogan."

25   They walked still farther and the girl said, "Is it true that long ago firemen put fires out instead of going to start them?"

26   "No. Houses have always been fireproof, take my word for it."

27   "Strange. I heard once that a long time ago houses used to burn by accident and they needed firemen to stop the flames."

28   He laughed.

29   She glanced quickly over. "Why are you laughing?"

30   "I don't know." He started to laugh again and stopped. "Why?"

31   "You laugh when I haven't been funny and you answer right off. You never stop to think what I've asked you."

Excerpted from *Fahrenheit 451* by Ray Bradbury, published by Simon & Schuster.

Copyright © BookheadEd Learning, LLC

THINK QUESTIONS

1. At what point in time is this novel set, and how can you tell? Cite textual evidence to explain your answer.

2. Who is Guy Montag and what do you know about him? Cite textual evidence to explain your response. Cite textual evidence and details that help you visualize his job.

3. Write two or three sentences explaining why you think Clarisse is talking to Montag. What do you think is her motivation for her asking these particular questions? Cite textual evidence to explain your inferences or predictions.

4. Use context, including antonyms, to determine the meaning of the word **hysterical** as it is used in *Fahrenheit 451*. Write your definition of *hysterical*.

5. The word **stolid** comes from the Latin root *stolidus*, meaning "dull or stupid." Read the word as it is used in the excerpt:

   "With his symbolic helmet numbered 451 on his **stolid** head, and his eyes all orange flame with the thought of what came next, he flicked the igniter and the house jumped up in a gorging fire that burned the evening sky red and yellow and black."

   Using the Latin root to determine the meaning, what does the word *stolid* tell readers about Montag?

CLOSE READ

Reread the excerpt from *Fahrenheit 451*. As you reread, complete the Focus Questions below. Then use your answers and annotations from the questions to help you complete the Writing Prompt.

FOCUS QUESTIONS

1. As you reread the excerpt from *Fahrenheit 451*, highlight several words and phrases that have negative or positive connotations. What inferences can you draw about Montag and the world he lives in based on these connotations? Make annotations to explain both the connotations and the inferences you made.

2. In paragraph 7, the author describes Montag's walk home from work. Highlight places where the structure of the sentences and the use of figures of speech help to show Montag's reliance on technology and other people to direct him. What does this reveal about the world of the novel? Write annotations to explain your choices.

3. Highlight figures of speech and other descriptive language in the dialogue between Montag and Clarisse in paragraphs 24–27. What is the role of this exchange in helping your understand the plot? Write annotations to explain the role of figurative language and other descriptions in this section.

4. Think about the narrator of *Fahrenheit 451* and his or her relationship to the characters and events. What is his or her point of view, and how does it reveal the main character? Highlight textual evidence over the course of the narrative to support your ideas and write annotations to explain your choices.

5. Think about the last section of the excerpt. What do Clarisse's questions introduce into the story that suggest a challenge to the rules? How does Montag feel about the appropriateness of this challenge? As you reread the text of *Fahrenheit 451*, highlight sentences and phrases that show a shift in the tone of the novel to this point. Write annotations to explain your choices.

WRITING PROMPT

Based on your understanding of figurative language, tone, and the characters in the excerpt, what can you infer about the society in which Montag and Clarisse live? What can you infer about the two characters and what makes them interested in each other? Finally, what predictions might you make about the rest of the novel? Cite textual evidence to support your ideas.

THE WHISPERERS:
PRIVATE LIFE IN STALIN'S RUSSIA

NON-FICTION
Orlando Figes
2007

INTRODUCTION

From the 1920s to the 1950s, a reign of terror gripped the Soviet Union under Josef Stalin. This book by British historian Orlando Figes goes beyond the show trials, executions, and gulag imprisonments to tell the stories of ordinary citizens in Stalinist Russia, who dared not speak above a whisper for fear of reprisals. The excerpt here concerns the persecution of "kulaks"—peasants who prospered by working outside the confines of the *kolkhoz* (collective farm).

"What were the motives of the men and women who carried out this brutal war against the peasantry?"

FIRST READ

NOTES

1   One Klavdiia Rublyova was born in 1913, the third of eleven children in a peasant family in the Irbei region of Krasnoiarsk in Siberia. Her mother died in 1924, while giving birth, leaving her father, Ilia, to bring up all the children on his own. An **enterprising** man, Ilia took advantage of the NEP [New Economic Policy] to branch out from farming to market gardening. He grew poppy seeds and cucumbers, which could easily be tended by his young children. For this he was branded a 'kulak', arrested and imprisoned, and later sent to a labour camp, leaving his children in the care of Klavdiia, who was then aged just seventeen. The children were deprived of all their father's property: the house, which he had built, was taken over by the village Soviet, while the horses, cows and sheep and the farm tools were transferred to the kolkhoz. For several weeks, the children lived in the bath-house, until officials came to take them all away to an orphanage. Klavdiia ran off with the youngest child to Kansk, near Krasnoiarsk, where her grown-up sister Raisa lived. Before they went they sold their last possessions to the other villagers. "We had nothing much to sell, we were just children," Klavdiia recalls. There was a fur-lined blanket and an old sheepskin, a feather mattress, and a mirror, which somehow we had rescued from our house. That was all we had to sell.

2   What were the motives of the men and women who carried out this brutal war against the peasantry? Most of the collectivizers were conscripted soldiers and workers — people anxious to carry out orders from above (and in some cases, to line their pockets). Hatred of the 'kulaks' had been drummed into them by their commanders and by propaganda which portrayed the 'kulak parasites' and 'bloodsuckers' as dangerous 'enemies of the people'. We were trained to see the kulaks, not as human beings, but as vermin, lice, which had to be destroyed,' recalls one young activist, the leader of a Komsomol brigade in the Kuban. 'Without the kolkhoz,' wrote another collectivizer in the 1980s, 'the kulaks would have grabbed us by the throat and skinned us all alive!'

NOTES

3　Others were carried away by their Communist enthusiasm. Inspired by the romantic revolutionary passions stirred up by the propaganda of the Five Year Plan, they believed with the Bolsheviks that any miracle could be achieved by sheer human will. As one student in those years recalls: 'We were convinced that we were creating a Communist society, that it would be achieved by the Five Year Plans, and we were ready for any sacrifice.' Today, it is easy to underestimate the emotional force of those messianic hopes and the **fanaticism** that it **engendered,** particularly in the younger generation, which had been brought up on the 'cult of struggle' and the romance of the Civil War. These young people wanted to believe that it was their calling to carry on the fight, in the words of the 'Internationale', for a 'new and better life'. In the words of one of the '25,000ers' — the urban army of enthusiasts sent into the countryside to help carry out the collectivization campaign: 'Constant struggle, struggle, and more struggle! This was how we had been taught to think — that nothing was achieved without struggle, which was a norm of social life.

4　According to this militant world-view, the creation of a new society would involve and indeed **necessitate** a bitter struggle with the forces of the old society (a logic reinforced by the propaganda of the Five Year Plan, with its constant talk of 'campaigns,' 'battles' and 'offensives' on the social, economic, international and internal 'fronts'). In this way the Communist idealists reconciled the 'anti-kulak' terror with their own utopian beliefs. Some were appalled by the brutal violence. Some were even sickened by their own role in it. But they all knew what they were doing (they could not plead that they were ignorant or that they were simply 'following orders'). And they all believed that the end justified the means.

5　Lev Kopelev, a young Communist who took part in some of the worst atrocities against the Ukrainian peasants, explained how he rationalized his actions. Kopelev had volunteered for a Komsomol brigade which requisitioned grain from the 'kulaks' in 1932. They took everything down to the last loaf of bread. Looking back on the experience in the 1970s, Kopelev recalled the children's screams and the appearance of the peasant men —'frightened, pleading, hateful, dully impassive, extinguished with despair or flaring up with half-mad daring ferocity':

6　It was excruciating to see and hear all this. And even worse to take part in it . . . And I persuaded myself, explained to myself. I mustn't give in to **debilitating** pity. We were realizing historical necessity. We were performing our revolutionary duty. We were obtaining grain for the socialist fatherland. For the Five Year Plan.

Excerpted from *The Whisperers: Private Life in Stalin's Russia* by Orlando Figes, published by Henry Holt and Company.

THINK QUESTIONS

1. Use details in the title and text to determine in what time and place the events described in this passage took place. Summarize who was affected by these events and why.

2. Use details from the text to explain how propaganda shaped the collectivizers' perceptions of the peasants and motivated their aggressive actions against these people.

3. The author indicates that the collectivizers believed that "the end justified the means." Explain the meaning of this expression as it applies to the collectivizers and use details from the text to explain why they believed in it.

4. Determine the meaning of the word **enterprising** as it is used in the first paragraph of the text and explain how context clues helped you arrive at this definition.

5. Use your knowledge of the word *necessary* as well as patterns of word changes to determine the meaning and part of speech of the word **necessitate**.

CLOSE READ

Reread the text excerpt from *The Whisperers: Private Life in Stalin's Russia*. As you reread, complete the Focus Questions below. Then use your answers and annotations from the questions to help you complete the Writing Prompt.

FOCUS QUESTIONS

1. Describe the author's attitude toward the "kulaks" and their treatment in Stalinist Russia, as evidenced by the story of Klavdiia and her family. Highlight evidence in the first paragraph, including specific word choices, that reinforces this attitude. Make annotations to support the details you select. Why do you think the author includes this paragraph at the beginning of the text?

2. Much of paragraph 2 describes the propaganda that led the collectivizers to fear the "kulaks" and motivated their attacks upon them. However, the paragraph also suggests that there were other motivations for the collectivizers' brutal actions. Highlight and annotate the textual evidence that identifies other potential reasons for the collectivizers' treatment of the "kulaks." In what way do these motivations paint the collectivizers in a more negative light?

3. Reread paragraph 3. Do you think that the first sentence is an effective summary of the paragraph's central or main idea? Write an annotation to explain your answer and highlight details that reinforce it.

4. What attitude does the author have toward the collectivizers? To what extent does he sympathize with the position in which they found themselves in that place and time, and to what extent does he think they should have challenged the rules? Highlight and annotate details in paragraph 4 that help convey the author's attitude.

5. Note this sentence in paragraph 4: *In this way the Communist idealists reconciled the 'anti-kulak' terror with their own utopian beliefs.* Highlight and annotate a sentence in paragraph 6 that reinforces this central idea through a first-person quotation.

WRITING PROMPT

Compare the excerpts from *Fahrenheit 451* and *The Whisperers: Private Life in Stalin's Russia*. Using textual evidence from both selections, explore how both authors illustrate that the utopian visions of totalitarian states can, in practice, lead to an experience of dystopia for the people. Be sure to summarize the central or main idea of each selection as it relates to this prompt.

Please note that excerpts and passages in the StudySync® library and this workbook are intended as touchstones to generate interest in an author's work. The excerpts and passages do not substitute for the reading of entire texts, and StudySync® strongly recommends that students seek out and purchase the whole literary or informational work in order to experience it as the author intended. Links to online resellers are available in our digital library. In addition, complete works may be ordered through an authorized reseller by filling out and returning to StudySync® the order form enclosed in this workbook.

Reading & Writing Companion 127

ANIMAL FARM

FICTION
George Orwell
1945

INTRODUCTION

studysync tv

"Every line of serious work that I have written since 1936 has been written, directly or indirectly, against totalitarianism and for democratic socialism as I understand it," George Orwell said, in "Why I Write." Nowhere is this more evident than *Animal Farm*, Orwell's allegorical novella that employs the uprising led by Napoleon, a pig, to satirize the corruption and dictatorship of 1917-1944 Russia. This excerpt begins just after Napoleon has lifted his leg to urinate on Snowball's plan for a technological innovation that would modernize the farm.

"By the time he had finished speaking, there was no doubt as to which way the vote would go."

 FIRST READ

Excerpt from Chapter 5

1   The whole farm was deeply divided on the subject of the windmill. Snowball did not deny that to build it would be a difficult business. Stone would have to be carried and built up into walls, then the sails would have to be made and after that there would be need for dynamos and cables. (How these were to be **procured,** Snowball did not say.) But he maintained that it could all be done in a year. And thereafter, he declared, so much labour would be saved that the animals would only need to work three days a week. Napoleon, on the other hand, argued that the great need of the moment was to increase food production, and that if they wasted time on the windmill they would all starve to death. The animals formed themselves into two **factions** under the slogan, "Vote for Snowball and the three-day week" and "Vote for Napoleon and the full manger." Benjamin was the only animal who did not side with either faction. He refused to believe either that food would become more plentiful or that the windmill would save work. Windmill or no windmill, he said, life would go on as it had always gone on--that is, badly.

2   Apart from the disputes over the windmill, there was the question of the defence of the farm. It was fully realised that though the human beings had been defeated in the Battle of the Cowshed they might make another and more determined attempt to recapture the farm and reinstate Mr. Jones. They had all the more reason for doing so because the news of their defeat had spread across the countryside and made the animals on the neighbouring farms more **restive** than ever. As usual, Snowball and Napoleon were in disagreement. According to Napoleon, what the animals must do was to procure firearms and train themselves in the use of them. According to Snowball, they must send out more and more pigeons and stir up rebellion among the animals on the other farms. The one argued that if they could not defend themselves they were bound to be conquered, the other argued that

if rebellions happened everywhere they would have no need to defend themselves. The animals listened first to Napoleon, then to Snowball, and could not make up their minds which was right; indeed, they always found themselves in agreement with the one who was speaking at the moment.

3   At last the day came when Snowball's plans were completed. At the Meeting on the following Sunday the question of whether or not to begin work on the windmill was to be put to the vote. When the animals had assembled in the big barn, Snowball stood up and, though occasionally interrupted by bleating from the sheep, set forth his reasons for advocating the building of the windmill. Then Napoleon stood up to reply. He said very quietly that the windmill was nonsense and that he advised nobody to vote for it, and promptly sat down again; he had spoken for barely thirty seconds, and seemed almost indifferent as to the effect he produced. At this Snowball sprang to his feet, and shouting down the sheep, who had begun bleating again, broke into a passionate appeal in favour of the windmill. Until now the animals had been about equally divided in their sympathies, but in a moment Snowball's eloquence had carried them away. In glowing sentences he painted a picture of Animal Farm as it might be when **sordid** labour was lifted from the animals' backs. His imagination had now run far beyond chaff-cutters and turnip-slicers. Electricity, he said, could operate threshing machines, ploughs, harrows, rollers, and reapers and binders, besides supplying every stall with its own electric light, hot and cold water, and an electric heater. By the time he had finished speaking, there was no doubt as to which way the vote would go. But just at this moment Napoleon stood up and, casting a peculiar sidelong look at Snowball, uttered a high-pitched whimper of a kind no one had ever heard him utter before.

4   At this there was a terrible baying sound outside, and nine enormous dogs wearing brass-studded collars came bounding into the barn. They dashed straight for Snowball, who only sprang from his place just in time to escape their snapping jaws. In a moment he was out of the door and they were after him. Too amazed and frightened to speak, all the animals crowded through the door to watch the chase. Snowball was racing across the long pasture that led to the road. He was running as only a pig can run, but the dogs were close on his heels. Suddenly he slipped and it seemed certain that they had him. Then he was up again, running faster than ever, then the dogs were gaining on him again. One of them all but closed his jaws on Snowball's tail, but Snowball whisked it free just in time. Then he put on an extra spurt and, with a few inches to spare, slipped through a hole in the hedge and was seen no more.

5   Silent and terrified, the animals crept back into the barn. In a moment the dogs came bounding back. At first no one had been able to imagine where these creatures came from, but the problem was soon solved: they were the

puppies whom Napoleon had taken away from their mothers and reared privately. Though not yet full-grown, they were huge dogs, and as fierce-looking as wolves. They kept close to Napoleon. It was noticed that they wagged their tails to him in the same way as the other dogs had been used to do to Mr. Jones.

6 Napoleon, with the dogs following him, now mounted on to the raised portion of the floor where Major had previously stood to deliver his speech. He announced that from now on the Sunday-morning Meetings would come to an end. They were unnecessary, he said, and wasted time. In future all questions relating to the working of the farm would be settled by a special committee of pigs, presided over by himself. These would meet in private and afterwards communicate their decisions to the others. The animals would still assemble on Sunday mornings to salute the flag, sing 'Beasts of England', and receive their orders for the week; but there would be no more debates.

7 In spite of the shock that Snowball's expulsion had given them, the animals were dismayed by this announcement. Several of them would have protested if they could have found the right arguments. Even Boxer was vaguely troubled. He set his ears back, shook his forelock several times, and tried hard to **marshal** his thoughts; but in the end he could not think of anything to say. Some of the pigs themselves, however, were more articulate. Four young porkers in the front row uttered shrill squeals of disapproval, and all four of them sprang to their feet and began speaking at once. But suddenly the dogs sitting round Napoleon let out deep, menacing growls, and the pigs fell silent and sat down again. Then the sheep broke out into a tremendous bleating of "Four legs good, two legs bad!" which went on for nearly a quarter of an hour and put an end to any chance of discussion.

8 Afterwards Squealer was sent round the farm to explain the new arrangement to the others.

9 "Comrades," he said, "I trust that every animal here appreciates the sacrifice that Comrade Napoleon has made in taking this extra labour upon himself. Do not imagine, comrades, that leadership is a pleasure! On the contrary, it is a deep and heavy responsibility. No one believes more firmly than Comrade Napoleon that all animals are equal. He would be only too happy to let you make your decisions for yourselves. But sometimes you might make the wrong decisions, comrades, and then where should we be? Suppose you had decided to follow Snowball, with his moonshine of windmills—Snowball, who, as we now know, was no better than a criminal?"

10 "He fought bravely at the Battle of the Cowshed," said somebody.

Please note that excerpts and passages in the StudySync® library and this workbook are intended as touchstones to generate interest in an author's work. The excerpts and passages do not substitute for the reading of entire texts, and StudySync® strongly recommends that students seek out and purchase the whole literary or informational work in order to experience it as the author intended. Links to online resellers are available in our digital library. In addition, complete works may be ordered through an authorized reseller by filling out and returning to StudySync® the order form enclosed in this workbook.

Reading & Writing Companion   **131**

NOTES

11 "Bravery is not enough," said Squealer. "Loyalty and obedience are more important. And as to the Battle of the Cowshed, I believe the time will come when we shall find that Snowball's part in it was much exaggerated."

Excerpted from *Animal Farm* by George Orwell, published by Harcourt Brace & Company.

THINK QUESTIONS

1. As the excerpt opens, who are Snowball and Napoleon, and what has led them to this point? How do you know? What is Snowball arguing for and why? Cite textual details that support your explanation.

2. Was the attack of the dogs planned? Cite textual evidence to support your response.

3. What reason does Napoleon give for ending the Sunday meetings? Why does he really end them? Cite evidence to support your response.

4. Use context to determine the meaning of the word **factions** as it is used in *Animal Farm*. Write your definition of *factions*.

5. The word **comrade** is often used to mean "friend." However, in Soviet Russia, *comrade* indicated a fellow member of the Communist party. Use context to determine the meaning of the word *comrade* as it is used in *Animal Farm*. Write your definition of *comrade*.

CLOSE READ

Reread the excerpt from *Animal Farm*, Chapter 5. As you reread, complete the Focus Questions below. Then use your answers and annotations from the questions to help you complete the Writing Prompt.

FOCUS QUESTIONS

1. As you reread the excerpt from *Animal Farm,* think about the how the author reveals the characters of Napoleon and Snowball. What do their names as well as their actions reveal about their characters? Highlight textual evidence, beginning in the first paragraph to support your ideas and inferences and write annotations to explain your choices.

2. How do the other animals react to Napoleon's and Snowball's differing ideas in paragraph 2 of the selection? How do the animals' reactions connect to Orwell's themes? Highlight evidence to support your ideas and write annotations to explain your choices.

3. In paragraph 5, the narrator explains the origin of Napoleon's dogs. What does this information reveal about Napoleon? Why does the author include this information at this moment? Highlight evidence to support your ideas and write annotations to explain your choices.

4. In this excerpt, only one character, Squealer, is shown to be speaking for himself through dialogue. Why do you think Orwell chose to include that character's speech while only summarizing the main points of Napoleon's and Snowball's speeches? Highlight textual evidence and write annotations to explain your ideas.

5. How did both Snowball and Napoleon both challenge the existing order? What makes Snowball and Napoleon different? Use your understanding of narrative point of view and character in this selection to identify the central message, or theme, that emerges in this excerpt of the novel. Annotate to explain the theme, and highlight evidence from the text that will help support your ideas.

WRITING PROMPT

Squealer says, "No one believes more firmly than Comrade Napoleon that all animals are equal." Squealer also tells the animals that only Napoleon can be trusted to make the right decisions for the group. In 250 words, analyze this apparent contradiction in terms of leadership, power, and general citizen participation in government. Relate your ideas to a theme from this excerpt of the novel.

Please note that excerpts and passages in the StudySync® library and this workbook are intended as touchstones to generate interest in an author's work. The excerpts and passages do not substitute for the reading of entire texts, and StudySync® strongly recommends that students seek out and purchase the whole literary or informational work in order to experience it as the author intended. Links to online resellers are available in our digital library. In addition, complete works may be ordered through an authorized reseller by filling out and returning to StudySync® the order form enclosed in this workbook.

Reading & Writing
Companion

133

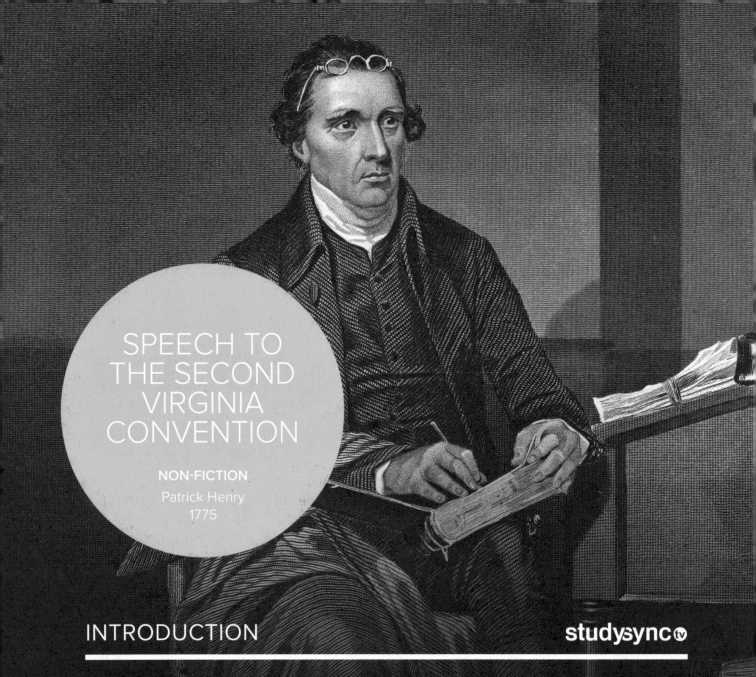

SPEECH TO THE SECOND VIRGINIA CONVENTION

NON-FICTION
Patrick Henry
1775

INTRODUCTION

"Different men often see the same subject in different lights," says Patrick Henry in his speech to the Second Virginia Convention, eloquently evoking reason to subtly persuade his audience. In 1775, on the eve of America's Revolutionary War, one of America's Founding Fathers, Patrick Henry, articulates his radical views with carefully constructed language intended to convince the Virginia's House of Burgesses to pass a resolution to support a war of independence against Britain. Hoping to convince Virginia to provide troops, Henry appealed to the patriotism of all those listening, including future presidents George Washington and Thomas Jefferson, with powerful oratory, including the famous line from the speech, "I know not what course others may take; but as for me, give me liberty or

"The war is inevitable and let it come!"

FIRST READ

NOTES

1   Mr. President, no man thinks more highly than I do of the patriotism, as well as abilities, of the very worthy gentlemen who have just addressed the House. But different men often see the same subject in different lights; and, therefore, I hope it will not be thought disrespectful to those gentlemen if, entertaining as I do, opinions of a character very opposite to theirs, I shall speak forth my **sentiments** freely, and without reserve. This is no time for ceremony. The question before the House is one of awful moment to this country. For my own part, I consider it as nothing less than a question of freedom or slavery; and in proportion to the magnitude of the subject ought to be the freedom of the debate. It is only in this way that we can hope to arrive at truth, and fulfill the great responsibility which we hold to God and our country. Should I keep back my opinions at such a time, through fear of giving offence, I should consider myself as guilty of treason towards my country, and of an act of disloyalty toward the majesty of heaven, which I **revere** above all earthly kings.

2   Mr. President, it is natural to man to indulge in the illusions of hope. We are apt to shut our eyes against a painful truth, and listen to the song of that siren till she transforms us into beasts. Is this the part of wise men, engaged in a great and **arduous** struggle for liberty? Are we disposed to be of the number of those who, having eyes, see not, and, having ears, hear not, the things which so nearly concern their temporal salvation? For my part, whatever anguish of spirit it may cost, I am willing to know the whole truth; to know the worst, and to provide for it.

3   I have but one lamp by which my feet are guided; and that is the lamp of experience. I know of no way of judging of the future but by the past. And judging by the past, I wish to know what there has been in the conduct of the British ministry for the last ten years, to justify those hopes with which gentlemen have been pleased to solace themselves, and the House? Is it that insidious smile with which our petition has been lately received? Trust it

not, sir; it will prove a snare to your feet. Suffer not yourselves to be betrayed with a kiss. Ask yourselves how this gracious reception of our petition comports with these war-like preparations which cover our waters and darken our land. Are fleets and armies necessary to a work of love and reconciliation? Have we shown ourselves so unwilling to be reconciled, that force must be called in to win back our love? Let us not deceive ourselves, sir. These are the implements of war and **subjugation;** the last arguments to which kings resort. I ask, gentlemen, sir, what means this martial array, if its purpose be not to force us to submission? Can gentlemen assign any other possible motive for it?

4 Has Great Britain any enemy, in this quarter of the world, to call for all this accumulation of navies and armies? No, sir, she has none. They are meant for us; they can be meant for no other. They are sent over to bind and rivet upon us those chains which the British ministry have been so long forging. And what have we to oppose to them? Shall we try argument? Sir, we have been trying that for the last ten years. Have we anything new to offer upon the subject? Nothing. We have held the subject up in every light of which it is capable; but it has been all in vain. Shall we resort to entreaty and humble **supplication?** What terms shall we find which have not been already exhausted? Let us not, I beseech you, sir, deceive ourselves. Sir, we have done everything that could be done, to avert the storm which is now coming on. We have petitioned; we have remonstrated; we have supplicated; we have prostrated ourselves before the throne, and have implored its interposition to arrest the tyrannical hands of the ministry and Parliament. Our petitions have been slighted; our remonstrances have produced additional violence and insult; our supplications have been disregarded; and we have been spurned, with contempt, from the foot of the throne. In vain, after these things, may we indulge the fond hope of peace and reconciliation. There is no longer any room for hope. If we wish to be free, if we mean to preserve inviolate those inestimable privileges for which we have been so long contending, if we mean not basely to abandon the noble struggle in which we have been so long engaged, and which we have pledged ourselves never to abandon until the glorious object of our contest shall be obtained, we must fight! I repeat it, sir, we must fight! An appeal to arms and to the God of Hosts is all that is left us!

5 They tell us, sir, that we are weak; unable to cope with so formidable an adversary. But when shall we be stronger? Will it be the next week, or the next year? Will it be when we are totally disarmed, and when a British guard shall be stationed in every house? Shall we gather strength by irresolution and inaction? Shall we acquire the means of effectual resistance, by lying supinely on our backs, and hugging the delusive phantom of hope, until our enemies shall have bound us hand and foot? Sir, we are not weak if we make a proper use of those means which the God of nature hath placed in our

power. Three millions of people, armed in the holy cause of liberty, and in such a country as that which we possess, are invincible by any force which our enemy can send against us. Besides, sir, we shall not fight our battles alone. There is a just God who presides over the destinies of nations; and who will raise up friends to fight our battles for us. The battle, sir, is not to the strong alone; it is to the vigilant, the active, the brave. Besides, sir, we have no election. If we were base enough to desire it, it is now too late to retire from the contest. There is no retreat but in submission and slavery! Our chains are forged! Their clanking may be heard on the plains of Boston! The war is inevitable and let it come! I repeat it, sir, let it come. It is in vain, sir, to extenuate the matter. Gentlemen may cry, Peace, Peace but there is no peace. The war is actually begun! The next gale that sweeps from the north will bring to our ears the clash of resounding arms! Our brethren are already in the field! Why stand we here idle? What is it that gentlemen wish? What would they have? Is life so dear, or peace so sweet, as to be purchased at the price of chains and slavery? Forbid it, Almighty God! I know not what course others may take; but as for me, give me liberty or give me death!

 THINK QUESTIONS

1. Who is Patrick Henry's audience for the speech? What passage from the speech helps you answer? Support your answer with textual evidence.

2. Explain how Patrick Henry alerts his listeners to the urgency of his message. What actions taken by the British in 1775 required an immediate response from the colonists, according to Henry? Support your answer with textual evidence.

3. The purpose of Henry's speech is to persuade his audience to take action. What specific action does Henry urge his audience to take? Provide textual evidence for your response. Why do you think the precise purpose of Henry's speech only becomes clear in the second half of the speech rather than the first?

4. Use context to identify a more familiar synonym of the word **sentiments,** which appears in paragraph 1 of the speech. Explain how this synonym in the same sentence helps you determine the meaning of the word *sentiments*.

5. Use context to identify a word that seems to be related to the word **subjugation,** which appears in paragraph 3 of the speech. Explain how this related word in the next sentence helps you determine the meaning of the word *subjugation*.

Please note that excerpts and passages in the StudySync® library and this workbook are intended as touchstones to generate interest in an author's work. The excerpts and passages do not substitute for the reading of entire texts, and StudySync® strongly recommends that students seek out and purchase the whole literary or informational work in order to experience it as the author intended. Links to online resellers are available in our digital library. In addition, complete works may be ordered through an authorized reseller by filling out and returning to StudySync® the order form enclosed in this workbook.

Reading & Writing Companion   **137**

CLOSE READ

Reread the excerpt from "Speech to the Second Virginia Convention." As you reread, complete the Focus Questions below. Then use your answers and annotations from the questions to help you complete the Writing Prompt.

FOCUS QUESTIONS

1. What point of view does Henry convey in the second paragraph of the speech and to what purpose? Highlight and annotate evidence to support your analysis.

2. The delegates at the Second Virginia Convention, Patrick Henry's audience, were largely in favor of diplomatic resolution. How does Henry address the concerns of those who wonder if another course of action besides war might be available? Highlight and annotate specific text evidence from paragraph 4 to support your response.

3. The British, as well as many delegates themselves, feared that the colonists were too weak to take on the British. What is Henry's point of view on this point? What tactics does he use to persuade his audience to share his point of view? Highlight and annotate specific text evidence from paragraph 5 to support your response.

4. What does Henry believe will happen if the colonists fail to act now against the British? Highlight and annotate emotional appeals and language Henry uses in the final lines of his speech to build momentum and accomplish his purpose of rousing his audience to immediate action.

5. Based on details presented throughout the speech, when does Patrick Henry believe it is not only appropriate but necessary to challenge authority? Reread the text in its entirety and then highlight and annotate revealing details within the text.

WRITING PROMPT

Identify an issue about which you have a strong point of view. How might challenging authority or the status quo be necessary to achieve the purpose of making your point of view a reality? Write a 300-word speech that, like Patrick Henry's "Speech to the Second Virginia Convention," supports a strong point of view, creates a powerful sense of urgency, and provokes listeners to take action and change the status quo. Be sure to make logical as well as emotional appeals and use rhetorical techniques such as figurative language, allusions, and rhetorical questions to advance your argument. Perhaps you might even coin a line worthy of going down in the history books alongside Henry's "Give me liberty or give me death!"

THE BALLAD OF BIRMINGHAM

POETRY
Dudley Randall
1965

INTRODUCTION

Dudley Randall was an African-American poet and publisher who served for a time as Poet Laureate of Detroit. "The Ballad of Birmingham" is the most well-known of his poems, many of which were written during the tumultuous period of the Civil Rights Movement. The poem, written from the point of view of a mother who has lost her child, evokes the pain and confusion caused by the 1963 Birmingham church bombing, which killed four young African

"No, baby, no, you may not go, For I fear those guns will fire."

FIRST READ

1 As "Mother dear, may I go downtown
2 Instead of out to play,
3 And march the streets of Birmingham
4 In a Freedom March today?"

5 "No, baby, no, you may not go,
6 For the dogs are **fierce** and **wild,**
7 And clubs and hoses, guns and jails
8 Aren't good for a little child."

9 "But, mother, I won't be alone.
10 Other children will go with me,
11 And march the streets of Birmingham
12 To make our country free."

13 "No, baby, no, you may not go,
14 For I fear those guns will fire.
15 But you may go to church instead,
16 And sing in the children's choir."

17 She has combed and brushed her night-dark hair,
18 And bathed rose petal sweet,
19 And **drawn** white gloves on her small brown hands,
20 And white shoes on her feet.

21 The mother smiled to know her child
22 Was in the **sacred** place,
23 But that smile was the last smile
24 To come upon her face.

25 For when she heard the explosion,
26 Her eyes grew wet and wild.
27 She raced through the streets of Birmingham
28 Calling for her child.

29 She **clawed** through bits of glass and brick,
30 Then lifted out a shoe.
31 "O, here's the shoe my baby wore,
32 But, baby, where are you?"

© 2009 by Dudley Randall, ROSES AND REVOLUTIONS: THE SELECTED WRITINGS OF DUDLEY RANDALL, Wayne State University Press. Reproduced by permission of Melba J. Boyd.

 ## THINK QUESTIONS

1. Why does the mother in the poem deny her child the chance to join one of the Freedom Marches in downtown Birmingham? Cite evidence from the poem to support your answer.

2. Based on details in the text, describe the purpose of the Freedom Marches and who participated in them.

3. What is ironic about the mother's decision to send her child to sing in the church choir instead of to march on the streets? Explain your answer using textual evidence.

4. To which place in the poem does the word **sacred** refer? How does this reference help you understand the meaning of the word *sacred*? Explain your answer.

5. Use context clues to determine what the speaker means when he or she says that the mother's eyes grew **wild**. Explain your answer.

CLOSE READ

Reread the poem "The Ballad of Birmingham". As you reread, complete the Focus Questions below. Then use your answers and annotations from the questions to help you complete the Writing Prompt.

FOCUS QUESTIONS

1. In the fourth stanza, highlight words that are associated with the church and words that are associated with the street. How do the different connotations of these words set up a contrast between the church and the street that later proves to be ironic? Make annotations to support your explanation.

2. Explain how vivid descriptions and words with strong connotations emphasize the child's purity and innocence in the fifth stanza.

3. What is the connotation of the word *clawed* in the eighth and last stanza? How is this connotation similar to that of the word *wild* in the seventh stanza, and how does each serve to convey the mother's state of mind?

4. Highlight other words in the eighth and last stanza that help create strong mental images for readers. What effect are such images likely intended to have and why?

5. Based on details in the text, what might have been the poet's purpose in writing this piece? What point of view might he have had toward the Civil Rights Movement and the costs of challenging the rules?

WRITING PROMPT

Dudley Randall wrote "The Ballad of Birmingham" after the real-life bombing that occurred in 1963 in Birmingham, Alabama, during the period of the Civil Rights Movement. Research details about the bombing and its historical context. Then use your research findings to analyze how the poem includes both facts from the historical record about actual events that took place in Birmingham, Alabama as well as literary dramatizations of these events. Which details can be confirmed by source materials? How does the fictionalized material enhance the description of the real-life events and their impact on readers? Finally, explain how the content of the poem may suggest Randall's point of view and message about the protests, the bombing, and the impact of the violence on families. Be sure to include specific examples from the text as well as information obtained from research to support your analysis.

REMARKS TO THE SENATE IN SUPPORT OF THE DECLARATION OF CONSCIENCE

NON-FICTION
Margaret Chase Smith
1950

INTRODUCTION

studysync🅣

Margaret Chase Smith, a Republican from Maine, was the first woman to serve in both the House of Representatives and the Senate. In this famous speech, delivered four months after Senator Joseph McCarthy made his inflammatory claim that the State Department was "infested" with Communists, beginning a dark period in Congressional history, Smith reaches out to her

"As an American, I want to see our nation recapture the strength and unity it once had..."

FIRST READ

Mr. President:

1   I would like to speak briefly and simply about a serious national condition. It is a national feeling of fear and frustration that could result in national suicide and the end of everything that we Americans hold dear. It is a condition that comes from the lack of effective leadership in either the Legislative Branch or the Executive Branch of our Government.

2   That leadership is so lacking that serious and responsible proposals are being made that national advisory commissions be appointed to provide such critically needed leadership.

3   I speak as briefly as possible because too much harm has already been done with irresponsible words of bitterness and selfish political **opportunism**. I speak as briefly as possible because the issue is too great to be obscured by eloquence. I speak simply and briefly in the hope that my words will be taken to heart.

4   I speak as a Republican. I speak as a woman. I speak as a United States Senator. I speak as an American.

5   The United States Senate has long enjoyed worldwide respect as the greatest deliberative body in the world. But recently that deliberative character has too often been **debased** to the level of a forum of hate and character assassination sheltered by the shield of congressional immunity.

6   It is ironical that we Senators can in debate in the Senate directly or indirectly, by any form of words, **impute** to any American who is not a Senator any conduct or motive unworthy or unbecoming an American—and without that non-Senator American having any legal redress against us—yet if we say the same thing in the Senate about our colleagues we can be stopped on the grounds of being out of order.

NOTES

7　It is strange that we can verbally attack anyone else without restraint and with full protection and yet we hold ourselves above the same type of criticism here on the Senate Floor. Surely the United States Senate is big enough to take self-criticism and self-appraisal. Surely we should be able to take the same kind of character attacks that we "dish out" to outsiders.

8　I think that it is high time for the United States Senate and its members to do some soul-searching—for us to weigh our consciences—on the manner in which we are performing our duty to the people of America—on the manner in which we are using or abusing our individual powers and privileges.

9　I think that it is high time that we remembered that we have sworn to uphold and defend the Constitution. I think that it is high time that we remembered that the Constitution, as amended, speaks not only of the freedom of speech but also of trial by jury instead of trial by accusation.

10　Whether it be a criminal prosecution in court or a character prosecution in the Senate, there is little practical distinction when the life of a person has been ruined.

11　Those of us who shout the loudest about Americanism in making character assassinations are all too frequently those who, by our own words and acts, ignore some of the basic principles of Americanism:

12　The right to criticize;
The right to hold unpopular beliefs;
The right to protest;
The right of independent thought.

13　The exercise of these rights should not cost one single American citizen his reputation or his right to a livelihood nor should he be in danger of losing his reputation or livelihood merely because he happens to know someone who holds unpopular beliefs. Who of us doesn't? Otherwise none of us could call our souls our own. Otherwise thought control would have set in.

14　The American people are sick and tired of being afraid to speak their minds lest they be politically smeared as "Communists" or "Fascists" by their opponents. Freedom of speech is not what it used to be in America. It has been so abused by some that it is not exercised by others.

15　The American people are sick and tired of seeing innocent people smeared and guilty people whitewashed. But there have been enough proved cases, such as the Amerasia case, the Hiss case, the Coplon case, the Gold case, to cause the nationwide distrust and strong suspicion that there may be something to the unproved, sensational accusations.

16   As a Republican, I say to my colleagues on this side of the aisle that the Republican Party faces a challenge today that is not unlike the challenge that it faced back in Lincoln's day. The Republican Party so successfully met that challenge that it emerged from the Civil War as the champion of a united nation -- in addition to being a Party that unrelentingly fought loose spending and loose programs.

17   Today our country is being psychologically divided by the confusion and the suspicions that are bred in the United States Senate to spread like cancerous tentacles of "know nothing, suspect everything" attitudes. Today we have a Democratic Administration that has developed a mania for loose spending and loose programs. History is repeating itself—and the Republican Party again has the opportunity to emerge as the champion of unity and prudence.

18   The record of the present Democratic Administration has provided us with sufficient campaign issues without the necessity of resorting to political smears. America is rapidly losing its position as leader of the world simply because the Democratic Administration has pitifully failed to provide effective leadership.

19   The Democratic Administration has completely confused the American people by its daily contradictory grave warnings and optimistic assurances— that show the people that our Democratic Administration has no idea of where it is going.

20   The Democratic Administration has greatly lost the confidence of the American people by its **complacency** to the threat of communism here at home and the leak of vital secrets to Russia though key officials of the Democratic Administration. There are enough proved cases to make this point without diluting our criticism with unproved charges.

21   Surely these are sufficient reasons to make it clear to the American people that it is time for a change and that a Republican victory is necessary to the security of this country. Surely it is clear that this nation will continue to suffer as long as it is governed by the present ineffective Democratic Administration.

22   Yet to displace it with a Republican regime embracing a philosophy that lacks political integrity or intellectual honesty would prove equally disastrous to this nation. The nation sorely needs a Republican victory. But I don't want to see the Republican Party ride to political victory on the Four Horsemen of Calumny—Fear, Ignorance, Bigotry, and Smear.

23   I doubt if the Republican Party could—simply because I don't believe the American people will uphold any political party that puts political exploitation above national interest. Surely we Republicans aren't that desperate for victory.

24 I don't want to see the Republican Party win that way. While it might be a fleeting victory for the Republican Party, it would be a more lasting defeat for the American people. Surely it would ultimately be suicide for the Republican Party and the two-party system that has protected our American liberties from the dictatorship of a one party system.

25 As members of the Minority Party, we do not have the primary authority to formulate the policy of our Government. But we do have the responsibility of rendering constructive criticism, of clarifying issues, of allaying fears by acting as responsible citizens.

26 As a woman, I wonder how the mothers, wives, sisters, and daughters feel about the way in which members of their families have been politically mangled in the Senate debate -- and I use the word "debate" advisedly.

27 As a United States Senator, I am not proud of the way in which the Senate has been made a publicity platform for irresponsible **sensationalism**. I am not proud of the reckless abandon in which unproved charges have been hurled from this side of the aisle. I am not proud of the obviously staged, undignified countercharges that have been attempted in retaliation from the other side of the aisle.

28 I don't like the way the Senate has been made a rendezvous for vilification, for selfish political gain at the sacrifice of individual reputations and national unity. I am not proud of the way we smear outsiders from the Floor of the Senate and hide behind the cloak of congressional immunity and still place ourselves beyond criticism on the Floor of the Senate.

29 As an American, I am shocked at the way Republicans and Democrats alike are playing directly into the Communist design of "confuse, divide, and conquer." As an American, I don't want a Democratic Administration "whitewash" or "cover-up" any more than I want a Republican smear or witch hunt.

30 As an American, I condemn a Republican "Fascist" just as much I condemn a Democratic "Communist." I condemn a Democrat "Fascist" just as much as I condemn a Republican "Communist." They are equally dangerous to you and me and to our country. As an American, I want to see our nation recapture the strength and unity it once had when we fought the enemy instead of ourselves.

31 It is with these thoughts that I have drafted what I call a "Declaration of Conscience." I am gratified that Senator Tobey, Senator Aiken, Senator Morse, Senator Ives, Senator Thye, and Senator Hendrickson have concurred in that declaration and have authorized me to announce their concurrence.

THINK QUESTIONS

1. Why is Senator Margaret Chase Smith addressing the U.S. Senate? To whom are the remarks delivered? Cite textual evidence to support your answer.

2. What, to Senator Smith, are the significant characteristics of the Republican Party and the Democratic Administration at the time she is delivering this speech? Why is she concerned about both of them? Cite textual evidence to support your answer.

3. Why do you think Chase Smith waits until Paragraph 13 to use the word "Communists" in her remarks? Cite textual evidence to explain your inference.

4. Use context to determine the meaning of the word **debased** as it is used in "Remarks to the Senate in Support of a Declaration of Conscience." Write your definition for *debased*.

5. Use your understanding of word parts and the context clues provided in the passage to determine the meaning of **sensationalism**. Explain how you figured out the meaning and write your definition of *sensationalism*.

CLOSE READ

Reread the text from "Remarks to the Senate in Support of a Declaration of Conscience." As you reread, complete the Focus Questions below. Then use your answers and annotations from the questions to help you complete the Writing Prompt.

FOCUS QUESTIONS

1. How does Smith contrast the rights of Senators with the rights of ordinary citizens? Highlight textual evidence to support your ideas. Annotate to explain the contrasts.

2. Highlight textual evidence that Smith gives to support the idea that Americans may have some reason to suspect their fellow citizens. Write annotations to explain how she supports her claims.

3. Smith makes it clear that she is speaking from a variety of points of view, all of which have joined together to express a single opinion. Highlight the text in which she identifies these points of view. Annotate to explain the value in identifying these points of view.

4. Like Patrick Henry in his "Speech to the Second Virginia Convention," Smith speaks to what she sees as an immediate and dangerous issue and challenges her colleagues to take a new course of action. Highlight some phrases she uses to convince her fellow Senators of the importance of the issue. Write annotations to explain how her rhetoric compares to that of Patrick Henry and how their use of language helped make their speeches effective in their times.

5. In this speech, Smith challenges her fellow Senators over what she perceives as an abuse of power. What words and phrases help to justify her criticism? Highlight textual evidence in the first five paragraphs of the speech that help clarify Smith's reasons for issuing the challenge. Then make annotations to explain your choices.

WRITING PROMPT

If you could make a speech on an issue, what would it be? Taking a cue from Margaret Chase Smith, write your own Declaration of Conscience. Identify an issue of national or global importance, and write an address of at least 250 words for an audience of your classmates. Remember to state claims supported with reasons and evidence, and make your purpose clear and point of view clear. Once you are finished, review Smith's speech. Write a brief explanation of how your speeches are alike and different.

Please note that excerpts and passages in the StudySync® library and this workbook are intended as touchstones to generate interest in an author's work. The excerpts and passages do not substitute for the reading of entire texts, and StudySync® strongly recommends that students seek out and purchase the whole literary or informational work in order to experience it as the author intended. Links to online resellers are available in our digital library. In addition, complete works may be ordered through an authorized reseller by filling out and returning to StudySync® the order form enclosed in this workbook.

Reading & Writing Companion **149**

TEXAS V. JOHNSON

NON-FICTION
U.S. Supreme Court
1989

INTRODUCTION

n 1989, the U.S. Supreme Court ruled that states could not prohibit citizens from desecrating the flag as a form of protest, determining that such an act constitutes protected speech under the First Amendment. This excerpt from the Court's ruling summarizes the case and provides passages from both the majority and the

"The American flag played a central role in our Nation's most tragic conflict…"

 FIRST READ

TEXAS v. JOHNSON
Argued March 21, 1989
Decided June 21, 1989

1   During the 1984 Republican National Convention in Dallas, Texas, respondent Johnson participated in a political **demonstration** to protest the policies of the Reagan administration and some Dallas-based corporations. After a march through the city streets, Johnson burned an American flag while protesters chanted. No one was physically injured or threatened with injury, although several witnesses were seriously offended by the flag burning. Johnson was convicted of desecration of a venerated object in violation of a Texas statute, and a State Court of Appeals affirmed. However, the Texas Court of Criminal Appeals reversed, holding that the State, consistent with the First Amendment, could not punish Johnson for burning the flag in these circumstances. The court first found that Johnson's burning of the flag was **expressive** conduct protected by the First Amendment. The court concluded that the State could not criminally sanction flag desecration in order to preserve the flag as a symbol of national unity. It also held that the statute did not meet the State's goal of preventing breaches of the peace, since it was not drawn narrowly enough to encompass only those flag burnings that would likely result in a serious disturbance, and since the flag burning in this case did not threaten such a reaction. Further, it stressed that another Texas statute prohibited breaches of the peace and could be used to prevent disturbances without punishing this flag desecration.

2   Held:

3   Johnson's conviction for flag desecration is inconsistent with the First Amendment.

…

4   JUSTICE BRENNAN delivered the opinion of the Court.

...

5   We are tempted to say, in fact, that the flag's deservedly cherished place in our community will be strengthened, not weakened, by our holding today. Our decision is a reaffirmation of the principles of freedom and inclusiveness that the flag best reflects, and of the conviction that our toleration of criticism such as Johnson's is a sign and source of our strength. Indeed, one of the proudest images of our flag, the one immortalized in our own national anthem, is of the bombardment it survived at Fort McHenry. It is the Nation's resilience, not its rigidity, that Texas sees reflected in the flag - and it is that resilience that we reassert today.

6   The way to preserve the flag's special role is not to punish those who feel differently about these matters. It is to persuade them that they are wrong. "To courageous, self-reliant men, with confidence in the power of free and fearless reasoning applied through the processes of popular government, no danger flowing from speech can be deemed clear and present, unless the incidence of the evil apprehended is so imminent that it may befall before there is opportunity for full discussion. If there be time to expose through discussion the falsehood and **fallacies,** to avert the evil by the processes of education, the remedy to be applied is more speech, not enforced silence." And, precisely because it is our flag that is involved, one's response to the flag burner may exploit the uniquely persuasive power of the flag itself. We can imagine no more appropriate response to burning a flag than waving one's own, no better way to counter a flag burner's message than by saluting the flag that burns, no surer means of preserving the dignity even of the flag that burned than by- as one witness here did - according its remains a respectful burial. We do not consecrate the flag by punishing its desecration, for in doing so we dilute the freedom that this cherished emblem represents.

...

7   CHIEF JUSTICE REHNQUIST, with whom JUSTICE WHITE and JUSTICE O'CONNOR join, dissenting.

8   For more than 200 years, the American flag has occupied a unique position as the symbol of our Nation, a uniqueness that justifies a governmental **prohibition** against flag burning in the way respondent Johnson did here.

9   At the time of the American Revolution, the flag served to unify the Thirteen Colonies at home, while obtaining recognition of national sovereignty abroad.

. . .

NOTES

10　The American flag played a central role in our Nation's most tragic conflict, when the North fought against the South. The lowering of the American flag at Fort Sumter was viewed as the start of the war. . . .

11　In the First and Second World Wars, thousands of our countrymen died on foreign soil fighting for the American cause. At Iwo Jima in the Second World War, United States Marines fought hand to hand against thousands of Japanese. By the time the Marines reached the top of Mount Suribachi, they raised a piece of pipe upright and from one end fluttered a flag. That ascent had cost nearly 6,000 American lives. . . .

12　Both Congress and the States have enacted numerous laws regulating misuse of the American flag. Until 1967, Congress left the regulation of misuse of the flag up to the States. Now, however, 18 U.S.C. 700(a) provides that:

13　"Whoever knowingly casts contempt upon any flag of the United States by publicly mutilating, defacing, defiling, burning, or trampling upon it shall be fined not more than $1,000 or imprisoned for not more than one year, or both."

…

14　The American flag, then, throughout more than 200 years of our history, has come to be the visible symbol embodying our Nation. It does not represent the views of any particular political party, and it does not represent any particular political philosophy. The flag is not simply another "idea" or "point of view" competing for recognition in the marketplace of ideas. Millions and millions of Americans regard it with an almost mystical **reverence** regardless of what sort of social, political, or philosophical beliefs they may have. I cannot agree that the First Amendment invalidates the Act of Congress, and the laws of 48 of the 50 States, which make criminal the public burning of the flag.

THINK QUESTIONS

1. What legal issue is this Supreme Court case about? What are the two points of view? Cite textual evidence to support your answer.

2. What was the winning decision? Write two or three sentences explaining Justice Brennan's majority opinion on this legal issue. Cite textual evidence that includes one or two reasons for the court's decision.

3. Write two or three sentences explaining the dissenting point of view as expressed by Chief Justice Rehnquist and two other justices in the minority opinion. In what ways do they disagree with Justice Brennan? Cite textual evidence to support your answer.

4. Use context to determine the meaning of the word **fallacies** as it is used in *Supreme Court Ruling: Texas versus Johnson, 1989*. Write your definition of *fallacies* and explain how you determined it.

5. Using the context of Chief Justice Rehnquist's opinion about the history of the American flag, determine the meaning of **reverence.** Write your definition of *reverence* and explain how you determined it.

CLOSE READ

Reread the *Supreme Court Ruling: Texas versus Johnson, 1989*. As you reread, complete the Focus Questions below. Then use your answers and annotations from the questions to help you complete the Writing Prompt.

FOCUS QUESTIONS

1. As you reread the first section of *Supreme Court Ruling: Texas versus Johnson, 1989*, analyze how the author unfolds a description of the events and how connections are made between the events. How and why did the Supreme Court conclude that Johnson's burning of the flag is protected by the First Amendment? Highlight textual evidence in the text. Make annotations to define technical language, as needed, and to explain how the author explains the outcome of the case.

2. Reread Chief Justice Rehnquist's dissent from the majority opinion. What is the main idea of his disagreement with the court's decision? What arguments does he use to support his disagreement? Highlight textual evidence, including technical language, and annotate to explain your ideas.

3. How does the technical language of the legal system affect the meaning and tone of this selection? What technical language does Brennan use to show how the reactions to the flag burning influence the applications of law to this case? Highlight your evidence and make annotations to explain your choices.

4. Compare and contrast the points of view of the two Justices when it comes to the challenge of deciding the rules on flag burning. On what points do the Justices agree? On what points do they disagree? Highlight evidence from the text that will help support your ideas, and write annotations to explain your understanding of their reasoning.

5. Reread Justice Brennan's decision. Analyze in detail how Brennan's ideas or claims are developed. What claim does he make about the value of the court's decision? Which key details support this claim? How does he support Johnson's challenge of the rules? Highlight evidence, including technical language, to support your ideas and write annotations to explain your choices.

Please note that excerpts and passages in the StudySync® library and this workbook are intended as touchstones to generate interest in an author's work. The excerpts and passages do not substitute for the reading of entire texts, and StudySync® strongly recommends that students seek out and purchase the whole literary or informational work in order to experience it as the author intended. Links to online resellers are available in our digital library. In addition, complete works may be ordered through an authorized reseller by filling out and returning to StudySync® the order form enclosed in this workbook.

Reading & Writing Companion **155**

WRITING PROMPT

Write an objective summary of each viewpoint on the issue of whether or not flag burning is an expressive conduct protected under free speech by the First Amendment. Determine the central idea of each viewpoint and analyze how it is supported by key points. Then write a paragraph stating which viewpoint you agree with and explain your reasons. Develop your explanation using relevant facts, extended definitions, concrete details, quotations, or other information and examples. Be sure to use legal technical language correctly and appropriately.

IMPASSIONED ARGUMENTS MARK HIGH COURT FLAG-BURNING DECISION

NON-FICTION
Judy Weissler
1989

INTRODUCTION

This newspaper article originally appeared in the *Houston Chronicle* on June 22, 1989. The article summarizes the U.S. Supreme Court decision on the Texas v. Johnson flag-burning case, which determined that Gregory Lee Johnson's conviction for burning the U.S. flag at a protest in Dallas was inconsistent

"Johnson soaked the flag in kerosene and set it afire."

FIRST READ

1   WASHINGTON—The Supreme Court's **fragmented** affirmation of First Amendment rights in a Texas flag-burning case was marked by impassioned **rhetoric** rom both the majority and the **dissent.**

2   The court split 5–4 in its decision, for the first time deciding the government may not impose criminal penalties to punish such activity as long as it is peaceful.

3   "We do not consecrate the flag by punishing its desecration, for in doing so we dilute the freedom that this cherished emblem represents," Justice William Brennan wrote for the court. He was joined in the opinion by Justices Thurgood Marshall, Harry Blackmun, Antonin Scalia and Anthony Kennedy.

4   But Chief Justice William Rehnquist—in a dissent notable for its extensive quotations of poetry and song—said the First Amendment should not be interpreted to **invalidate** laws passed by Congress and by 48 of the 50 states prohibiting the burning of the flag.

5   "The government may conscript men into the armed forces where they must fight and perhaps die for the flag, but the government (under the new ruling) may not prohibit the public burning of the banner under which they fight," Rehnquist wrote. The other dissenting justices were Byron White, Sandra O'Connor and John Paul Stevens.

6   The court's opinion wipes out the conviction of former Houston resident Gregory Lee (Joey) Johnson, a member of the Revolutionary Communist Youth Brigade who was sentenced to a year in jail and fined $2,000 for burning a flag in downtown Dallas during the 1984 Republican National Convention.

7   The Texas Court of Criminal Appeals reversed the conviction, on **grounds** that the Texas law was overbroad and inconsistent with the First Amendment guarantees of free speech. The Supreme Court affirmed the lower court's ruling.

8   Texas officials had argued that the state law prohibiting desecration of the flag is justified as a way to preserve a symbol of national unity and to prevent breaches of the peace.

9   But Brennan said the flag will be an even stronger symbol of freedom under the new court finding, he said, and there was never any real threat of breach of the peace from Johnson's symbolic act.

10 "The First Amendment literally forbids the abridgement only of 'speech,' but we have long recognized that its protection does not end at the spoken or written word," Brennan wrote.

11 "If there is a bedrock principle underlying the First Amendment, it is that the government may not prohibit the expression of an idea simply because society finds the idea itself offensive or disagreeable . . . We have not recognized an exception to this principle even where our flag has been involved."

12 Johnson, who said he lived in Houston for four years following the flag-burning incident, said his case was "an important victory . . . but I refuse to attribute this to the Supreme Court, the Constitution, to justice having prevailed . . . because this is the same Supreme Court and the same Constitution that's being used to carry out vicious and oppressive decisions against all the civil rights cases of the 1960s."

13 Johnson said he is "looking forward to coming back" to Houston. "I'm going to be politically preparing the ground for revolution there . . . I don't know at this point when that's going to happen."

14 The Dallas prosecutors who used the state law to convict Johnson continued to insist that flag-burning is not protected by the First Amendment.

15 "Texas had sought to punish Mr. Johnson for his destruction of the flag, not for any ideas he sought to convey by the act. We agree with Justice Stevens that sanctioning the public destruction of the flag may tarnish its value for all Americans," Dallas Assistant District Attorney Kathi A. Drew said in a written statement.

16 Alan Slobodin, attorney for the conservative Washington Legal Foundation, said the decision is "outrageous" and "offensive to deeply held views about the flag and respect for the flag and people who've died for the flag.

NOTES

The court is apparently going to give carte blanche to a bunch of extremist groups."

17 The Texas law used to prosecute Johnson made it a criminal offense to "intentionally or knowingly desecrate . . . a state or national flag . . . in a way the actor knows will seriously offend one or more persons likely to observe or discover his actions."

18 Johnson was among a group of protesters outside Dallas City Hall on Aug. 22, 1984. They staged "die-ins" by collapsing on the ground in a symbol of nuclear war and spray-painted buildings and tore up potted plants and papers.

19 The flag-burning occurred when about 50 people formed a circle and chanted, "America, the red, white and blue—we spit on you."

20 Johnson soaked the flag in kerosene and set it afire.

21 Brennan wrote that Johnson was prosecuted not because his actions might cause a breach of the peace—since there was no violence associated with the demonstration—but because his expression could offend others.

22 But Rehnquist invoked the 200-year history of the nation to show that the flag has "a uniqueness" in the nation that justifies a governmental prohibition against flag burning.

23 He quoted passages about the flag from Ralph Waldo Emerson's *Concord Hymn,* from the *Star Spangled Banner* and extensively from the poem Barbara Frietchie by John Greenleaf Whittier, which includes the famous lines:

24 Shoot if you must
This old grey head
But spare your country's flag.

Republished with permission of Houston Chronicle Publishing Co., from "Impassioned Arguments Mark High Court Flag-Burning Decision" by Judy Weissler, June 22, 1989 Edition of the Houston Chronicle, section A, p.11. Permission conveyed through Copyright Clearance Center, Inc.

THINK QUESTIONS

1. How does the first sentence, or lead, of the article effectively introduce the content to come as well as capture readers' attention and interest? Cite textual evidence to support your answer.

2. Identify both practical and emotional arguments Chief Justice Rehnquist used as the basis for his dissent against the court's decision. Cite textual evidence to support your answer.

3. Explain Justice Brennan's view of Johnson's prosecution. Why did Brennan believe the prosecution was unjust? Use evidence from the passage to support your ideas and inferences.

4. Use context to determine the meaning of the word **dissent**. Explain how clues in the article helped you arrive at this meaning.

5. Use context to determine the meaning of the word **fragmented** as it is used in the article. Explain how clues in the article helped you arrive at this meaning.

Please note that excerpts and passages in the StudySync® library and this workbook are intended as touchstones to generate interest in an author's work. The excerpts and passages do not substitute for the reading of entire texts, and StudySync® strongly recommends that students seek out and purchase the whole literary or informational work in order to experience it as the author intended. Links to online resellers are available in our digital library. In addition, complete works may be ordered through an authorized reseller by filling out and returning to StudySync® the order form enclosed in this workbook.

Reading & Writing
Companion

161

CLOSE READ

Reread the text from "Impassioned Arguments Mark High Court Flag Burning Decision." As you reread, complete the Focus Questions below. Then use your answers and annotations from the questions to help you complete the Writing Prompt.

FOCUS QUESTIONS

1. Compare and contrast the opening of the newspaper article with the opening of the court decision excerpt. How does the writer of the article use language to "tell a story" rather than list facts about a topic? Consider in your analysis the writer's use of the word *fragmented*. What connotations does this word have, and how does it impact the opening of the article? How might a word with a similar denotation but different connotation change the tone? Highlight evidence and annotate to support your ideas.

2. What is the purpose of paragraphs 6 and 7 in the article? How do they enhance readers' understanding of the Supreme Court's decision, the main event explored in the article? Highlight evidence and annotate to support your ideas.

3. How would you describe the way the writer organizes the information in this newspaper article? Are the paragraphs long or short? Why? Highlight evidence in the paragraphs –11 to support your ideas. Make annotations to explain your choices.

4. Reread the final three paragraphs of the article. What effect is this section likely to have on readers? Why might the writer have chosen to end the article with Chief Justice Rehnquist's quotation? Highlight evidence and make annotations to support your ideas.

5. How does the Supreme Court's decision about flag-burning shed legal light on the question of when it is appropriate to challenge the rules? Highlight evidence and annotate to support your ideas.

WRITING PROMPT

In a 300-word analysis, compare and contrast the newspaper article "Impassioned Arguments Mark High Court Flag-Burning Decision" with the library excerpt of the court opinion *Texas v. Johnson*. Identify similarities and differences in information, organizational structure, and language in the two pieces. Offer reasons why differences might exist and speculate about what effects they might have on readers. Why might a reader exploring this landmark case about the the flag and its use in acts of symbolic protest benefit from experiencing both texts? Cite specific evidence from both texts to support your analysis.

BURNING THE FLAG

NON-FICTION

2014

INTRODUCTION

In these two articles the writers make arguments for and against the rights of American citizens to burn the country's flag as a form of political protest. This debate has been going on since American activist Gregory Lee Johnson was arrested in Dallas, Texas, for burning the American flag outside of the Republican National Convention in 1984. Both writers present strong arguments and support their claims with evidence. Which one does the better job convincing you that his or her view is correct?

"All citizens must understand that the right to burn the flag is protected by America's Constitution."

FIRST READ

The Burning the American Flag: First Amendment Right or a Crime?

Point: The Right to Burn the Flag Is Protected by Freedom of Speech

1　When a citizen of a nation is dissatisfied with the government, what can he or she do to try to create change? What if voting in elections and participating in local government doesn't seem to be enough? This is exactly the position some citizens find themselves in when they make the choice to burn the flag as a form of protest. Many see it as a last resort. All citizens must understand that the right to burn the flag is protected by America's Constitution.

2　There are many people who do not support the legal right to burn the flag. They feel that burning the flag is **callous** toward the military servicemen and women who have fought and died for their country. Anyone can see how this act would be hurtful toward members of the armed forces. However, it is not **plausible** to say that in order to protect freedom, you must limit the very freedoms you are trying to protect. Even some service members agree. According to a veteran of the Vietnam War, Richard Savage, "...Those who would burn the flag destroy the symbol of freedom, but amending the Constitution would destroy part of freedom itself."

3　The United States Supreme Court agrees that it would be unethical to limit citizens' personal freedoms with laws against burning the flag. In 1984, Gregory Lee Johnson burned the American flag at the Republican National Convention in Dallas because he was dissatisfied with the government of the United States. At the time it was illegal in the state of Texas to burn the flag, so Johnson was arrested. Johnson fought the case and it went all the way to the Supreme Court. The Court ruled in 1989 that burning a flag is symbolically the same as exercising your right to free speech, and therefore it is protected by the First Amendment to the Constitution. Since the Constitution is the

Copyright © BookheadEd Learning, LLC

supreme law of the land, states are no longer allowed to make or enforce laws against burning the flag.

5   Citizens like Gregory Lee Johnson who make the decision to burn the American flag in protest probably do not take the decision lightly. Instead, they are weighing their reverence for the flag carefully with their civic duty to stand up for what they believe in. One of the most important patriotic ideals in the United States is that the government is for the people and by the people. By burning a flag in protest, a citizen is participating in politics and therefore fulfilling his or her civic duty. It is far more unpatriotic to either not act to try to improve the government, or to use inadequate methods to try to bring about change.

6   To those who say flag burning should be illegal despite this evidence, I have a few questions. What exactly would be protected by a law that makes it illegal to burn flags? Clothing featuring American flags? Fourth of July picnic napkins and plates? Although it sounds a bit absurd, this is not very far-fetched. According to the Federal Flag Code, which was signed by President Franklin Roosevelt in 1942, a flag is anything "by which the average person seeing the same without deliberation may believe the same to represent the flag." A law against burning flags could have the negative, unintended consequence of unnecessary litigation against people that harm an image of the flag with no intention of protest.

7   The Supreme Court got this one right. When someone burns the flag in protest they are exercising their right to free speech, and that is a freedom that should never be tarnished by the government. The men and women who decide to burn the flag in protest would not bother to take action if they were not devoted to the betterment of the United States.

8   **Counterpoint:** Burning the American Flag Is a Threat to Our Country

9   The American flag is one of the most sacred symbols of the United States. When six Marines raised the American flag over Iwo Jima in 1945, it symbolized the United States' strength in the face of world powers that wanted to destroy us. Three of the Marines that raised that flag would make the ultimate sacrifice for their country when they were killed in action. When Neil Armstrong placed an American Flag on the moon in 1969, it was a symbol of the United States' resolve to be a leader in science and technology despite competition from the repressive Communist regimes. When New York City firefighters raised the flag over the ruins of the World Trade Center in 2001, it was a symbol of solidarity and strength after an **atrocious** attack on the American people. To burn the United States flag for any reason is disrespectful and should be outlawed.

10   Unfortunately, there are some people who think it is acceptable to burn this sacred symbol as a form of protest against the government. They mistakenly believe that it is **feasible** to fight for freedom while simultaneously destroying one if its most cherished symbols. On the contrary, burning the American flag is deeply disrespectful to those that actually fight for freedom: members of the armed forces. Anyone that thinks that it should be legal to burn the flag should consider the following points of view.

11   Think how it must feel to be an American service member injured in battle. You are happy to be alive but you have a long road to recovery. Then you come home to the injurious act of the same citizens you fought to protect, burning a symbol of the freedom you fought for. Now picture tears in the eyes of the child or spouse of a soldier that went missing in action while fighting for our country. Imagine how it must feel for them to see people disrespecting a symbol of the freedom their missing loved one fought for, not knowing if their family member will ever have their own freedom again. Consider a serviceman or woman that fought in battle and made it home, but carries the memory of his or her comrades that were not so lucky to make it back to their families alive. How would it feel to see the memory of their fallen comrades degraded by the burning of the flag?

12   People who think it should be legal to burn the American flag argue that the Supreme Court ruled it is a right protected by the Constitution. However, this is not a sufficient reason to let the issue lie. The Supreme Court has been wrong before. There was a time when the Supreme Court ruled that African Americans could not be American citizens (Dred Scott v. Sandford, 1857). Then only a little more than ten years later the Thirteenth, Fourteenth, and Fifteenth Amendments to the Constitution were passed, reversing this decision and ensuring that all Americans enjoy the protection of the law. One of the wonderful things about the United States is that the Constitution is flexible, and it is **imperative** that it be adjusted to reflect respect for the American flag as well.

13   In fact, the majority of Americans think that it should be illegal to burn the flag. In a poll conducted in 1990, 69% of Americans said that they supported a Constitutional Amendment that would make it legal for Congress or individual states to pass laws against flag burning. Since the United States government is for the people and by the people, public opinion should matter in deciding this issue.

14   And perhaps the most compelling reason to make burning the American flag illegal, is that it is a threat to national security. Simply put, when American citizens burn the flag it makes us look weak to our enemies. The world we live in today is increasingly threatening. It is essential that the United States show a united and strong nation that will not tolerate aggression from others.

15　Internationally there is a precedent for limiting freedom of expression in the interest of national security. The European Convention on Human Rights is an international treaty that has been in place in Europe since 1953. Article 10 (the section on freedom of expression) of the ECHR states: "The exercise of these freedoms, since it carries with it duties and responsibilities, may be subject to such formalities, conditions, restrictions or penalties as are prescribed by law and are necessary in a democratic society, in the interests of national security, territorial integrity or public safety...."

16　The clear message here is that it is more important to protect our citizens than to allow such an extreme display of freedom of speech. If you are dissatisfied with the government, there are many options available to you. Go out and vote. Speak or write about your point of view in a public forum so that your message can be heard. Run for office. Any of these would be better than the disrespectful, depraved act of burning the most sacred symbol of the freedoms you enjoy.

THINK QUESTIONS

1. For what reasons does the author of the PRO statement support the right to burn the flag as a protest? Support your answer with both ideas that are directly stated and ideas that you have inferred from textual evidence.

2. For what reasons does the author of the CON statement oppose giving people the right to burn the flag as a protest? Support your answer with both ideas that are directly stated and ideas that you have inferred from clues in the text.

3. Use the reading comprehension technique of asking and answering questions to compare the two opinions (PRO and CON) on this issue. How do the authors appeal to the readers? What kind of evidence does each author use to back up his or her opinion? Support your answer with evidence from the text.

4. Use context to determine the meaning of the word **callous** as it is used in *PRO: The Right to Burn the Flag Is Protected by Freedom of Speech*. Write your definition of **callous** and explain how you determined it.

5. Remembering that the Latin suffix *-ible* means "able to" and using context clues, determine the meaning of the word **feasible** as it is used in *CON: Burning the American Flag Is a Threat to Our Country*. Write your definition of *feasible* and explain how you determined it.

Please note that excerpts and passages in the StudySync® library and this workbook are intended as touchstones to generate interest in an author's work. The excerpts and passages do not substitute for the reading of entire texts, and StudySync® strongly recommends that students seek out and purchase the whole literary or informational work in order to experience it as the author intended. Links to online resellers are available in our digital library. In addition, complete works may be ordered through an authorized reseller by filling out and returning to StudySync® the order form enclosed in this workbook.

Reading & Writing Companion　**167**

CLOSE READ

Reread the text "Burning the Flag." As you reread, complete the Focus Questions below. Then use your answers and annotations from the questions to help you complete the Writing Prompt.

FOCUS QUESTIONS

1. In paragraph 4 of the pro statement, the author claims that "By burning a flag in protest, a citizen is participating in politics and therefore fulfilling his or her civic duty. It is far more unpatriotic to either not act to try to improve the government, or to use inadequate methods to try to bring about change." How does the author support this claim? Explain why you think his argument is reasonable or fallacious. Highlight text evidence to support your evaluation. Make annotations to explain your thinking.

2. In paragraph 9, the author of the con statement argues that the flag is a symbol of freedom and that burning the flag causes emotional distress to many Americans, especially members of the armed forces and their families. Does the author provide relevant evidence for this argument? How does rhetoric affect the argument? Highlight evidence in the text that you would consider relevant. Make annotations to explain why this evidence does or does not convince you that flag burning as protest should be banned.

3. In paragraph 12, the author of the con statement claims that flag burning is a threat to our national security. Evaluate the reasons and evidence that the author supplies. Are the reasons faulty or reasonable? Is there sufficient and relevant evidence for the author's argument? Highlight evidence from the text and make annotations to support your evaluation.

4. In paragraph 13, a precedent for limiting freedom of expression in the interest of national security is presented. The author concludes that: "The clear message here is that it is more important to protect our citizens than to allow such an extreme display of freedom of speech." Explain why you think this is a reasonable or a fallacious argument. What does the author mean by "extreme display of freedom of speech"? What makes it extreme or not extreme? Highlight evidence from the text and make annotations to support your explanation.

5. Read the following excerpt from paragraph 10 and think about the importance of both setting and being able to challenge the rules. Does the author provide convincing arguments for amending the Constitution to prohibit flag burning? Why or why not? Highlight textual evidence and make annotations to explain and support your answers.

6. People who think it should be legal to burn the American flag argue that the Supreme Court ruled it is a right protected by the Constitution. However, this is not a sufficient reason to let the issue lie. The Supreme Court has been wrong before. There was a time when the Supreme Court ruled that African Americans could not be American citizens (Dred Scott v. Sandford, 1857). However, ten years later, the Thirteenth, Fourteenth, and Fifteenth Amendments to the Constitution were passed, reversing this decision and ensuring that all Americans enjoy the protection of the law.

7. The author of the pro statement believes that flag burning is an appropriate way to challenge the rules. What claim does the author make about flag burning and citizenship? How does this claim support the idea that flag burning is an appropriate way to challenge the rules? Highlight text evidence to support your evaluation. Make annotations to explain your thinking.

WRITING PROMPT

Imagine that you have an opportunity to argue for or against a law or rule in front of the U.S. Supreme Court. Write an argument concerning a law or rule that you are familiar with and have an opinion about. You can use an actual rule, law, or legal decision or a plausible one that you invent. Clearly state the rule, law, or legal decision and use your understanding of valid reasons and evidence to support your pro or con argument. Use the appropriate rhetoric to explain your reasoning. Be aware of fallacious or faulty reasoning and correct it. Provide relevant and adequate evidence for your argument.

Please note that excerpts and passages in the StudySync® library and this workbook are intended as touchstones to generate interest in an author's work. The excerpts and passages do not substitute for the reading of entire texts, and StudySync® strongly recommends that students seek out and purchase the whole literary or informational work in order to experience it as the author intended. Links to online resellers are available in our digital library. In addition, complete works may be ordered through an authorized reseller by filling out and returning to StudySync® the order form enclosed in this workbook.

Reading & Writing Companion

169

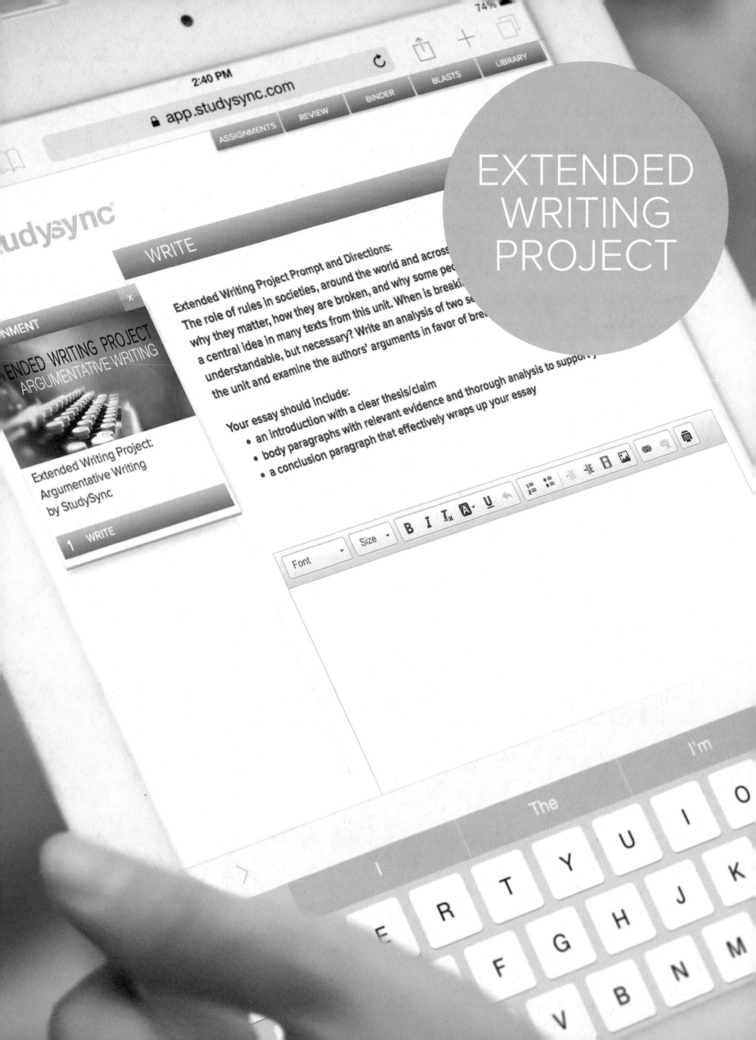

EXTENDED WRITING PROJECT

app.studysync.com

74%

2:40 PM

ASSIGNMENTS   REVIEW   BINDER   BLASTS   LIBRARY

StudySync®

WRITE

Extended Writing Project Prompt and Directions:
The role of rules in societies, around the world and across
why they matter, how they are broken, and why some peo
a central idea in many texts from this unit. When is breaki
understandable, but necessary? Write an analysis of two se
the unit and examine the authors' arguments in favor of bre

Your essay should include:
- an introduction with a clear thesis/claim
- body paragraphs with relevant evidence and thorough analysis to support
- a conclusion paragraph that effectively wraps up your essay

EXTENDED WRITING PROJECT
ARGUMENTATIVE WRITING

Extended Writing Project:
Argumentative Writing
by StudySync

1   WRITE

Font   Size   **B** *I* I̶ **A** ~U~

ARGUMENTATIVE WRITING

WRITING PROMPT

The role of rules in societies, around the world and across the ages—what the rules are, why they matter, how they are broken, and why some people feel they must break them—is a central idea in many texts from this unit. When is breaking the rules not only understandable, but necessary? Write an analysis of two selections you have read during the unit and examine the authors' arguments in favor of breaking the rules.

Your essay should include:

- an introduction with a clear thesis/claim
- body paragraphs with relevant evidence and thorough analysis to support your thesis
- a conclusion paragraph that effectively wraps up your essay

Argumentative writing asks the student to make a claim or take a position on a topic and then to identify, evaluate, and provide textual evidence that offers reasonable support for the claim. Literary analysis is a form of argumentative writing. In a **literary analysis,** a writer takes a position on one or more works of literature to demonstrate why authors used particular text structures, word choices, ideas, images, or literary devices in their work. Literary analysis is not a summary of the literature. Instead, it is an opportunity for a writer to share his or her personal perspectives, critical thinking, or interpretation of works of literature.

Strong argumentative writing begins with an introductory paragraph that provides a general context for the topic and then presents a reasonably narrow thesis statement that explicitly states the writer's position on the topic. The body paragraphs of an argumentative essay involving a literary analysis are focused on relevant textual details that provide evidentiary support for the main idea. Argumentative essays focused on literary analysis often

Please note that excerpts and passages in the StudySync® library and this workbook are intended as touchstones to generate interest in an author's work. The excerpts and passages do not substitute for the reading of entire texts, and StudySync® strongly recommends that students seek out and purchase the whole literary or informational work in order to experience it as the author intended. Links to online resellers are available in our digital library. In addition, complete works may be ordered through an authorized reseller by filling out and returning to StudySync® the order form enclosed in this workbook.

Reading & Writing Companion

171

contain direct quotations, or citations, from the texts being analyzed. The writing in an argumentative essay is clear, coherent, formal in tone, and appropriate to its task, purpose, and intended audience. Argumentative essays stay focused on the main idea and claim by using transition words to help create flow and make connections between supporting details and citations. Strong argumentative essays end with a conclusion that revisits the main point of the thesis statement and synthesizes the evidence that has been provided. The features of argumentative writing include:

- clear and logical organizational structure
- an introductory with a clear thesis statement
- body paragraphs that offer supporting details
- precise language and domain-specific vocabulary
- citations of sources
- a concluding paragraph that summarizes the analysis and restates the thesis

STUDENT MODEL

Before you get started on your own argumentative essay, begin by reading this essay that one student wrote in response to the writing prompt. As you read this student model, highlight and annotate the features of argumentative writing that the student included in his essay.

Breaking the Rules

Rules are often thought of as the bricks and mortar that people use to construct the societies they live in. Rules, we are told, keep the wheels of society turning, provide people with basic necessities, keep peace and order, and secure the well-being of citizens. Without rules, nations and whole cultures would likely descend into chaos and eventual self-destruction. Yet rules can be perverted and used to violate the needs and rights of the people they are meant to serve. Sophocles's play *Antigone* and George Orwell's novel *Animal Farm* provide examples of events and situations where it is clear that rules sometimes can be challenged and broken but not without consequences.

In the opening scene of *Antigone*, Sophocles introduces the audience to the initial conflict of the play: whether or not to obey King Creon's decree. Antigone and Ismene's brothers—Polyneices and Eteocles—have killed each other during battle. Eteocles, who fought on the side of the victorious city of Thebes, has been buried with the full rituals of a Greek citizen and soldier. However, Creon, the new king of Thebes, has ordered that Polyneices, who fought against Thebes, should remain unburied. His body is to remain on the open battlefield, and his spirit is condemned to roam the land without peace. Antigone has asked to meet her sister outside the gates of Thebes to plea for help in taking Polyneices' body for proper burial. Should Antigone break the law or not? This is the problem Sophocles explores.

Immediately, the two sisters begin to argue over the whether or not Creon's decree should be followed. As the sisters show their differences, the audience gets a chance to see both sides of the argument. Ismene believes that it is the role of Greek citizens, especially women, to follow the rules set down by the male leaders of their society. Ismene warns, "Shall we not perish wretchedness of all,/ If in defiance of the law we cross/A monarch's will?" To the contrary, Antigone feels that Creon's decree should be disobeyed because it violates the basic rules of loving family relationships and the eternal laws of the Greek Gods. Ismene, trying to use reason, continues to object to Antigone's plan and cautions Antigone that she will likely be killed if she follows through on it. Sophocles shows that Antigone is making her choice to break the rules partly on tradition, but mostly on emotion. Antigone scornfully replies to Ismene, "Go thine own way; myself will bury him,/How sweet to die in such employ, to rest—/Sister and brother linked in love's embrace—/A sinless sinner, banned awhile on earth,/But by the dead commended; and with them I shall abide for ever. As for thee,/Scorn if thou wilt, the eternal laws of Heaven" (Sophocles). For Antigone, the unfair rule of a vengeful but victorious leader may be rightfully broken so that the more important rules of family and faith can prevail. Should the heart rule the head? Sophocles shows that Antigone, whatever her choice, will have to live, or die, with the consequences of her actions.

In his novel *Animal Farm,* George Orwell also deals with the importance of rules to social order. As it was for Antigone in Thebes, the rules of Animal Farm seem to be justifiably broken, but for different reasons and with different consequences. Orwell uses this story of farm animals to explore the limits of rules and the uses of power. After the animals' initial overthrow of Mr. Jones's rule, Snowball and Napoleon vie for leadership. A debate over the building of the windmill precedes what is supposed to be a democratic vote by all the animals. To the animals' surprise, the democratic rules of debate and voting are violated when the meeting turns into a military-style coup as Napoleon uses his trained dogs to viciously attack Snowball and chase him off the farm. Having seized power, Napoleon immediately changes the existing rules so he can maintain iron-fisted control. "He [Napoleon] announced that from now on the Sunday-morning meetings would come to an end…. In future all questions relating to the working of the farm would be settled by a special committee of pigs, presided over by himself" (Orwell). Later, Napoleon sends Squeaker around the farm to explain the new rules. Squeaker tells the animals, "No one believes more firmly than Comrade Napoleon that all animals are equal. He would be only too happy to let you make your decisions for yourselves. But sometimes you might make the wrong decisions, comrades, and then where should we be?" (Orwell). Previously, the animals had justifiably broken rules when they overthrew their human masters. The animals are eventually subjected to the same type of autocratic control that they had sought to overthrow.

In summary, the main characters of both texts think they are right to overthrow what they see as unfair rules. That said, the breaking of rules may result in dire consequences. For Antigone, death may be the punishment she pays for disobeying Creon's edict. For the creatures living on Animal Farm, the breaking of the rules merely changes the leadership of the farm, but it does not improve the lives of the animals. Both Sophocles and Orwell seem to asking readers if there is any chance of a middle ground, a true compromise, and seem to suggest that this tension will never be resolved. In short, rules may be justifiably broken, but not without unintended and often unpleasant consequences.

THINK QUESTIONS

1. What is the central or main idea of this essay? How do you know? Cite textual evidence to support your ideas.

2. How is the text in "Breaking the Rules" organized?

3. What types of evidence does the writer provide in the body paragraphs of this argumentative essay?

4. Thinking about the writing prompt, which selections or other resources would you like to use to create your own literary analysis?

5. Based on what you have read, listened to, or researched, how would you answer the question: *When is breaking the rules not only understandable, but necessary?* What are some examples of situations where you think rules should be broken?

PREWRITE

WRITING PROMPT

The role of rules in societies, around the world and across the ages—what the rules are, why they matter, how they are broken, and why some people feel they must break them—is a central idea in many texts from this unit. When is breaking the rules not only understandable, but necessary? Write an analysis of two selections you have read during the unit and examine the authors' arguments in favor of breaking the rules.

Your essay should include:

- an introduction with a clear thesis/claim
- body paragraphs with relevant evidence and thorough analysis to support your thesis
- a conclusion paragraph that effectively wraps up your essay

---

You have been reading stories and other texts that feature people breaking the rules. You have also been learning about literary analysis as a form of argumentative writing. Now you will use those argumentative writing techniques to compose your own literary analysis in response to the prompt.

Remember that literary analysis asks you to make a claim or take a position on a topic and then to identify, evaluate, and provide textual evidence that offers reasonable support for the claim. Consider the situation in George Orwell's *Animal Farm*. How did the characters break the rules? Why did they believe that it was necessary to break the rules? What were the results of breaking the rules? Think about not only the message that Orwell conveys but how he conveys it.

Make a list of the answers to these questions for *Animal Farm* and at least two other texts you have encountered in this unit. **You must use at least one work of fiction or drama, though the second text may be fiction, drama,**

---

poetry, or nonfiction, depending on your topic. As you write down your ideas, consider whether the author presents a fair case for breaking the rules. Do you agree with the situations presented in the text? Why or why not? Determining the answers to these questions will help you craft the claim of your argumentative essay. Also look for patterns to emerge. Do these texts have anything in common? What important differences do they have? Look for these patterns to help you build support for your main claim. Use this model to help you get started with your own prewriting:

Model Text: *Animal Farm* by George Orwell

How the Characters Broke the Rules: The animals have overthrown their human leader, Mr. Jones, to establish democratic rule on the farm. Snowball and Napoleon then vie for leadership.

Reasons It Was Necessary to Break the Rules: Democratic rule was enacted to ensure that the farm ran properly, under animal (rather than human) control.

Results of Breaking the Rules: When the power-hungry Napoleon believes that Snowball is making the wrong decision about the windmill, he instructs his trained dogs to chase Snowball from the farm. He then seizes an autocratic role and changes the rules of the farm, so that he will make all final decisions.

Author's Message: Different people react to rules in different ways, and not everyone will have the same point of view about breaking them. Some people make it impossible to work for a compromise.

Does the Author Make a Fair Case? Author's Point of View: Orwell shows, through the animals' actions, how human beings struggle for power over who controls the rules. He shows it is an ugly business by showing how some people get impatient with democracy.

SKILL:
THESIS
STATEMENT

 DEFINE

The thesis statement is the most important sentence in an argumentative essay, including a literary analysis, because it introduces what the writer is going to explore or attempt to prove in the essay or analysis. The thesis statement expresses the writer's central or main idea about that topic, which is the position the writer will develop in the body of the essay. The thesis statement usually appears in the essay's introductory paragraph and is often the introduction's last sentence. The rest of the paragraphs in the essay all support the thesis statement with specific details, facts, evidence, quotations, and examples. The thesis statement should reappear in some form in the essay's concluding paragraph.

 IDENTIFICATION AND APPLICATION

A thesis statement:

- makes a clear statement about the writer's central idea.
- lets the reader know what to expect in the body of the essay.
- responds fully and completely to an essay prompt.
- is presented in the introduction paragraph and restated in the conclusion.
- is a work-in-progress and should be revised and improved, as needed, during the early stages of the writing process.

 MODEL

The following is the introductory paragraph from the student model essay "Breaking the Rules":

> Rules are often thought of as the bricks and mortar that people use to construct the societies they live in. Rules we are told keep the wheels of

Please note that excerpts and passages in the StudySync® library and this workbook are intended as touchstones to generate interest in an author's work. The excerpts and passages do not substitute for the reading of entire texts, and StudySync® strongly recommends that students seek out and purchase the whole literary or informational work in order to experience it as the author intended. Links to online resellers are available in our digital library. In addition, complete works may be ordered through an authorized reseller by filling out and returning to StudySync® the order form enclosed in this workbook.

Reading & Writing
Companion

177

society turning, provide people with basic necessities, keep peace and order, and secure the well-being of citizens. Without rules, nations and whole cultures will likely descend into chaos and eventual self-destruction. Yet rules can be perverted and used to violate the needs and rights of the people they are meant to serve. **Sophocles' play Antigone and George Orwell's novel Animal Farm provide examples of events and situations where it is clear that rules sometimes can be challenged and broken but not without consequences.**

Notice the boldfaced thesis statement. This student's thesis statement responds to the prompt, identifying the selections they will analyze, the authors of those selections, and the point he will be making about the selections. It reminds readers of the topic of the essay, in this case, situations when people feel they are right to break the rules. It also specifically states the writer's particular central or main idea about that topic. In this writer's view, these authors show that in certain situations rules should be broken but consequences should be expected.

 ## PRACTICE

Draft a thesis statement with pen and paper that states your main idea in a clear and engaging way. Be sure that your thesis statement addressed the prompt. When you are done writing, switch papers with a partner to evaluate each other's work. How clearly did the writer state the main point? Does the thesis statement answer the question or topic posed in the prompt? Does the thesis statement clearly state the focus of the rest of the essay? Offer suggestions, and remember that they are most helpful when they are informative and constructive.

 DEFINE

A purpose of argumentative writing focused on literary analysis is to make a claim or take a position on a topic, and then to identify, evaluate, and present relevant textual evidence that supports the position. To do this effectively, writers need to organize and present their claims, topics, ideas, facts, details, and other information in a logical way that makes it easy for readers to follow and understand.

Students are often asked to write argumentative essays that analyze literary texts as part of their studies in English language arts classes. A common method for writing a strong argumentative essay is organizing the writing using the **five-paragraph strategy**. As you saw in the introductory lesson, this consists of an **introductory paragraph** that presents the **topic** and the writer's position in a **thesis statement**. The introduction is then followed by **three body paragraphs**, each of which presents evidentiary details and ideas that support some aspect of the essay's thesis. The fifth paragraph is a **conclusion** that provides a unique restatement of the thesis, reviews the evidence presented, and ends with a concluding sentence that wraps up the topic. The five-paragraph approach is straightforward, concise, and effective. However, it is not the only organizational structure that may be used to write a strong argumentative essay.

The content of the essay—that is the type of prompt the writer is responding to, the nature of the textual evidence to be presented for support and analysis, and the characteristics of the selections to be analyzed—must also be considered in choosing an overall **organizational structure** that suits the topic and the literary texts a writer plans to analyze. For example, in comparing the treatment of a topic from two historical novels, the writer might decide that a **sequential** or chronological structure might work best since events can then be discussed in the order they occurred. On the other hand, if the writer is analyzing the similarity and differences of the actions of characters in resolving conflicts from several short stories or plays, a **compare and contrast** structure might be the most effective organizational method for an argumentative essay. Other organizational structures include: **problem and solution** and **cause-and-effect**. It is important to remember that while an essay or a paragraph may use an overall organizational method, it may be necessary to introduce another organizational technique to get across an important point.

IDENTIFICATION AND APPLICATION

- When selecting an organizational structure, writers must consider the purpose of their writing. They often ask themselves questions about the nature of the writing task they are engaging in. They might ask themselves the following questions:

  › Can I express my thoughts effectively within a five-paragraph structure?
  › What is the claim or thesis that I am making about the topic?
  › Am I comparing and contrasting different viewpoints held by different characters about the same topic, issue, or conflict?
  › Would it make sense to relay events in the order they occurred?
  › What is the problem and what solutions did the characters find or the events lead to?
  › Is there a natural cause and effect relationship in my analysis of evidence I use to support my thesis?

- Writers often use word choice to create connections between details and hint at the organizational structure being used:

  › Sequential order: *first, next, then, finally, last, initially, ultimately*
  › Cause and effect: *because, accordingly, as a result, effect, so*
  › Compare and contrast: *like, unlike, also, both, similarly, although, while, but, however*

- Sometimes, within the overall structure, writers may find it necessary to organize individual paragraphs using other structures—for instance, a paragraph that compares and contrasts might benefit from a quick summary of events presented in chronological order. Be careful that such mixed strategies do not muddy the overall organization.

MODEL

The writer of the student model understood from his prewriting that he was mostly comparing and contrasting the viewpoints of characters faced with deciding whether or not to break the rules of the societies they live in.

The student writer of the literary analysis "Breaking the Rules" knew that in his discussion of *Antigone* he would be comparing and contrasting Ismene's and Antigone's beliefs about whether or not Creon's decree concerning the burial of Polyneices should be obeyed or broken. He created a Pro and Con diagram to compare and contrast these two characters' points of view.

 PRACTICE

Using a *SmartArt Graphic Organizer* (Microsoft Word) like the one you have just studied, a traditional Venn diagram, or a graphic organizer of your own creation, fill in the information you gathered in the Prewrite stage of writing your essay.

Ismene
Follow Creon's Decree

- Women must always follow rules of male leaders
- Will be stoned to dealth if the decree is disobeyed

Antigone
Disobey Creon's Decree

- The spirits of the unburied can't find peace
- Family relationships obligate sisters to bury brothers
- Gods say Greek soldiers should be buried

Please note that excerpts and passages in the StudySync® library and this workbook are intended as touchstones to generate interest in an author's work. The excerpts and passages do not substitute for the reading of entire texts, and StudySync® strongly recommends that students seek out and purchase the whole literary or informational work in order to experience it as the author intended. Links to online resellers are available in our digital library. In addition, complete works may be ordered through an authorized reseller by filling out and returning to StudySync® the order form enclosed in this workbook.

Reading & Writing Companion

181

SKILL: SUPPORTING DETAILS

DEFINE

Texts that take a side on an issue or a specific view on a topic are made up of claims and counterclaims. A **claim** is the idea, often written in the form of a thesis statement, put forth by the writer. A **counterclaim** is an opposing idea, one that disagrees with the author's claim. Writers must present **details** to support any claim: reasons and evidence must not only support their own claim, but also disprove any counterclaims. Showing the inaccuracies of a counterclaim does more than just lessen its credibility in the minds of readers. It also increases the audience's willingness to side with the author's claim.

Supporting details should be backed up with textual evidence that supports the author's analysis and argument. Writers should choose evidence that helps them to develop a central idea—the **thesis**—over the course of the text. The specific details a writer chooses to include help to shape and refine the central idea.

Details are chosen because of their appropriateness for the task, purpose, and audience. Choose the details that will be most convincing to your particular audience and that will most effectively achieve the purpose of the text. When including quotes and ideas from other texts and media in informational and argumentative writing, students should cite all of their sources.

IDENTIFICATION AND APPLICATION

For a literary analysis:

- Provide details in the form of **reasons** backed up by **evidence** found in the literary text or texts being discussed. **Direct quotations,** followed by the writer's analysis of the quotations in connection to the thesis, make the strongest evidence.

- Choose details for inclusion according to the audience's background knowledge, concerns, and beliefs. Use only details that will help prove your point. Too many details, or unorganized details, can confuse a point rather than prove it.

- Choose details to best point out the strengths and limitations of claims and counterclaims.

- Use the details to develop main claim of the paper—often called the thesis—over the course of the entire text. Every detail chosen should support the thesis

 ## MODEL

The most common use of informational and argumentative writing is to convince readers that the writer's stand on an issue or view of a topic—his or her thesis—is the correct one and should be adopted by the reader. The best way to convince readers of the correctness of a thesis is to provide plenty of details that support it.

A common mistake in student writing is to venture off topic and introduce details that may be interesting, but are not **relevant,** or related to the argument being discussed. It is important to always consider how a detail is related to the thesis. If a connection cannot be drawn, the detail may need to be deleted. Including too many irrelevant details will convince many readers to not believe in a writer's thesis.

In *The Whisperers: Private Life in Stalin's Russia* by Orlando Figes, all of the details unite together to prove the author's thesis: that Communist citizens were brainwashed to take part in and support horrible atrocities as their "revolutionary duty." Figes makes a point of telling individual stories to engage readers' emotions. He begins the text with a personal story that shows the cruelty of the "collectivizers":

> **Klavdiia Rublyova** was born in 1913, the third of **eleven children** in a peasant family in the Irbei region of Krasnoiarsk in Siberia. **Her mother died in 1924, while giving birth, leaving her father, Ilia, to bring up all the children on his own.** An enterprising man, Ilia took advantage of the NEP [New Economic Policy] to branch out from farming to market gardening. **He grew poppy seeds and cucumbers, which could easily be tended by his young children. For this he was branded a 'kulak', arrested and imprisoned, and later sent to a labour camp**, leaving his children in the care of Klavdiia, who was then aged just seventeen. The children were deprived of all their father's property: the house, which he had built, was taken over by the village Soviet, while the horses, cows and sheep and the farm tools were transferred to the kolkhoz.

NOTES

This essay focuses on the cruelty of the gulags, which imprisoned over a million "kulaks". Why does the author include so many details of just one individual, Klavdiia Rublyova, and her family? When eliciting reader emotions, one personal story can be more powerful than a list of facts about the large nameless numbers who suffered. Figes instead focuses on one single family in which a father creatively tried to feed his eleven children, and for his attempts, was "branded a 'kulak', arrested and imprisoned, and later sent to a labour camp." This one powerful example shows readers what they need to know about the unfairness and cruelty peasants experienced.

An important reminder to writers of formal academic essays, such as a literary analysis, is to work to maintain **objectivity**. That is, in a formal paper, writers should explain the details with strong analysis, and think carefully before adding words with specific connotations, such as "branded." Writers might begin to list the details they will use in a graphic organizer before writing about them. This sort of forethought helps writers to avoid the mistake of including details that do not support the thesis. Fill in this graphic organizer to evaluate the details of an essay and see how they are relevant to the thesis. One detail is already filled in as an example.

DETAIL	WHAT POINT DOES THIS DETAIL MAKE?	HOW DOES THIS DETAIL SUPPORT THE THESIS?
The children were deprived of all their father's property: the house, which he had built, was taken over by the village Soviet, while the horses, cows and sheep and the farm tools were transferred to the kolkhoz.	The Siberian peasants were treated cruelly and unfairly during this period in history.	This detail shows how inhumane citizens under Stalin became during the time of the gulags.

PLAN

WRITING PROMPT

The role of rules in societies, around the world and across the ages—what the rules are, why they matter, how they are broken, and why some people feel they must break them—is a central idea in many texts from this unit. When is breaking the rules not only understandable, but necessary? Write an analysis of two selections you have read during the unit and examine the authors' arguments in favor of breaking the rules.

Your essay should include:

- an introduction with a clear thesis/claim
- body paragraphs with relevant evidence and thorough analysis to support your thesis
- a conclusion paragraph that effectively wraps up your essay

Review the information you recorded in your graphic organizer during the Organize Argumentative Writing lesson. This organized information and your thesis statement will help you to create a road map to use for writing your literary analysis.

Consider the following questions as you develop your paragraph topics and supporting details in the road map:

- How do the characters in these texts gain an understanding of the rules?
- Do the characters in these texts think that the rules matter?
- What beliefs or ideals do the characters in these texts hold to be most important?
- What kind of relationships do the characters in these texts have with those in power?
- What situations do the characters face that cause them to consider breaking the rules?

- How do the characters break the rules?
- Do you think it is necessary for these characters to break the rules? Why or why not?
- What consequences do these characters face as a result of breaking the rules?

Use this model to get started with your road map:

Literary Analysis Road Map

Thesis statement: Sophocles's play *Antigone* and George Orwell's novel *Animal Farm* provide examples of events and situations where it is clear that rules sometimes can be challenged and broken but not without consequences.

Paragraph 1 Topic: Rules are intended to keep society in order and help meet the needs of citizens.

Supporting Detail #1: Rules are necessary to prevent chaos and destruction of society.

Supporting Detail #2: Rules sometimes violate the needs and rights of those they are meant to serve, as seen in Sophocles's play *Antigone* and George Orwell's novel *Animal Farm*.

Paragraph 2 Topic: In *Antigone,* Antigone must decide if she will obey King Creon's decree or break the rules by burying her brother, Polyneices.

Supporting Detail #1: Her brother Eteocles has been buried with the full rituals of a Greek citizen and soldier because he fought for Thebes, but Creon has ordered that Polyneices, who fought against Thebes, should remain unburied.

Supporting Detail #2: Leaving Polyneices' body unburied will condemn his spirit to roam the land without peace.

Paragraph 3 Topic: Sisters Antigone and Ismene are at odds about what is the right action to take.

Supporting Detail #1: Ismene believes that it is the role of Greek citizens, especially women, to follow the rules set down by the male leaders of their society. She operates on reason, stating: "Shall we not perish wretchedness of all, / If in defiance of the law we cross/A monarch's will?"

Supporting Detail #2: Antigone feels that Creon's decree violates the basic rules of loving family relationships and the eternal laws of the Greek Gods. She is driven by emotion. Sophocles shows that Antigone's choice will have consequences, no matter which course of action she chooses.

Paragraph 4 Topic: In *Animal Farm,* Orwell uses the story of farm animals to explore the limits of rules and the uses of power.

Supporting Detail #1: After the animals' overthrow the human Mr. Jones's rule, they attempt to establish a democracy, though Snowball and Napoleon vie for leadership.

Supporting Detail #2: During a debate over the building of the windmill, Napoleon enacts a military-style coup and seizes power of the farm, so that he will make all final decisions on behalf of the other animals. "He [Napoleon] announced that from now on the Sunday-morning meetings would come to an end.... In future all questions relating to the working of the farm would be settled by a special committee of pigs, presided over by himself."

Paragraph 5 Topic: the main characters of both texts think they are right to overthrow what they see as unfair rules, but they will have to suffer the consequences of this choice.

Supporting Detail #1: Antigone faces death as punishment for disobeying Creon's edict.

Supporting Detail #2: In *Animal Farm,* the overthrow of human leadership causes great change, but it does not seem to improve the lives of the animals.

Please note that excerpts and passages in the StudySync® library and this workbook are intended as touchstones to generate interest in an author's work. The excerpts and passages do not substitute for the reading of entire texts, and StudySync® strongly recommends that students seek out and purchase the whole literary or informational work in order to experience it as the author intended. Links to online resellers are available in our digital library. In addition, complete works may be ordered through an authorized reseller by filling out and returning to StudySync® the order form enclosed in this workbook.

Reading & Writing Companion

187

SKILL:
INTRODUCTIONS

DEFINE

In any type of writing, the **introduction** plays a very important role. The first paragraph is where writers grab the audience's attention, establish their purpose, and make it clear what information that is coming next. After reading the first paragraph, the reader should be aware of a writer's claim. A **claim,** usually located in a **thesis statement,** is an idea about an issue, a stand in a debate, or a position on a topic. An introduction should also suggest the **organization** of a piece of writing, or the order in which the writer will present the claims, any **counterclaims** (opposing viewpoints), and supporting details in the form of reasons and evidence.

IDENTIFICATION AND APPLICATION

When introducing a literary analysis, consider the following:

- The introduction identifies the topic and states what the writer will prove in a **thesis statement**. This is also the writer's central or main idea. The thesis will be restated, and often enhanced, in the conclusion.
- Writers can begin an introduction with a variety of techniques, including:
  - › anecdotes, or brief stories based on either personal experiences or the experiences of others.
  - › references to a specific event or occasion.
  - › direct questions, which the essay will try to answer.
  - › direct quotations from texts or famous sayings.
  - › descriptions of particular events or people.
- Writers can reference specific textual evidence in the introduction to give readers an understanding of how the claims will be supported, but most of the reasons and evidence should be saved for the main body of the text.

- Before drafting an introduction, consider the **audience,** the people who will read your writing, and your **purpose,** which will be to persuade or convince readers of the claim or claims in the thesis statement.

Copyright © BookheadEd Learning, LLC

MODEL

When setting up an argument, introductions can take many forms and have different tones. Some texts open with direct questions that the writer wants to answer. Others might begin in an adversarial way, challenging the audience from the beginning to consider the writer's point of view. The introduction of Patrick Henry's *Speech to the Second Virginia Convention,* to highlight another example, shows the most charming way possible for a speaker to to tell an audience that he wholeheartedly disagrees with them:

> Mr. President, no man thinks more highly than I do of the patriotism, as well as abilities, of the very worthy gentlemen who have **just addressed the House**. But different men often see the same subject in different lights; and, therefore, I hope it will not be thought disrespectful to those gentlemen if, entertaining as I do, **opinions of a character very opposite to theirs, I shall speak forth my sentiments freely, and without reserve**. This is no time for ceremony. The question before the House is one of awful moment to this country. For my own part, I consider it as nothing less than a question of freedom or slavery; and **in proportion to the magnitude of the subject ought to be the freedom of the debate. It is only in this way that we can hope to arrive at truth**, and fulfill the great responsibility which we hold to God and our country. **Should I keep back my opinions at such a time, through fear of giving offence, I should consider myself as guilty of treason towards my country**, and of an act of disloyalty toward the majesty of heaven, which I revere above all earthly kings.

Henry starts by establishing his respect for the speakers who "just addressed the House," a move that encourages the audience to show him the same respect. This respect will be very important because the speaker sets his thesis on the line early on in his speech: His "opinions [are] of a character very opposite to theirs," but he strongly believes his views are right. That sort of confidence in an introduction is very effective. A common mistake in essay writing is not taking a strong enough stance on an issue. A good thesis states an educated opinion with confidence. If the author does not fully believe in the ideas, why should the audience?

Henry knows his audience admires patriotism and allegiance to the nation's cause, so he emphasizes that his views, though widely opposed to many others, should be considered because they are the *most* patriotic. He lets listeners know that he will speak "freely and without reserve," for a true patriot knows that "in proportion to the magnitude of the subject ought to be the freedom of the debate. It is only in this way that we can hope to arrive at truth." Henry positions himself as a respectful, patriotic citizen even as he lets his colleagues know he disagrees with many of them. To be less than honest would cause him to feel "guilty of treason" toward his country. While many of the people in this audience may have disregarded Henry right from the start because of his message, Henry successfully garnered their interest in his controversial message supporting revolution.

⚡ PRACTICE

Write an introduction for your essay that includes the thesis statement you have already worked on, as well as a hook to capture your readers' interest. Trade with a peer review partner when you are finished and offer feedback on each other's introductions. Remember that suggestions for improvement are most helpful when they are supportive and kind.

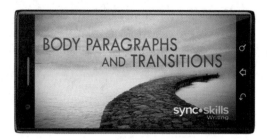

SKILL: BODY
PARAGRAPHS
AND
TRANSITIONS

 DEFINE

Body paragraphs are the section of the essay between the introduction and conclusion paragraphs. This is where you support your thesis statement by developing your main points with evidence from the text and analysis. Typically, each body paragraph will focus on one main point or idea to avoid confusing their reader. The main idea or focus of each body paragraph must help develop and support the thesis statement.

It's important to structure your body paragraph clearly. One strategy for structuring the body paragraph for an argumentative essay is the following:

Write a topic sentence: The topic sentence is the first sentence of your body paragraph and clearly states the main idea or focus of the paragraph. In the first body paragraph, the topic sentence should connect your thesis statement to the first set of evidence you will use to support the thesis statement.

Provide evidence: Be sure to support your topic sentence with evidence. Evidence can be a summary of relevant facts, concrete details, quotations, definitions or other information and examples.

Analyze/Explain: After presenting evidence to support your topic sentence, you will need to analyze that evidence and explain how it supports your topic sentence and, in effect, your thesis.

Repeat, as needed: Use the process above for each body paragraph you add, since you may find that you want to provide another piece of related evidence and analysis. Be sure that all the evidence in each body paragraph supports the same idea.

Concluding sentence: After presenting your evidence in a body paragraph, you need to wrap up your main idea. In addition, this sentence should help lead to the next body paragraph or to the conclusion.

Transitions are connecting words and phrases that clarify the relationships among ideas in a text. Transitions work at three different levels: 1) within a sentence, 2) within a paragraph, and 3) between paragraphs, providing an organizational structure.

IDENTIFICATION AND APPLICATION

- Body paragraphs of an argumentative essay appear between the introduction and conclusion paragraphs. Body paragraphs provide the evidence and explanation needed to support the thesis statement. Typically, writers develop one main idea per body paragraph.
  - › Topic sentences clearly state the main idea of that paragraph.
  - › Evidence consists of relevant facts, concrete details, quotations, definitions, or other information and examples.
  - › Analysis and explanation are needed to explain how the evidence supports the topic sentence.
  - › The conclusion sentence wraps up the main point and transitions to the next body paragraph.

- Transition words are a necessary element of a successful piece of argumentative writing.
  - › Transition words help readers understand the text structure of an argumentative text. Here are some transition words that are frequently used in three different text structures:
    - › Cause-effect: *because, accordingly, as a result, effect, so, for, since*
    - › Compare-contrast: *like, unlike, also, both, similarly, although, while, but, however, whereas, conversely, meanwhile, on the contrary, and yet, still*
    - › Chronological order: *first, next, then, finally, last, initially, ultimately*

- Transition words and phrases help authors make connections between words within a sentence. Conjunctions such as *and, or,* and *but* and prepositions such as *with, beyond, inside,* show the relationships between words. Transitions help readers understand how words fit together to make meaning.

- Transition words help readers understand the flow of ideas and concepts in a paragraph. Some of the most useful transitions are words that indicate that the ideas in one paragraph are building on or adding to those in another. Examples include: *furthermore, therefore, in addition, moreover, by extension, in order to, etc.*

Copyright © BookheadEd Learning, LLC

- Authors of argumentative texts involving literary analysis use transitions to help readers connect one author to another, one text to another, and recognize the connections among the ideas. Transitions are a key organizational tool for essays like this. Transitions to connect paragraphs can be indicated in your concluding sentence of one paragraph and at the beginning of the next paragraph.

 ## MODEL

The Student Model uses a body paragraph structure to develop the essay's thesis statement. The writer uses transitions to help the reader connect ideas within sentences and paragraphs, as well as between paragraphs.

Reread the body paragraphs from the student model essay "Breaking the Rules." Look closely at the structure and note the transition words in bold. Think about the purpose of the essay. Do the details effectively develop the main points made in each topic sentence? How do the transition words help you to how the ideas are related to each other and to the thesis statement?

In the opening scene of Antigone, Sophocles introduces the audience to the initial conflict of the play: whether or not to obey King Creon's decree. Antigone and Ismene's brothers—Polyneices and Eteocles—have killed each other during battle. Eteocles, who fought on the side of the victorious city of Thebes, has been buried with the full rituals of a Greek citizen and soldier. **However,** Creon, the new king of Thebes, has ordered that Polyneices, who fought against Thebes, should remain unburied. His body is to remain on the open battlefield, and his spirit is condemned to roam the land without peace. Antigone has asked to meet her sister outside the gates of Thebes to plea for help in taking Polyneices' body for proper burial. Should Antigone break the law or not? **This is the problem Sophocles explores.**

Immediately, the two sisters begin to argue over the whether or not Creon's decree should be followed. As the sisters show their differences, the audience gets a chance to see both sides of the argument. Ismene believes that it is the role of Greek citizens, especially women, to follow the rules set down by the male leaders of their society. Ismene warns, "Shall we not perish wretchedness of all,/If in defiance of the law we cross/A monarch's will?" **To the contrary,** Antigone feels that Creon's decree should be disobeyed because it violates the basic rules of loving family relationships and the

Please note that excerpts and passages in the StudySync® library and this workbook are intended as touchstones to generate interest in an author's work. The excerpts and passages do not substitute for the reading of entire texts, and StudySync® strongly recommends that students seek out and purchase the whole literary or informational work in order to experience it as the author intended. Links to online resellers are available in our digital library. In addition, complete works may be ordered through an authorized reseller by filling out and returning to StudySync® the order form enclosed in this workbook.

Reading & Writing Companion **193**

NOTES

eternal laws of the Greek Gods. Ismene, trying to use reason, continues to object to Antigone's plan and cautions Antigone that she will likely be killed if she follows through on it. **Sophocles shows that Antigone is making her choice to break the rules partly on tradition, but mostly on emotion.** Antigone scornfully replies to Ismene, "Go thine own way; myself will bury him,/How sweet to die in such employ, to rest—/Sister and brother linked in love's embrace—/A sinless sinner, banned awhile on earth,/But by the dead commended; and with them I shall abide for ever. As for thee,/Scorn if thou wilt, the eternal laws of Heaven" (Sophocles). For Antigone, the unfair rule of a vengeful but victorious leader may be rightfully broken so that the more important rules of family and faith can prevail. Should the heart rule the head? **Sophocles shows that Antigone, whatever her choice, will have to live, or die, with the consequences of her actions.**

In his novel Animal Farm, George Orwell **also** deals with the importance of rules to social order. **As it was for Antigone in Thebes, the rules of Animal Farm seem to be justifiably broken, but** for different reasons and with different consequences. Orwell uses this story of farm animals to explore the limits of rules and the uses of power. **After** the animals' initial overthrow of Mr. Jones's rule, Snowball and Napoleon vie for leadership. A debate over the building of the windmill precedes what is supposed to be a democratic vote by all the animals. **To the animals' surprise,** the democratic rules of debate and voting are violated when the meeting turns into a military-style coup as Napoleon uses his trained dogs to viciously attack Snowball and chase him off the farm. Having seized power, Napoleon immediately changes the existing rules so he can maintain iron-fisted control. "He [Napoleon] announced that from now on the Sunday-morning meetings would come to an end.... In future all questions relating to the working of the farm would be settled by a special committee of pigs, presided over by himself" (Orwell). **Later,** Napoleon sends Squeaker around the farm to explain the new rules. Squeaker tells the animals, "No one believes more firmly than Comrade Napoleon that all animals are equal. He would be only too happy to let you make your decisions for yourselves. But sometimes you might make the wrong decisions, comrades, and then where should we be?" (Orwell). **Previously,** the animals had justifiably broken rules when they overthrew their human masters. The animals are eventually subjected to the same type of autocratic control that they had sought to overthrow.

The first two body paragraphs of the Student Model are concerned with developing ideas from *Antigone* that support the thesis statement expressed in the introduction. The first body paragraph begins by stating, "In the opening scene of *Antigone,* we are introduced to the initial conflict of the play: whether or not to obey King Creon's decree." This **topic sentence** clearly establishes the purpose and main idea of this body paragraph. This topic sentence is immediately followed by **evidence** in the form of specific details from the play that introduces all the main characters and the key events that lead up to the focus of the first scene. He closes the paragraph by pointing out the author's purpose, which to explore this question: "Should Antigone break the law or not?"

The second body paragraph narrows the focus to the specific terms of the conflict by recounting Ismene's and Antigone's positions concerning Creon's decree. The student writer summarizes the argument each sister makes and supports his analysis with details and direct quotations from the text. Notice how the concluding sentence of this paragraph—"For Antigone, the unfair rule of a vengeful but victorious leader may be rightfully broken so that the more important rules of family and faith can prevail"—concisely summarizes Antigone's position and ties directly to the writing prompt and the thesis statement made in the introduction. The student closes by returning, and dramatically, to Sophocles's purpose as he sees it: "Sophocles shows that Antigone, whatever her choice, will have to live, or die, with the consequences of her actions."

All three body paragraphs use **transition words** to show relationships between the main points within and between the body paragraphs. Words and phrases such as ***In the opening scene, immediately, initial*** and ***later*** signal sequential, or chronological, transitions. Other transitional words and phrases, such as ***however, to the contrary,*** and ***also,*** indicate that comparisons and contrasts are being used as transitions. In this context, a text-specific line such as ***To the animals' surprise*** is a transitional phrase as well. Without transitions as a guide, connecting such different works as *Antigone* and *Animal Farm* would be difficult to follow.

 PRACTICE

Write one body paragraph for your literary analysis essay that follows the suggested format. When you are finished, trade with a partner and offer each other feedback. How effective is the topic sentence at stating the main point of the paragraph? How strong is the evidence used to support the topic sentence? Does the analysis thoroughly support the topic sentence? Does the analysis contain good organization and strong transitions to connect and clarify ideas? Offer each other suggestions, and remember that they are most helpful when they are constructive.

SKILL: CONCLUSIONS

 DEFINE

Conclusions are the paragraphs that show how the key ideas developed in an informational, argumentative, or analytical text prove the thesis. They often include a final point that emphasizes the writer's message. There are several approaches to writing a strong conclusion. Perhaps the most common way is to simply summarize the key ideas, in the order they were presented, to show how the thesis statement was proven. Other conclusions try to take the material in another direction, such as calling on a reader to take action, or suggesting that more thinking needs to be done on the subject.

As with the rest of the text, it is important to consider the audience and purpose when writing a conclusion. Do you want to rile readers to action? Make them reflect deeply on their own opinions on a hotbed issue? Calm readers' worries about a social problem? Your purpose can help you to craft the tone as well as the content of your conclusion. Think about what is important to your audience and what final statement will be most effective in achieving your purpose.

 IDENTIFICATION AND APPLICATION

When writing conclusions for a literary analysis:

- Provide a concluding paragraph that follows the body paragraphs and supports the thesis statement presented in the introduction.
- Reference key points, supporting details, and the names of work and authors discussed.
- Avoid including new information not previously mentioned or developed.
- When summarizing the argument made in the analysis, keep main points in the order in which they were introduced.
- Consider other options besides summarizing, such as a call to action, or motivation from the author toward whatever action or opinion the writer suggests taking after reading the text.

Copyright © BookheadEd Learning, LLC

- Consider audience and purpose when creating tone and selecting supporting details to include.

MODEL

A great conclusion sums up the argument of the entire essay and spurs the audience on to some sort of desired effect. The conclusion of the student model, "Breaking the Rules," the writer returns to ideas in the introduction, summarizes the information that helped prove the thesis, and concludes with a restatement of the original thesis.

> **In summary,** the main characters of both texts think they are right to overthrow what they see as unfair rules. That said, the breaking of rules may result in dire consequences. For Antigone, death may be the punishment she pays for disobeying Creon's edict. For the creatures living on Animal Farm, the breaking of the rules merely changes the leadership of the farm, but it does not improve the lives of the animals. **In short, rules may be justifiably broken, but not without unintended and often unpleasant consequences.**

The transition *In summary* lets the reader know that this is the concluding paragraph, but there are other ways to create stronger transitions. Since the author draws similarities between literature and life, another way of beginning the concluding paragraph might be, *As often happens with people even today,* or *Despite the pressures not to go too far.* However, both the introduction and conclusion of "Breaking the Rules" focus on the themes of the two selections, and also show how these stories are reflected in reality, that "rules may be justifiably broken, but not without unintended and often unpleasant consequences."

The author summarizes not only the thesis, but also the details presented over the course of the text—the situations explored in the two pieces of literature that prove the thesis. While the writer used the body of the essay to delve deeply into the details of the sources, the conclusion contains a short summary of what was proven.

PRACTICE

Write a conclusion for your essay. Your essay should include reinforcement or a restatement of the thesis you have already worked on and a final thought you want to leave with readers. Trade with a peer review partner when you are finished and offer feedback on each other's conclusion.

Copyright © BookheadEd Learning, LLC

NOTES

DRAFT

WRITING PROMPT

The role of rules in societies, around the world and across the ages— what the rules are, why they matter, how they are broken, and why some people feel they must break them—is a central idea in many texts from this unit. When is breaking the rules not only understandable, but necessary? Write an analysis of two selections you have read during the unit and examine the authors' arguments in favor of breaking the rules.

Your essay should include:

- an introduction with a clear thesis/claim

- body paragraphs with relevant evidence and thorough analysis to support your thesis

- a conclusion paragraph that effectively wraps up your essay

You have already made progress toward writing your own literary analysis. You have thought about your purpose and examined the texts you've read in this unit to choose two you will address in your essay. You have created a thesis statement and analyzed the text evidence to choose details that will support the claim in that thesis statement. You have considered audience and purpose to help guide your writing. You have decided how to organize information, and generated supporting reasons. Now it is time to write a draft of your literary analysis.

Use your outline, essay road map, and your other prewriting materials to help you as you write. Remember that argumentative writing begins with an introduction and presents a claim in the form of a thesis statement. Body paragraphs develop the claim in the thesis statement with strong supporting reasons, details, quotations, and other relevant information from the texts. Transitions help the reader understand the relationship among the claim, supporting reasons, and evidence. A concluding paragraph summarizes or

Copyright © BookheadEd Learning, LLC

reflects on the information in the essay and restates the thesis statement to remind readers why the thesis statement is sound and correct.

When drafting, ask yourself these questions:

- What is the most important thing I want to say in this essay?
- How can I best present the claim in my thesis statement?
- What facts, details, and quotations can I draw from the texts to provide strong support for my claims?
- Have I taken the time to analyze each piece of evidence I have chosen?
- Am I remembering to relate all the evidence to my thesis statement?
- Does the evidence I've chosen represent a thorough understanding of the texts?
- How can I use precise language to present my claims and evidence in a way that is interesting to the reader?
- How well have I communicated each writer's portrayal of a situation in which it is necessary to break the rules?
- What do I want my readers to believe or think about once they have finished reading my essay?

Before you submit your draft, read it over carefully. You want to be sure that you have responded to all aspects of the prompt.

REVISE

WRITING PROMPT

The role of rules in societies, around the world and across the ages—what the rules are, why they matter, how they are broken, and why some people feel they must break them—is a central idea in many texts from this unit. When is breaking the rules not only understandable, but necessary? Write an analysis of two selections you have read during the unit and examine the authors' arguments in favor of breaking the rules.

Your essay should include:

- an introduction with a clear thesis/claim
- body paragraphs with relevant evidence and thorough analysis to support your thesis
- a conclusion paragraph that effectively wraps up your essay

You have written a draft of your literary analysis. You have also received input from your peers about how to improve it. Now you are going to revise your draft.

Here are some recommendations to help you revise:

- Review the suggestions made by your peers.
- Focus on maintaining a formal style. A formal style suits your purpose—making a claim about academic texts. It is also appropriate for an audience of peers, teachers, and other readers interested in learning more about the themes and messages of literary texts.
  - As you revise, replace slang with formal diction.
  - Remove any first-person pronouns such as "I," "me," or "mine" or instances of addressing readers as "you," as well as any contractions or other shorthand. This will help you maintain a formal, rather than conversational or personal, writing style.

- › Remove any emotional or biased language from your writing that interferes with an objective tone.
- › Find places where you have shifted verb tense, could combine short sentences and break up run-on sentences, or might otherwise adjust your writing to elevate its quality.
- › Verify that your claims are supported by textual evidence and not personal opinion.
- › Use active voice rather than passive voice whenever possible in supporting your claims.

- After you have revised elements of style, think about ways to improve your essay's content and organization.

  - › Is your claim stated clearly in your thesis statement?
  - › Does your introduction present your thesis statement and the texts you will discuss in your essay?
  - › Do the reasons and evidence in your body paragraphs support your thesis statement?
  - › Do you need to add any new textual evidence to fully support the claim in your thesis statement?
  - › Have you evaluated the strengths and weaknesses of any of the evidence you used to support your claim? Did you remove or edit weak evidence?
  - › Do your word choices make sense and engage the reader?
  - › Do your body paragraphs contain clear transitions and smoothly link the ideas in your essay?
  - › Have you presented readers with a strong conclusion that also supports your thesis statement?

Please note that excerpts and passages in the StudySync® library and this workbook are intended as touchstones to generate interest in an author's work. The excerpts and passages do not substitute for the reading of entire texts, and StudySync® strongly recommends that students seek out and purchase the whole literary or informational work in order to experience it as the author intended. Links to online resellers are available in our digital library. In addition, complete works may be ordered through an authorized reseller by filling out and returning to StudySync® the order form enclosed in this workbook.

Reading & Writing Companion **201**

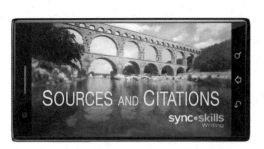

SKILL: SOURCES AND CITATIONS

 DEFINE

Sources are the documents and information that an author uses to develop his or her writing. Some sources are **primary sources**. A primary source is a document or object from the time being studied. In the case of an argumentative essay involving a literary analysis, the primary source is the original literary text being analyzed, such as the novel *Animal Farm*. Other sources are **secondary sources**. Secondary sources analyze and interpret primary sources. For example, an essay or article *about* the novel *Animal Farm* is a secondary source that a writer might consult when writing about the novel. Writers need to cite any sources they use. **Citations** are notes that give information about the sources an author used in his or her writing. Citations are required whenever authors quote others' words or refer to others' ideas in their writing. Citations let readers know who originally came up with those words and ideas.

 IDENTIFICATION AND APPLICATION

- Sources can be primary or secondary in nature. Primary sources are original literary texts, first-hand accounts, artifacts, or other original materials. Examples of primary sources include:
  › Original works of literature
  › Letters or other correspondence
  › Autobiographies or memoirs
  › Diaries or journals
  › Photographs
  › Official documents
  › Eyewitness accounts and interviews
  › Audio recordings and radio broadcasts
  › Works of art
  › Artifacts

- Secondary sources are usually texts. Secondary sources are the written interpretation and analysis of primary source materials. Some examples of secondary sources include:
  - › Commentary or criticisms
  - › Encyclopedia articles
  - › Textbooks
  - › Histories
  - › Documentary films
  - › News analyses
- Whether sources are primary or secondary, they must be **credible** and **accurate**. Writers of informative/explanatory texts look for sources from experts in the topic they are writing about.
  - › When researching online, they look for URLs that contain .gov (government agencies), .edu (colleges and universities), and .org (museums and other non-profit organizations).
  - › Writers also use respected print and online news and information sources.
- Anytime a writer uses words from another source exactly as they are written, the words must appear in quotation marks. Quotation marks show that the words are not the author's own words but are borrowed from another source. In the student model essay, the writer uses quotation marks around words taken directly from the source *Antigone*:

  "Go thine own way; myself will bury him,/How sweet to die in such employ, to rest—/Sister and brother linked in love's embrace—/A sinless sinner, banned awhile on earth,/But by the dead commended; and with them I shall abide for ever. As for thee,/Scorn if thou wilt, the eternal laws of Heaven" (Sophocles).

- A writer includes a citation to give credit to any source, whether primary or secondary, that is quoted exactly. There are several different ways to cite a source. One way is to put the author's last name in parenthesis at the end of the sentence in which the quote appears. This is what the writer of the student model essay does after the quotation above. Notice that the punctuation goes after the second parenthesis.
- Citations are also necessary when a writer borrows ideas from another source, even if the writer paraphrases, or puts those ideas in his or her own words. Citations demonstrate that the writer did credible work, but they also help readers discover where they can learn more.

Please note that excerpts and passages in the StudySync® library and this workbook are intended as touchstones to generate interest in an author's work. The excerpts and passages do not substitute for the reading of entire texts, and StudySync® strongly recommends that students seek out and purchase the whole literary or informational work in order to experience it as the author intended. Links to online resellers are available in our digital library. In addition, complete works may be ordered through an authorized reseller by filling out and returning to StudySync® the order form enclosed in this workbook.

Reading & Writing Companion   **203**

MODEL

In this excerpt from the student model essay, the writer uses quotations from the primary literary source material.

> In his novel *Animal Farm,* George Orwell also deals with the importance of rules to social order. As in Antigone, the rules of Animal Farm seem to be justifiably broken, but for different reasons and with different consequences. After the animal's initial overthrow of Mr. Jones's rule, Snowball and Napoleon vie for leadership. A debate over the building of the windmill precedes what is supposed to be a democratic vote by all the animals. To the animals' surprise, the democratic rules of debate and voting are violated when the meeting turns into a military-style coup as Napoleon uses his trained dogs to viciously attack Snowball and chase him off the farm. Having seized power, Napoleon immediately changes the existing rules so he can maintain iron-fisted control. **"He [Napoleon] announced that from now on the Sunday-morning meetings would come to an end.... In future all questions relating to the working of the farm would be settled by a special committee of pigs, presided over by himself" (Orwell).** Later, Napoleon sends Squeaker around the farm to explain the new rules. **Squeaker tells the animals, "No one believes more firmly than Comrade Napoleon that all animals are equal. He would be only too happy to let you make your decisions for yourselves. But sometimes you might make the wrong decisions, comrades, and then where should we be?" (Orwell).** The animals had justifiably broken rules when they overthrew their human masters. Nonetheless, the animals are eventually subjected to the same type of autocratic control that they had sought to overthrow.

The writer announces the name of the text and the author of that text from the paragraph's opening. When quoting directly, the writer included the author's name in parentheses "(Orwell)" and placed a period after each citation. There are two kinds of quotations, though they are treated the same way: The first is by the narrator, and the other is a character's dialogue. To avoid an awkward quote-within-a-quote in the second quotation, the writer identifies the speaker, Squeaker, and then punctuates the dialogue in regular quotation marks. Notice, too, how the writer uses a bracketed note to clarify who "He" is in a long quotation: "[Napoleon]." This is used when a quotation makes reference to previous lines and includes, then, an ambiguous pronoun. All of this effort on the part of the writer makes the work of reading that much easier for the audience.

Copyright © BookheadEd Learning, LLC

EDIT, PROOFREAD AND PUBLISH

WRITING PROMPT

The role of rules in societies, around the world and across the ages—what the rules are, why they matter, how they are broken, and why some people feel they must break them—is a central idea in many texts from this unit. When is breaking the rules not only understandable, but necessary? Write an analysis of two selections you have read during the unit and examine the authors' arguments in favor of breaking the rules.

Your essay should include:

- an introduction with a clear thesis/claim
- body paragraphs with relevant evidence and thorough analysis to support your thesis
- a conclusion paragraph that effectively wraps up your essay

You have revised your literary analysis essay and received input from your peers on that revision. Now it's time to edit and proofread your essay to produce a final version. Here are some questions you asked yourself prior to this stage. Review this list once more to ensure that your essay is appropriate to the task and meets the requirements of a literary analysis:

- Have I fully developed the claim in my thesis statement?
- Have I included strong reasons and sound evidence to support my analysis claim?
- Have I accurately cited the sources I have included as supporting evidence?
- Does the evidence I've chosen represent a thorough analysis of the texts?
- Have I organized my essay so that my body paragraphs each contain a clear topic and supporting details?

NOTES

- Have I used clear transitions between the body paragraphs of my essay?
- Have I presented the reader with a conclusion that effectively wraps up my essay?

When you are satisfied with your work, move on to proofread it for errors:

- Check that you have formatted your essay according to approved guidelines and standards. This includes title page or title placement, margins, font, spacing, paragraphing, bibliographic information, and other technical considerations.
- Check your spelling, including names of authors, titles, and characters.
- Check sentence structure, including use of compound sentences and parallel structure. Look for missing or misplaced commas. Check your use of semicolons, colons, and other punctuation.
- Check content and punctuation of quotations and citations.

Once you have made all your corrections, you are ready to submit and publish your work. You can distribute your writing to family and friends, hang it on a bulletin board, or post it on your blog. If you publish online, create links to your sources and citations, to help readers investigate your sources and learn more about the texts you have analyzed.

studysync®

Reading & Writing Companion

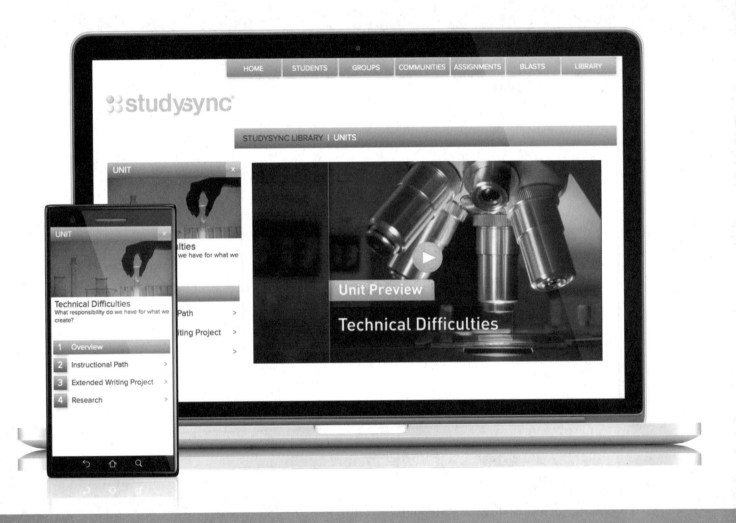

What responsibility do we have for what we create?

Technical Difficulties

Technical Difficulties

 TEXTS

EXTENDED WRITING PROJECT

425

Text Fulfillment
through
StudySync

Please note that excerpts and passages in the StudySync® library and this workbook are intended as touchstones to generate interest in an author's work. The excerpts and passages do not substitute for the reading of entire texts, and StudySync® strongly recommends that students seek out and purchase the whole literary or informational work in order to experience it as the author intended. Links to online resellers are available in our digital library. In addition, complete works may be ordered through an authorized reseller by filling out and returning to StudySync® the order form enclosed in this workbook.

Reading & Writing
Companion   **209**

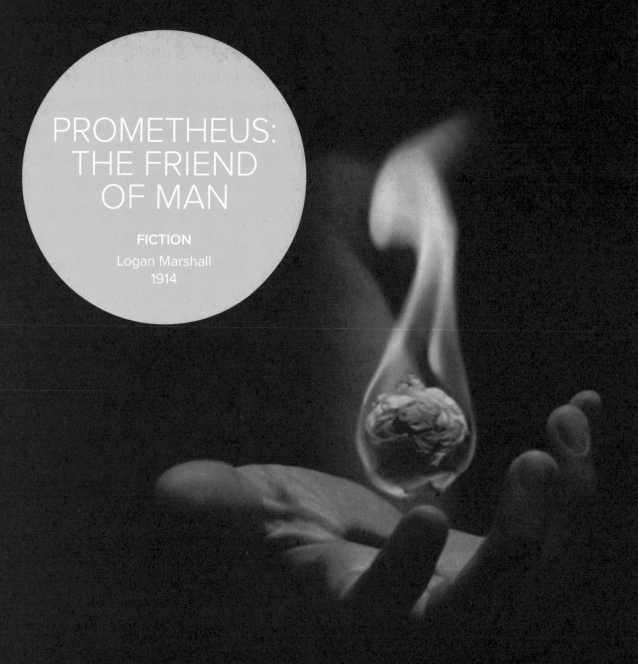

PROMETHEUS: THE FRIEND OF MAN

FICTION
Logan Marshall
1914

INTRODUCTION

Ancient Greeks and other cultures developed myths and legends to explain the origins of their gods, heroes and practices, as well as the laws of nature. These dramatic and often tragic narratives offer insight into the political, religious, and social structures in place at the time. The selection here from author Logan Marshall's collection of myths and legends tells the story of Prometheus, the Titan who defies Jupiter's command and provides fire to humans. Although motivated by a desire to promote progress and prosperity, Prometheus is severely punished by the gods for his act.

"And from your race shall spring the hero who will break my chains and set me free."

 FIRST READ

1 Many, many centuries ago there lived two brothers, Prometheus or Forethought, and Epimetheus or Afterthought. They were the sons of those Titans who had fought against Jupiter and been sent in chains to the great prison-house of the lower world, but for some reason had escaped punishment.

2 Prometheus, however, did not care for **idle** life among the gods on Mount Olympus. Instead he preferred to spend his time on the earth, helping men to find easier and better ways of living. For the children of earth were not happy as they had been in the golden days when Saturn ruled. Indeed, they were very poor and wretched and cold, without fire, without food, and with no shelter but miserable caves.

3 "With fire they could at least warm their bodies and cook their food," Prometheus thought, "and later they could make tools and build houses for themselves and enjoy some of the comforts of the gods."

4 So Prometheus went to Jupiter and asked that he might be permitted to carry fire to the earth. But Jupiter shook his head in wrath.

5 "Fire, indeed!" he exclaimed. "If men had fire they would soon be as strong and wise as we who dwell on Olympus. Never will I give my **consent**."

6 Prometheus made no reply, but he didn't give up his idea of helping men. "Some other way must be found," he thought.

7 Then, one day, as he was walking among some reeds he broke off one, and seeing that its hollow stalk was filled with a dry, soft pith, exclaimed:

8 "At last! In this I can carry fire, and the children of men shall have the great gift in spite of Jupiter."

NOTES

9 Immediately, taking a long stalk in his hands, he set out for the dwelling of the sun in the far east. He reached there in the early morning, just as Apollo's chariot was about to begin its journey across the sky. Lighting his reed, he hurried back, carefully guarding the precious spark that was hidden in the hollow stalk.

10 Then he showed men how to build fires for themselves, and it was not long before they began to do all the wonderful things of which Prometheus had dreamed. They learned to cook and to **domesticate** animals and to till the fields and to mine precious metals and melt them into tools and weapons. And they came out of their dark and gloomy caves and built for themselves beautiful houses of wood and stone. And instead of being sad and unhappy they began to laugh and sing. "Behold, the Age of Gold has come again," they said.

11 But Jupiter was not so happy. He saw that men were gaining daily greater power, and their very prosperity made him angry.

12 "That young Titan!" he cried out, when he heard what Prometheus had done. "I will punish him."

13 But before punishing Prometheus he decided to vex the children of men. So he gave a lump of clay to his blacksmith, Vulcan, and told him to mold it in the form of a woman. When the work was done he carried it to Olympus.

14 Jupiter called the other gods together, bidding them give her each a gift. One bestowed upon her beauty, another, kindness, another, skill, another, curiosity, and so on. Jupiter himself gave her the gift of life, and they named her Pandora, which means "all-gifted."

15 Then Mercury, the messenger of the gods, took Pandora and led her down the mountain side to the place where Prometheus and his brother were living.

16 "Epimetheus, here is a beautiful woman that Jupiter has sent to be your wife," he said.

17 Epimetheus was delighted and soon loved Pandora very deeply, because of her beauty and her goodness.

18 Now Pandora had brought with her as a gift from Jupiter a golden casket. Athena had warned her never to open the box, but she could not help wondering and wondering what it contained. Perhaps it held beautiful jewels. Why should they go to waste?

19 At last she could not contain her curiosity any longer. She opened the box just a little to take a peep inside. Immediately there was a buzzing, whirring sound, and before she could snap down the lid ten thousand ugly little creatures had jumped out. They were diseases and troubles, and very glad they were to be free.

20 All over the earth they flew, entering into every household, and carrying sorrow and distress wherever they went.

21 How Jupiter must have laughed when he saw the result of Pandora's curiosity!

22 Soon after this the god decided that it was time to punish Prometheus. He called Strength and Force and bade them seize the Titan and carry him to the highest peak of the Caucasus Mountains. Then he sent Vulcan to bind him with iron chains, making arms and feet fast to the rocks. Vulcan was sorry for Prometheus, but dared not disobey.

23 So the friend of man lay, miserably bound, naked to the winds, while the storms beat about him and an eagle tore at his liver with its cruel talons. But Prometheus did not utter a groan in spite of all his sufferings. Year after year he lay in agony, and yet he would not complain, beg for mercy or repent of what he had done. Men were sorry for him, but could do nothing.

24 Then one day a beautiful white cow passed over the mountain, and stopped to look at Prometheus with sad eyes.

25 "I know you," Prometheus said. "You are Io, once a fair and happy maiden dwelling in Argos, doomed by Jupiter and his jealous queen to wander over the earth in this **guise**. Go southward and then west until you come to the great river Nile. There you shall again become a maiden, fairer than ever before, and shall marry the king of that country. And from your race shall spring the hero who will break my chains and set me free."

26 Centuries passed and then a great hero, Hercules, came to the Caucasus Mountains. He climbed the rugged peak, slew the fierce eagle, and with mighty blows broke the chains that bound the friend of man.

THINK QUESTIONS

1. How does Jupiter respond to Prometheus's request to take fire to the earth, and why? What does Jupiter's response indicate about his character? Cite strong textual evidence to support your answer.

2. Who has more power, Jupiter or Prometheus? How do you know? Use evidence from the text to support your answer.

3. What does the story of Prometheus reveal about the gods and their characters? In what ways are the gods both like and unlike typical human beings?

4. Use context to determine the meaning of the word **consent** as it is used in "Prometheus: The Friend of Man." Write your definition of "consent" and explain the basis for your definition. Then look "consent" up in a dictionary and compare your definition with the one in the dictionary. How accurate was your initial definition?

5. Use context to determine the meaning of the word **vex** as it is used in "Prometheus: The Friend of Man." Write your definition of "vex" and explain the basis for your definition. Verify your preliminary definition by checking it in context and then in a dictionary.

CLOSE READ

Reread the excerpt from "Prometheus: The Friend of Man." As you reread, complete the Focus Questions below. Then use your answers and annotations from the questions to help you complete the Writing Prompt.

FOCUS QUESTIONS

1. In what different ways does the text distinguish Prometheus's character from that of the other gods on Mount Olympus?

2. The third paragraph describes Prometheus's intent in helping man. How does he expect to improve life for man and help him live a better life? What do his goals for man reveal about his perception of the relationship between the gods and men?

3. Why do you think Prometheus is punished so severely for his actions? How does Prometheus respond to his punishment, and what does this response reveal about his character?

4. What different and perhaps conflicting messages does the Prometheus myth convey about challenging the authority of the gods?

5. According to Greek legend, Prometheus created men from mud. Then, as this story makes clear, he gave them the gift of fire. To what extent can Prometheus's act of giving men fire be considered another act of creation? What responsibility does he assume when he gives men the gift of fire?

WRITING PROMPT

Find an image of the painting Prometheus Bound by Peter Paul Rubens. Write a response in which you compare and contrast the representation of the Prometheus myth in the text and in the painting. In your response, discuss what is emphasized and absent in each treatment. How does the painting contribute to your understanding of Prometheus's character and the themes that are developed through it?

Please note that excerpts and passages in the StudySync® library and this workbook are intended as touchstones to generate interest in an author's work. The excerpts and passages do not substitute for the reading of entire texts, and StudySync® strongly recommends that students seek out and purchase the whole literary or informational work in order to experience it as the author intended. Links to online resellers are available in our digital library. In addition, complete works may be ordered through an authorized reseller by filling out and returning to StudySync® the order form enclosed in this workbook.

Reading & Writing Companion 215

FRANKENSTEIN

FICTION
Mary Shelley
1818

INTRODUCTION

studysync tv

Mary Shelley began *Frankenstein* as a teenager, part of a competition among her friends to write the best horror story. First published in 1818, this gothic tale of scientific experimentation gone wrong is now considered one of the earliest examples of science fiction. Her character, Dr. Frankenstein, has discovered a way to re-animate dead tissue using an electrical current. His experiment is a success, but the result is a monster brought to life. Horrified by the creature he has created, the doctor flees. Alone and confused, the monster accidentally kills Dr. Frankenstein's younger brother and then murders his best friend. In the excerpt below, the creature explains his actions

"Life, although it may only be an accumulation of anguish, is dear to me, and I will defend it."

 FIRST READ

Excerpt from Chapter 5

1   It was on a dreary night of November that I beheld the accomplishment of my toils. With an anxiety that almost amounted to agony, I collected the instruments of life around me, that I might **infuse** a spark of being into the lifeless thing that lay at my feet. It was already one in the morning; the rain pattered dismally against the panes, and my candle was nearly burnt out, when, by the glimmer of the half-extinguished light, I saw the dull yellow eye of the creature open; it breathed hard, and a convulsive motion agitated its limbs.

2   How can I describe my emotions at this catastrophe, or how delineate the wretch whom with such infinite pains and care I had endeavoured to form? His limbs were in proportion, and I had selected his features as beautiful. Beautiful! Great God! His yellow skin scarcely covered the work of muscles and arteries beneath; his hair was of a lustrous black, and flowing; his teeth of a pearly whiteness; but these luxuriances only formed a more horrid contrast with his watery eyes, that seemed almost of the same colour as the dun-white sockets in which they were set, his shrivelled complexion and straight black lips.

3   The different accidents of life are not so changeable as the feelings of human nature. I had worked hard for nearly two years, for the sole purpose of infusing life into an inanimate body. For this I had deprived myself of rest and health. I had desired it with an ardour that far exceeded moderation; but now that I had finished, the beauty of the dream vanished, and breathless horror and disgust filled my heart. Unable to endure the aspect of the being I had created, I rushed out of the room and continued a long time traversing my bed-chamber, unable to compose my mind to sleep. At length lassitude succeeded to the tumult I had before endured, and I threw myself on the bed in my clothes, endeavouring to seek a few moments of forgetfulness. But it was in vain; I slept, indeed, but I was disturbed by the wildest dreams. I thought I saw Elizabeth, in the bloom of health, walking in the streets of Ingolstadt. Delighted

and surprised, I embraced her, but as I imprinted the first kiss on her lips, they became livid with the hue of death; her features appeared to change, and I thought that I held the corpse of my dead mother in my arms; a shroud enveloped her form, and I saw the grave-worms crawling in the folds of the flannel. I started from my sleep with horror; a cold dew covered my forehead, my teeth chattered, and every limb became convulsed; when, by the dim and yellow light of the moon, as it forced its way through the window shutters, I beheld the wretch—the miserable monster whom I had created. He held up the curtain of the bed; and his eyes, if eyes they may be called, were fixed on me. His jaws opened, and he muttered some inarticulate sounds, while a grin wrinkled his cheeks. He might have spoken, but I did not hear; one hand was stretched out, seemingly to detain me, but I escaped and rushed downstairs. I took refuge in the courtyard belonging to the house which I inhabited, where I remained during the rest of the night, walking up and down in the greatest agitation, listening attentively, catching and fearing each sound as if it were to announce the approach of the demoniacal corpse to which I had so miserably given life.

Excerpt from Chapter 10

4   ...I suddenly beheld the figure of a man, at some distance, advancing towards me with superhuman speed. He bounded over the crevices in the ice, among which I had walked with caution; his stature, also, as he approached, seemed to exceed that of man. I was troubled; a mist came over my eyes, and I felt a faintness seize me, but I was quickly restored by the cold gale of the mountains. I perceived, as the shape came nearer (sight tremendous and abhorred!) that it was the wretch whom I had created. I trembled with rage and horror, resolving to wait his approach and then close with him in mortal combat. He approached; his **countenance** bespoke bitter anguish, combined with disdain and malignity, while its unearthly ugliness rendered it almost too horrible for human eyes. But I scarcely observed this; rage and hatred had at first deprived me of utterance, and I recovered only to overwhelm him with words expressive of furious detestation and contempt.

5   "Devil," I exclaimed, "do you dare approach me? And do not you fear the fierce vengeance of my arm wreaked on your miserable head? Begone, vile insect! Or rather, stay, that I may trample you to dust! And, oh! That I could, with the extinction of your miserable existence, restore those victims whom you have so diabolically murdered!"

6   "I expected this reception," said the daemon. "All men hate the wretched; how, then, must I be hated, who am miserable beyond all living things! Yet you, my creator, detest and spurn me, thy creature, to whom thou art bound by ties only dissoluble by the annihilation of one of us. You purpose to kill me. How dare you sport thus with life? Do your duty towards me, and I will do

Copyright © BookheadEd Learning, LLC

mine towards you and the rest of mankind. If you will comply with my conditions, I will leave them and you at peace; but if you refuse, I will glut the maw of death, until it be satiated with the blood of your remaining friends."

7   "Abhorred monster! Fiend that thou art! The tortures of hell are too mild a vengeance for thy crimes. Wretched devil! You reproach me with your creation, come on, then, that I may extinguish the spark which I so negligently bestowed."

8   My rage was without bounds; I sprang on him, impelled by all the feelings which can arm one being against the existence of another.

9   He easily eluded me and said,

10   "Be calm! I entreat you to hear me before you give vent to your hatred on my devoted head. Have I not suffered enough, that you seek to increase my misery? Life, although it may only be an accumulation of anguish, is dear to me, and I will defend it. Remember, thou hast made me more powerful than thyself; my height is superior to thine, my joints more supple. But I will not be tempted to set myself in opposition to thee. I am thy creature, and I will be even mild and docile to my natural lord and king if thou wilt also perform thy part, which thou owest me. Oh, Frankenstein, be not equitable to every other and trample upon me alone, to whom thy justice, and even thy **clemency** and affection, is most due. Remember that I am thy creature; I ought to be thy Adam, but I am rather the fallen angel, whom thou drivest from joy for no misdeed. Everywhere I see bliss, from which I alone am irrevocably excluded. I was benevolent and good; misery made me a fiend. Make me happy, and I shall again be **virtuous**."

 ## THINK QUESTIONS

1. What is the setting of the opening scene of this chapter? What details mentioned in the opening paragraph contribute to the overall mood of the scene? Refer to details from the text to support your answer.

2. How do Dr. Frankenstein's feelings about his activities change after he brings his creature to life? What does this change reveal about his character? Quote specific textual evidence to support your answer.

3. What does the creature want from Frankenstein? Support your answer with textual evidence.

4. Use context to determine the meaning of the word **countenance** as it is used in Frankenstein. Write your definition of "countenance" and tell how you arrived at this meaning.

5. Use the context clues provided in the passage to determine the meaning of **virtuous**. Write your definition of "virtuous" and explain how you determined its meaning. Afterward, check your definition against a dictionary definition and explain how accurate it was.

Please note that excerpts and passages in the StudySync® library and this workbook are intended as touchstones to generate interest in an author's work. The excerpts and passages do not substitute for the reading of entire texts, and StudySync® strongly recommends that students seek out and purchase the whole literary or informational work in order to experience it as the author intended. Links to online resellers are available in our digital library. In addition, complete works may be ordered through an authorized reseller by filling out and returning to StudySync® the order form enclosed in this workbook.

Reading & Writing Companion   **219**

CLOSE READ

Reread the excerpt from *Frankenstein*. As you reread, complete the Focus Questions below. Then use your answers and annotations from the questions to help you complete the Writing Prompt.

FOCUS QUESTIONS

1. After reviewing details in the paragraphs 2 and 3, what ideas about "playing god" do you think Shelley might be conveying through the character of Dr. Frankenstein? How does the film version's characterization of the doctor address these ideas in both similar and different ways?

2. What inferences can you make about the significance of Frankenstein's dream in Chapter 5? What might it suggest about the doctor's state of mind? How might it connect to one or more themes explored in the novel?

3. Review the paragraphs 6–9. Contrast the characters of Frankenstein and his creature based on their language, tone, and behavior. Who appears to be the more rational being at this point?

4. Both Frankenstein and the creature make Biblical allusions in Chapter 10. How do the Biblical allusions in the text help the reader to understand Dr. Frankenstein's point of view about his creature, the creature's point of view about Dr. Frankenstein, and each one's view of himself?

5. In the final paragraph of the excerpt from Chapter 10, the creature calls on Frankenstein to accept responsibility for bringing him into existence and for turning him into the monster he has become. To what extent do you think Frankenstein is responsible for the creature's actions?

WRITING PROMPT

The full title of Mary Shelley's famous novel is *Frankenstein; or, the Modern Prometheus*. To what extent do you think Mary Shelley's association of Frankenstein (the doctor who creates new life from dead tissue) with Prometheus (the Titan from Greek mythology who steals fire from the gods to give to man) is appropriate? Consider similarities and differences in their characters, motivations, actions, fates, and impacts in your response. Then briefly connect ideas explored in Shelley's Romantic novel with scientific issues under debate in today's world. What scientific endeavor might have the potential to produce "the Modern Frankenstein"? Support your arguments with evidence from the text as well as from your reading and knowledge of current events.

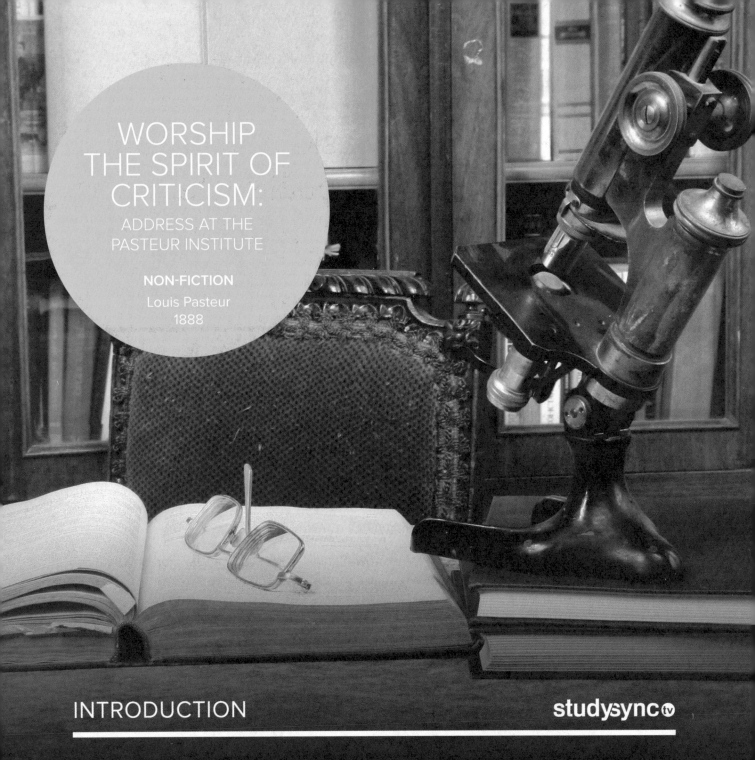

WORSHIP THE SPIRIT OF CRITICISM:
ADDRESS AT THE PASTEUR INSTITUTE

NON-FICTION
Louis Pasteur
1888

INTRODUCTION

Renowned French scientist Louis Pasteur's research into infectious diseases led to longer and healthier lives for countless millions of people. On November 14, 1888, he addressed his colleagues at the opening of the Pasteur Institute in Paris. In an effort to encourage the advancement of science, Pasteur exhorted his peers to "worship the spirit of criticism" by questioning their own findings. Pasteur's speech also helped define the relationship between science and society as he pressed future generations of scientists to seek "new means of delivering man from the scourges which beset him."

"What I am now asking you, and you will ask of your pupils later on, is what is most difficult to an inventor."

FIRST READ

1   It is now finished, this great building, of which it might be said that there is not a stone but what is the material sign of a generous thought. All the virtues have subscribed to build this dwelling place for work.

2   Alas! mine is the bitter grief that I enter it, a man "vanquished by time," deprived of my masters, even of my companions in the struggle, Dumas, Bouley, Paul Bert, and lastly Vulpian, who, after having been with you, my dear Grancher, my counselor at the very first, became the most energetic, the most convinced champion of this method.

3   However, if I have the sorrow of thinking that they are no more, after having valiantly taken their part in discussions which I have never provoked but I have had to endure; if they cannot hear me proclaim all that I owe to their counsels and support; if I feel their absence as deeply as on the morrow of their death, I have at least the **consolation** of believing that all we struggled for together will not perish. The **collaborators** and students who are now here share our scientific faith.... Keep your early enthusiasm, dear collaborators, but let it ever be regulated by rigorous examinations and tests. Never advance anything that cannot be proved in a simple and decisive fashion.

4   Worship the spirit of criticism. If reduced to itself, it is not an awakener of ideas or a stimulant to great things, but, without it, everything is **fallible**; it always has the last word. What I am now asking you, and you will ask of your pupils later on, is what is most difficult to an inventor.

5   It is indeed a hard task, when you believe you have found an important scientific fact and are feverishly anxious to publish it, to constrain yourself for days, weeks, years sometimes, to fight with yourself, to try and ruin your own experiments and only to proclaim your discovery after having exhausted all contrary hypotheses.

6   But when, after so many efforts, you have at last arrived at a certainty, your joy is one of the greatest which can be felt by a human soul, and the thought that you have contributed to the honor of your country renders that joy still deeper.

7   If science has no country, the scientist should have one, and ascribe to it the influence which his works may have in this world.... Two contrary laws seem to be wrestling with each other nowadays; the one, a law of blood and death, ever imagining new means of destruction and forcing nations to be constantly ready for the battlefield—the other, a law of peace, work and health, ever evolving new means of delivering man from the **scourges** which beset him.

8   The one seeks violent conquests; the other, the relief of humanity. The latter places one human life above any victory; while the former would sacrifice hundreds and thousands of lives to the **ambition** of one. The law of which we are the instruments seeks, even in the midst of carnage, to cure the sanguinary ills of the law of war; the treatment inspired by our sanguinary methods may preserve thousands of soldiers. Which of those two laws will ultimately prevail, God alone knows. But we may assert that French science will have tried, by obeying the law of humanity, to extend the frontiers of life.

THINK QUESTIONS

1.   What people are uppermost in Louis Pasteur's mind at the opening of the Pasteur Institute? What are his feelings towards them? Use evidence from the text to support your answer.

2.   Use details from the text to explain what Pasteur advises scientists to do before they proclaim their discoveries.

3.   Write two or three sentences explaining the two "contrary laws" that Pasteur sees at work in the world. Support your answer with textual evidence.

4.   Use context clues to determine the meaning of the word **consolation** as it is used in Pasteur's speech. Write the meaning you determine, and explain how you determined it. Then, check your preliminary determination in a dictionary.

5.   Use context clues to determine the meaning of the word **collaborators** as it is used in Pasteur's speech. Write the meaning you determine, and explain how you determined it. Then, check your preliminary determination in a dictionary.

Please note that excerpts and passages in the StudySync® library and this workbook are intended as touchstones to generate interest in an author's work. The excerpts and passages do not substitute for the reading of entire texts, and StudySync® strongly recommends that students seek out and purchase the whole literary or informational work in order to experience it as the author intended. Links to online resellers are available in our digital library. In addition, complete works may be ordered through an authorized reseller by filling out and returning to StudySync® the order form enclosed in this workbook.

Reading & Writing   **223**
Companion

CLOSE READ

Reread the excerpt from Pasteur's speech. As you reread, complete the Focus Questions below. Then use your answers and annotations from the questions to help you complete the Writing Prompt.

FOCUS QUESTIONS

1. Identify words in the second and third paragraphs that carry positive connotations. How do these particular word choices help to convey Pasteur's attitude toward his colleagues? How might his attitude help explain his observation in the first paragraph that "all the virtues" have helped build the new institute? Highlight textual evidence and make annotations to explain your ideas.

2. In the fourth paragraph, Pasteur expresses his attitude toward the role of criticism in the scientific process. Sum up this attitude, citing particular words that help to reveal it. Highlight textual evidence and make annotations to explain your choices.

3. In the fifth paragraph, what does Pasteur recognize about the process of scientific research? What strong words help to convey this message? Make annotations about the connotations of those words and tell how they help reinforce Pasteur's ideas.

4. What are the two "contrary laws," or types of human behavior, that Pasteur discusses in the last two paragraphs? What strong words help to make the contrast clear? Support your answer with textual evidence and make annotations to explain your answer choices.

5. Consider this speech in conjunction with the Essential Question for this unit. What responsibility does Pasteur seem to think scientists have for what they create? Highlight and annotate details in the last two paragraphs that support your answer.

WRITING PROMPT

From the details in this speech, what do you conclude is Pasteur's general attitude toward the field of science and those who engage in it? What goals does he think science should pursue? Analyze specific word choices that help to convey Pasteur's positions. Explain how the connotations of the words help to build a tone and to emphasize Pasteur's message.

THE IMMORTAL LIFE OF HENRIETTA LACKS

NON-FICTION
Rebecca Skloot
2010

INTRODUCTION

studysynctv

Author Rebecca Skloot was a freshman biology student when she learned of a unique and moving human story. It was a tale of medical discoveries, of ethics, of race, of big business, and of the struggles of an underprivileged family in East Baltimore. Though scientists worldwide know her as HeLa, at the center of this controversy is Henrietta Lacks. She was a poor black tobacco farmer whose cells were removed without her consent as she lay dying of cervical cancer in 1951. The years Skloot spent researching Henrietta exposed the truth—those cells taken from her and kept alive have contributed to great medical breakthroughs including the polio vaccine, cloning, and much more. Yet, Henrietta has remained unknown and her family was never compensated. The world has benefited and many people have profited from Henrietta without even knowing she existed.

"HeLa cells were one of the most important things that happened to medicine in the last hundred years..."

FIRST READ

Excerpt from Prologue

THE WOMAN IN THE PHOTOGRAPH

1   There's a photo on my wall of a woman I've never met, its left corner torn and patched together with tape. She looks straight into the camera and smiles, hands on hips, dress suit neatly pressed, lips painted deep red. It's the late 1940s and she hasn't yet reached the age of thirty. Her light brown skin is smooth, her eyes still young and playful, oblivious to the tumor growing inside her—a tumor that would leave her five children motherless and change the future of medicine. Beneath the photo, a caption says her name is "Henrietta Lacks, Helen Lane or Helen Larson."

2   No one knows who took that picture, but it's appeared hundreds of times in magazines and science textbooks, on blogs and laboratory walls. She's usually identified as Helen Lane, but often she has no name at all. She's simply called HeLa, the code name given to the world's first immortal human *cells—her* cells, cut from her cervix just months before she died.

3   Her real name is Henrietta Lacks.

4   I've spent years staring at that photo, wondering what kind of life she led, what happened to her children, and what she'd think about cells from her cervix living on forever—bought, sold, packaged, and shipped by the trillions to laboratories around the world. I've tried to imagine how she'd feel knowing that her cells went up in the first space missions to see what would happen to human cells in zero gravity, or that they helped with some of the most important advances in medicine: the polio vaccine, chemotherapy, cloning, gene mapping, in vitro fertilization. I'm pretty sure that she—like most of us—

would be shocked to hear that there are trillions more of her cells growing in laboratories now than there ever were in her body.

5   There's no way of knowing exactly how many of Henrietta's cells are alive today. One scientist estimates that if you could pile all HeLa cells ever grown onto a scale, they'd weigh more than 50 million metric tons—an inconceivable number, given that an individual cell weighs almost nothing. Another scientist calculated that if you could lay all HeLa cells ever grown end-to-end, they'd wrap around the Earth at least three times, spanning more than 350 million feet. In her prime, Henrietta herself stood only a bit over five feet tall.

6   I first learned about HeLa cells and the woman behind them in 1988, thirty-seven years after her death, when I was sixteen and sitting in a community college biology class. My instructor, Donald Defler, a gnomish balding man, paced at the front of the lecture hall and flipped on an overhead projector. He pointed to two diagrams that appeared on the wall behind him. They were schematics of the cell reproduction cycle, but to me they just looked like a neon-colored mess of arrows, squares, and circles with words I didn't understand, like "MPF Triggering a Chain Reaction of Protein Activations."

7   I was a kid who'd failed freshman year at the regular public high school because she never showed up. I'd transferred to an alternative school that offered dream studies instead of biology, so I was taking Defler's class for high-school credit, which meant that I was sitting in a college lecture hall at sixteen with words like *mitosis* and *kinase inhibitors* flying around. I was completely lost.

8   "Do we have to memorize everything on those diagrams?" one student yelled.

9   Yes, Defler said, we had to memorize the diagrams, and yes, they'd be on the test, but that didn't matter right then. What he wanted us to understand was that cells are amazing things: There are about one hundred trillion of them in our bodies, each so small that several thousand could fit on the period at the end of this sentence. They make up all our tissues—muscle, bone, blood—which in turn make up our organs.

10 Under the microscope, a cell looks a lot like a fried egg: It has a white (the *cytoplasm*) that's full of water and proteins to keep it fed, and a yolk (the *nucleus*) that holds all the genetic information that makes you *you*. The cytoplasm buzzes like a New York City street. It's crammed full of molecules and vessels endlessly shuttling enzymes and sugars from one part of the cell to another, pumping water, nutrients, and oxygen in and out of the cell. All the while, little cytoplasmic factories work 24/7, cranking out sugars, fats, proteins, and energy to keep the whole thing running and feed the nucleus—the brains of the operation. Inside every nucleus within each cell in your body, there's

NOTES

an identical copy of your entire genome. That genome tells cells when to grow and divide and makes sure they do their jobs, whether that's controlling your heartbeat or helping your brain understand the words on this page.

11   Defler paced the front of the classroom telling us how mitosis—the process of cell division—makes it possible for embryos to grow into babies, and for our bodies to create new cells for healing wounds or replenishing blood we've lost. It was beautiful, he said, like a perfectly choreographed dance.

12   All it takes is one small mistake anywhere in the division process for cells to start growing out of control, he told us. Just one enzy me misfiring, just one wrong protein activation, and you could have cancer. Mitosis goes haywire, which is how it spreads.

13   "We learned that by studying cancer cells in culture," Defler said. He grinned and spun to face the board, where he wrote two words in enormous print: HENRIETTA LACKS.

14   Henrietta died in 1951 from a vicious case of cervical cancer, he told us. But before she died, a surgeon took samples of her tumor and put them in a petri dish. Scientists had been trying to keep human cells alive in culture for decades, but they all eventually died. Henrietta's were different: they reproduced an entire generation every twenty-four hours, and they never stopped. They became the first immortal human cells ever grown in a laboratory.

15   "Henrietta's cells have now been living outside her body far longer than they ever lived inside it," Defler said. If we went to almost any cell culture lab in the world and opened its freezers, he told us, we'd probably find millions—if not billions—of Henrietta's cells in small vials on ice.

16   Her cells were part of research into the genes that cause cancer and those that suppress it; they helped develop drugs for treating herpes, leukemia, influenza, hemophilia, and Parkinson's disease; and they've been used to study lactose digestion, sexually transmitted diseases, appendicitis, human longevity, mosquito mating, and the negative cellular effects of working in sewers. Their chromosomes and proteins have been studied with such detail and precision that scientists know their every quirk. Like guinea pigs and mice, Henrietta's cells have become the standard laboratory workhorse.

17   "HeLa cells were one of the most important things that happened to medicine in the last hundred years," Defler said.

18   Then, matter-of-factly, almost as an afterthought, he said, "She was a black woman." He erased her name in one fast swipe and blew the chalk from his hands. Class was over.

19   As the other students filed out of the room, I sat thinking, *That's it? That's all we get? There has to be more to the story.*

20   I followed Defler to his office.

21   "Where was she from?" I asked. "Did she know how important her cells were? Did she have any children?"

22   "I wish I could tell you," he said, "but no one knows anything about her."

23   After class, I ran home and threw myself onto my bed with my biology textbook. I looked up "cell culture" in the index, and there she was, a small parenthetical:

24   In culture, cancer cells can go on dividing indefinitely, if they have a continual supply of nutrients, and thus are said to be "immortal." A striking example is a cell line that has been reproducing in culture since 1951. (Cells of this line are called HeLa cells because their original source was a tumor removed from a woman named Henrietta Lacks.)

25   That was it. I looked up HeLa in my parents' encyclopedia, then my dictionary: No Henrietta.

26   As I graduated from high school and worked my way through college toward a biology degree, HeLa cells were omnipresent. I heard about them in histology, neurology, pathology; I used them in experiments on how neighboring cells communicate. But after Mr. Defler, no one mentioned Henrietta.

27   When I got my first computer in the mid-nineties and started using the Internet, I searched for information about her, but found only confused snippets: most sites said her name was Helen Lane; some said she died in the thirties; others said the forties, fifties, or even sixties. Some said ovarian cancer killed her, others said breast or cervical cancer.

28   Eventually I tracked down a few magazine articles about her from the seventies. *Ebony* quoted Henrietta's husband saying, "All I remember is that she had this disease, and right after she died they called me in the office wanting to get my permission to take a sample of some kind. I decided not to let them." *Jet* said the family was angry—angry that Henrietta's cells were being sold for twenty-five dollars a vial, and angry that articles had been published about the cells without their knowledge. It said, "Pounding in the back of their heads was a gnawing feeling that science and the press had taken advantage of them."

Please note that excerpts and passages in the StudySync® library and this workbook are intended as touchstones to generate interest in an author's work. The excerpts and passages do not substitute for the reading of entire texts, and StudySync® strongly recommends that students seek out and purchase the whole literary or informational work in order to experience it as the author intended. Links to online resellers are available in our digital library. In addition, complete works may be ordered through an authorized reseller by filling out and returning to StudySync® the order form enclosed in this workbook.

Reading & Writing Companion   **229**

29　The articles all ran photos of Henrietta's family: her oldest son sitting at his dining room table in Baltimore, looking at a genetics textbook. Her middle son in military uniform, smiling and holding a baby. But one picture stood out more than any other: in it, Henrietta's daughter, Deborah Lacks, is surrounded by family, everyone smiling, arms around each other, eyes bright and excited. Except Deborah. She stands in the foreground looking alone, almost as if someone pasted her into the photo after the fact. She's twenty-six years old and beautiful, with short brown hair and catlike eyes. But those eyes glare at the camera, hard and serious. The caption said the family had found out just a few months earlier that Henrietta's cells were still alive, yet at that point she'd been dead for twenty-five years.

30　All of the stories mentioned that scientists had begun doing research on Henrietta's children, but the Lackses didn't seem to know what that research was for. They said they were being tested to see if they had the cancer that killed Henrietta, but according to the reporters, scientists were studying the Lacks family to learn more about Henrietta's cells. The stories quoted her son Lawrence, who wanted to know if the immortality of his mother's cells meant that he might live forever too. But one member of the family remained voiceless: Henrietta's daughter, Deborah.

31　As I worked my way through graduate school studying writing, I became fixated on the idea of someday telling Henrietta's story. At one point I even called directory assistance in Baltimore looking for Henrietta's husband, David Lacks, but he wasn't listed. I had the idea that I'd write a book that was a biography of both the cells and the woman they came from—someone's daughter, wife, and mother.

32　I couldn't have imagined it then, but that phone call would mark the beginning of a decadelong adventure through scientific laboratories, hospitals, and mental institutions, with a cast of characters that would include Nobel laureates, grocery store clerks, convicted felons, and a professional con artist. While trying to make sense of the history of cell culture and the complicated ethical debate surrounding the use of human tissues in research, I'd be accused of conspiracy and slammed into a wall both physically and metaphorically, and I'd eventually find myself on the receiving end of something that looked a lot like an exorcism. I did eventually meet Deborah, who would turn out to be one of the strongest and most resilient women I'd ever known. We'd form a deep personal bond, and slowly, without realizing it, I'd become a character in her story, and she in mine.

33　Deborah and I came from very different cultures: I grew up white and agnostic in the Pacific Northwest, my roots half New York Jew and half Midwestern Protestant; Deborah was a deeply religious black Christian from the South. I tended to leave the room when religion came up in conversation because it made me uncomfortable; Deborah's family tended toward preaching, faith healings, and sometimes voodoo. She grew up in a black neighborhood that was one of the poorest and most dangerous in the country; I grew up in a safe, quiet middle-class neighborhood in a predominantly white city and went to high school with a total of two black students. I was a science journalist who referred to all things supernatural as "woo-woo stuff"; Deborah believed Henrietta's spirit lived on in her cells, controlling the life of anyone who crossed its path. Including me.

34 "How else do you explain why your science teacher knew her real name when everyone else called her Helen Lane?" Deborah would say. "She was trying to get your attention." This thinking would apply to everything in my life: when I married while writing this book, it was because Henrietta wanted someone to take care of me while I worked. When I divorced, it was because she'd decided he was getting in the way of the book. When an editor who insisted I take the Lacks family out of the book was injured in a mysterious accident, Deborah said that's what happens when you piss Henrietta off.

35 The Lackses challenged everything I thought I knew about faith, science, journalism, and race. Ultimately, this book is the result. It's not only the story of HeLa cells and Henrietta Lacks, but of Henrietta's family—particularly Deborah—and their lifelong struggle to make peace with the existence of those cells, and the science that made them possible.

Excerpt from THE IMMORTAL LIFE OF HENRIETTA LACKS by Rebecca Skloot, copyright © 2010, 2011 by Rebecca Skloot. Used by permission of Crown Books, an imprint of the Crown Publishing Group, a division of Random House LLC. All rights reserved.

 THINK QUESTIONS

1. According to the author, how do scientists typically refer to Henrietta Lacks? Cite details from the text to support your response.

2. Why does the author begin to research the life of Henrietta Lacks? What does she discover, and why does it make her want to know more? Cite details from the text to support your answer.

3. The author compares and contrasts herself to Deborah Lacks, the daughter of Henrietta. Which differences does she note within the text?

4. Based on the text, what does the word **haywire** mean? Explain which context clues help you arrive at a definition. Then rephrase the sentence in which "haywire" appears.

5. Use context to determine the meaning of the word chromosomes as it is used within the text. Write your definition of "chromosomes" and tell how you arrived at it.

CLOSE READ

Reread the excerpt from *The Immortal Life of Henrietta Lacks*. As you reread, complete the Focus Questions below. Then use your answers and annotations from the questions to help you complete the Writing Prompt.

FOCUS QUESTIONS

1. What is the meaning of the term "nucleus" in paragraph 10? What words and phrases in the paragraph help you determine the meaning? Highlight textual evidence and make annotations to help you decode this technical language.

2. Based on the text, what does the term "petri dish" in paragraph 14 mean? What words and phrases in the paragraph help you determine the meaning? Highlight textual evidence and make annotations to help you decode this technical language.

3. Read the paragraphs that describe the information in the articles from Ebony and Jet. What do the details in these paragraphs add to your understanding of Henrietta Lacks? What might they suggest about science's responsibility for the use of her cells? Highlight textual evidence and make annotations to explain your answer.

4. In the third-to-last paragraph, what contrast does the author draw between herself and Deborah? Why is this contrast important to the story? Highlight textual evidence and make annotations to explain your answer.

5. How does the last paragraph sum up the events that led to the writing of the book? Highlight textual evidence and make annotations to explain your answer.

WRITING PROMPT

What would you want to say to the Lacks family about the contribution to science their mother made through her immortal cells? Write a letter of at least 300 words to Henrietta Lacks's family that lays out what you would like to tell them. Be sure to include details about the events that occurred after Lacks's cells were preserved. Use outside research and this excerpt to support your ideas.

SILENT SPRING

NON-FICTION
Rachel Carson
1962

INTRODUCTION

In 1962, scientist and author Rachel Carson published *Silent Spring* as a warning to the public about the environmental risks of pesticides like DDT. Carson's work presented a serious critique of the chemical industry and of the public officials who knowingly condoned the use of harmful chemicals. Immediately, the chemical industry, agricultural organizations, and many government officials questioned the validity of the book's findings. However, scientific studies ordered by President John F. Kennedy found evidence to support Carson's research. These studies spurred an environmental movement across the country, leading to the creation of the Environmental Protection Agency (EPA) in 1970, and a federal ban on DDT

"Then a strange blight crept over the area and everything began to change."

NOTES

FIRST READ

From Chapter I: A Fable for Tomorrow

1   There was once a town in the heart of America where all life seemed to live in harmony with its surroundings. The town lay in the midst of a checkerboard of **prosperous** farms, with fields of grain and hillsides of orchards where, in spring, white clouds of bloom drifted above the green fields. In autumn, oak and maple and birch set up a blaze of color that flamed and flickered across a backdrop of pines. Then foxes barked in the hills and deer silently crossed the fields, half hidden in the mists of the fall mornings.

2   Along the roads, laurel, viburnum and alder, great ferns and wildflowers delighted the traveler's eye through much of the year. Even in winter the roadsides were places of beauty, where countless birds came to feed on the berries and on the seed heads of the dried weeds rising above the snow. The countryside was, in fact, famous for the abundance and variety of its bird life, and when the flood of migrants was pouring through in spring and fall people traveled from great distances to observe them. Others came to fish the streams, which flowed clear and cold out of the hills and contained shady pools where trout lay. So it had been from the days many years ago when the first settlers raised their houses, sank their wells, and built their barns.

3   Then a strange **blight** crept over the area and everything began to change. Some evil spell had settled on the community: mysterious maladies swept the flocks of chickens; the cattle and sheep sickened and died. Everywhere was a shadow of death. The farmers spoke of much illness among their families. In the town the doctors had become more and more puzzled by new kinds of sickness appearing among their patients. There had been several sudden and unexplained deaths, not only among adults but even among children, who would be stricken suddenly while at play and die within a few hours.

4   There was a strange stillness. The birds, for example—where had they gone? Many people spoke of them, puzzled and disturbed. The feeding stations in the backyards were deserted. The few birds seen anywhere were moribund;they trembled violently and could not fly. It was a spring without voices. On the mornings that had once throbbed with the dawn chorus of robins, catbirds, doves, jays, wrens, and scores of other bird voices there was now no sound; only silence lay over the fields and woods and marsh.

5   On the farms the hens brooded, but no chicks hatched. The farmers complained that they were unable to raise any pigs—the litters were small and the young survived only a few days. The apple trees were coming into bloom but no bees droned among the blossoms, so there was no pollination and there would be no fruit.

6   The roadsides, once so attractive, were now lined with browned and withered vegetations as though swept by fire. These, too, were silent, deserted by all living things. Even the streams were now lifeless. Anglers no longer visited them, for all the fish had died.

7   In the gutters under the eaves and between the shingles of the roofs, a white granular powder still showed a few patches; some weeks before it had fallen like snow upon the roofs and the lawns, the fields and the streams.

8   No witchcraft, no enemy action had silenced the rebirth of new life in this stricken world. The people had done it themselves.

9   This town does not actually exist, but it might easily have a thousand **counterparts** in America or elsewhere in the world. I know of no community that has experienced all the misfortunes I describe. Yet every one of these disasters has actually happened somewhere, and many real communities have already suffered a substantial number of them. A grim specter has crept upon us almost unnoticed, and this imagined tragedy may easily become a stark reality we all shall know.

Excerpted from *Silent Spring* by Rachel Carson, published by Houghton Mifflin Company.

THINK QUESTIONS

1. Use details from the text to explain what sort of town the author describes in the first two paragraphs. Why does the author describe this town in such detail for readers?

2. What details does the author provide in the fourth through seventh paragraphs to show the impact of the "strange blight" that suddenly descends upon the town? What main idea does the author wish to convey in this section of the text?

3. Why do you think the author waits until the final paragraph of the section to explain that the town she describes does not actually exist? Support your answer with textual evidence.

4. Use context to determine the meaning of the word **counterparts** as it is used in *Silent Spring*. Write your definition of "counterparts" and tell how you arrived at it.

5. Remembering that the Latin verb *mori* means "to die" and the Latin word *moribundus* means "dying, at the point of death," use the context clues provided in the passage to determine the meaning of **moribund**. Write your definition of "moribund" and tell how you arrived at it.

CLOSE READ

Reread the excerpt from *Silent Spring*. As you reread, complete the Focus Questions below. Then use your answers and annotations from the questions to help you complete the Writing Prompt.

FOCUS QUESTIONS

1. Explain why Rachel Carson wrote this section of her book *Silent Spring* as a fable, considering the fact that the text as a whole is a scientific analysis of how pesticides have entered the food chain and threatened life forms.

2. What does the language in the third paragraph suggest has caused the change in the town? Why do you think Carson uses this language here? Why might Carson have chosen not to identify the specific cause of the blight in the opening chapter of the book, except to say in the second-to-last paragraph that "the people brought it on themselves"?

3. The fourth, fifth, and sixth paragraphs present the town after the blight. How do the details in this section emphasize the town's state? How do these details help to clarify the meaning of the book's title, *Silent Spring*?

4. In the last sentence, Rachel Carson uses the term "grim specter." What do you think this term means and what words help you understand its meaning? How does the meaning of the term match the effect she is trying to achieve? Discuss how this term also connects to the overall structure of the opening chapter of *Silent Spring*.

5. What does the fictional town described in the opening chapter of *Silent Spring*, representative of many towns all over America, suggest about the responsibility humans have for environmental problems such as those created by the use of pesticides like DDT?

WRITING PROMPT

Think of an environmental issue about which you have strong beliefs, such as global warming, use of agricultural hormones, fracking, etc. What actual or potential problems have debates about this issue raised? How has human activity created or contributed to these problems? How might you, like Rachel Carson in the opening chapter of *Silent Spring*, use a fable to introduce your analysis of this issue? Write an introduction to an argument in the form of a fable or some other literary text structure designed to alert readers to an environmental problem and capture their attention and interest. Be sure that your introduction uses this fable—or other literary text structure—as well as additional informational text structures to illustrate the problem and its effects. Include a moral, or lesson that readers might take away from the experience of reading this introduction. Use your analysis of the chapter from *Silent Spring* as a model.

Please note that excerpts and passages in the StudySync® library and this workbook are intended as touchstones to generate interest in an author's work. The excerpts and passages do not substitute for the reading of entire texts, and StudySync® strongly recommends that students seek out and purchase the whole literary or informational work in order to experience it as the author intended. Links to online resellers are available in our digital library. In addition, complete works may be ordered through an authorized reseller by filling out and returning to StudySync® the order form enclosed in this workbook.

Reading & Writing Companion   **237**

A CIVIL ACTION

NON-FICTION
Jonathan Harr
1996

INTRODUCTION

When 28 children contracted leukemia in a Massachusetts town, local residents Donna Robbins and Anne Anderson formed a citizen action group and attorney Jan Schlichtmann took the case to court. Jonathan Harr's *A Civil Action* tells the story, including the heavy toll the case took on Schlichtmann. In this excerpt, Anne Anderson gathers information and begins to

"The water had never tasted right, it never looked right, and it never smelled right."

FIRST READ

Excerpt from Chapter 2

1   Anne thought it strange that three cases of leukemia should occur in the same neighborhood, within a few blocks of each other. She wondered if it was coincidence or if a virus of some sort was circulating. Dr. Truman, she remembered, had mentioned that some cancer researchers suspected a virus might cause childhood leukemia. Although she knew that was an unproven **hypothesis**, she and Carol Gray spent hours speculating about it. ...

2   During a visit to the clinic at Massachusetts General that spring, Anne told Dr. Truman about the Zonas and the Nagles. Wasn't it unusual, she asked, that there were three cases in the same neighborhood?

3   Truman listened in his polite, attentive manner, tall frame slightly stooped, but he would admit later that he did not give Anne's question any serious consideration. He'd learned over the years that parents of children with leukemia tended to develop a heightened awareness of the illness. Everywhere they turned it seemed they encountered a reference to it, or someone else whose child had it. To Truman, this was not an uncommon psychological phenomenon. Many years later, in a deposition, Truman recalled his reaction to Anne's queries: "My response was that on the basis of the number of children with leukemia that I was aware of at the time, and considering the population of the city of Woburn, I did not think the **incidence** of leukemia appeared to be increased. In essence, I dismissed her suggestion."

4   Nor did it occur to Truman a year later, in June 1973, that there was anything unusual about the illness of a two-and-a-half-year-old boy from Woburn named Kevin Kane, Jr. The boy had been referred to Truman from Winchester Hospital where his mother, a nurse, had taken him because of a persistent fever, pallor, and irritability. Two weeks earlier he had been treated unsuccessfully for a respiratory infection that did not respond to penicillin. His

history on presentation at Winchester Hospital included several respiratory infections as well as recurrent episodes of earaches. Winchester referred Kevin Kane to Dr. Truman at Massachusetts General with a "high suspicion" of acute lymphocytic leukemia. Truman confirmed the suspicion. He began treating Kevin Kane on a chemotherapy **regimen** similar to the St. Jude protocol. The child responded well. At four weeks, a bone marrow aspiration revealed that he was in remission.

5   Kevin Kane, Sr., and his wife, Patricia, lived with their four children on Henry Avenue in east Woburn. Henry Avenue curved around the perimeter of a low bluff overlooking the Aberjona marsh. From the back door of the Kane's house, looking east across the expanse of marsh, you could see the houses of the Pine Street neighborhood a quarter of a mile away. If you looked closely, you could see Orange Street and, through the trees, the red-shingled ranch house of the Andersons.

6   Anne found out about the Kane's child from Carol Gray, whose fourteen-year-old son delivered the *Woburn Daily Times* every afternoon along Henry Avenue. In the summer of 1973, as Carol's son made his rounds, he learned that one of the Kane's children had leukemia. He reported the news to his mother, who went immediately to the phone and called Anne. "What the hell is going on here?" Carol said to Anne.

7   With the discovery of yet another leukemia case, Anne began writing down some of her thoughts. She made the first of many lists of the cases she knew about, writing in a spiral notebook the names of the children, their addresses, their ages, and the dates when she figured they had been diagnosed.

8   The **notion** that each case shared some common cause began to obsess her. "The water and the air were the two things we all shared," she said in a deposition some years later. "And the water was bad. I thought there was a virus that might have been transmitted through the water, some kind of a leukemia virus. The water had never tasted right, it never looked right, and it never smelled right. There were times when it was worse than others, usually during the summer, and then it was almost impossible to drink. My mother would bring some water from Somerville to the house on weekends, probably about three quarts, which we used as drinking water. The rest of the time, when we could mask the flavor of it with Zarex or orange juice or coffee or whatever, then we used water from the tap. But you couldn't even mask it. It ruined the dishwasher. The door **corroded** to such a degree that it had to be replaced. The prongs that hold the dishes just gave way and broke off. On a regular basis, the pipes under the kitchen sink would leak, and under the bathroom sink. The faucets had to be replaced. The bathroom faucet dripped constantly. It seemed like no sooner would I get everything fixed and we'd have another problem."

Copyright © BookheadEd Learning, LLC

Excerpted from *A Civil Action* by Jonathan Harr, published by Vintage Books.

 THINK QUESTIONS

1. Refer to one or more details (both from ideas that are directly stated as well as context clues) from the text to support your understanding of the facts that led Anne to think that the children's leukemia might be caused by a virus in their environment.

2. Use details from the text to write two or three sentences describing why Dr. Truman rejected Anne's claims about a virus causing the leukemia. Support your ideas with textual evidence.

3. Write two or three sentences describing why Anne suspected that the source of the virus might be the neighborhood water supply. Support your answer with textual evidence.

4. Use context to determine the meaning of the word **incidence** as it is used in *A Civil Action*. Write your definition of "incidence" and tell how you arrived at it.

5. Use context to determine the meaning of the word **hypothesis** as it is used in *A Civil Action*. Write your definition of "hypothesis" and tell how you arrived at it.

Please note that excerpts and passages in the StudySync® library and this workbook are intended as touchstones to generate interest in an author's work. The excerpts and passages do not substitute for the reading of entire texts, and StudySync® strongly recommends that students seek out and purchase the whole literary or informational work in order to experience it as the author intended. Links to online resellers are available in our digital library. In addition, complete works may be ordered through an authorized reseller by filling out and returning to StudySync® the order form enclosed in this workbook.

Reading & Writing Companion

241

CLOSE READ

Reread the excerpt from *A Civil Action*. As you reread, complete the Focus Questions below. Then use your answers and annotations from the questions to help you complete the Writing Prompt.

FOCUS QUESTIONS

1. Which key details in paragraph 3 reveal Dr. Truman's experience with the parents of children with leukemia? How does this experience influence his dismissal of Anne's hypothesis about a virus causing leukemia? Highlight evidence from the text and make annotations to support your inferences.

2. In paragraph 4, the text relates that another child in the neighborhood has developed leukemia. Paragraphs 6 and 7 reveal the reactions of Carol and Anne, both mothers of a child with leukemia, to the news. Contrast their actions and attitudes with those of Dr. Truman. Why are they different? Support your answer with textual evidence and make annotations to explain your answer choices.

3. Why is the information in paragraph 5 about the location of the Kane home a key detail? What does it suggest to Anne and Carol? Highlight your textual evidence and make annotations to explain your inferences.

4. In the final paragraph, why does the author focus on Anne's observations about the neighborhood's problems with local water? How does this paragraph support the main idea of the selection? Highlight textual evidence and make annotations to explain your ideas.

5. How does this selection and its central or main idea relate to the Essential Question: "What responsibility do we have for what we create?" Explain what the text suggests about the importance of finding out the truth about the causes of problems such as disease. Highlight text evidence and make annotations to support your explanation.

WRITING PROMPT

Imagine you are Anne. Write a letter to the editor of the local newspaper about the dangers of the local water supply and its possible effect on the health of the children of the community. Have Anne summarize her central ideas about the suspicious nature of the leukemia cases, supporting the ideas with key details. Also have Anne recount the challenges she has faced while trying to get people to pay attention to the problem.

SHADING THE EARTH

NON-FICTION
Robert Kunzig
2009

INTRODUCTION

studysync🅣ⓥ

Geoengineering, or the application of science and technology to change the Earth, is currently being proposed as a possible solution to the problem of climate change. With the evidence mounting that the earth's temperature is rising, many believe we should be curbing our fossil fuel dependency and reducing CO_2 emissions. Since 2006, improbable ideas such as mirrors in space, whitening clouds, and dropping trees from planes like bombs have moved from the fringes of the scientific community to the mainstream. But have we reached the point where we should seriously consider manipulating our environment on such a large scale? Would doing so be a smart application of manmade technology or an example of science run amok? In "Shading the Earth," an article published in National Geographic in August 2009, Robert Kunzig presents the debate over geoengineering the climate.

"We are already modifying climate by accident..."

 FIRST READ

1 If we don't cut fossil fuels fast enough, global warming may get out of hand. Some scientists say we need a plan B: a giant sunshade that would cool the whole planet.

2 Some call it **hubris**; others call it cool reason. But the idea that we might combat global warming by deliberately engineering a cooler climate—for instance, by constructing some kind of planetary sunshade—has lately migrated from the **fringe** to the scientific mainstream. We are already modifying climate by accident, say **proponents** of geoengineering; why not do something intentional and intelligent to stop it? Hold on, say critics. Global warming shows we understand the Earth too little to engineer it without unintended and possibly disastrous consequences. Both sides worry that facts on the ground—rising seas melting ice, failing crops—may cut short the geoengineering debate. "If a country starts thinking it's in their vital interests to do this, and they have the power, I find it hard to imagine them not doing it," says Ken Caldeira, a climate expert at the Carnegie Institution.

3 Caldeira is talking about the easiest, cheapest form of geoengineering: building a sunshade in the stratosphere out of millions of tons of tiny reflective particles, such as sulfate. Planes, balloons, battleship guns pointed upward— there is no shortage of possible delivery vehicles. And there is little doubt you could cool Earth that way, because volcanoes already do it. After Mount Pinatubo erupted in the Philippines in 1991, launching ten million tons of sulfur into the stratosphere and spreading a sun-dimming haze around the planet, the average temperature dropped by about a degree Fahrenheit for a year. With carefully designed particles, geoengineers might make do with a fraction of that tonnage—though because they fall out of the stratosphere, the particles would have to be delivered continually, year after year. Still, says Caldeira, the sulfate scheme would be "essentially free compared with the other costs of **mitigating** climate change."

NOTES

4   Not so the idea suggested by Roger Angel, an **eminent** astronomer and telescope designer at the University of Arizona. Angel has proposed launching trillions of two-foot-wide, thinner-than- Kleenex disks of silicon nitride—each disk an autonomous robot weighing less than a gram—into space between Earth and the sun, where they could deflect sunlight. By Angel's own reckoning, the scheme would take decades and cost trillions of dollars. With that much time and money, we could wean ourselves from fossil fuels and actually solve the climate problem—by far the better outcome, as Angel and most proponents of geoengineering would agree. Unfortunately, though the recession has temporarily slowed the rise in carbon dioxide emissions, we've made no real progress toward that goal. Some say we're running out of time.

5   If we put up a sunshade without restraining emissions and the sunshade later fails, the climate accident would become a train wreck: The global warming we'd been masking would come rushing at us all at once. That might be the worst unintended consequence of geoengineering, but there could be others—damage to the ozone layer, perhaps, or an increase in drought. If CO2 keeps rising, though, we may face greater emergencies. And what once seemed insane hubris just might become reality.

"Shading the Earth" by Robert J. Kunzig. National Geographic Magazine (August 2009). Used by Permission of National Geographic Creative.

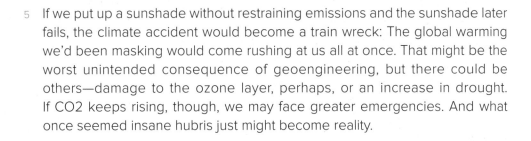

THINK QUESTIONS

1. In what ways has the perception of geoengineering changed in recent years, and why? Cite evidence from the text in your response.

2. State **three** approaches to addressing the problem of global warming that are either stated or implied in the article. Does the author take a clear position? Explain, citing examples from the text in your answer.

3. Based on evidence presented in the third and fourth paragraphs, which do you think is likely a more plausible solution to the problem of global warming: building a sunshade in the stratosphere from reflective particles or launching disks of silicon nitride into the space between Earth and the sun? Use text evidence to support your position.

4. Use context to determine the meaning of the word **hubris** as it is used in "Shading the Earth." Write your definition of "hubris" and tell how you arrived at it.

5. Remembering that the Latin prefix pro- means "for" and the Latin suffix -ent means "signifying action or being," use the context clues provided in the passage to determine the meaning of **proponents**. Write your definition of "proponents" and tell how you arrived at it.

Please note that excerpts and passages in the StudySync® library and this workbook are intended as touchstones to generate interest in an author's work. The excerpts and passages do not substitute for the reading of entire texts, and StudySync® strongly recommends that students seek out and purchase the whole literary or informational work in order to experience it as the author intended. Links to online resellers are available in our digital library. In addition, complete works may be ordered through an authorized reseller by filling out and returning to StudySync® the order form enclosed in this workbook.

Reading & Writing Companion   **245**

CLOSE READ

Reread the excerpt from "Shading the Earth." As you reread, complete the Focus Questions below. Then use your answers and annotations from the questions to help you complete the Writing Prompt.

FOCUS QUESTIONS

1. What reasons from supporters of geoengineering does Kunzig present in the second paragraph? What counterclaim, reasons, and evidence from critics of geoengineering does he present afterward? On what point are both sides united, according to Kunzig? How does this paragraph alert you to Kunzig's purpose in writing this article?

2. What claim does Kunzig present in the opening of the third paragraph? What evidence does he supply to support this claim? What evidence does he provide to support the claim he presents later that the sunshade would work? How might this evidence be considered fallacious?

3. Select one technical word or phrase from the fourth paragraph and one from the fifth paragraph of "Shading the Earth." Identify the terms' meanings, using context clues and, as necessary, reference materials. What effect do such technical words have on the tone and effect of the article?

4. Paraphrase claims against the sunshade that Kunzig presents in the fifth paragraph. Then quote or paraphrase a counterclaim he presents in response. Does this counterclaim effectively address issues raised by critics of geoengineering? Use reasons and evidence to support your point of view.

5. Based on the ideas that Robert Kunzig has presented in the article, how do you think he would answer the Essential Question, "What responsibility do we have for what we create?" Write two or three sentences, using textual evidence to support your response.

WRITING PROMPT

Based on the arguments and evidence presented in "Shading the Earth" and on your prior knowledge, do you think geoengineering is a good solution to the problem of global warming? Construct a persuasive, well-organized argument in support of your position, using reasons and evidence from the text to support your claims. You should critically evaluate opposing arguments presented in the article in order to support your own view. Use technical terms where appropriate.

Copyright © BookheadEd Learning, LLC

EINSTEIN'S LETTER TO THE PRESIDENT

NON-FICTION
Albert Einstein
1939

INTRODUCTION

studysync tv

I n 1933, with the rise of Hitler's Nazi party and its aggression toward Jews, Albert Einstein left Germany and settled in New Jersey, where he took a position as Professor of Theoretical Physics at Princeton University. Lobbied by fellow physicists to use his influence, Einstein sent the following carefully worded letter to President Franklin D. Roosevelt regarding Germany and the development of nuclear weapons.

"Certain aspects of the situation which has arisen seem to call for watchfulness..."

FIRST READ

Albert Einstein
Old Grove Road
Nassau Point
Peconic, Long Island

August 2nd, 1939

F.D. Roosevelt
President of the United States
White House
Washington, D.C.

Sir:

1   Some recent work by E. Fermi and L. Szilard, which has been communicated to me in **manuscript**, leads me to expect that the element uranium may be turned into a new and important source of energy in the immediate future. Certain aspects of the situation which has arisen seem to call for watchfulness and if necessary, quick action on the part of the Administration. I believe therefore that it is my duty to bring to your attention the following facts and recommendations.

2   In the course of the last four months it has been made probable through the work of Joliot in France as well as Fermi and Szilard in America—that it may be possible to set up a nuclear **chain reaction** in a large mass of uranium, by which vast amounts of power and large quantities of new radium-like elements would be generated. Now it appears almost certain that this could be achieved in the immediate future.

3   This new phenomenon would also lead to the construction of bombs, and it is **conceivable**—though much less certain—that extremely powerful bombs of this type may thus be constructed. A single bomb of this type, carried by boat and exploded in a port, might very well destroy the whole port together with some of the surrounding territory. However, such bombs might very well prove too heavy for transportion by air.

4   The United States has only very poor ores of uranium in **moderate** quantities. There is some good ore in Canada and former Czechoslovakia, while the most important source of uranium is in the Belgian Congo.

5   In view of this situation you may think it desirable to have some permanent contact maintained between the Administration and the group of physicists working on chain reactions in America. One possible way of achieving this might be for you to **entrust** the task with a person who has your confidence and who could perhaps serve in an unofficial capacity. His task might comprise the following:

6   a) to approach Government Departments, keep them informed of the further development, and put forward recommendations for Government action, giving particular attention to the problem of securing a supply of uranium ore for the United States.

7   b) to speed up the experimental work, which is at present being carried on within the limits of the budgets of University laboratories, by providing funds, if such funds be required, through his contacts with private persons who are willing to make contributions for this cause, and perhaps also by obtaining co-operation of industrial laboratories which have necessary equipment.

8   I understand that Germany has actually stopped the sale of uranium from the Czechoslovakian mines which she has taken over. That she should have taken such early action might perhaps be understood on the ground that the son of the German Under-Secretary of State, von Weizsacker, is attached to the Kaiser-Wilhelm Institute in Berlin, where some of the American work on uranium is now being repeated.

Yours very truly,

Albert Einstein

THINK QUESTIONS

1. Refer to one or more details from the text to support your understanding of why Einstein felt that he needed to write this letter to the president.

2. What exactly is the "new phenomenon" Einstein mentions in the second and third paragraphs? Support your answer with textual evidence.

3. What are some of the ways that Einstein suggests the president deal with this information? Support your answer with textual evidence.

4. Use context to determine the meaning of the word **manuscript** as it is used in "Einstein's Letter to the President." Write your definition of "manuscript" and tell how you arrived at it.

5. Use context to determine the meaning of the word **conceivable** as it is used in "Einstein's Letter to the President." Write your definition of "conceivable" and tell how you arrived at it.

CLOSE READ

Reread the excerpt from "Einstein's Letter to the President." As you reread, complete the Focus Questions below. Then use your answers and annotations from the questions to help you complete the Writing Prompt.

FOCUS QUESTIONS

1. Explain how Einstein uses the first paragraph to grab the reader's attention and introduce his purpose. Highlight evidence from the text and make annotations to explain your choices.

2. In paragraph 2, what words does Einstein use to reinforce that his ideas are possibilities, not certainties, about the future? Why do you think he includes all of these words? Highlight evidence from the text and make annotations to explain your choices.

3. In the indented paragraphs, Einstein outlines the responsibilities of a new government official that he is recommending be appointed. What are the responsibilities? Why do you think Einstein gives this information through indented text and lettered paragraphs? Highlight evidence from the text and make annotations to support your explanation.

4. What is the significance of the information in the final paragraph? How has Einstein given readers information throughout the letter to prepare them to understand the final paragraph? Highlight evidence from the text and make annotations to support your answer.

5. How is Einstein taking responsibility for the scientific and political situation of his time in this text? Highlight evidence from the text and make annotations to explain your choices.

WRITING PROMPT

Reread Albert Einstein's letter to President Roosevelt. Then respond to Einstein in a 300-word memo. In your memo, explain your understanding of Einstein's purpose for writing and point of view. Your response should be written from you, in the present, to Einstein at the time he wrote the letter.

Please note that excerpts and passages in the StudySync® library and this workbook are intended as touchstones to generate interest in an author's work. The excerpts and passages do not substitute for the reading of entire texts, and StudySync® strongly recommends that students seek out and purchase the whole literary or informational work in order to experience it as the author intended. Links to online resellers are available in our digital library. In addition, complete works may be ordered through an authorized reseller by filling out and returning to StudySync® the order form enclosed in this workbook.

Reading & Writing Companion   **251**

COUNTER-ATTACK

POETRY
Siegfried Sassoon
1918

INTRODUCTION

Siegfried Sassoon was an English soldier, poet, and author who wrote much of his poetry about World War I. Commended for bravery on the Western Front, Sassoon became disillusioned with the conduct of the war, and eventually began speaking out in opposition. As can be seen in "Counter-Attack," his poetry vividly conveys the horrors of trench warfare while sarcastically questioning the motives of those in charge the war effort. Sassoon was a close friend of fellow soldier and poet Wilfred Owen, who was killed in action in 1918.

"O Christ, they're coming at us!"

FIRST READ

NOTES

1 We'd gained our first **objective** hours before
2 While dawn broke like a face with blinking eyes,
3 Pallid, unshaved and thirsty, blind with smoke.
4 Things seemed all right at first. We held their line,
5 With bombers posted, Lewis guns well placed,
6 And clink of shovels deepening the shallow trench.
7 The place was rotten with dead; green clumsy legs
8 High-booted, sprawled and grovelled along the saps
9 And trunks, face downward, in the sucking mud,
10 Wallowed like trodden sand-bags loosely filled;
11 And naked sodden buttocks, mats of hair,
12 Bulged, clotted heads slept in the plastering slime.
13 And then the rain began,—the jolly old rain!

14 A yawning soldier knelt against the bank,
15 Staring across the morning **blear** with fog;
16 He wondered when the Allemands would get busy;
17 And then, of course, they started with five-nines
18 **Traversing**, sure as fate, and never a dud.
19 Mute in the clamour of shells he watched them burst
20 Spouting dark earth and wire with gusts from hell,
21 While **posturing** giants dissolved in drifts of smoke.
22 He crouched and flinched, dizzy with galloping fear,
23 Sick for escape,—loathing the strangled horror
24 And butchered, frantic gestures of the dead.

25 An officer came blundering down the trench:
26 'Stand-to and man the fire-step! 'On he went...
27 Gasping and bawling, 'Fire- step...counter-attack!'
28 Then the haze lifted. Bombing on the right
29 Down the old sap: machine- guns on the left;

30   And stumbling figures looming out in front.
31   'O Christ, they're coming at us!' Bullets spat,
32   And he remembered his rifle...rapid fire...
33   And started blazing wildly...then a bang
34   Crumpled and spun him sideways, knocked him out
35   To grunt and wriggle: none heeded him; he choked
36   And fought the flapping **veils** of smothering gloom,
37   Lost in a blurred confusion of yells and groans...
38   Down, and down, and down, he sank and drowned,
39   Bleeding to death. The counter-attack had failed.

THINK QUESTIONS

1. Refer to one or more details from the text to support your understanding of who the speaker in this poem is and what the speaker is describing in the opening six lines of the poem. Base your answers on ideas that are directly stated and ideas that you have inferred from clues in the text.

2. What does the poet describe in the last seven lines of stanza 1? Write two or three sentences that explain the images the poet uses to paint a picture of the scene.

3. Write two or three sentences exploring the different responses of the infantryman and the officer who are participating in the counter-attack. Whose death is described in the last stanza? Support your answer with textual evidence.

4. Use context to determine the meaning and connotation of the word **blear** as it is used in "Counter-Attack." Write your definition of "blear" and tell how you determined its meaning.

5. Remembering that the Latin prefix *trans-* means "across" and the Latin root versus means "turn toward or against," use the context clues provided in the passage to determine the meaning of **traversing**. Write your definition of "traversing" and tell how you determined its meaning.

CLOSE READ

Reread the poem "Counter-Attack." As you reread, complete the Focus Questions below. Then use your answers and annotations from the questions to help you complete the Writing Prompt.

FOCUS QUESTIONS

1. Describe the overall structure of the poem. How many stanzas and lines does the poet use? What features do you notice about the lines of the poem? What does this structure indicate about the poet's intentions? Highlight evidence from the text and make annotations to explain your responses.

2. What does Sassoon compare the dawn to in stanza 1 of "Counter-Attack"? How does this comparison connect with the theme of the poem? Make annotations highlighting your inferences about the text and its deeper meaning. Support your ideas with textual evidence.

3. How does the tone of the poem shift in the last line of stanza 1? What does this shift in tone reveal about the poet's attitude toward war? How does the poet connect this shift in tone to the images and emotions explored in stanza 2?

Highlight evidence from the text and make annotations to support your explanations.

4. How do the officer's actions and what happens in stanza 3 connect to the tone of the poem developed in stanza 2? Which images in the final stanza connect to the poem's central theme? Support your answer with textual evidence and make annotations to explain your ideas.

5. What is the central theme and message of "Counter-Attack"? According to Sassoon, what is the ultimate result of war for those who fight? Based on what you know about Sassoon from the Introduction to the poem, whom do you think he would hold responsible for these consequences? Make annotations and cite evidence from the selection to support your answers.

WRITING PROMPT

Siegfried Sassoon served as a soldier in the British Army for the entirety of World War I. What is the message of Siegfried Sassoon's poem "Counter-Attack"? What does the poem's tone and structure reveal about the poet's experience in and attitude toward the war? Can a poem about a century-old war have the same impact today as it did when it was written? Write a response of at least 300 words exploring answers to these questions.

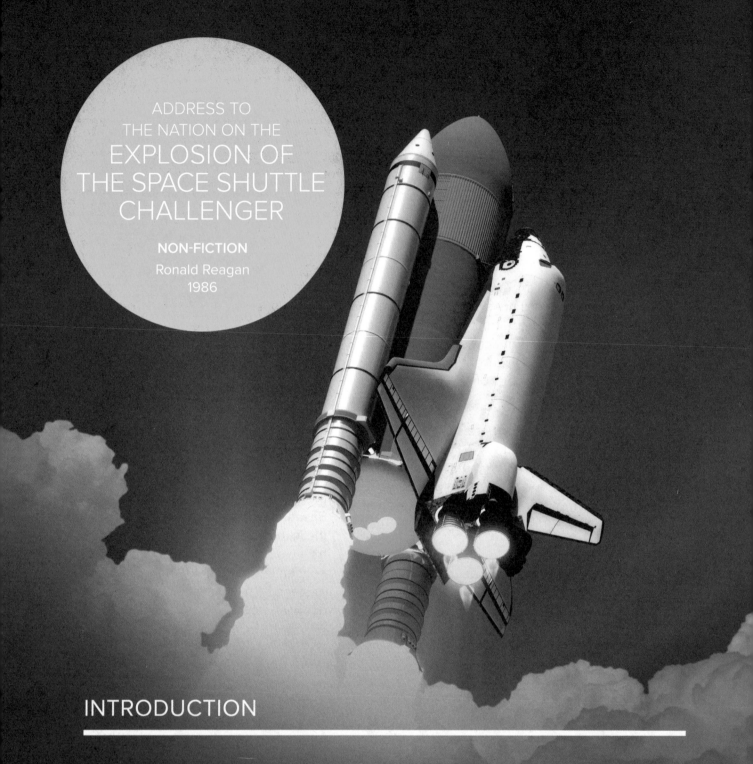

ADDRESS TO
THE NATION ON THE
EXPLOSION OF
THE SPACE SHUTTLE
CHALLENGER

NON-FICTION
Ronald Reagan
1986

INTRODUCTION

On January 28, 1986, millions of Americans watched on live TV as the Space Shuttle *Challenger* violently exploded just 73 seconds after takeoff, killing all seven people on board. It was the tenth mission for *Challenger*, but the first scheduled to carry an ordinary citizen into space, a teacher from New Hampshire named Christa McAuliffe. That evening, President Ronald Reagan addressed the nation, including the many school children who witnessed the disaster, and lauded the bravery of the fallen crew.

"Today is a day for mourning and remembering."

 FIRST READ

January 28, 1986

1 Ladies and gentlemen, I'd planned to speak to you tonight to report on the state of the Union, but the events of earlier today have led me to change those plans. Today is a day for mourning and remembering. Nancy and I are pained to the core by the tragedy of the shuttle *Challenger*. We know we share this pain with all of the people of our country. This is truly a national loss.

2 Nineteen years ago, almost to the day, we lost three astronauts in a terrible accident on the ground. But we've never lost an astronaut in flight; we've never had a tragedy like this. And perhaps we've forgotten the courage it took for the crew of the shuttle. But they, the *Challenger* Seven, were aware of the dangers, but overcame them and did their jobs brilliantly. We mourn seven heroes: Michael Smith, Dick Scobee, Judith Resnik, Ronald McNair, Ellison Onizuka, Gregory Jarvis, and Christa McAuliffe. We mourn their loss as a nation together.

3 For the families of the seven, we cannot bear, as you do, the full impact of this tragedy. But we feel the loss, and we're thinking about you so very much. Your loved ones were daring and brave, and they had that special **grace**, that special spirit that says, "Give me a challenge, and I'll meet it with joy." They had a hunger to explore the universe and discover its truths. They wished to serve, and they did. They served all of us. We've grown used to wonders in this century. It's hard to dazzle us. But for 25 years the United States space program has been doing just that. We've grown used to the idea of space, and perhaps we forget that we've only just begun. We're still pioneers. They, the members of the *Challenger* crew, were pioneers.

4 And I want to say something to the schoolchildren of America who were watching the live coverage of the shuttle's takeoff. I know it is hard to

NOTES

understand, but sometimes painful things like this happen. It's all part of the process of exploration and discovery. It's all part of taking a chance and expanding man's **horizons**. The future doesn't belong to the fainthearted; it belongs to the brave. The *Challenger* crew was pulling us into the future, and we'll continue to follow them.

5   I've always had great faith in and respect for our space program, and what happened today does nothing to diminish it. We don't hide our space program. We don't keep secrets and cover things up. We do it all up front and in public. That's the way freedom is, and we wouldn't change it for a minute. We'll continue our quest in space. There will be more shuttle flights and more shuttle crews and, yes, more volunteers, more civilians, more teachers in space. Nothing ends here; our hopes and our journeys continue. I want to add that I wish I could talk to every man and woman who works for NASA or who worked on this mission and tell them: "Your dedication and **professionalism** have moved and impressed us for decades. And we know of your **anguish**. We share it."

6   There's a **coincidence** today. On this day 390 years ago, the great explorer Sir Francis Drake died aboard ship off the coast of Panama. In his lifetime the great frontiers were the oceans, and an historian later said, "He lived by the sea, died on it, and was buried in it." Well, today we can say of the *Challenger* crew: Their dedication was, like Drake's, complete.

7   The crew of the space shuttle *Challenger* honored us by the manner in which they lived their lives. We will never forget them, nor the last time we saw them, this morning, as they prepared for their journey and waved goodbye and "slipped the surly bonds of earth" to "touch the face of God."

THINK QUESTIONS

1. Refer to one or more details from the text to support your understanding of the significance of the space shuttle tragedy. What words and phrases in the first two paragraphs indicate this significance?

2. Use details from the text to write two or three sentences detailing how President Reagan describes the astronauts.

3. Write two or three sentences explaining how President Reagan feels about the space program. What details does he offer to support his ideas? Cite textual evidence in your answer.

4. Use context to determine the meaning of the word **horizons** as it is used in this speech. Write your definition of "horizons" and tell how you arrived at it.

5. Remembering that the Latin prefix co- means "together," use the context clues provided in the passage to determine the meaning of **coincidence**. Write your definition of "coincidence" and tell how you arrived at it it.

CLOSE READ

Reread President Reagan's speech about the space shuttle disaster. As you reread, complete the Focus Questions below. Then use your answers and annotations from the questions to help you complete the Writing Prompt.

FOCUS QUESTIONS

1. Which words and phrases in the first two paragraphs help establish the topic of the speech? Highlight evidence from the text and make annotations to explain your answer.

2. What does the formal, elevated language in paragraph 3 help to emphasize? Highlight evidence from the text and make annotations to support your answer.

3. In paragraphs 4 and 5, what argument does the president make about the space program? Highlight evidence from the text and make annotations to support your ideas.

4. Highlight the quotation in paragraph 6. What ideas does this quotation help the president to express about the *Challenger* astronauts? Make annotations to explain the president's ideas in your own words.

5. Throughout the address, President Reagan expresses his confidence in the space program, and he compliments the people who work for NASA. How do his words relate to the unit's Essential Question? Highlight textual evidence and make annotations to explain your ideas.

WRITING PROMPT

Write a response in which you analyze the choice of words and phrases in the speech. Which words and phrases would be unlikely to appear in a newspaper or magazine article or in a news broadcast? Why are they included in the speech? Support your answer with textual evidence.

ADDRESS TO STUDENTS AT MOSCOW STATE UNIVERSITY

NON-FICTION
Ronald Reagan
1988

INTRODUCTION

I n May 1988, during the final year of Ronald Reagan's presidency and just one year after he admonished Gorbachev to tear down the Berlin wall, the president met with the USSR's leader in Moscow to discuss arms reductions. During his visit, he delivered a stirring speech to students at Moscow State University setting forth his vision for the expansion of liberty across the globe. Highlighting the opportunities afforded by freedom and entrepreneurship, Reagan focused on the advances of technology in the United States, as well as Russian contributions to

"The key is freedom—freedom of thought, freedom of information, freedom of communication."

FIRST READ

NOTES

1   As you know, I've come to Moscow to meet with one of your most distinguished graduates. In this, our fourth summit, General Secretary Gorbachev and I have spent many hours together, and I feel that we're getting to know each other well. Our discussions, of course, have been focused primarily on many of the important issues of the day, issues I want to touch on with you in a few moments. But first I want to take a little time to talk to you much as I would to any group of university students in the United States. I want to talk not just of the realities of today but of the possibilities of tomorrow.

2   Standing here before a mural of your revolution, I want to talk about a very different revolution that is taking place right now, quietly sweeping the globe without bloodshed or conflict. Its effects are peaceful, but they will **fundamentally** alter our world, shatter old assumptions, and reshape our lives. It's easy to underestimate because it's not accompanied by banners or fanfare. It's been called the technological or information revolution, and as its emblem, one might take the tiny silicon chip, no bigger than a fingerprint. One of these chips has more computing power than a roomful of old-style computers.

3   As part of an exchange program, we now have an **exhibition** touring your country that shows how information technology is transforming our lives—replacing manual labor with robots, forecasting weather for farmers, or mapping the genetic code of DNA for medical researchers. These microcomputers today aid the design of everything from houses to cars to spacecraft; they even design better and faster computers. They can translate English into Russian or enable the blind to read or help Michael Jackson produce on one synthesizer the sounds of a whole orchestra. Linked by a network of satellites and fiber-optic cables, one individual with a desktop computer and a telephone commands resources unavailable to the largest governments just a few years ago.

NOTES

4   Like a chrysalis, we're emerging from the economy of the Industrial Revolution—an economy confined to and limited by the Earth's physical resources—into, as one economist titled his book, "The Economy in Mind," in which there are no bounds on human imagination and the freedom to create is the most precious natural resource. Think of that little computer chip. Its value isn't in the sand from which it is made but in the microscopic architecture designed into it by ingenious human minds. Or take the example of the satellite relaying this broadcast around the world, which replaces thousands of tons of copper mined from the Earth and molded into wire. In the new economy, human invention increasingly makes physical resources obsolete. We're breaking through the material conditions of existence to a world where man creates his own destiny. Even as we explore the most advanced reaches of science, we're returning to the age-old wisdom of our culture, a wisdom contained in the book of Genesis in the Bible: In the beginning was the spirit and it was from this spirit that the material abundance of creation issued forth.

5   But progress is not **foreordained**. The key is freedom—freedom of thought, freedom of information, freedom of communication. The renowned scientist, scholar, and founding father of this university, Mikhail Lomonosov, knew that. "It is common knowledge," he said, "that the achievements of science are considerable and rapid, particularly once the yoke of slavery is cast off and replaced by the freedom of philosophy."

6   You know, one of the first contacts between your country and mine took place between Russian and American explorers. The Americans were members of Cook's last voyage on an expedition searching for an Arctic passage; on the island of Unalaska, they came upon the Russians, who took them in, and together with the native inhabitants, held a prayer service on the ice.

7   The explorers of the modern era are the entrepreneurs, men with vision, with the courage to take risks and faith enough to brave the unknown. These entrepreneurs and their small enterprises are responsible for almost all the economic growth in the United States. They are the prime movers of the technological revolution. In fact, one of the largest personal computer firms in the United States was started by two college students, no older than you, in the garage behind their home. Some people, even in my own country, look at the riot of experiment that is the free market and see only waste. What of all the entrepreneurs that fail? Well, many do, particularly the successful ones; often several times. And if you ask them the secret of their success they'll tell you it's all that they learned in their struggles along the way; yes, it's what they learned from failing. Like an athlete in competition or a scholar in pursuit of the truth, experience is the greatest teacher.

8   And that's why it's so hard for government planners, no matter how sophisticated, to ever substitute for millions of individuals working night and day to make their dreams come true.

. . .

9   We Americans make no secret of our belief in freedom. In fact, it's something of a national pastime. Every 4 years the American people choose a new President, and 1988 is one of those years. At one point there were 13 major candidates running in the two major parties, not to mention all the others, including the Socialist and Libertarian candidates—all trying to get my job.

10 About 1,000 local television stations, 8,500 radio stations, and 1,700 daily newspapers—each one an independent, private enterprise, fiercely independent of the Government—report on the candidates, grill them in interviews, and bring them together for debates. In the end, the people vote; they decide who will be the next President.

11 But freedom doesn't begin or end with elections. Go to any American town, to take just an example, and you'll see dozens of churches, representing many different beliefs—in many places, synagogues and mosques—and you'll see families of every conceivable nationality worshiping together. Go into any schoolroom, and there you will see children being taught the Declaration of Independence, that they are endowed by their Creator with certain unalienable rights—among them life, liberty, and the pursuit of happiness—that no government can justly deny; the guarantees in their Constitution for freedom of speech, freedom of assembly, and freedom of religion.

12 Go into any courtroom, and there will preside an independent judge, **beholden** to no government power. There every defendant has the right to a trial by a jury of his peers, usually 12 men and women—common citizens; they are the ones, the only ones, who weigh the evidence and decide on guilt or innocence. In that court, the accused is innocent until proven guilty, and the word of a policeman or any official has no greater legal standing than the word of the accused.

13 Go to any university campus, and there you'll find an open, sometimes heated discussion of the problems in American society and what can be done to correct them. Turn on the television, and you'll see the legislature conducting the business of government right there before the camera, debating and voting on the legislation that will become the law of the land. March in any demonstration, and there are many of them; the people's right of assembly is guaranteed in the Constitution and protected by the police. Go into any union hall, where the members know their right to strike is protected by law. As a

Please note that excerpts and passages in the StudySync® library and this workbook are intended as touchstones to generate interest in an author's work. The excerpts and passages do not substitute for the reading of entire texts, and StudySync® strongly recommends that students seek out and purchase the whole literary or informational work in order to experience it as the author intended. Links to online resellers are available in our digital library. In addition, complete works may be ordered through an authorized reseller by filling out and returning to StudySync® the order form enclosed in this workbook.

Reading & Writing Companion   **263**

matter of fact, one of the many jobs I had before this one was being president of a union, the Screen Actors Guild. I led my union out on strike, and I'm proud to say we won.

14   But freedom is more even than this. Freedom is the right to question and change the established way of doing things. It is the continuing revolution of the marketplace. It is the understanding that allows us to recognize shortcomings and seek solutions. It is the right to put forth an idea, scoffed at by the experts, and watch it catch fire among the people. It is the right to dream—to follow your dream or stick to your conscience, even if you're the only one in a sea of doubters. Freedom is the recognition that no single person, no single authority or government has a monopoly on the truth, but that every individual life is infinitely precious, that every one of us put on this world has been put there for a reason and has something to offer.

. . .

15   But I hope you know I go on about these things not simply to **extol** the virtues of my own country but to speak to the true greatness of the heart and soul of your land. Who, after all, needs to tell the land of Dostoyevski about the quest for truth, the home of Kandinski and Scriabin about imagination, the rich and noble culture of the Uzbek man of letters Alisher Navoi about beauty and heart? The great culture of your diverse land speaks with a glowing passion to all humanity. Let me cite one of the most eloquent contemporary passages on human freedom. It comes, not from the literature of America, but from this country, from one of the greatest writers of the 20th century, Boris Pasternak, in the novel "Dr. Zhivago." He writes: "I think that if the beast who sleeps in man could be held down by threats—any kind of threat, whether of jail or of retribution after death—then the highest emblem of humanity would be the lion tamer in the circus with his whip, not the prophet who sacrificed himself. But this is just the point—what has for centuries raised man above the beast is not the cudgel, but an inward music—the irresistible power of unarmed truth."

THINK QUESTIONS

1. President Reagan says that the technological or information revolution will "alter our world" and "reshape our lives." What changes does the president note are already happening? Support your answer with textual evidence.

2. Use details from the text to write two or three sentences about the evidence President Reagan offers to support his claim that freedom is "a national pastime" for Americans.

3. What connection does President Reagan make between freedom and progress? Support your answer with textual evidence and your own inferences.

4. You may remember that the Anglo-German prefix *for-* means "before" or "first," and the Latin root ord refers to order. Use these roots and the context clues provided in the passage to determine the meaning of **foreordained**. Write your definition of "foreordained" and explain how you arrived at it.

5. Use context to determine the meaning of the word **extol** as it is used in "Address to Students at Moscow State University." Write your definition of "extol" and explain how you arrived at it.

CLOSE READ

Reread President Reagan's speech to the students in Moscow. As you reread, complete the Focus Questions below. Then use your answers and annotations from the questions to help you complete the Writing Prompt.

FOCUS QUESTIONS

1. In paragraph 2 of his Moscow address, President Reagan introduces the word "revolution." He compares and contrasts the Russian Revolution of 1917 with the "technological or information revolution" of his own day. How are these two revolutions alike? How are they different? What exactly does he mean by calling the changes in technology a "revolution"? Support your answer with textual evidence and make annotations to support your explanations.

2. Summarize President Reagan's main points about daily life in America. What is his purpose in speaking at such length about Americans' experiences with politics, law, home, work, and community? Highlight evidence from the text and make annotations to explain your ideas.

3. In the second-to-last paragraph of the speech, how does the president define freedom? What ideas from earlier in the speech does this section help to reinforce? Highlight evidence from the text and make annotations to support your explanations.

4. In the final paragraph of the speech, President Reagan quotes from Boris Pasternak's *Dr. Zhivago*. Summarize Pasternak's main point. How does Pasternak's message relate to the main message Reagan wants to convey to the Moscow students? Highlight evidence from the text and make annotations to support your answer.

5. In this speech, President Reagan alludes to the openness of the American system of government. What relationship do you see between openness and responsibility? Highlight evidence from the text and make annotations to support your answer.

WRITING PROMPT

Compare and contrast the main themes and concepts contained in "Address to Students at Moscow State University" and in "Address to the Nation on the Explosion of the Space Shuttle *Challenger*." What claims about society and progress do both speeches make? What kinds of details do the speeches use to support the claims? Are the details similar or different? Finally, which speech is the more effective or convincing? Support your answer with evidence from both speeches.

DE-EXTINCTION:
THE SCIENCE AND ETHICS OF BRINGING LOST SPECIES BACK TO LIFE

NON-FICTION
2014

INTRODUCTION

Advances in biological science may soon make it possible to bring animals and plants back from extinction. This prospect has wildly exciting implications: by reversing extinction, we could restore biodiversity to the planet and potentially solve some of our environmental problems. However, de-extinction has the potential for dangerous, evenly deadly consequences. Is this a case of "just because we can doesn't mean we should?" Read two essays that explore the issue from different sides and decide for yourself. Which argument do you feel is more convincing?

"What sounds like science fiction may soon be scientific fact."

FIRST READ

The Science and Ethics of De-Extinction: Should We Recreate Lost Species?

Point: "De-Extinction Is Ethical, and Compelled by Science"

1 Which of the following animals would you most like to see up close and in person? Would it be the dodo, those flightless, squat birds from Mauritius? Sadly, dodos were victims of overhunting and the destruction of their habitat and now they are extinct. The last one died in the late 1800's. How about the passenger pigeon? This species went from being the most common bird in North America to being hunted to extinction. The last passenger pigeon died in an Illinois zoo in 1914. Why not meet a saber-toothed tiger, a creature as fierce as its name suggests? Sorry: this species vanished from Earth more than 10,000 years ago. Once a creature is extinct, it is gone forever...or is it?

2 What sounds like science fiction may soon be scientific fact. De-extinction, or bringing back extinct animals and plants, is becoming increasingly possible. That is because sci-en-tists are now working to develop technology that will enable them to clone extinct species and bring them back to life. But just because we can do something, should we do it? Yes! Scientists should vigorously pursue their experiments in de-extinction. People who say that de-extinction is unethical are wrong. Here's why.

3 The first ethical reason for bringing creatures back from extinction is that it helps preserve biodiversity, repair damaged ecosystems, and preserve the world for future generations. Stewart Brand, creator of the *Whole Earth Catalog*, argued in favor of de-extinction in *National Geographic* magazine. Brand described how some long-gone species were especially important to their region, calling these species "keystones" after the central stone at the top of an arch. Brand says: "Woolly mammoths, for instance, were the dominant herbivore of the mammoth steppe in the far north, once the largest biome on Earth. In their absence, the grasslands they helped sustain were

Copyright © BookheadEd Learning, LLC

replaced by species-poor tundra and boreal forest. Their return to the north would bring back carbon-fixing grass and reduce greenhouse-gas-releasing tundra."

4   Brand is not alone in his support of de-extinction for preserving biodiversity. "I think de-extinction can enrich conservation efforts," says Ryan Phelan, executive director of the Revive & Restore project at the Long Now Foundation. Phelan continues: "As controversial as all of it is, and possibly because it's controversial, it's going to help drive interest in [species loss], in a way that conservation by itself couldn't do...The species that we are talking about bringing back, they really are part of the continuum of life. And I think that's the real power in what we are trying to do. We're calling attention to the extinction threat."

5   Since every species is linked to every other one, resurrecting extinct animals may help us control the ravages of global warming and human overpopulation, too. De-extinction might even be able to repair some of the damage we have **incurred** by cutting down rainforests and building too many homes. De-extinction can certainly help restore traditional values, strengthen families, and encourage education. It is a win-win proposition.

6   What about the price tag? A scientific endeavor of this complexity and magnitude may not come cheaply, but it is worth the cost. De-extinction is an ethical use of research funding because it helps us undo harm that humans have caused in the past, such as the appalling slaughter of the passenger pigeon. In his article "The Story of the Passenger Pigeon," author Clive Ponting notes that passenger pigeons were so common 150 years ago that a hunter could kill 30-40 birds with a single bullet. Soon, the birds were hunted to death for food. On just one day in 1860, over 200,000 birds were killed and shipped from the Midwest to the East. By 1914, a species that had once numbered five billion had been totally **eradicated**. Don't we owe it to these harmless, beautiful birds to bring them back?

7   Finally, bringing back extinct creatures advances science, which helps us in myriad ways. For instance, people have been critical about the space program since its inception, saying that we would never get anything useful from blasting into the skies. However, in a speech celebrating NASA's 50th anniversary, NASA administrator Michael Griffin noted that the technology to come out of the space program has greatly improved our lives. Thanks to space exploration, we have weather satellites that warn us of coming storms, heart defibrillators that save lives, personal computers that foster communication, bigger and better crops, and much more. The genome manipulation used in de-extinction research might bring about even more marvels. Maybe these experiments will lead to a cure for cancer or let us live to be 200! We won't know unless we try.

NOTES

Counterpoint: "De-Extinction Is Immoral, and Bad Science All Around"

8   A scientist cobbles together a creature from old body parts and brings it to life. The scientist is aghast at his creation, a horrific monster. The monster, shunned by the human race, kills his creator's brother in an attempt to punish his creator. An innocent young girl is convicted of the crime and executed. Can it get any worse? Yes, it can. Fortunately, this story is fiction, the plot of the novel *Frankenstein* by Mary Shelley. Make-believe can become reality, thanks to research on de-extinction. De-extinction is immoral, unethical, and dangerous. It should not be pursued.

9   To start, it is unethical for humans to mess with Mother Nature because, as the story of *Frankenstein* illustrates, we have no idea what **havoc** we might cause in doing so. Many extinct creatures were fearsome killers that would be very dangerous to humans. The extinct saber-toothed tiger, for instance, was a terrifying predator armed with razor-sharp long sharp teeth used to tear open its prey. We should be glad we are not living in the Ice Age and facing off against such a dangerous creature! Fortunately, de-extinction of such long-ago creatures is not yet possible, but *National Geographic* reports that a different kind of lethal organism *has* been brought back—the flu virus of 1918, which killed 50 million people. Scientists are keeping the virus under lock and key, so no one has been exposed. Extinct animal predators like the saber-toothed tiger are dangerous enough, but what if the tigers or other animals also bring back treacherous viruses on their bodies? The harm to humanity cannot be calculated.

10   Let's imagine that scientists do succeed in bringing back ancient creatures through de-extinction. To do so, scientists would create multiple creatures from a single piece of genetic material. As a result, the creatures would lack genetic variety, which would be unfair to the creatures because genetic variety is essential to survival. These creatures would be less capable of adapting to new challenges and so they would be **susceptible** to all sorts of threats. The cloned sheep Dolly illustrates this. Born in 1996, she lived until 2003, a total of six and a half years. Sheep can live to be twelve years old, but Dolly was euthanized after only half her natural life span because she had severe arthritis and lung disease. Some sources say her diseases were caused by cloning; others because she was raised indoors rather than outdoors. We don't know why her lifespan was half of what it should have been, which is arguably reason enough to reject de-extinction through cloning.

11   It is likely that de-extinction cannot be accomplished in a humane way, which is troublesome. Let's return to Dolly as an example. "From 277 cell fusions, 29 early embryos developed and were implanted into 13 surrogate mothers. But only one pregnancy went to full term," according to Animal Research. Info. That

amounts to thirteen sheep that were used to clone just one lamb, a creature that was not extinct. How many elephants, serving as surrogate mothers, would it take bring back the **primeval** woolly mammoth? Conservationist Rory Young, interviewed in the *Huffington Post*, is "absolutely convinced" that African elephants could be extinct in less than a decade if they are not protected. Using them to incubate wooly mammoths hardly qualifies as protection—it is not ethical to harm one species to bring back another.

12 Here is yet another reason why de-extinction is immoral: bringing back extinct creatures distracts us from the real and pressing environmental issues we face today. De-extinction research, not to mention the actual process of cloning these creatures from their DNA, costs a prohibitive amount of money. This funding can be put to far better use by finding ways to prevent extinction in the first place through saving natural habitats, reducing pollution, and researching climate change. As Bob Strauss, a dinosaur expert, writes in "De-Extinction—The Resurrection of Extinct Animals," "De-extinction is a PR gimmick that detracts from real environmental issues. What is the point of resurrecting the Gastric-Brooding Frog when hundreds of amphibian species are on the brink of succumbing to global warming? A successful de-extinction effort may give people the false, and dangerous, impression that scientists have 'solved' all of our environmental problems."

13 The creatures that scientists bring back would require food, so we would have to alter the land and introduce new—perhaps previously extinct—crops. These new crops would interfere with the habitats of existing species, plus the returned animals would also need safe homes, further displacing the existing species. It would be a vicious cycle.

14 Finally, there are significant reasons why some creatures went extinct in the first place. With the exception of animals driven to extinction by humans, such as passenger pigeons, extinct animals are extinct for valid reasons. In some cases their environments changed so that food and water supplies decreased or disappeared. And what happens if we bring back extinct creatures like woolly mammoths and saber-toothed tigers and humans hunt them back into extinction a second time? According to "8 Endangered Species Still Hunted," great white sharks, cheetahs, polar bears, and hippos are just a few of the vulnerable species hunted despite laws designed to protect them.

15 Being *able* to do something doesn't mean we should do it. Where will allowing de-extinction lead? Will scientists bring back a few oddities for show? This is unethical, but establishing a stable population and returning it to the wild is even more unethical because we have no idea what impact it would have on the environment. If we resurrect extinct species, humans might become extinct! And would saber-toothed tigers and wooly mammoths want to bring *us* back?

THINK QUESTIONS

1. The specific issue of de-extinction is part of a broader issue that faces humanity. What is that broader issue, and where in the text of the debate does each author address it? Cite specific passages in your response.

2. What is each author's perspective on the idea that "just because we can doesn't mean we should?" Why is this a relevant idea to explore in relation to the issue of de-extinction and other possibilities created by scientific advancements? Cite text evidence in your answer.

3. This debate is an example of persuasive writing. What role does information play in it? Provide specific examples from the debate.

4. Use context to determine the meaning of the word **susceptible** as it is used in *De-Extinction: The Science and Ethics of Bringing Lost Species Back to Life* Write your definition of "susceptible" and tell how you arrived at it.

5. Use the context clues provided in the passage to determine the meaning of the word **eradicated**. Write your definition of "eradicated" and tell how you arrived at it.

CLOSE READ

Reread the debate about de-extinction. As you reread, complete the Focus Questions below. Then use your answers and annotations from the questions to help you complete the Writing Prompt.

FOCUS QUESTIONS

1. How does the Point argument entitled "De-Extinction Is Ethical, and Compelled by Science" use problem-and-solution structure in the fifth paragraph? What is the problem, and what solution is presented? Is the logic used to support this problem and solution sound? Why or why not?

2. Review the sixth paragraph of the Point argument and the fifth paragraph of the Counterpoint argument, entitled "De-Extinction Is Immoral, and Bad Science All Around." What strategy do both arguments use in these paragraphs to support their claims? Identify the claim and evidence in each paragraph.

3. What is the relevance of the discussion of Dolly the sheep in the third paragraph of the Counterpoint argument? How does this subtopic fit into the structure of the argument as a whole?

4. How does the sixth paragraph of the Counterpoint argument use cause-and-effect text structure in support of a point?

5. Based on ideas presented throughout the debate, what responsibility does each author think humans bear for the world in its present state, and how should they best address that responsibility in the future? Address similarities and differences in the two authors' points of view.

WRITING PROMPT

In your estimation, which argument—Point or Counterpoint—won the debate in *De-Extinction: The Science and Ethics of Bringing Lost Species Back to Life?* In a structured argument of approximately one page, explain why you think either the Point or the Counterpoint argument is more successful than the other, addressing the validity of both arguments' reasoning, the amount and relevance of their evidence, and whether or not they contain any fallacious reasoning. In what way did the argument you feel won best use text structure and persuasive techniques to help organize and enhance its claims? Cite specific passages from both the Point and the Counterpoint sides of the de-extinction debate as evidence for your evaluation.

Please note that excerpts and passages in the StudySync® library and this workbook are intended as touchstones to generate interest in an author's work. The excerpts and passages do not substitute for the reading of entire texts, and StudySync® strongly recommends that students seek out and purchase the whole literary or informational work in order to experience it as the author intended. Links to online resellers are available in our digital library. In addition, complete works may be ordered through an authorized reseller by filling out and returning to StudySync® the order form enclosed in this workbook.

Reading & Writing
Companion **273**

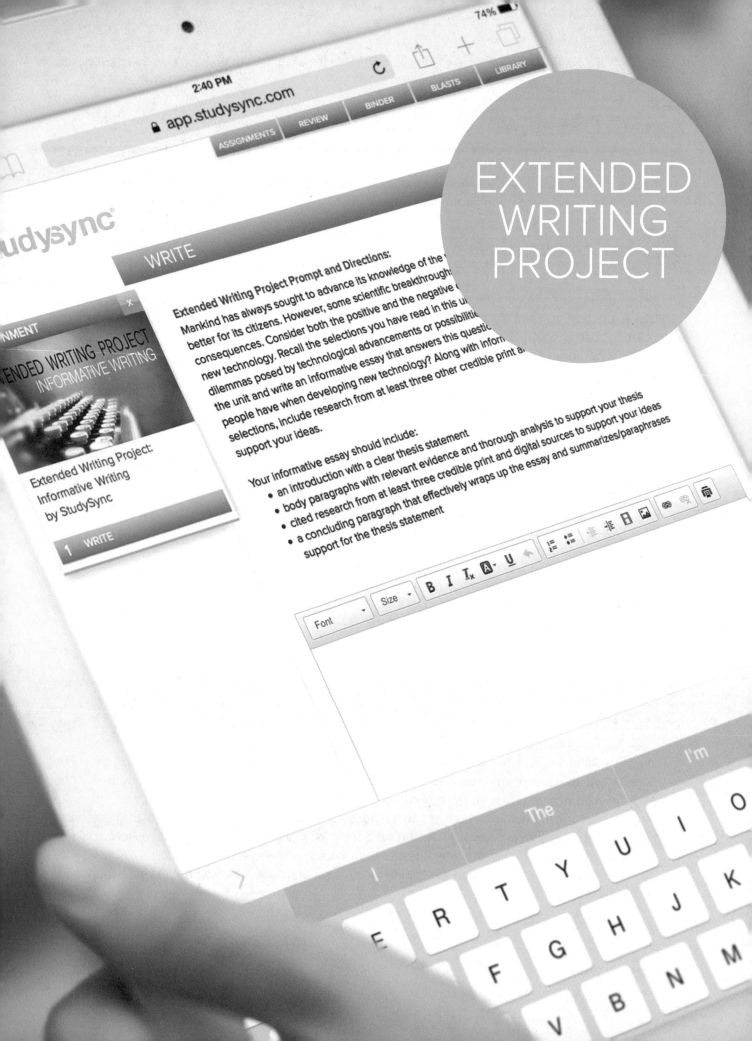

EXTENDED
WRITING
PROJECT

WRITE

Extended Writing Project Prompt and Directions:

Mankind has always sought to advance its knowledge of the
better for its citizens. However, some scientific breakthrough
consequences. Consider both the positive and the negative
new technology. Recall the selections you have read in this u
dilemmas posed by technological advancements or possibiliti
the unit and write an informative essay that answers this quest
people have when developing new technology? Along with infor
selections, include research from at least three other credible print a
support your ideas.

Your informative essay should include:
- an introduction with a clear thesis statement
- body paragraphs with relevant evidence and thorough analysis to support your thesis
- cited research from at least three credible print and digital sources to support your ideas
- a concluding paragraph that effectively wraps up the essay and summarizes/paraphrases
  support for the thesis statement

**Extended Writing Project:
Informative Writing
by StudySync**

1 **WRITE**

INFORMATIVE/ EXPLANATORY WRITING

Informative/explanatory writing explains, compares and contrasts, describes, and informs. One purpose of informative writing is to convey accurate information to the reader. In addition, informative writing serves to increase readers' knowledge of a subject, to help readers better understand processes, and to enhance readers' comprehension of a certain concept. Some examples of informative writing include analytical essays, scientific studies, reports, research papers, newspaper articles, and other non-fiction texts.

Strong informative writing introduces a main idea, often in the form of a thesis statement. The writing then develops that main idea with supporting details. Information, ideas, and concepts are organized so that each new element builds on what preceded it, to create a piece that is unified and whole. The writing stays focused on the main idea, using transition words to help create flow and make clear connections between supporting details. Although informative writing draws a conclusion to support the thesis, the writing is always objective, unbiased, and free of opinion.

Finally, informative writing incorporates strong, accurate outside research to help make and support ideas and claims. Outside research is a valuable writing element that is essential to the development of a topic. Research enables writers to not only discover and confirm facts, but to draw new conclusions. Sources used in research must be formally cited—that is, referenced and identified using specific guidelines.

Main features of informative/explanatory writing include:

- a clear and logical organizational structure
- an introduction with a clear thesis statement
- relevant facts, supporting details, and quotations used to develop the topic
- information from research sources with formal citations
- precise language and domain-specific vocabulary
- a concluding statement that supports the thesis, information, and topic

NOTES

In order to present these features accurately and engagingly as they write their essays, students must pay careful attention to:

- a formal and objective style
- logical and varied transitions to connect ideas

As you continue with this extended writing project, you will receive more instructions and practice to help you craft each of the elements of informative/explanatory writing in your own essay. You will also learn more about incorporating research into your essays to make and support ideas and claims. The student model for this lesson incorporates one method for citing sources; you will learn more about this method as well as others in a later lesson.

Before you get started on your own informative/explanatory essay, begin by reading this essay that one student wrote in response to the writing prompt. As you read this student model, highlight and annotate the features of informative writing that the student included in the essay.

Your informative essay should include:

- an introduction with a clear thesis statement
- body paragraphs with relevant evidence and thorough analysis to support your thesis
- cited research from at least three credible print and digital sources to support your ideas
- a concluding paragraph that effectively wraps up the essay and summarizes/paraphrases support for the thesis statement

WRITING PROMPT

Mankind has always sought to advance its knowledge of the world and to make life easier and better for its citizens. However, some scientific breakthroughs have led to unintended consequences. Consider both the positive and the negative outcomes that may result from new technology. Recall the selections you have read in this unit and how they explore moral dilemmas posed by technological advancements or possibilities. Choose two selections from the unit and write an informative essay that answers this question: What responsibility do people have when developing new technology? Along with information from the unit selections, include research from at least three other credible print and/or digital sources to support your ideas.

STUDENT MODEL

The Moral Dilemma of Technology: Benefit versus Harm

Technology is often viewed as inherently good. When technology improves the human condition, such as enabling cures for disease, society sees it as a benefit. A moral dilemma arises, however, when negative effects, such as physical or emotional pain, accompany the benefit. Society must then weigh the benefit of the value against its human costs, and an important question must be answered: What responsibility do we have when developing new technology? Louis Pasteur, in his speech "Worship the Spirit of Criticism: Address at the Pasteur Institute," and Rebecca Skloot, in the biography *The Immortal Life of Henrietta Lacks*, address this dilemma and its questions. Each focuses on a shared belief: Society bears a responsibility to ensure that, when developing new technology, it addresses unintended consequences that threaten the sanctity of human life.

In 1888, the Pasteur Institute in Paris—a place where Louis Pasteur and his pupils "could work together for science and the cure of disease"—officially opened (Keim and Lumet 176). In his address upon its opening, Pasteur urged his colleagues and students to scrutinize their work and bear moral responsibility for their research, advising them to "Worship the spirit of criticism...without it, everything is fallible . . ." He added that although science binds itself to no country, a scientist must be aware of "the influence which his works may have in this world" (Pasteur 443–444). Pasteur felt that awareness applied to science and to its impact on humanity. "Louis Pasteur was a humanist who put himself and science to work to improve the human condition" (Persson 44). In closing his address, Pasteur presented his "philosophic reflections" about scientific advancement and making choices between positive and negative impacts of science (Keim and Lumet 182). "Two contrary laws seem to be wrestling with each other nowadays," Pasteur stated. "[T]he one, a law of blood and death, ever imagining new means of destruction and forcing nations to be constantly ready for the battlefield—the other, a law of peace, work and health, ever evolving new means of delivering man from the scourges which beset him." For Pasteur, the choice between the conflicting laws of science—one that "seeks violent conquests" and destruction in war, and the other that finds "relief of humanity" that "places one human life above any victory"—was clear. He would obey "the law of humanity, to extend the frontiers of life" (Pasteur 444).

Pasteur undeniably saw the conflict surrounding technological advancement of his time. He encouraged taking responsibility for research and its consequences. Rebecca Skloot sees a similar conflict over advancing medical technology and an "ethical debate surrounding the use of human tissues in research . . ." (Skloot 6). In particular, as Skloot's writing points out, the dilemma she deals with concerns the important medical advancements made through the discovery and use of HeLa cells and, in part, the problems medical advances created for the family of Henrietta Lacks, for whom the cells were named. The problems stemmed from the family's anger over the removal of cells from Henrietta's body without permission after she died, over the sale of vials of the cells for $25 for research, and the publication of articles about the cells without their knowledge. Family members felt that the scientific community had taken advantage of them (Skloot 5). In addition, Henrietta's contribution was not properly acknowledged by the scientific community; indeed, early Internet research conducted by Skloot revealed that most sites referred to her as Helen Lane (Skloot 5). As background, Skloot tells us that HeLa cells are "said to be 'immortal'" because they were taken from a cancerous tumor that killed Henrietta Lacks and now live on outside her body in culture. (Skloot 5). She also says that billions of HeLa cells are used in laboratories around the world, and that they helped with some of the most important advances in medicine (Skloot 2). She further tells us that only after completing some of her own biological research using HeLa cells, Skloot learned through reading magazine articles she read of the Lacks family's anger (Skloot 5). As a researcher attempting to discover and tell the whole story of Henrietta Lacks, of HeLa cells, and of technological advances using them, Skloot dug deeper into information about the Lacks family and tried to make sense of the history of cell culture and the ethical debate about human tissue research (Skloot 5–6). Ultimately, she became one voice calling for the scientific community to acknowledge the harm done to the Lacks family as medical advancements were made with HeLa cells. Then, another ethical controversy erupted. German researchers published data from a study of the HeLa genome—the complete genetic material present in a line of HeLa cells. It was "data with the potential to reveal some very private information about Ms. Lacks' descendants, including their risks of various diseases" (Collins). Many people joined in the demand for moral responsibility. "After outcries from the Lacks family, scientists, bioethicists, and many others, the HeLa genome sequence was removed from a public database" (Collins). Ultimately, the U.S. National Institutes of Health made amends. An agreement was struck taking into account both the advancement of medical research and

NOTES

the concerns of Lacks' descendants. "In addition, the agreement asks researchers who use or derive genomic data from HeLa cells to acknowledge the contribution of Ms. Lacks and her family in their publications" (Collins).

The works of Pasteur and Skloot illustrate sharp contrasts in how society addresses the consequences of a technological benefit. Two anecdotes—one of Pasteur's approach to research and his human subjects and the other about Skloot's discovery of Henrietta Lacks—further illustrate the contrast in connections, lost or kept, between research and an individual's impact on it. In 1885, "Pasteur tested his pioneering rabies treatment on man for the first time" (Dhoke). The patient was a 9-year-old boy and "The child stood it admirably, but Pasteur became anxious, distressed to the point of sleeplessness, when it came time to pass on the ...vaccines" (Keim and Lumet 171). "This was done at some personal risk for Pasteur, since he was not a licensed physician and could have faced prosecution for treating the boy. After consulting with colleagues, he decided to go ahead with the treatment." (Wikipedia 1). The vaccine soon became widely used and "Pasteur took an interest in the children who he treated . . . trying to keep watch on their subsequent lives . . . " (Keim and Lumet 175). On the other hand, Skloot tells of asking her high school science teacher for details about Henrietta Lacks. Her teacher's response was "I wish I could tell you...but no one knows anything about her" (Skloot 4).

Although a span of some 120 years separates Pasteur's and Skloot's writings, the common thread binding them is an underlying moral principle: Society has a twofold responsibility in the development of technology. It must ensure that benefit of technology to humanity is evaluated in conjunction with its potential unintended, harmful consequences.

Works Cited

Collins, Francis. "HeLa Cells: A New Chapter in An Enduring Story." *National Institutes of Health*. U.S. Department of Health and Human Services, 7 Aug. 2013. Web. 10 Oct. 2014.

Dhoke, Ruchira. "LOUIS PASTEUR: the man who built the foundation for the science of microbiology and modern medicine." *The National*, 20 Oct. 2014. Web. 21 Oct. 2014.

Keim, Albert, and Louis Lumet. *Louis Pasteur*. Trans. Frederic Taber Cooper. New York: Frederick A. Stokes, 1914. Print.

Pasteur, Louis. "Worship the Spirit of Criticism." *The Life of Pasteur*. René Vallery-Radot. Forgotten Books. 2012. Print.

Persson, Sheryl. *Smallpox, Syphilis, and Salvation: Medical Breakthroughs that Changed the World*. Australia: Exisle Publishing, 2010. Print.

Skloot, Rebecca. *The Immortal Life of Henrietta Lacks*. New York: Crown Publishing Group, a division of Random House. 2011. Print.

THINK QUESTIONS

1. What is the central idea of the model essay? Where does the writer introduce the central idea in the essay?

2. How are the writer's ideas developed and refined by sentences, paragraphs, or larger portions of the text?

3. How does the writer sound in this essay? Is she casual or formal? How does the writer remain objective? Explain.

4. In thinking about the student model and writing your own informative essay, what types of sources can you use to respond to the prompt?

5. Based on what you have read, listened to, or researched, how would you answer the question *What responsibility do we have for what we create?* What are some issues associated with this question today?

PREWRITE

When beginning the process of writing your informative essay, think about strategies you have used in the past to gather and organize your ideas. You likely used one of the following techniques—questioning, brainstorming, list making, creating a word web, outlining, or free writing—to develop your essays.

Before you begin your essay, think about specific questions related to the Extended Writing Project prompt to help guide your brainstorming and focus on the topic dictated by the prompt. The prompt encourages you to consider the positive and negative effects of new technology and how the unit texts address moral dilemmas posed by technological advancements or possibilities. It also directs you to explain what responsibility people must assume when developing technology that is intended to benefit humanity.

Think about what you read in "Worship the Spirit of Criticism: Address at the Pasteur Institute" and *The Immortal Life of Henrietta Lacks*. What moral dilemmas with regard to technology do the texts explore? What benefits and drawbacks to humanity that result from new technology do the texts identify? In each text, what responsibility or lack of responsibility does the scientific community exhibit as a result of its endeavors? Make a list of the answers to these questions. You might put your ideas into a chart or create a web of clustered ideas. Here is one example of how you might answer and compare questions in a chart:

	PASTEUR	SKLOOT
What moral dilemma(s) does each text explore?	What kinds of technology are acceptable to pursue? (only those intended to save and improve lives, as opposed to those intended to destroy or kill?) Is the potential for new medicines worth the risk to test subjects?	How must the scientific community behave toward the individual human beings (and their families) from whom the tissue used in medical research comes?
What benefits to humanity does each text identify?	saving lives and helping people live longer	changing and improving medical science using HeLa cells that lead to important advancements in medicine
What costs to humanity does each text identify?	technology that leads to the destruction of lives	personal, hurtful consequences for Henrietta Lacks's family
According to each text, what responsibility do people have when developing new technology?	Pasteur holds the scientific community responsible for ensuring that technology benefits rather than harms humanity.	Skloot's discoveries suggest that the scientific community has a responsibility to be open, honest, and respectful toward those individuals and their families who contribute to science through the use of their personal tissue.

PRACTICE

Make a similar list of questions for two selections from the unit you have read. As you write down your ideas, look for patterns that emerge. Do the technological advancements examined have anything in common? In what similar or different ways do the authors of the selections explore moral dilemmas posed by technology? What key benefits and costs to humanity result from the technological advancements mentioned in the two selections? What responsibility do people have when developing new technology according to the two texts? Looking for similarities as well as differences between how the texts treat the subject may help you solidify the ideas you want to discuss in your essay.

Now brainstorm a list of questions you would like to have answered as you research. Questions might include: What information, such as that found in other sources (research studies, biographical or historical accounts, print or electronic publications), is available on the topic? What do other sources say about technology and its benefits and costs to humanity? Do other authors agree or disagree with the information in the unit selections you chose, and if so, how? What new or additional data or information about a particular technology explored in one of the unit texts is now available? Keep these questions in mind as you research your topic. Other questions may arise as you progress.

SKILL:
RESEARCH AND
NOTE-TAKING

 DEFINE

Researching is the process of gathering data, such as facts and other information about a topic of interest or importance to you. Research helps writers narrow or broaden their inquiry into a topic, develop a point of view, and draw conclusions by providing relevant evidence and details that support claims. The point of view and conclusions you draw from research help solidify the main idea, or thesis, of a topic. Good research will not only help you formulate ideas, but will also increase your understanding of a topic and strengthen your writing.

Research involves the systematic investigation of general and specific factual information from several reliable sources that are credible, or trustworthy and accurate. As you research, it is important to explore a variety of both print and digital resources that specifically relate to your topic to discover pertinent facts and information. When conducting research online, for example, you can do an advanced search in order to find sources that are most relevant to your topic.

Information collected from sources must be carefully evaluated in order to determine how strongly it suits the writer's task, purpose, and audience. When gathering information, you will need to scrutinize and analyze it to determine if it is accurate and relevant to your topic. Ask some questions about your sources:

- Is the information provided by the source specific, and does it contain facts about the topic that can be proven?
- Is the information, including conclusions drawn by the source, over-generalized without data or evidence to support it, or are the conclusions drawn well-founded?
- Is the author of the information you want to use mentioned, and if so, is the author credible?

- Is the source considered reliable; can you find information to support its validity such as acceptable publication information and author credentials?
  - › Reliable sources can either be primary or secondary.
    - Primary sources are documents or physical objects that were created and present during an experience or time period and offer a firsthand account or interpretation of a particular event. Some types of primary sources include:
      - Original documents: diaries, speeches, manuscripts, letters, interviews, news film footage, photographs, autobiographies, official records
      - Creative works: novels, poetry, plays, music, art
      - Relics or artifacts: Pottery, furniture, clothing, buildings

  - › Secondary sources interpret and analyze primary sources. Secondary sources may have pictures, quotes, or graphics of primary sources in them, but they are one or more steps removed from the event. Types of secondary sources include:
    - textbooks, magazine articles, histories, criticisms, commentaries, documentaries, encyclopedias

  - › Unreliable sources should NEVER be used in research and note-taking because they are considered inaccurate and are not credible. Simply put, they are a waste of your researching time. Any research you glean from these sources will not validate your overall message, so be careful to refrain from using any information you find in:
    - anything that is purely personal opinion (blogs, personal websites)
    - anything that is a collaborative work and open to revision or augmentation (Wikipedia and all other Wiki sites)
    - movies (they may contain some truth, but are made for entertainment and therefore cannot be considered credible)
    - historical novels (similar to movies, fictional novels may be based on true stories or real events, but they are written for entertainment and cannot serve as supporting evidence)
    - IF you find some information in an unreliable source you think might be interesting or true, research that information and find a primary or secondary source on the same subject to reference

An essential part of the research process is note-taking. **Note-taking** is a process, or consistent and systematic way, of writing down select pieces of information, either in your own words or as direct quotes taken from a source. Notes will help you develop or support a topic about which you are writing. Information you choose for your notes should strongly support your topic and

Please note that excerpts and passages in the StudySync® library and this workbook are intended as touchstones to generate interest in an author's work. The excerpts and passages do not substitute for the reading of entire texts, and StudySync® strongly recommends that students seek out and purchase the whole literary or informational work in order to experience it as the author intended. Links to online resellers are available in our digital library. In addition, complete works may be ordered through an authorized reseller by filling out and returning to StudySync® the order form enclosed in this workbook.

Reading & Writing Companion   **285**

answer questions you encounter while researching. Good notes can help you keep your topic focused, make connections between ideas, and become evidence you cite to support or broaden ideas. Since notes help you keep track of information, they need to be organized and document not only information you are going to use, but also tell where, from whom, and when you found the information. Documenting information will help you track it down later if you need to find it again as you are writing.

When researching and taking notes, you need to choose the method, or combination of methods, that works best for you. Think about what you have learned from research presentations you prepared for previous units or have been working on in the current unit. Consider what worked well for keeping your information organized and systematic. Here are some methods used by researchers when taking notes:

- **Note cards** with information written on standard 3×5", 4×6", or 5×8" index cards:
  - › **Source cards** are note cards that document the author (Last name first), title of an article or book, publication information, and location where the source can be found, such as a library or the Internet. Include URLs (Uniform Resource Locators) or reference addresses for information found on the Internet. It is a good idea to number each source card.
  - › **Note cards** include key words, phrases, direct quotations or paraphrased quotations, and summaries that specifically relate to the topic. The information on the cards should be relatively short and to the point. Use a new card for each piece of information you want to consider or use. Write **direct quotes or phrases** using the exact words of the source and put the words in quotation marks so there is no mistake that the words belong to someone else. If you **paraphrase** in your own words what a source says in a short passage, you need to make a note and attribute the information to that source. For longer pieces of work, such as chapters or sections, **summarize** main ideas in your own words. Note cards should include the source and a page number, or paragraph number, where the information can be found. If you use the system of numbering source cards, write the number of the source card related to the piece of information you are considering using on the note card where you can find it easily.
  - › **Online note cards** help some researchers organize, document, and print the information they find. There are a variety of sources that sell computer programs for creating cards or some that offer access to online systems or programs that compile and organize information. Online systems often require the user to set up an account. Consumers of online products need to weigh the benefits, such as saving time writing and organizing, against difficulty or ease of use and cost.

- **Bibliographic information lists** are another way some researchers keep track of sources. They create computer-generated lists of bibliographic information to help document and organize their source material. Bibliographic information is the same as the information included on a source card.

Regardless of which methods you choose, you must always avoid **plagiarizing**, or taking another person's work and passing it off as your own, whether intentionally or not. If the notes you take from a source and information you use is accurate and attributed to the source on your note cards, you will avoid plagiarizing anyone's work when you are writing. There are specific, formal guidelines for writing research papers and including source information that you should learn to use. You will learn more about how to do this in the Sources and Citations lesson.

No matter the subject, any time you are writing an informational/explanatory essay, you can use the following roadmap to help you as you research your topic. This roadmap will help you to focus on important ideas as well as guide you toward the kind of information you'll want to include in your essay:

- Create a web or diagram of ideas and facts pertaining to your chosen subject; use the information to help you think of relevant issues or questions regarding your subject.

- Find sources and references that support and explain your subject; read general and specific information in books as well as magazine and newspaper articles in print and on the Internet. You might also look to video, poetry, songs, or artwork that would help to validate or authenticate your focus. Find information that is relevant to your topic and audience. Be mindful of what sources are considered valid or not valid— Wikipedia, for example, is not considered a valid source because it is a "collaborative project" that anyone can add to or edit; therefore, it is not verifiable or considered credible.

- Make a bibliographic list of references.

- Read information in sources and make cards for sources and references.

- Create note cards with quotes, paraphrases, or summaries of information.

 MODEL

Before considering the research and note-taking apparent in the student model essay, have another look at the writing prompt:

WRITING PROMPT

Mankind has always sought to advance its knowledge of the world and to make life easier and better for its citizens. However, some scientific breakthroughs have led to unintended consequences. Consider both the positive and the negative outcomes that may result from new technology. Recall the selections you have read in this unit and how they explore moral dilemmas posed by technological advancements or possibilities. Choose two selections from the unit and write an informative essay that answers this question: What responsibility do people have when developing new technology? Along with information from the unit selections, include research from at least three other credible print and/ or digital sources to support your ideas.

Here is the roadmap the author used in researching and taking notes to develop the second paragraph of the essay. While the writer could have used a graphic organizer to guide her organization, she chose to use an outline of questions to answer:

Student Outline for Paragraph Two

> *Main Idea: What were Pasteur's beliefs about advancements in science and technology? What were his beliefs about taking responsibility for them?*
>
> A. Where, when, why did Pasteur present his ideas and beliefs in a speech?
> B. What did Pasteur believe? What responsibility do scientists have ...?
>   a. For evaluating their work
>   b. As scientists in general
> C. What kind of person was Pasteur in the context of science?
> D. What philosophical beliefs did Pasteur have about advancements in science and technology?
>   a. Beneficial
>   b. Harmful
> E. What did Pasteur believe was the right way to develop or advance science and technology?

As the student read from Pasteur's speech and other sources to find answers to her questions, she made a list of sources to use for Paragraph 2.

NOTES

Works Cited

Keim, Albert, and Louis Lumet. *Louis Pasteur*. Trans. Frederic Taber Cooper. New York: Frederick A. Stokes, 1914. Print.

Pasteur, Louis. "Worship the Spirit of Criticism." *The Life of Pasteur*. René Vallery-Radot. Forgotten Books. 2012. Print.

Persson, Sheryl. *Smallpox, Syphilis, and Salvation: Medical Breakthroughs that Changed the World*. Australia: Exisle Publishing, 2010. Print.

Then the writer made source cards with information about the sources and numbered them.

Sample Source Cards

Source Number 1		Source Number 2
Keim, Albert, and Louis Lumet. Louis Pasteur. Trans. Frederic Taber Cooper. New York: Frederick A. Stokes, 1914. Print.		Pasteur, Louis. from "Worship the Spirit of Criticism: Address at the Pasteur Institute." StudySync. Web. 10 Oct 2014.
Source Number 3		
Persson, Sheryl. Smallpox, Syphilis, and Salvation: Medical Breakthroughs that Changed the World. Australia: Exisle Publishing, 2010. Print.		

Next, she made note cards with information she wanted to use that helped answer her questions.

Please note that excerpts and passages in the StudySync® library and this workbook are intended as touchstones to generate interest in an author's work. The excerpts and passages do not substitute for the reading of entire texts, and StudySync® strongly recommends that students seek out and purchase the whole literary or informational work in order to experience it as the author intended. Links to online resellers are available in our digital library. In addition, complete works may be ordered through an authorized reseller by filling out and returning to StudySync® the order form enclosed in this workbook.

Reading & Writing Companion   **289**

NOTES

Sample Note Cards

Where, when, why did Pasteur present his ideas in a speech?	What did Pasteur believe? What responsibility do scientists have for evaluating their work?
In 1888, the Pasteur Institute in Paris—a place where Louis Pasteur and his pupils "could work together for science and the cure of disease" —officially opened. (Keim and Lumet p. 176)	"Worship the spirit of criticism...without it, everything is fallible . . ." (Pasteur speech p. 1)
What did Pasteur believe? What responsibility do scientists have in general?	**What kind of person was Pasteur in the context of science?**
(paraphrase) although science binds itself to no country, a scientist must be aware of (quote) "the influence that his work may have in this world" (Pasteur speech p. 1)	"Louis Pasteur was a humanist who put himself and science to work to improve the human condition" (Persson p. 44)

After taking notes and completing her research, the author began to write the second paragraph of her essay. Here is what she wrote:

In 1888, the Pasteur Institute in Paris—a place where Louis Pasteur and his pupils **"could work together for science and the cure of disease"**—officially opened (Keim and Lumet 176). In his address upon its opening, Pasteur urged his colleagues and students to scrutinize their work and bear moral responsibility for their research, advising them to **"Worship the spirit of criticism...without it, everything is fallible ..."** He added that although science binds itself to no country, a scientist must be aware of **"the influence that his work may have in this world" (Pasteur 443–444).** Pasteur felt that awareness applied to science and to its impact on humanity. **"Louis Pasteur was a humanist who put himself and science to work to improve the human condition" (Persson 44).**

Notice that her essay contains citations in parentheses for her sources and the page numbers where the information is found. These citations follow MLA style, although other style guides may dictate the use of footnotes or endnotes.

 PRACTICE

Create four note cards that properly record quoted or paraphrased information from your sources. When you are finished, trade with a partner and offer each other feedback. Do the cards contain all of the necessary source information? Do direct quotes appear in quotations? Do the notes address the writer's questions? Offer each other suggestions, and remember that they are most helpful when they are constructive.

NOTES

SKILL:
THESIS
STATEMENT

DEFINE

The **thesis statement** is one of the most important elements in an informative/
explanatory essay. It introduces what the writer is going to say about the topic
of the essay, helps control and focus the information the writer provides, and
summarizes the central or main idea. It also gives the reader an overview of
the ideas the writer will develop in the body of the essay. Ideas presented in
a good thesis statement, although somewhat general, must also be focused
on, or specific to, the topic. Words used in the thesis statement should narrow
the focus of the topic without too many details. For example, a thesis statement
that says, "drugs are bad," is too broad and vague. It could be strengthened
by a more specific focus by stating what kinds of drugs are bad, for whom
they are bad, and why. The details about the topic will come later in the body
of the essay as the writer develops his or her central idea. The thesis
statement usually appears near the end of the essay's introductory paragraph.
The rest of the paragraphs in the essay all support the thesis statement with
facts, evidence, and examples.

A thesis statement:

- is a short, focused statement that makes a strong, clear assertion
  identifying and previewing the writer's central idea
- lets the reader know the direction the writer will take in the body of the
  essay, especially what the writer plans to discuss, support, or prove
- is presented in the introductory paragraph, usually near the end
- helps the writer focus on relationships among pieces of evidence from
  multiple sources used to support ideas, arguments, or conclusions
- responds fully, or completely, and specifically to an essay prompt

MODEL

The following is the introductory paragraph from the student model essay "The Moral Dilemma of Technology: Benefit versus Harm":

Technology is often viewed as inherently good. When technology improves the human condition, such as enabling cures for disease, society sees it as a benefit. A moral dilemma arises, however, when negative effects, such as physical or emotional pain, accompany the benefit. Society must then weigh the benefit of the value against its human costs, and an important question must be answered: What responsibility do we have when developing new technology? Louis Pasteur, in his speech "Worship the Spirit of Criticism: Address at the Pasteur Institute," and Rebecca Skloot, in the biography The Immortal Life of Henrietta Lacks, *address this dilemma and its questions. Each focuses on a shared belief:* **Society bears a responsibility to ensure that, when developing new technology, it addresses unintended consequences that threaten the sanctity of human life.**

Notice the bold-faced thesis statement at the end of the introductory paragraph. This student's thesis statement asserts the writer's central or main idea about that topic: that society must take responsibility for addressing unintended consequences of technology.

 PRACTICE

Write a thesis statement for your informative essay that articulates your central idea in relation to the essay prompt. When you are finished, trade with a partner and offer each other feedback. How clear was the writer's central idea? Is it obvious what this essay will focus on? Does it specifically address the prompt? Offer each other suggestions, and remember that they are most helpful when they are constructive.

SKILL:
ORGANIZE
INFORMATIVE
WRITING

 DEFINE

The purpose of writing an informative/explanatory text is to inform readers. To do this effectively, writers need to organize and present their ideas, facts, details, and other information in a logical sequence that is easy to understand.

Students are often asked to write informative essays as part of their studies in English language arts classes. A common method for writing a strong informative essay is organizing the writing using the **five-paragraph strategy**. As you saw in the introductory lesson, this consists of an **introductory paragraph** that presents the **topic** and the writer's position in a **thesis statement**. The introduction is then followed by **three body paragraphs**, each of which presents evidentiary details and ideas that support some aspect of the essay's thesis. The fifth paragraph is a **conclusion** that provides a unique restatement of the thesis, reviews the evidence presented, and ends with a concluding sentence that wraps up the topic. The five-paragraph approach is straightforward, concise, and effective; however, it is not the only organizational structure that may be used to write a strong informative essay.

Experienced writers carefully choose an **organizational structure** that best suits their material. They often use an outline or other graphic organizer to determine which organizational structure will help them express their ideas most effectively.

For example, scientific reports and studies often use a **cause and effect** structure. This mirrors the information scientists need to relay—the experiment and the results of the experiment. Historians and memoirists often use a **sequential** or a chronological structure, discussing events in the order they occurred. Topical essays by historians may use a **problem and solution** structure in which a social or historical problem such as the Great Depression is presented and is followed by a discussion of how the problem was solved.

A common organizational structure for informative writing involves using a **comparison and contrast** strategy. There are several ways this strategy may be implemented. The writer might focus on one idea or example after the introductory paragraph and then a second idea or example in the subsequent paragraph. Another technique is to compare and contrast related ideas within each paragraph. Sometimes, the writer might choose to mix-and-match the approaches for a more complex structure. In this case, the first section might be dedicated to similarities, but the writer might feel the need to have two paragraphs within this section, one dedicated to each text. The reader would then expect a similar substructure in the second section, with each text being given one paragraph as differences are explained and analyzed.

It is important to remember that while an informative essay or a paragraph may use an overall organizational method, it may be necessary to introduce another organizational technique to convey an important point. Keep the following points in mind when beginning to craft your essay:

- When selecting an organizational structure, writers must consider the purpose of their writing. They often ask themselves questions about the kind of information they are writing about. Questions they might consider are:
  › "What organizational structure does the language of the prompt suggest?"
  › "What is the main idea I'd like to convey?"
  › "Would it make sense to relay events in the order they occurred?"
  › "What is the problem?"
  › "What solutions seem like possible answers to the problem?"
  › "Is there a natural cause and effect relationship in my information?"
  › "Can I compare and contrast different examples of my thesis statement?"
  › "Am I teaching readers how to do something?"

- Writers often use word choice to create connections between details and hint at the organizational structure being used:
  › Sequential order: *first, next, then, finally, last, initially, ultimately*
  › Cause and effect: *because, accordingly, therefore, as a result, effect, so*
  › Compare and contrast: *like, unlike, also, both, similarly, although, while, but, however*

- Sometimes, within the overall structure, writers may find it necessary to organize individual paragraphs using other substructures—a definition paragraph in a chronological structure, for instance. This should not affect the overall organization.

MODEL

The writer of the student model understood—from the prompt itself, which calls upon students to examine two texts, and from her prewriting—that her overall organizational plan should focus on comparing and contrasting examples of how the scientific community responds to unintended consequences of technology.

In this excerpt from the introduction of the student model, the writer makes the organizational structure clear with her word choice:

> **Each [selection] focuses on a shared belief:** Society bears a responsibility to ensure that, when new developing technology, it addresses unintended consequences that threaten the sanctity of human life.

The writer uses the clause "Each [selection] focuses on a shared belief" to make clear that she will show how the two writers—Pasteur and Skloot—explore both the positive and negative effects of technological advancement in science, specifically medicine.

In order to organize her ideas during the prewriting process, the writer used a three-column chart like the one shown below. In the first column, she listed key questions related to her topic: What moral dilemma(s) does each text explore? What benefits to humanity does each text identify? What costs to humanity does each text identify? What was society's role in the development of technology designed to benefit humanity? In the next two columns, she listed the response to each question that she found in the selections by Pasteur and Skloot. She added comments to her prewriting notes about the similarities and differences of these two authors' point of view and highlighted them in yellow.

	PASTEUR	SKLOOT
What moral dilemma(s) does each text explore?	What kinds of technology are acceptable to pursue? (only those intended to save and improve lives, as opposed to those intended to destroy or kill?)	How must the scientific community behave toward the individual human beings (and their families) from whom the tissue used in medical research comes?

What benefits to humanity does each text identify?	saving lives and helping people live longer	changing and improving medical science using HeLa cells that lead to important advancements in medicine
What costs to humanity does each text identify?	technology that leads to the destruction of lives	personal, hurtful consequences for Henrietta Lacks's family
According to each text, what responsibility do people have when developing new technology?	Pasteur holds the scientific community responsible for ensuring that technology benefits rather than harms humanity.	Skloot's discoveries suggest that the scientific community has a responsibility to ensure that individuals (and their families) are not harmed in the process of advancing medicine.

PRACTICE

Using an *Organize Informative/Explanatory Writing* Three Column Chart like the one you have just examined or another type of graphic organizer, fill in the information you gathered in the Prewrite stage of writing your essay.

Please note that excerpts and passages in the StudySync® library and this workbook are intended as touchstones to generate interest in an author's work. The excerpts and passages do not substitute for the reading of entire texts, and StudySync® strongly recommends that students seek out and purchase the whole literary or informational work in order to experience it as the author intended. Links to online resellers are available in our digital library. In addition, complete works may be ordered through an authorized reseller by filling out and returning to StudySync® the order form enclosed in this workbook.

Reading & Writing Companion **297**

NOTES

SKILL: SUPPORTING DETAILS

 DEFINE

In informative writing, writers develop their main idea with relevant information called **supporting details.** These details can be drawn both from units texts as well as from outside research, which helps writers formulate their ideas and provides support for their thesis statements and main points. Relevant information includes all of the following:

- Facts and concrete details relevant to understanding the topic drawn from reliable sources
- Inferences drawn from texts that are important to understanding the topic
- Research and statistics related to the main idea or thesis
- Quotations and anecdotes from experts, eyewitnesses, or other source material
- Conclusions of scientific findings and studies
- Definitions from reference material

Writers can choose supporting details from many sources, including encyclopedias, research papers, newspaper and magazine articles, graphs, memoirs, biographies, criticism, documentaries, and reliable online references. Although information is plentiful and the source material varied, the writer must be careful to evaluate the quality of information to determine what information is most important and most closely related to the thesis. If the information does not support the topic, does not strengthen the writer's point, or is not appropriate to the audience's knowledge of the topic, it is not relevant.

Keep the following steps in mind when organizing your supporting details:

Step 1:

Review your thesis statement. To identify relevant supporting details, ask these question: What do I want my audience to know about the topic? What is my main idea? Is my thesis statement clear and concrete, *not* vague or abstract? Consider the following sample thesis statement about the Internet:

Copyright © BookheadEd Learning, LLC

Although global information available on the Internet is a valuable resource, **individual users are responsible for ensuring that materials accessed or posted are true, do not invade the privacy of others, and do not cause personal harm.**

The writer wants readers to know that the Internet is resource that must be used carefully. The writer's main idea is that "individual users are responsible for ensuring that materials accessed or posted are true, do not invade the privacy of others, and do not cause personal harm." This thesis statement is clear and specific.

Step 2:

Ask what a reader needs to know about the topic in order to understand the main idea. What details will support your thesis? Consider the details in this sample body paragraph, which follows the thesis statement:

A first step in taking responsibility for what you might use or cite from the Internet is to know the reliability of your sources. The Internet is an unregulated resource. People can post information that is both true and false. There are no universal filters required to prove that information is factual.

In order to understand the thesis statement, which includes three responsibilities individual Internet users have, readers will need more information about what each responsibility entails. The second body paragraph explains reasons why users cannot assume that all Internet material is true. This information, which is accurate and concise, relates to the overall purpose of the text and supports the writer's thesis.

Step 3:

Look for facts, quotations, research, and the conclusions of others as evidence for your points and support for your thesis. Consider the sample supporting details that follow the reasons described above:

In fact, some recent studies indicate that between 10% and 50% of information posted on the Internet is unreliable. One rule of thumb for increasing the likelihood that the information you access and use is accurate and reliable is to check the domain name extension of the source. Some of the more reliable sources use .edu, .gov, and sometimes .org within their domain names.

As evidence for his or her point that not all information on the Internet is true, the writer provides a statistic. Now that readers have a better understanding of why the information on the Internet cannot always be trusted, the writer provides a useful tip for how to increase the likelihood that the information Internet users access is reliable.

Use the following reader/writer checklists when assessing your essay's supporting details:

- Ask questions to determine if the readers' needs are met:
  › Is the information relevant to the audience?
  › Do the details hold the audience's interest with elements such as facts, statistics, quotations, and anecdotes?
  › Are the details and the language used clear and understandable?
  › Is this information necessary to the reader's understanding of the topic?

- Ask questions to determine if the writer's goals and needs are met:
  › Are the details relevant to the writer's goal?
  › Does the information prove the writer's point or achieve the writer's goal?
  › Is any information weak or should it be replaced with stronger evidence that makes the same point?
  › Are connections made between ideas and supported by details and relevant information?
  › Is information selectively integrated into the text to maintain a logical flow of ideas from the thesis, through the body paragraphs, and finally to the conclusion?

 MODEL

In the following excerpt from *Einstein's Letter to the President*—a letter written by Albert Einstein to U.S. President Franklin Delano Roosevelt in 1939—Einstein presents the idea that uranium is a powerful and potentially dangerous energy source that requires watchfulness and possibly quick action by the President and his administration.

> Some recent work by E. Fermi and L. Szilard, which has been communicated to me in manuscript, leads me to expect that the element uranium may be turned into a new and important source of energy in the immediate future. Certain aspects of the situation which has arisen seem to call for watchfulness and if necessary, quick action on the part of the Administration. I believe therefore that it is my duty to bring to your attention the following facts and recommendations.

In the course of the last four months it has been made probable through the work of Joliot in France as well as Fermi and Szilard in America—that it may be possible to set up a nuclear chain reaction in a large mass of uranium, by which vast amounts of power and large quantities of new radium-like elements would be generated. Now it appears almost certain that this could be achieved in the immediate future.

This new phenomenon would also lead to the construction of bombs, and it is conceivable—though much less certain—that extremely powerful bombs of this type may thus be constructed. A single bomb of this type, carried by boat and exploded in a port, might very well destroy the whole port together with some of the surrounding territory. However, such bombs might very well prove too heavy for transportation by air.

In the first paragraph, Einstein alerts President Roosevelt about some new information he has acquired about uranium and its potential. He begins to develop the idea that uranium requires monitoring and possibly quick action by the government. He is vague about his exact concern and why the government needs to monitor it or take action, but he infers that is an important matter that warrants the President's attention.

In the second and third paragraphs, Einstein provides additional details and selectively integrates information about the power of uranium and its potentially destructive capability in order to heighten the president's sense of urgency while maintaining the flow of ideas. During the course of the three paragraphs, Einstein goes from general to more specific to build connections and create more impact.

 PRACTICE

Review the information you have collected in your *Organize Informative/ Explanatory Writing* Three Column Chart. This organized information and your thesis will help you to create a road map to use for writing your essay.

Consider the following questions as you develop your main paragraph topics and their supporting details in the road map:

- What technological advancements does each text discuss?
- How do these advancements benefit society?
- What moral dilemma(s) in relation to the advances does each text explore?
- How do members of the scientific community and others featured in the texts respond to this moral dilemma?

Copyright © BookheadEd Learning, LLC

- How did their reactions make an impact—on themselves, the people around them, and on society?
- What do the situations described in the texts teach us about the different ways we can negotiate the conflict between technological advancement and morality?

Use this model to get started with your road map:

Essay Road Map

Thesis statement: Society bears a responsibility to ensure that, when developing new technology, it addresses unintended consequences that threaten the sanctity of human life.

Paragraph 1 Topic: Pasteur urged his colleagues and students to value human life.

Supporting Detail #1: Pasteur felt that it was essential that science be aware of its impact on humanity.

Supporting Detail #2: Pasteur valued life above scientific advancement purely for the sake of advancement.

Paragraph 2 Topic: Skloot also sees a conflict between medical advancements and the use of human tissue in research.

Supporting Detail #1: Henrietta Lack's family was angered by the use of Lack's cells without permission after she died.

Supporting Detail #2: Though Lack's cells are still used and have helped with essential medical advances, the privacy of her family was once compromised.

Paragraph 3 Topic: There can sometimes be conflicting values or controversy regarding scientific experimentation and those affected by it.

Supporting Detail #1: Pasteur valued his human subjects a great deal and was often anxious and curious about their well-being.

Supporting Detail #2: Though Henrietta Lacks's cells were essential to much research and discovery, her story had been virtually untold until Skloot took it upon herself to do so.

Reading & Writing Companion

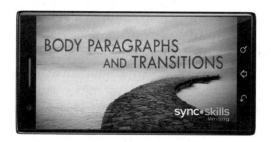

SKILL:
BODY
PARAGRAPHS AND
TRANSITIONS

 DEFINE

Body paragraphs are the section of the essay between the introduction and conclusion paragraphs. This is where you support your thesis statement by developing your main points with evidence from the text and your own analysis. Typically, each body paragraph will focus on one main point or idea to avoid confusing the reader. The main point of each body paragraph must support the thesis statement.

It is important to structure each of your body paragraphs clearly. One strategy for structuring a body paragraph for an informational essay is the following:

Topic sentence: The topic sentence is the first sentence of your body paragraph and clearly states the main point of the paragraph. It is important that your topic sentence develop the main assertion or central idea you presented in your thesis statement.

Evidence #1: It is important to support your topic sentence with evidence. Evidence can be relevant facts, definitions, concrete details, quotations, or other information and examples derived from the unit texts or sources identified during research.

Analysis/Explanation #1: After presenting evidence to support your topic sentence, you will need to analyze that evidence and explain how it supports your topic sentence and, in effect, your thesis.

Evidence #2: Continue to develop your topic sentence with a second piece of evidence.

Analysis/Explanation #2: Analyze this second piece of evidence and explain how it supports your topic sentence and, in effect, your thesis.

Concluding sentence: After presenting your evidence, you will need to wrap up your main idea and transition to the next paragraph in your concluding sentence.

Transitions are connecting words and phrases that clarify the relationships among ideas in a text. Authors of informative/explanatory texts use transitions to help readers recognize the overall organizational structure of the text. Transitions also help readers make connections among ideas within and across sentences and paragraphs. Also, by adding transition words or phrases to the beginning or end of a paragraph, authors guide readers smoothly through the text.

In addition, transition words and phrases help authors make connections between words within a sentence. Conjunctions such as *and*, *or*, and *but* and prepositions such as *with*, *beyond*, *inside*, show the relationships between words. Transitions help readers understand how words fit together to make meaning. Consider the following points when thinking about the transitions you will use in your essay:

- Body paragraphs are the section of the essay between the introduction and conclusion paragraphs. The body paragraphs provide the evidence and analysis/explanation needed to support the thesis statement. Typically, writers develop one main idea per body paragraph.
  › A topic sentence clearly state the main idea of the paragraph.
  › Evidence consists of relevant facts, definitions, concrete details, quotations, or other information and examples derived from the unit texts or sources obtained from research.
  › Analysis and explanation are needed to explain how the evidence supports the topic sentence.
  › The conclusion sentence wraps up the main point and transitions to the next body paragraph.

- Transition words are a necessary element of a successful piece of informative writing.
  › Transition words help readers understand the text structure of an informative text. Here are some transition words that are frequently used in three different text structures:
    - Cause-effect: *because, accordingly, as a result, therefore, effect, so, for, since*
    - Compare-contrast: *like, unlike, also, both, similarly, although, while, but, however, whereas, conversely, meanwhile, on the contrary, on the other hand, and yet, still*
    - Chronological order: *first, next, then, finally, last, initially, ultimately*

- Transition words help readers understand the flow of ideas and concepts in a text. Some of the most useful transitions are words that indicate that the ideas in one paragraph are building on or adding to those in another.

NOTES

Examples include: *furthermore, therefore, in addition, moreover, by extension, in order to,* etc.

MODEL

The Student Model uses a body paragraph structure to develop the main ideas presented in the thesis statement and transitions to help the reader understand the relationship between ideas in the text.

Read the body paragraphs from the student model essay "The Moral Dilemma of Technology: Benefit versus Harm." Look closely at the structure and note the transition words in bold. Think about the purpose of the information presented. Does each body paragraph effectively develop the main point made in each topic sentence? How do transition words help you to understand the similarities and differences between ideas and experiences in the two texts?

In 1888, the Pasteur Institute in Paris—a place where Louis Pasteur and his pupils "could work together for science and the cure of disease"—officially opened (Keim and Lumet 176). **In his address upon its opening,** Pasteur urged his colleagues and students to scrutinize their work and bear moral responsibility for their research, advising them to "Worship the spirit of criticism...without it, everything is fallible . . ." **He added that** although science binds itself to no country, a scientist must be aware of "the influence which his works may have in this world" (Pasteur 443–444). Pasteur felt that awareness applied to science and to its impact on humanity. "Louis Pasteur was a humanist who put himself and science to work to improve the human condition" (Persson 44). **In closing his address,** Pasteur presented his "philosophic reflections" (Keim and Lumet 182) about scientific advancement and making choices between positive and negative impacts of science. "Two contrary laws seem to be wrestling with each other nowadays," Pasteur stated. "[T]he one, a law of blood and death, ever imagining new means of destruction and forcing nations to be constantly ready for the battlefield— the other, a law of peace, work and health, ever evolving new means of delivering man from the scourges which beset him." **For Pasteur,** the choice between the conflicting laws of science—one that "seeks violent conquests" and destruction in war, and the other that finds "relief of humanity" that "places one human life above any victory"—was clear. He would obey "the law of humanity, to extend the frontiers of life" (Pasteur 444).

Pasteur undeniably saw the conflict surrounding technological advancement of his time. He encouraged taking responsibility for research and its consequences. **Rebecca Skloot sees a similar conflict** over advancing medical technology and an "ethical debate surrounding the use of human tissues in research . . ." (Skloot 6). **In particular,** as Skloot's writing points out, the dilemma she deals with concerns the important medical advancements in the discovery and use of HeLa cells and, in part, the problems medical advances created for the family of Henrietta Lacks, for whom the cells were named. The problems stemmed from the family's anger over the removal of cells from Henrietta's body without permission after she died, over the sale of vials of the cells for $25 for research, and the publication of articles about the cells without their knowledge. Family members felt that the scientific community had taken advantage of them (Skloot 5). **In addition,** Henrietta's contribution was not properly acknowledged by the scientific community; indeed, early Internet research conducted by Skloot revealed that most sites referred to her as Helen Lane (Skloot 5). **As background,** Skloot tells us that HeLa cells are "said to be 'immortal'" because they were taken from a cancerous tumor that killed Henrietta Lacks and now live on outside her body in culture (Skloot 5). **She also says** that billions of HeLa cells are used in laboratories around the world, and that they helped with some of the most important advances in medicine (Skloot 2). **She further tells us** that only after completing some of her own biological research using HeLa cells, Skloot learned through reading magazine articles she read of the Lacks family's anger (Skloot 5). **As a researcher** attempting to discover and tell the whole story of Henrietta Lacks, of HeLa cells, and of technological advances using them, Skloot dug deeper into information about the Lacks family and tried to make sense of the history of cell culture and the ethical debate about human tissue research (Skloot 5–6). **Ultimately,** she became one voice calling for the scientific community to acknowledge the harm done to the Lacks family as medical advancements were made with HeLa cells. Then, another ethical controversy erupted. German researchers published data from a study of the HeLa genome—the complete genetic material present in a line of HeLa cells. It was "data with the potential to reveal some very private information about Ms. Lacks' descendants, including their risks of various diseases" (Collins). Many people joined in the demand for moral responsibility. "After outcries from the Lacks family, scientists, bioethicists,

Reading & Writing Companion

and many others, the HeLa genome sequence was removed from a public database" (Collins). **Ultimately,** the U.S. National Institutes of Health made amends. An agreement was struck taking into account both the advancement of medical research and the concerns of Lacks' descendants. "In addition, the agreement asks researchers who use or derive genomic data from HeLa cells to acknowledge the contribution of Ms. Lacks and her family in their publications" (Collins).

The works of Pasteur and Skloot illustrate sharp contrasts in how society addresses the consequences of a technological benefit. Two anecdotes—one of Pasteur's approach to research and his human subjects and the other about Skloot's discovery of Henrietta Lacks—**further illustrate** the contrast in connections, lost or kept, between research and an individual's impact on it. **In 1885,** "Pasteur tested his pioneering rabies treatment on man for the first time" (Dhoke). The patient was a 9-year-old boy and "The child stood it admirably, but Pasteur became anxious, distressed to the point of sleeplessness, when it came time to pass on the ...vaccines" (Keim and Lumet 171). "This was done at some personal risk for Pasteur, since he was not a licensed physician and could have faced prosecution for treating the boy. After consulting with colleagues, he decided to go ahead with the treatment." (Wikipedia 1). The vaccine **soon** became widely used and "Pasteur took an interest in the children who he treated . . . trying to keep watch on their subsequent lives . . . " (Keim and Lumet 175). **On the other hand,** Skloot tells of asking her high school science teacher for details about Henrietta Lacks. Her teacher's response was "I wish I could tell you...but no one knows anything about her" (Skloot 4).

The first body paragraph of the Student Model is concerned with developing ideas expressed by Louis Pasteur in his address at the opening of the Pasteur Institute in 1888. The paragraph is built on the **topic sentence,** "In his address upon its opening, Pasteur urged his colleagues and students to scrutinize their work and bear moral responsibility for their research. . ." This topic sentence is supported by **evidence**, which includes direct quotations from Pasteur's actual address before the institute. In addition, the writer also quotes Pasteur's biographers and a noted science writer to support the idea that Pasteur was a humanist who believed passionately in taking moral responsibility for the progressive work that scientists do. Toward the end of the paragraph, the writer offers evidence in the form of another quotation from Pasteur's address, one that demonstrates the level of commitment the

Copyright © BookheadEd Learning, LLC

great scientist believed was necessary when considering the consequences of technological progress in one's work: "'Two contrary laws seem to be wrestling with each other nowadays,' Pasteur stated. '[T]he one, a law of blood and death, ever imagining new means of destruction and forcing nations to be constantly ready for the battlefield—the other, a law of peace, work and health, ever evolving new means of delivering man from the scourges which beset him.'" The paragraph ends with a summary statement that expresses the Pasteur's position on the topic.

Notice how the writer carefully integrates several quotations from different types of sources—primary and secondary—to help develop and support the main idea of this paragraph. The writer does not break up the text to indicate the sources from which he is quoting. Rather, she makes quoted material evident through the use of quotation marks, transitional phrases, and source citations. We are introduced to Pasteur's idea of worshipping "the spirit of criticism" as well as the idea of a scientist being aware of "the influence that his work may have in the world" through the citation of his speech that appears at the end of the quotation. Similarly, we are introduced to the idea of Pasteur's position as a humanist through a cited quotation from a noted science writer—"'Louis Pasteur was a humanist who put himself and science to work to improve the human condition' (Persson)"—and to his "philosophical reflections" through his biographers Keim and Lumet.

While the text of the paragraph flows smoothly, as if it was all the creation of the writer, we know exactly when and where the writer is choosing her words and when they are not her own. The flow of ideas is aided by the use of transitions such as "In his address upon its opening," "He added," "In closing his address," and "For Pasteur." The reader is given a sense of how the ideas connect to each other as well as the sequence in which they occurred or were presented.

In the second body paragraph, the writer turns her attention to ideas from *The Immortal Life of Henrietta Lacks* by Rebecca Skloot. Notice that the writer's use of transitional words and phrases, such as "Rebecca Skloot sees a similar conflict" and "on the other hand," help the reader understand that the overall text structure of the essay is comparison and contrast—that is, the essay explores ways in which the ideas and experiences presented in the two texts are similar and different. These transitional words and phrases also help readers identify specific bases upon which the two texts address similar or different ideas.

PRACTICE

Write one body paragraph for your informative essay that follows the suggested format. When you are finished, trade with a partner and offer each other feedback. How effective is the topic sentence at stating the main point of the paragraph? How strong is the evidence used to support the topic sentence? Are all quotes and paraphrased evidence cited properly? Did the analysis thoroughly support the topic sentence? How effectively are transitions used to clarify the relationships among the ideas in the text? Offer each other suggestions, and remember that they are most helpful when they are constructive.

DRAFT

⭐ DEFINE

As you prepare to write your draft, gather all of your prewriting and planning information, including outlines, organizers, and any other information you feel is essential to begin the process. Keep in mind all of the skills you have learned up to this point: how your audience and purpose inform your writing style; how to research outside sources and take relevant, detailed, useful notes; how to craft a clear and purposeful thesis statement; how to organize your research as well as your thoughts in order to conceptualize your overall intent and purpose for writing; how to plan where to put the information you have gathered according to the outline of an informative/explanatory essay; how to use supporting details to bolster the main ideas of your body paragraphs; how to write an effective introduction to engage the reader and frame the purpose of your essay as well as an impactful conclusion to summarize your points, restate your thesis, and soundly bring your essay to a close; how to use engaging and smooth transitions throughout your essay to connect all of the ideas and subtopics that support your thesis.

Remember that your draft is not the final essay. While you should maintain an essay format in keeping with informational/explanatory writing, you can use this Draft stage to experiment with different ideas you might have regarding the positive and negative impacts of technology—you can always remove or delete an idea, but an idea unrecorded is gone forever.

When drafting, ask yourself these questions:

- What can I do to engage my reader? How can I improve my hook to make it more appealing?

- Does my essay follow the format of an introduction, body paragraphs, and a conclusion?

- Is my thesis statement part of my introduction? Have I presented my thesis statement clearly? What can I do to clarify my thesis statement?

- In each body paragraph, which relevant facts, strong details, and interesting quotations derived from the unit texts and outside research

NOTES

support the thesis statement? Are the main ideas of each paragraph relevant to my overall purpose for writing?

- Would more precise language or different details about the controversy behind technology make the text more exciting and vivid?

- How effectively does the information I obtained from research enhance my analysis of the unit texts?

- How well have I communicated what moral dilemmas the texts explore in the context of new technology? How have I shown my reader that I have considered both the positive and negative consequences of technology?

- Does my conclusion restate my thesis and effectively summarize the main points of my essay?

- Have I made sure that all of my resources are properly cited both in-text and in my Works Cited page? Have I checked that every in-text citation corresponds to a Works Cited reference? Have I made sure to use *only* acceptable (primary and secondary) source material?

- With what final thought do I want to leave my readers?

Please note that excerpts and passages in the StudySync® library and this workbook are intended as touchstones to generate interest in an author's work. The excerpts and passages do not substitute for the reading of entire texts, and StudySync® strongly recommends that students seek out and purchase the whole literary or informational work in order to experience it as the author intended. Links to online resellers are available in our digital library. In addition, complete works may be ordered through an authorized reseller by filling out and returning to StudySync® the order form enclosed in this workbook.

Copyright © BookheadEd Learning, LLC

NOTES

SKILL:
SOURCES AND
CITATIONS

SOURCES AND CITATIONS

sync•skills
Writing

⭐ DEFINE

When writing an informative/explanatory essay, writers cannot simply make up information or rely on their own subjective experiences or opinions. To thoroughly support the treatment and analysis of their topics, writers need to include information from relevant, accurate, and reliable sources and cite, or acknowledge, them properly. Writers should keep track of these sources as they research and plan their work. When it comes time to write, they can use this information to acknowledge the sources when necessary within the text. If they don't, writers can be accused of **plagiarism**, or stealing someone else's words and ideas. In some academic texts, writers may be asked to provide sources and citations in **footnotes** or **endnotes**, which link specific references within the essay to the correlating pages or chapters in an outside source. In addition to internal citations, writers may also need to provide a full list of sources in a **Works Cited** section or standard **bibliography**.

Keep the following points in mind as you organize your source materials for your essay:

- As you identify possible sources for reference in your work, consider the **accuracy** and **reliability** of the material:
  › Is it published by a well-known and reliable person or company?
  › Is the material contemporary and current, or is it possible that the facts and data may have changed by now?
  › Would a reader be able to find this source easily if he or she were interested?
  › Does the Web site have a reliable extension (.edu and .gov, for example), or is more research needed to verify the truth and objectivity of the information?
  › Remember, some seemingly popular or reliable sources, such as Wikipedia, have been known to include misinformation. It's a good idea to have a backup source listed for any information that might attract an editor's or reader's doubts or concerns.

- When performing research online using a search engine, consider using accurate keywords and online filters to narrow the results and limit the number of distracting and irrelevant results. Try a variety of words for different searches in order to come up with the widest range of options.

- When including outside sources and references in your work, think of them as additional pieces of relevant information. In other words, they should clearly fit the purpose and context of your explanation or analysis. If this is not obvious from the citation itself, you might need to add text that establishes this relevance or relationship.

- When gathering sources and information for an informative/explanatory text, writers should take note of as much of the following information as possible:

  › Title of the work
  › Author(s) or editor(s) of the work
  › Pages referenced (relate this to specific quotations or information)
  › Date of publication
  › Publisher name and address (city, state, and/or country)
  › Web address (if online; provide the full hyperlink if possible)

- Always avoid plagiarism by either quoting the original text directly and crediting the author or paraphrasing the original idea and crediting the author.

- Different organizations and agencies have different ways of handling the proper formatting of citations and sources. When you receive an assignment, always check for and follow the proper formatting requirements. A scholarly article may have stricter requirements than a newspaper article, for example, though both will expect that your information is factually accurate and can be supported by a secondary source if needed.

- Familiarize yourself with the footnote and citation features of your word processing software. These can often make the task of tracking sources much less challenging. They may also be able to assist you in creating a final bibliography, or Works Cited page, once your document is complete.

 MODEL

In this excerpt from the Student Model essay, the writer uses quotations from primary and secondary source material and includes parenthetical citations.

> In 1888, the Pasteur Institute in Paris—a place where Louis Pasteur and his pupils "could work together for science and the cure of disease"—officially opened (**Keim and Lumet 176**). In his address upon its opening, Pasteur

NOTES

urged his colleagues and students to scrutinize their work and bear moral responsibility for their research, advising them to "Worship the spirit of criticism...without it, everything is fallible . . ." He added that although science binds itself to no country, a scientist must be aware of "the influence which his works may have in this world" (Pasteur 443–44). Pasteur felt that awareness applied to science and to its impact on humanity. "Louis Pasteur was a humanist who put himself and science to work to improve the human condition" (Persson 44). In closing his address, Pasteur presented his "philosophic reflections" (Keim and Lumet 182) about scientific advancement and making choices between positive and negative impacts of science. "Two contrary laws seem to be wrestling with each other nowadays," Pasteur stated. "[T]he one, a law of blood and death, ever imagining new means of destruction and forcing nations to be constantly ready for the battlefield— the other, a law of peace, work and health, ever evolving new means of delivering man from the scourges which beset him." For Pasteur, the choice between the conflicting laws of science—one that "seeks violent conquests" and destruction in war, and the other that finds "relief of humanity" that "places one human life above any victory"—was clear. He would obey "the law of humanity, to extend the frontiers of life" (Pasteur 444).

Notice that all the works referenced in the essay are listed here. For each work cited, complete bibliographic information is presented including the authors' names, the title of the work, the place of publication, the publisher, and the date of publication. In the case of Keim and Lumet, we learn that the work being cited is a biography entitled *Louis Pasteur* that was translated by Frederic Taber Cooper and published in New York in 1914 by Frederick A. Stokes, the name of a publishing company. In the citation, you can see that the author's name is presented with the last name first, followed by a comma and then the first name. If there is a second author, that name is presented as the first name followed by the last name. The names of the authors are followed by a period.

After the author's name, the citation presents the title of the work. It is common practice to present the titles of full-length works such as books, plays, and movies in italics. Shorter works, such as titles of articles, chapters, short stories, poems, and songs are presented within quotation marks. A period is used at the end of all titles of works. Since the biography by Keim and Lumet was translated from another language into English, the name of the translator appears after the English title and is also followed by a period. The publication information comes last in the citation and includes, in order: the place of publication, the name of the publisher, and the year of publication. Each item is set off with commas and ends with a period. Since there are many different types of sources used, the last element of the citation indicates that this particular item is "Print," which his means it was published on paper.

If you scan the items in the Works Cited list, you will see that all types of sources follow the same general sequence: author, title of the work, publication information. Commas are used to set off elements within each of these general groupings, but each grouping ends with a period. Notice how, when a source is electronic, the last element of the citation indicates that the item is from the "Web."

The style for the material presented in this Works Cited list is based on standards established by the Modern Language Association (MLA). However, there are many other acceptable forms of citation. When completing academic writing, it is important to determine if any other particular style of citation is required by your teacher.

 PRACTICE

Write citations for quoted information in your informative essay. When you are finished, trade with a partner and offer each other feedback. How successful was the writer in citing sources for the essay? How well did the writer make use of varied sources? Offer each other suggestions, and remember that they are most helpful when they are constructive.

REVISE

You have written a draft of your informative/explanatory text. You have also received input from your peers about how to improve it. Now you are going to revise your draft.

Here are some recommendations to help you revise.

- Review the suggestions made by your peers.
- Focus on maintaining a formal style. A formal style suits your purpose—that is, giving information about a serious topic. It also fits your audience—that is, students, teachers, and other readers interested in learning more about your topic.
  - › As you revise, eliminate any slang.
  - › Look for imprecise language. Can you substitute a more precise word for a word that is general or dull?
  - › Remove any first-person pronouns such as "I," "me," or "mine" or instances of addressing readers as "you." These are more suitable to a writing style that is informal, personal, and conversational. Check that you have used all pronouns correctly.
  - › If you include your personal opinions, remove them. Your essay should be objective and unbiased.
- After you have revised elements of style, think about whether there is anything else you can do to improve your essay's information or organization.
  - › Do you need to add any new textual evidence to fully support your thesis statement or engage the interest of readers? For example, is there a detail about someone's moral struggle that a reader might find compelling?
  - › Did one of your subjects say something special that you forgot to quote? Quotations can add life to your essay. Be sure to cite your sources.
  - › Consider your organization. Would your essay flow better if you strengthened the transitions between paragraphs?

NOTES

- Double check all your citations and your Works Cited list.
  - › Have you cited all direct quotations and paraphrased ideas within the body of the essay?
  - › Is every source you cited in the body of your essay included in your Works Cited list?
  - › Is there a source on your Works Cited list that you did not include in the essay? Delete that source from the list.
  - › Are your internal citations and Works Cited list formatted appropriately, according to the assigned style (MLA, APA, or Chicago)?

- As you add new details or change information, check your grammar and punctuation.
  - › Check that you have utilized parallel structure in sentences that include a series.
  - › Be sure to use semicolons and colons correctly.
  - › Check carefully for misspelled words.

Please note that excerpts and passages in the StudySync® library and this workbook are intended as touchstones to generate interest in an author's work. The excerpts and passages do not substitute for the reading of entire texts, and StudySync® strongly recommends that students seek out and purchase the whole literary or informational work in order to experience it as the author intended. Links to online resellers are available in our digital library. In addition, complete works may be ordered through an authorized reseller by filling out and returning to StudySync® the order form enclosed in this workbook.

Reading & Writing Companion   **317**

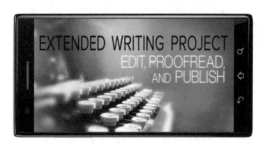

EDIT,
PROOFREAD,
AND PUBLISH

You have revised your informative/explanatory essay and received input from your peers on that revision. Now it is time to edit and proofread your essay to produce a final version. As you edit your final version, ask yourself the following questions:

- Does my essay follow the basic structure of an informative/explanatory essay (introduction, body paragraphs, conclusion)?

- Does my introduction grab the readers' attention in an interesting yet relevant way? Is my thesis statement part of my introduction as well as my conclusion? Does it respond to the prompt clearly and effectively?

- Have I included strong main ideas, supporting details, and relevant evidence to support my thesis and create a cohesive, vivid presentation of what I want to say?

- Have all of my outside sources been cited properly both within the body of my essay and in my Works Cited list? Are all of my outside sources appropriate (credible, comprised of both primary and secondary, NOT Wikipedia, etc.)?

- Do I use appropriate and smooth transitions to connect ideas and details within paragraphs as well as between paragraphs?

- Have I presented my readers with a conclusion that summarizes my purpose and intent as well as coherently restates my thesis?

- Have I incorporated all the valuable suggestions from my peers?

When you are satisfied with your work, move on to proofread it for errors. For example, check that you have used correct punctuation for quotations, citations, and restrictive/nonrestrictive phrases and clauses. Have you used pronouns correctly? Have you corrected any misspelled words?

- Check that you have formatted your essay according to approved guidelines and standards. This includes proper headings, title placement, margins, font, spacing, essay structure, and bibliographic information, as well as any other technical considerations that come to mind. For example, articles, speeches, and poem titles should be regular font, Title

Copyright © BookheadEd Learning, LLC

Case, with quotation marks; excerpts from books or novels should be Title Case in italics.

- Check sentence structure, including use of compound sentences and parallel structure. Check your use of sentence punctuation, confirming the appropriate use of commas, semicolons, colons, periods, and any other punctuation. Check carefully for punctuation that might be missing or misplaced.

- Check the content and punctuation of quotations and citations.

- Check that each in-text citation matches a complete reference in your Works Cited list.

- Check your spelling, paying special attention to the names of authors, titles, and individuals described in the texts.

Once you have made all your corrections, you are ready to publish your work. You can distribute your writing to family and friends, hang it on a bulletin board, or post it on your blog. If you publish online, create links to your sources and citations. That way, readers can follow-up on what they have learned from your essay and read more on their own.

Please note that excerpts and passages in the StudySync® library and this workbook are intended as touchstones to generate interest in an author's work. The excerpts and passages do not substitute for the reading of entire texts, and StudySync® strongly recommends that students seek out and purchase the whole literary or informational work in order to experience it as the author intended. Links to online resellers are available in our digital library. In addition, complete works may be ordered through an authorized reseller by filling out and returning to StudySync® the order form enclosed in this workbook.

Reading & Writing Companion **319**

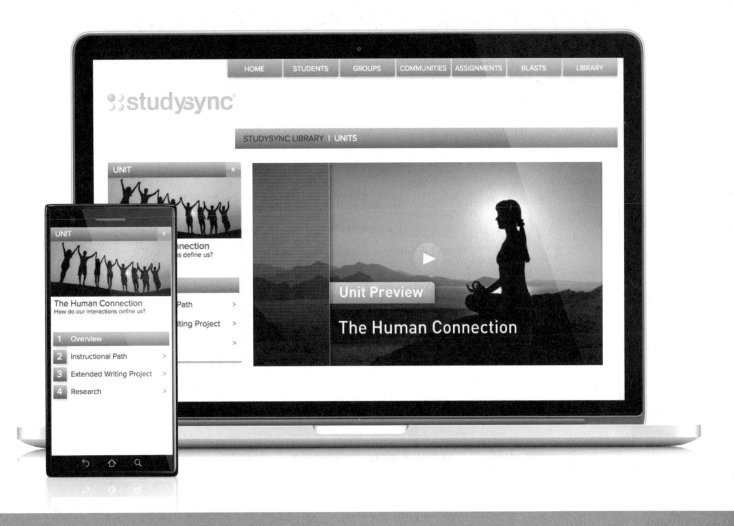

studysync®

Reading & Writing Companion

How do our interactions define us?

The Human Connection

UNIT 4   How do our interactions define us?

The Human Connection

 TEXTS

EXTENDED WRITING PROJECT

PLUTARCH'S LIVES

NON-FICTION
Plutarch
1579

INTRODUCTION

Plutarch, an ancient Greek historian, biographer, and essayist, is most famous for his series of parallel biographies about Greek and Roman leaders, known as *Plutarch's Lives*. Plutarch explored the qualities of each leader in order to establish a link between their character and political destiny. In the 16th century, Sir Thomas North translated Plutarch's work into English, and it was North's translation that Shakespeare consulted when writing several of his historical plays, including *Julius Caesar*. The excerpts here come from three different chapters in *Plutarch's Lives*, but all describe the same event—the riot that erupted at Caesar's

"Brutus committed two great faults..."

FIRST READ

NOTES

From Volume 7: Caesar

Caesar's funerals

1   The next morning, Brutus and his confederates came into the market-place to speak unto the people, who gave them such audience, that it seemed they neither greatly **reproved,** nor allowed the fact: for by their great silence they shewed, that they were sorry for Caesar's death, and also that they did reverence Brutus. Now the Senate granted general pardon for all that was past, and to pacify every man, ordained besides, that Caesar's funerals should be honoured as a god, and established all things that he had done: and gave certain provinces also, and convenient honours unto Brutus and his confederates, whereby every man thought all things were brought to good peace and quietness again. But when they had opened Caesar's testament, and found a liberal legacy of money, bequeathed unto every citizen of Rome, and that they saw his body (which was brought into the market-place) all bemangled with gashes of swords: then there was no order to keep the multitude and common people quiet, but they plucked up forms, tables, and stools, and laid them all about the body, and setting them afire, burnt the corpse. Then when the fire was well kindled, they took the firebrands, and went unto their houses that had slain Caesar, to set them afire.

From Volume 9: Brutus

Brutus committed two great faults

2   Then Antonius thinking good [Caesar's] testament should be read openly, and also that his body should be honourably buried, and not in hugger-mugger, lest the people might thereby take occasion to be worse offended if they did otherwise: Cassius stoutly spake against it. But Brutus went with the

motion, and agreed unto it: wherein it seemeth he committed a second fault. For the first fault he did was, when he would not consent to his fellow-conspirators, that Antonius should be slain. And therefore he was justly accused, that thereby he had saved and strengthened a strong and grievous enemy of their conspiracy. The second fault was, when he agreed that Caesar's funerals should be as Antonius would have them: the which indeed **marred** all. For first of all, when Caesar's testament was openly read among them, whereby it appeared that he bequeathed unto every citizen of Rome, seventy-five drachmas a man, and that he left his gardens and arbours unto the people, which he had on this side of the river of Tiber, in the place where now the temple of Fortune is built: the people then loved him, and were marvellous sorry for him. Afterwards when Caesar's body was brought into the market-place, Antonius making his funeral oration in praise of the dead, according to the ancient custom of Rome, and perceiving that his words moved the common people to compassion: he framed his **eloquence** to make their hearts yearn the more, and taking Caesar's gown all bloody in his hand, he laid it open to the sight of them all, shewing what a number of cuts and holes it had upon it. Therewithal the people fell presently into such a rage and mutiny, that there was no more order kept amongst the common people.

From Volume 9: Antonius

Antonius maketh uproar among the people

3   But now, the opinion he conceived of himself after he had a little felt the goodwill of the people towards him, hoping thereby to make himself the chiefest man if he might overcome Brutus: did easily make him alter his first mind. And therefore when Caesar's body was brought to the place where it should be buried, he made a funeral oration in **commendation** of Caesar, according to the ancient custom of praising noblemen at their funerals. When he saw that the people were very glad and desirous also to hear Caesar spoken of, and his praises uttered: he mingled his orations with lamentable words, and by amplifying of matters did greatly move their hearts and affections unto pity and compassion. In fine to conclude his oration, he unfolded before the whole assembly the bloody garments of the dead, thrust through in many places with their swords, and called the **malefactors,** cruel and cursed murtherers. With these words he put the people into such a fury, that they presently took Caesar's body, and burnt it in the market-place, with such tables and forms as they could get together. Then when the fire was kindled, they took firebrands, and ran to the murtherer's houses to set them on fire, and to make them come out to fight.

THINK QUESTIONS

1. According to the biography of Caesar, how did the people's attitude toward him change during his funeral, and why?

2. In the excerpt from the biography of Brutus, what made the people fall "into such a rage and mutiny"? Use evidence from the text to support your response.

3. What does the excerpt from Antonius's biography suggest about his motivation for speaking at Caesar's funeral and thus reveal about his character? Use evidence from the text to support your response.

4. Use context to determine the meaning of the word **malefactors** as it is used in the text. Write your definition of "malefactors" and describe how you arrived at it. Then look up "malefactors" in a dictionary and compare the dictionary definition with your own.

5. Recall that the Latin suffix *-tion* forms a noun from a verb form. Based on this knowledge, provide a definition of the word **commendation** as it is used in the text, and explain how you arrived at it.

CLOSE READ

Reread the excerpt from *Plutarch's Lives*. As you reread, complete the Focus Questions below. Then use your answers and annotations from the questions to help you complete the Writing Prompt.

FOCUS QUESTIONS

1. What is the central or main idea of the excerpt from Caesar's biography, entitled "Caesar's funerals"? Write a summary of the paragraph.

2. According to Plutarch, what two "faults" does Brutus commit? What do you think Brutus's interactions with his co-conspirators suggest about his character?

3. What is the central or main idea of the excerpt from Antonius's biography? How effectively does the title express the main idea of the passage?

4. Analyze the persuasive tactics Antonius uses during his funeral oration, as described by Plutarch.

5. What do Antonius's interactions with the crowd suggest about his character?

WRITING PROMPT

What do Plutarch's descriptions of the people and events in this part of Roman history reveal about his own point of view or attitude toward them? Analyze the central ideas that emerge from Plutarch's descriptions of Caesar, Brutus, and Antonius and what these reveal about how Plutarch perceives their characters and about the links he attempts to draw between their qualities as leaders and their political destinies. Based on his description of events, do you think Plutarch approves or disapproves of how this part of Roman history unfolded? Cite evidence from the text to support your response.

JULIUS CAESAR

DRAMA

William Shakespeare
1599

INTRODUCTION

Shakespeare's *Julius Caesar* was modeled on historic events in Rome, 44 B.C, with the central characters based on members of the Senate, where infighting and power struggles were the order of the day. Believing that Caesar had acquired too much power, Cassius and Brutus led a successful campaign to assassinate him on March 15, the infamous Ides of March. Shakespeare re-enacts these events and the dramatic consequences that follow while exploring the conflict between loyalty and nationalism. In this passage, Brutus and Antony offer alternate interpretations of Caesar's murder in order to sway the plebeians.

"Friends, Romans, countrymen, lend me your ears..."

FIRST READ

Excerpt from ACT III SCENE II. The Forum.

1 *[Enter Brutus and Cassius, with a throng of Citizens.]*

2 CITIZENS.
3 We will be satisfied; let us be satisfied.

4 BRUTUS.
5 Then follow me, and give me audience, friends.—
6 Cassius, go you into the other street
7 And part the numbers.—
8 Those that will hear me speak, let 'em stay here;
9 Those that will follow Cassius, go with him;
10 And public reasons shall be **rendered**
11 Of Caesar's death.

12 FIRST CITIZEN.
13 I will hear Brutus speak.

14 SECOND CITIZEN.
15 I will hear Cassius; and compare their reasons,
16 When severally we hear them rendered.

17 *[Exit Cassius, with some of the Citizens. Brutus goes into the rostrum.]*

18 THIRD CITIZEN.
19 The noble Brutus is ascended: silence!

20 BRUTUS.
21 Be patient till the last.
22 Romans, countrymen, and lovers! Hear me for my cause; and be
23 silent, that you may hear: believe me for mine honour, and have

24 respect to mine honor, that you may believe: **censure** me in your
25 wisdom; and awake your senses, that you may the better judge.
26 If there be any in this assembly, any dear friend of Caesar's, to
27 him I say that Brutus' love to Caesar was no less than his. If
28 then that friend demand why Brutus rose against Caesar, this is
29 my answer,—Not that I loved Caesar less, but that I loved Rome
30 more. Had you rather Caesar were living, and die all slaves, than
31 that Caesar were dead, to live all freemen? As Caesar loved me, I
32 weep for him; as he was fortunate, I rejoice at it; as he was
33 valiant, I honour him; but, as he was ambitious, I slew him.
34 There is tears for his love; joy for his fortune; honour for his
35 valour; and death for his ambition. Who is here so base that
36 would be a bondman? If any, speak; for him have I offended. Who
37 is here so rude that would not be a Roman? If any, speak; for him
38 have I offended. Who is here so vile that will not love his
39 country? If any, speak; for him have I offended. I pause for a
40 reply.

41 CITIZENS.
42 None, Brutus, none.

43 BRUTUS.
44 Then none have I offended. I have done no more to Caesar
45 than you shall do to Brutus. The question of his death is
46 enroll'd in the Capitol, his glory not **extenuated,** wherein he
47 was worthy; nor his offenses enforced, for which he suffered
48 death.

49 *[Enter Antony and others, with Caesar's body.]*

50 Here comes his body, mourned by Mark Antony, who, though he had
51 no hand in his death, shall receive the benefit of his dying, a
52 place in the commonwealth; as which of you shall not? With this
53 I depart— that, as I slew my best lover for the good of Rome, I
54 have the same dagger for myself, when it shall please my country
55 to need my death.

56 CITIZENS.
57 Live, Brutus! live, live!

58 FIRST CITIZEN.
59 Bring him with triumph home unto his house.

60 SECOND CITIZEN.
61 Give him a statue with his ancestors.

Please note that excerpts and passages in the StudySync® library and this workbook are intended as touchstones to generate interest in an author's work. The excerpts and passages do not substitute for the reading of entire texts, and StudySync® strongly recommends that students seek out and purchase the whole literary or informational work in order to experience it as the author intended. Links to online resellers are available in our digital library. In addition, complete works may be ordered through an authorized reseller by filling out and returning to StudySync® the order form enclosed in this workbook.

62 THIRD CITIZEN.
63 Let him be Caesar.

64 FOURTH CITIZEN.
65 Caesar's better parts
66 Shall be crown'd in Brutus.

67 FIRST CITIZEN.
68 We'll bring him to his house with shouts and clamours.

69 BRUTUS.
70 My countrymen,—

71 SECOND CITIZEN.
72 Peace! silence! Brutus speaks.

73 FIRST CITIZEN.
74 Peace, ho!

75 BRUTUS.
76 Good countrymen, let me depart alone,
77 And, for my sake, stay here with Antony:
78 Do grace to Caesar's corpse, and grace his speech
79 Tending to Caesar's glory; which Mark Antony,
80 By our permission, is allow'd to make.
81 I do entreat you, not a man depart,
82 Save I alone, till Antony have spoke.

83 [Exit.]

84 FIRST CITIZEN.
85 Stay, ho! and let us hear Mark Antony.

86 THIRD CITIZEN.
87 Let him go up into the public chair;
88 We'll hear him.—Noble Antony, go up.

89 ANTONY.
90 For Brutus' sake, I am beholding to you.

91 [Goes up.]

92 FOURTH CITIZEN.
93 What does he say of Brutus?

94 THIRD CITIZEN.
95 He says, for Brutus' sake,
96 He finds himself beholding to us all.

97 FOURTH CITIZEN.
98 'Twere best he speak no harm of Brutus here.

99 FIRST CITIZEN.
100 This Caesar was a tyrant.

101 THIRD CITIZEN.
102 Nay, that's certain:
103 We are blest that Rome is rid of him.

104 SECOND CITIZEN.
105 Peace! let us hear what Antony can say.

106 ANTONY.
107 You gentle Romans,—

108 CITIZENS.
109 Peace, ho! let us hear him.

110 ANTONY.
111 Friends, Romans, countrymen, lend me your ears;
112 I come to bury Caesar, not to praise him.
113 The evil that men do lives after them;
114 The good is oft interred with their bones:
115 So let it be with Caesar. The noble Brutus
116 Hath told you Caesar was ambitious:
117 If it were so, it was a grievous fault;
118 And grievously hath Caesar answer'd it.
119 Here, under leave of Brutus and the rest,—
120 For Brutus is an honourable man;
121 So are they all, all honorable men,—
122 Come I to speak in Caesar's funeral.
123 He was my friend, faithful and just to me:
124 But Brutus says he was ambitious;
125 And Brutus is an honourable man.
126 He hath brought many captives home to Rome,
127 Whose ransoms did the general **coffers** fill:
128 Did this in Caesar seem ambitious?
129 When that the poor have cried, Caesar hath wept:
130 Ambition should be made of sterner stuff:
131 Yet Brutus says he was ambitious;
132 And Brutus is an honourable man.

133 You all did see that on the Lupercal

134 I thrice presented him a kingly crown,

135 Which he did thrice refuse: was this ambition?

136 Yet Brutus says he was ambitious;

137 And, sure, he is an honourable man.

138 I speak not to disprove what Brutus spoke,

139 But here I am to speak what I do know.

140 You all did love him once,—not without cause:

141 What cause withholds you, then, to mourn for him?—

142 O judgment, thou art fled to brutish beasts,

143 And men have lost their reason!—Bear with me;

144 My heart is in the coffin there with Caesar,

145 And I must pause till it come back to me.

146 FIRST CITIZEN.

147 Methinks there is much reason in his sayings.

148 SECOND CITIZEN.

149 If thou consider rightly of the matter,

150 Caesar has had great wrong.

151 THIRD CITIZEN.

152 Has he not, masters?

153 I fear there will a worse come in his place.

154 FOURTH CITIZEN.

155 Mark'd ye his words? He would not take the crown;

156 Therefore 'tis certain he was not ambitious.

157 FIRST CITIZEN.

158 If it be found so, some will dear abide it.

159 SECOND CITIZEN.

160 Poor soul! his eyes are red as fire with weeping.

161 THIRD CITIZEN.

162 There's not a nobler man in Rome than Antony.

163 FOURTH CITIZEN.

164 Now mark him; he begins again to speak.

165 ANTONY.

166 But yesterday the word of Caesar might

167 Have stood against the world: now lies he there,

168 And none so poor to do him reverence.

169 O masters, if I were disposed to stir

170 Your hearts and minds to mutiny and rage,
171 I should do Brutus wrong and Cassius wrong,
172 Who, you all know, are honourable men:
173 I will not do them wrong; I rather choose
174 To wrong the dead, to wrong myself, and you,
175 Than I will wrong such honourable men.
176 But here's a parchment with the seal of Caesar,—
177 I found it in his closet,—'tis his will:
178 Let but the commons hear this testament,—
179 Which, pardon me, I do not mean to read,—
180 And they would go and kiss dead Caesar's wounds,
181 And dip their napkins in his sacred blood;
182 Yea, beg a hair of him for memory,
183 And, dying, mention it within their wills,
184 **Bequeathing** it as a rich legacy
185 Unto their issue.

186 FOURTH CITIZEN.
187 We'll hear the will: read it, Mark Antony.

188 CITIZENS.
189 The will, the will! We will hear Caesar's will.

190 ANTONY.
191 Have patience, gentle friends, I must not read it;
192 It is not meet you know how Caesar loved you.
193 You are not wood, you are not stones, but men;
194 And, being men, hearing the will of Caesar,
195 It will inflame you, it will make you mad.
196 'Tis good you know not that you are his heirs;
197 For if you should, O, what would come of it!

198 FOURTH CITIZEN.
199 Read the will! we'll hear it, Antony;
200 You shall read us the will,—Caesar's will!

201 ANTONY.
202 Will you be patient? will you stay awhile?
203 I have o'ershot myself to tell you of it:
204 I fear I wrong the honorable men
205 Whose daggers have stabb'd Caesar; I do fear it.

206 FOURTH CITIZEN.
207 They were traitors: honourable men!

208   CITIZENS.
209   The will! The testament!

210   SECOND CITIZEN.
211   They were villains, murderers. The will! read the will!

212   ANTONY.
213   You will compel me, then, to read the will?
214   Then make a ring about the corpse of Caesar,
215   And let me show you him that made the will.
216   Shall I descend? and will you give me leave?

217   CITIZENS.
218   Come down.

219   SECOND CITIZEN.
220   Descend.

221   *[He comes down.]*

222   THIRD CITIZEN.
223   You shall have leave.

224   FOURTH CITIZEN.
225   A ring! stand round.

226   FIRST CITIZEN.
227   Stand from the hearse, stand from the body.

228   SECOND CITIZEN.
229   Room for Antony!—most noble Antony!

230   ANTONY.
231   Nay, press not so upon me; stand far' off.

232   CITIZENS.
233   Stand back; room! bear back.

234   ANTONY.
235   If you have tears, prepare to shed them now.
236   You all do know this mantle: I remember
237   The first time ever Caesar put it on;
238   'Twas on a Summer's evening, in his tent,
239   That day he overcame the Nervii.
240   Look, in this place ran Cassius' dagger through:
241   See what a rent the envious Casca made:

242 Through this the well-beloved Brutus stabb'd;
243 And as he pluck'd his cursed steel away,
244 Mark how the blood of Caesar follow'd it,—
245 As rushing out of doors, to be resolved
246 If Brutus so unkindly knock'd, or no;
247 For Brutus, as you know, was Caesar's angel:
248 Judge, O you gods, how dearly Caesar loved him!
249 This was the most unkindest cut of all;
250 For when the noble Caesar saw him stab,
251 Ingratitude, more strong than traitors' arms,
252 Quite vanquish'd him: then burst his mighty heart;
253 And, in his mantle muffling up his face,
254 Even at the base of Pompey's statua,
255 Which all the while ran blood, great Caesar fell.
256 O, what a fall was there, my countrymen!
257 Then I, and you, and all of us fell down,
258 Whilst bloody treason flourish'd over us.
259 O, now you weep; and, I perceive, you feel
260 The dint of pity: these are gracious drops.
261 Kind souls, what, weep you when you but behold
262 Our Caesar's vesture wounded? Look you here,
263 Here is himself, marr'd, as you see, with traitors.

264 FIRST CITIZEN.
265 O piteous spectacle!

266 SECOND CITIZEN.
267 O noble Caesar!

268 THIRD CITIZEN.
269 O woeful day!

270 FOURTH CITIZEN.
271 O traitors, villains!

272 FIRST CITIZEN.
273 O most bloody sight!

274 SECOND CITIZEN.
275 We will be revenged.

276 CITIZENS.
277 Revenge,—about,—seek,—burn,—fire,—kill,—slay,—let not a
278 traitor live!

279 ANTONY.
280 Stay, countrymen.

281 FIRST CITIZEN.
282 Peace there! hear the noble Antony.

283 SECOND CITIZEN.
284 We'll hear him, we'll follow him, we'll die with him.

285 ANTONY.
286 Good friends, sweet friends, let me not stir you up
287 To such a sudden flood of mutiny.
288 They that have done this deed are honourable:
289 What private griefs they have, alas, I know not,
290 That made them do it; they're wise and honourable,
291 And will, no doubt, with reasons answer you.
292 I come not, friends, to steal away your hearts:
293 I am no orator, as Brutus is;
294 But, as you know me all, a plain blunt man,
295 That love my friend; and that they know full well
296 That gave me public leave to speak of him:
297 For I have neither wit, nor words, nor worth,
298 Action, nor utterance, nor the power of speech,
299 To stir men's blood: I only speak right on;
300 I tell you that which you yourselves do know;
301 Show you sweet Caesar's wounds, poor dumb mouths,
302 And bid them speak for me: but were I Brutus,
303 And Brutus Antony, there were an Antony
304 Would ruffle up your spirits, and put a tongue
305 In every wound of Caesar, that should move
306 The stones of Rome to rise and mutiny.

307 CITIZENS.
308 We'll mutiny.

309 FIRST CITIZEN.
310 We'll burn the house of Brutus.

311 THIRD CITIZEN.
312 Away, then! come, seek the conspirators.

313 ANTONY.
314 Yet hear me, countrymen; yet hear me speak.

315 CITIZENS.
316 Peace, ho! hear Antony; most noble Antony!

Copyright © BookheadEd Learning, LLC

317 ANTONY.
318 Why, friends, you go to do you know not what.
319 Wherein hath Caesar thus deserved your loves?
320 Alas, you know not; I must tell you then:
321 You have forgot the will I told you of.

322 CITIZENS.
323 Most true; the will!—let's stay, and hear the will.

324 ANTONY.
325 Here is the will, and under Caesar's seal.
326 To every Roman citizen he gives,
327 To every several man, seventy-five drachmas.

328 SECOND CITIZEN.
329 Most noble Caesar!—we'll revenge his death.

330 THIRD CITIZEN.
331 O, royal Caesar!

332 ANTONY.
333 Hear me with patience.

334 CITIZENS.
335 Peace, ho!

336 ANTONY.
337 Moreover, he hath left you all his walks,
338 His private arbors, and new-planted orchards,
339 On this side Tiber: he hath left them you,
340 And to your heirs forever; common pleasures,
341 To walk abroad, and recreate yourselves.
342 Here was a Caesar! when comes such another?

343 FIRST CITIZEN.
344 Never, never.—Come, away, away!
345 We'll burn his body in the holy place,
346 And with the brands fire the traitors' houses.
347 Take up the body.

348 SECOND CITIZEN.
349 Go, fetch fire.

350 THIRD CITIZEN.
351 Pluck down benches.

352 FOURTH CITIZEN.
353 Pluck down forms, windows, any thing.

354 *[Exeunt Citizens, with the body.]*

355 ANTONY.
356 Now let it work.—Mischief, thou art afoot,
357 Take thou what course thou wilt!—

THINK QUESTIONS

1. Use details from the text to support your understanding of why, according to Brutus, he and other senators killed Caesar. Provide evidence that is directly stated in the selection as well as ideas that you have inferred from clues in the text.

2. Write a few sentences explaining why Mark Antony refers to Brutus and the other conspirators as "honourable" men? What examples of Caesar's ambition does Mark Antony raise and why? Cite evidence from the text to support your answers.

3. How does Mark Antony use Caesar's will to sway the emotions of the citizens? Support your answer with evidence from the text.

4. Use context to determine the meaning of the word **rendered** as it is used in *Julius Caesar*. Write your definition of "rendered" and tell how you arrived at it.

5. Use context to determine the meaning of the word **coffers** as it is used in *Julius Caesar*. Write your definition of "coffers" and tell how you arrived at it.

CLOSE READ

Reread the excerpt from *Julius Caesar*. As you reread, complete the Focus Questions below. Then use your answers and annotations from the questions to help you complete the Writing Prompt.

FOCUS QUESTIONS

1. Explain how Shakespeare uses Brutus's opening speech to set the scene. Then analyze the persuasive tactics Brutus uses in this speech and to what effect. What does Brutus mean when he says after it, "Then none have I offended"?

2. Reread Brutus's final words to the crowd before he leaves the Forum. Why do you think Brutus requests that "not a man depart" until Mark Antony has spoken of Caesar? How might the film clip of these lines from the 2012 Royal Shakespeare Company stage production shed light on this question?

3. Compare and contrast Plutarch's treatment of Antony's remarks about Caesar's garments with Shakespeare's treatment of the same. What was Antony's motivation for this display?

4. Compare and contrast the role of the crowd in Plutarch's text with the role it plays in Shakespeare's play. Why are the crowds important? In what ways are the two crowds alike and different?

5. Compare and contrast the characters of Brutus and Antony as they are revealed in Act III, Scene II of *Julius Caesar*. How are they most alike and most different? How do their actions and interactions define them?

WRITING PROMPT

How does Shakespeare transform the source material from Sir Thomas North's translation of *Plutarch's Lives* in Act III, Scene II of his play *Julius Caesar*? In what ways are the two texts similar and different? Use your understanding of comparison and contrast to explore how and why Shakespeare incorporated, expanded upon, and deviated from Plutarch's accounts of Caesar's funeral in the biographies of Caesar, Brutus, and Antonius. How did such transformations enhance the development of character and theme in the play? What dramatic effects might these artistic decisions on Shakespeare's part have been intended to have the audience, and how have different film versions illustrated these effects in different ways? Support your writing with evidence from the text.

Please note that excerpts and passages in the StudySync® library and this workbook are intended as touchstones to generate interest in an author's work. The excerpts and passages do not substitute for the reading of entire texts, and StudySync® strongly recommends that students seek out and purchase the whole literary or informational work in order to experience it as the author intended. Links to online resellers are available in our digital library. In addition, complete works may be ordered through an authorized reseller by filling out and returning to StudySync® the order form enclosed in this workbook.

Reading & Writing Companion   341

CIVIL PEACE

FICTION
Chinua Achebe
1972

INTRODUCTION

Chinua Achebe was a Nigerian novelist, poet, essayist and lecturer. Amid some controversy, Achebe elected to write in English, "the language of colonizers," in order to reach the broadest possible audience. He is best known for his novel *Things Fall Apart*, which remains today the most widely read work of African literature. In the short story here, "Civil Peace," Achebe provides a true-to-life description of Nigeria in the early 1970s, shortly after the Biafran War

"Nothing puzzles God."

 ## FIRST READ

NOTES

1   Jonathan Iwegbu counted himself extraordinarily lucky. "Happy survival!" meant so much more to him than just a current fashion of greeting old friends in the first hazy days of peace. It went deep to his heart. He had come out of the war with five inestimable blessings—his head, his wife Maria's head and the heads of three out of their four children. As a bonus he also had his old bicycle—a miracle too but naturally not to be compared to the safety of five human heads.

2   The bicycle had a little history of its own. One day at the height of the war it was commandeered "for urgent military action." Hard as its loss would have been to him he would still have let it go without a thought had he not had some doubts about the genuineness of the officer. It wasn't his disreputable rags, nor the toes peeping out of one blue and one brown canvas shoes, nor yet the two stars of his rank done obviously in a hurry in biro, that troubled Jonathan; many good and heroic soldiers looked the same or worse. It was rather a certain lack of grip and firmness in his manner. So Jonathan, suspecting he might be **amenable** to influence, rummaged in his raffia bag and produced the two pounds with which he had been going to buy firewood which his wife, Maria, retailed to camp officials for extra stock-fish and corn meal, and got his bicycle back. That night he buried it in the little clearing in the bush where the dead of the camp, including his own youngest son, were buried. When he dug it up again a year later after the surrender all it needed was a little palm-oil greasing. "Nothing puzzles God," he said in wonder.

3   He put it to immediate use as a taxi and accumulated a small pile of Biafran money ferrying camp officials and their families across the four-mile stretch to the nearest tarred road. His standard charge per trip was six pounds and those who had the money were only glad to be rid of some of it in this way. At the end of a fortnight he had made a small fortune of one hundred and fifteen pounds.

4   Then he made the journey to Enugu and found another miracle waiting for him. It was unbelievable. He rubbed his eyes and looked again and it was still

standing there before him. But, needless to say, even that monumental blessing must be accounted also totally inferior to the five heads in the family. This newest miracle was his little house in Ogui Overside. Indeed nothing puzzles God! Only two houses away a huge concrete edifice some wealthy contractor had put up just before the war was a mountain of rubble. And here was Jonathan's little zinc house of no regrets built with mud blocks quite intact! Of course the doors and windows were missing and five sheets off the roof. But what was that? And anyhow he had returned to Enugu early enough to pick up bits of old zinc and wood and soggy sheets of cardboard lying around the neighbourhood before thousands more came out of their forest holes looking for the same things. He got a **destitute** carpenter with one old hammer, a blunt plane and a few bent and rusty nails in his tool bag to turn this assortment of wood, paper and metal into door and window shutters for five Nigerian shillings or fifty Biafran pounds. He paid the pounds, and moved in with his overjoyed family carrying five heads on their shoulders.

5   His children picked mangoes near the military cemetery and sold them to soldiers' wives for a few pennies—real pennies this time—and his wife started making breakfast akara balls for neighbours in a hurry to start life again. With his family earnings he took his bicycle to the villages around and bought fresh palm-wine which he mixed generously in his rooms with the water which had recently started running again in the public tap down the road, and opened up a bar for soldiers and other lucky people with good money.

6   At first he went daily, then every other day and finally once a week, to the offices of the Coal Corporation where he used to be a miner, to find out what was what. The only thing he did find out in the end was that the little house of his was even a greater blessing than he had thought. Some of his fellow ex-miners who had nowhere to return at the end of the day's waiting just slept outside the doors of the offices and cooked what meal they could **scrounge** together in Bournvita tins. As the weeks lengthened and still nobody could say what was what Jonathan discontinued his weekly visits altogether and faced his palm-wine bar.

7   But nothing puzzles God. Came the day of the windfall when after five days of endless scuffles in queues and counter-queues in the sun outside the Treasury he had twenty pounds counted into his palms as ex-gratia award for the rebel money he had turned in. It was like Christmas for him and for many others like him when the payments began. They called it (since few could manage its proper official name) egg-rasher.

8   As soon as the pound notes were placed in his palm Jonathan simply closed it tight over them and buried fist and money inside his trouser pocket. He had to be extra careful because he had seen a man a couple of days earlier collapse into near-madness in an instant before that oceanic crowd because no sooner had he got his twenty pounds than some heartless **ruffian** picked

it off him. Though it was not right that a man in such an extremity of agony should be blamed yet many in the queues that day were able to remark quietly on the victim's carelessness, especially after he pulled out the innards of his pocket and revealed a hole in it big enough to pass a thief's head. But of course he had insisted that the money had been in the other pocket, pulling it out too to show its comparative wholeness. So one had to be careful.

9 Jonathan soon transferred the money to his left hand and pocket so as to leave his right free for shaking hands should the need arise, though by fixing his gaze at such an elevation as to miss all approaching human faces he made sure that the need did not arise, until he got home.

10 He was normally a heavy sleeper but that night he heard all the neighbourhood noises die down one after another. Even the night watchman who knocked the hour on some metal somewhere in the distance had fallen silent after knocking one o'clock. That must have been the last thought in Jonathan's mind before he was finally carried away himself. He couldn't have been gone for long, though, when he was violently awakened again.

11 'Who is knocking?' whispered his wife lying beside him on the floor.

12 "I don't know," he whispered back breathlessly.

13 The second time the knocking came it was so loud and imperious that the rickety old door could have fallen down.

14 "Who is knocking?" he asked then, his voice parched and trembling.

15 "Na tief-man and him people," came the cool reply. "Make you hopen de door." This was followed by the heaviest knocking of all.

16 Maria was the first to raise the alarm, then he followed and all their children.

17 *"Police-o! Thieves-o! Neighbours-o! Police-o! We are lost! We are dead! Neighbours, are you asleep? Wake up! Police-o!"*

18 This went on for a long time and then stopped suddenly. Perhaps they had scared the thief away. There was total silence. But only for a short while.

19 "You done finish?" asked the voice outside. "Make we help you small. Oya, everybody!"

20 *"Police-o! Tief-man-o! Neighbours-o! we done loss-o! Police-o!. . ."*

21 There were at least five other voices besides the leader's.

22 Jonathan and his family were now completely paralysed by terror. Maria and the children sobbed inaudibly like lost souls. Jonathan groaned continuously.

23 The silence that followed the thieves' alarm vibrated horribly. Jonathan all but begged their leader to speak again and be done with it.

24 "My frien," said he at long last, "we don try our best for call dem but I tink say dem all done sleep-o. . . So wetin we go do now? Sometaim you wan call soja? Or you wan make we call dem for you? Soja better pass police. No be so?"

25 "Na so!" replied his men. Jonathan thought he heard even more voices now than before and groaned heavily. His legs were sagging under him and his throat felt like sand-paper.

26 "My frien, why you no de talk again. I de ask you say you wan make we call soja?"

27 "No."

28 "Awrighto. Now make we talk business. We no be bad tief. We no like for make trouble. Trouble done finish. War done finish and all the katakata wey de for inside. No Civil War again. This time na Civil Peace. No be so?"

29 "Na so!" answered the horrible chorus.

30 'What do you want from me? I am a poor man. Everything I had went with this war. Why do you come to me? You know people who have money. We. . .'

31 "Awright! We know say you no get plenty money. But we sef no get even anini. So derefore make you open dis window and give us one hundred pound and we go commot. Orderwise we de come for inside now to show you guitar-boy like dis. . ."

32 A volley of automatic fire rang through the sky. Maria and the children began to weep aloud again.

33 "Ah, missisi de cry again. No need for dat. We done talk say we na good tief. We just take our small money and go nwayorly. No molest. Abi we de molest?"

34 "At all!" sang the chorus.

35 "My friends," began Jonathan hoarsely. "I hear what you say and I thank you. If I had one hundred pounds. . ."

36 "Lookia my frien, no be play we come play for your house. If we make mistake and step for inside you no go like am-o. So derefore. . ."

37 "To God who made me; if you come inside and find one hundred pounds, take it and shoot me and shoot my wife and children. I swear to God. The only money I have in this life is this twenty-pounds egg-rasher they gave me today. . ."

NOTES

38 "OK. Time de go. Make you open dis window and bring the twenty pound. We go manage am like dat."

39 There were now loud murmurs of dissent among the chorus: 'Na lie de man de lie; e get plenty money. . . Make we go inside and search properly well... Wetin be twenty pound?. . .

40 "Shurrup!" rang the leader's voice like a lone shot in the sky and silenced the murmuring at once. "Are you dere? Bring the money quick!"

41 "I am coming," said Jonathan fumbling in the darkness with the key of the small wooden box he kept by his side on the mat.

42 At the first sign of light as neighbours and others assembled to **commiserate** with him he was already strapping his five-gallon demijohn to his bicycle carrier and his wife, sweating in the open fire, was turning over akara balls in a wide clay bowl of boiling oil. In the corner his eldest son was rinsing out dregs of yesterday's palm wine from old beer bottles.

43 "I count it as nothing," he told his sympathizers, his eyes on the rope he was tying. "What is egg-rasher? Did I depend on it last week? Or is it greater than other things that went with the war? I say, let egg-rasherperish in the flames! Let it go where everything else has gone. Nothing puzzles God."

"Civil Peace," copyright © 1972 , 1973 by Chinua Achebe; from GIRLS AT WAR: AND OTHER STORIES by Chinua Achebe. Used by permission of Doubleday, an imprint of the Knopf Doubleday Publishing Group, a division of Random House LLC. All rights reserved.

THINK QUESTIONS

1. How did the civil war affect Jonathan and his neighbors? How does Jonathan begin to rebuild his life after the war? Cite textual evidence to support your answer.

2. What is Jonathan like as a person? Support your answer with textual evidence.

3. How do Jonathan's neighbors respond when he calls for help? Make an inference about why, and support it with evidence.

4. Use context to determine the meaning of the word **scrounge** as it is used in *Civil Peace*. Write your definition of "scrounge" and tell how you arrived it.

5. Remembering that the Latin prefix *com-* means "together with" and the Latin suffix *-ate* indicates an action, and comparing "commiserate" to the familiar words "miserable" and "misery," use the context clues provided in the passage to determine the meaning of **commiserate.** Write your definition of "commiserate" and tell how you arrived at it.

CLOSE READ

Reread the short story "Civil Peace." As you reread, complete the Focus Questions below. Then use your answers and annotations from the questions to help you complete the Writing Prompt.

FOCUS QUESTIONS

1. In the first two paragraphs of "Civil Peace," Jonathan's bicycle is one of the main topics. Why is the bicycle so important in setting up the story? What is the author conveying about the cultural context by focusing on the bicycle? Highlight evidence from the text and make annotations to support your interpretation.

2. Returning to the city of Enugu, Jonathan and his family begin a new life. What do their activities tell you about the cultural context? Support your answer with textual evidence and make annotations to explain your answer.

3. In the eighth paragraph, Jonathan thinks about the incident of the man who was robbed of his *ex gratia* award. He also thinks about the response of onlookers to the robbery. State two inferences that you make about the cultural context based on that incident. Highlight your textual evidence and make annotations to support your inferences.

4. The last third of the story describes Jonathan's encounter with the robbers. What is the leader of the robbers like? How do his interactions with Jonathan help define who he is? Highlight and annotate evidence from the text to support your analysis.

5. In the concluding two paragraphs, Jonathan's neighbors commiserate with him, and he explains his feelings to them. What theme do his words convey? Highlight textual evidence and make annotations to support your point.

WRITING PROMPT

What theme is conveyed by the story's repeated statement, "Nothing puzzles God"? What does the statement reveal about Jonathan's character? What does it show about the cultural context of Jonathan's life? Write a response to these questions. Cite evidence from the story to support your response.

THE BOOK THIEF

FICTION
Markus Zusak
2005

INTRODUCTION

Australian author Markus Zusak's acclaimed novel is set in Nazi Germany, where foster child Liesel Meminger develops an unusual passion—stealing books. Narrated by Death, who describes how busy he was at the time, the story focuses on Liesel's love for books as well as her relationships with her parents, her neighbors, and a Jewish fighter hiding in her basement. In the excerpt below, Death tells of his first encounter with the protagonist, then nine years old.

"It's the leftover humans.
The survivors."

 ## FIRST READ

Part 1: DEATH AND CHOCOLATE

1   First the colors.

2   Then the humans.

3   That's usually how I see things.

4   Or at least, how I try.

5   *****HERE IS A SMALL FACT *****
                            You are going to die.

6   I am in all truthfulness attempting to be cheerful about this whole topic, though most people find themselves hindered in believing me, no matter my **protestations**. Please, trust me. I most definitely can be cheerful. I can be amiable. Agreeable. **Affable**. And that's only the A's. Just don't ask me to be nice. Nice has nothing to do with me.

7   *****Reaction to the *****
                            AFOREMENTIONED fact
                            Does this worry you? urge you
                            —don't be afraid.
                            I'm nothing if not fair.

8   —Of course, an introduction.

9   A beginning.

10 Where are my manners?

11   I could introduce myself properly, but it's not really necessary. You will know me well enough and soon enough, depending on a diverse range of variables. It suffices to say that at some point in time, I will be standing over you, as genially as possible. Your soul will be in my arms. A color will be perched on my shoulder. I will carry you gently away.

12   At that moment, you will be lying there (I rarely find people standing up). You will be caked in your own body. There might be a discovery; a scream will dribble down the air. The only sound I'll hear after that will be my own breathing, and the sound of the smell, of my footsteps.

13   The question is, what color will everything be at that moment when I come for you? What will the sky be saying?

14   Personally, I like a chocolate-colored sky. Dark, dark chocolate. People say it suits me. I do, however, try to enjoy every color I see—the whole spectrum. A billion or so flavors, none of them quite the same, and a sky to slowly suck on. It takes the edge off the stress. It helps me relax.

15   *****A SMALL THEORY *****
People observe the colors of a day only at its beginnings and ends, but to me it's quite clear that a day merges through a multitude of shades and intonations, with each passing moment. A single hour can consist of thousands of different colors.Waxy yellows, cloud-spat blues. Murky darknesses.
In my line of work, I make it a point to notice them.

16   As I've been alluding to, my one saving grace is distraction. It keeps me sane. It helps me cope, considering the length of time I've been performing this job. The trouble is, who could ever replace me? Who could step in while I take a break in your stock-standard resort-style vacation destination, whether it be tropical or of the ski trip variety? The answer, of course, is nobody, which has prompted me to make a conscious, deliberate decision—to make distraction my vacation. Needless to say, I vacation in **increments.** In colors.

17   Still, it's possible that you might be asking, why does he even need a vacation? What does he need distraction from?

18   Which brings me to my next point.

19   It's the leftover humans. The survivors.

20   They're the ones I can't stand to look at, although on many occasions I still fail. I deliberately seek out the colors to keep my mind off them, but now and then, I witness the ones who are left behind, crumbling among the jigsaw

puzzle of realization, despair, and surprise. They have punctured hearts. They have beaten lungs.

21 Which in turn brings me to the subject I am telling you about tonight, or today, or whatever the hour and color. It's the story of one of those perpetual survivors—an expert at being left behind.

22 It's just a small story really, about, among other things:

23 › A girl
   › Some words
   › An accordionist
   › Some fanatical Germans* A Jewish fist fighter
   › And quite a lot of thievery

24 I saw the book thief three times.

Part 2: BESIDE THE RAILWAY LINE

25 First up is something white. Of the blinding kind.

26 Some of you are most likely thinking that white is not really a color and all of that tired sort of nonsense. Well, I'm here to tell you that it is. White is without question a color, and personally, I don't think you want to argue with me.

27 *****A REASSURING ANNOUNCEMENT *****
Please, be calm, despite that previous threat.
I am all bluster—
I am not violent.
I am not malicious.
I am a result.

28 Yes, it was white.

29 It felt as though the whole globe was dressed in snow. Like it had pulled it on, the way you pull on a sweater.

30 Next to the train line, footprints were sunken to their shins. Trees wore blankets of ice.

31 As you might expect, someone had died.

32 They couldn't just leave him on the ground. For now, it wasn't such a problem, but very soon, the track ahead would be cleared and the train would need to move on.

33 There were two guards.

34   There was one mother and her daughter.

35   One corpse.

36   The mother, the girl, and the corpse remained stubborn and silent.

37   "Well, what else do you want me to do?"

38   The guards were tall and short. The tall one always spoke first, though he was not in charge. He looked at the smaller, rounder one. The one with the juicy red face.

39   "Well," was the response, "we can't just leave them like this, can we?"

40   The tall one was losing patience. "Why not?"

41   And the smaller one damn near exploded. He looked up at the tall one's chin and cried, "Spinnst du! Are you stupid?!" The abhorrence on his cheeks was growing thicker by the moment. His skin widened. "Come on," he said, traipsing over the snow. "We'll carry all three of them back on if we have to. We'll notify the next stop."

42   As for me, I had already made the most elementary of mistakes. I can't explain to you the severity of my self-disappointment. Originally, I'd done everything right:

43   I studied the blinding, white-snow sky who stood at the window of the moving train. I practically inhaled it, but still, I wavered. I buckled—I became interested. In the girl. Curiosity got the better of me, and I resigned myself to stay as long as my schedule allowed, and I watched.

44   Twenty-three minutes later, when the train was stopped, I climbed out with them.

45   A small soul was in my arms.

46   I stood a little to the right.

47   The dynamic train guard duo made their way back to the mother, the girl, and the small male corpse. I clearly remember that my breath was loud that day. I'm surprised the guards didn't notice me as they walked by. The world was sagging now, under the weight of all that snow.

48   Perhaps ten meters to my left, the pale, empty-stomached girl was standing, frost-stricken.

49   Her mouth jittered.

50   Her cold arms were folded.

51   Tears were frozen to the book thief's face.

Excerpted from The Book Thief by Markus Zusak, published by Alfred A. Knopf.

THINK QUESTIONS

1. Which aspect of the world most fascinates the narrator of *The Book Thief*? Why? Cite details from the text to support your response.

2. How does Death react to the survivors after he takes a life? Why does he react this way? Cite details from the text in your response.

3. Based on your knowledge of Europe during the 1940s, why do you think the author chose Death to narrate this story? Provide reasons or evidence to explain your response.

4. Look up the definition of **protestation** in a dictionary. Then rewrite the sentence in which the word "protestations" appears in the selection, replacing this term with a synonym.

5. Use context to determine the meaning of the word **increments** as it is used within the text. Write your definition of "increments," and tell how you arrived at it.

CLOSE READ

Reread the excerpt from *The Book Thief*. As you reread, complete the Focus Questions below. Then use your answers and annotations from the questions to help you complete the Writing Prompt.

FOCUS QUESTIONS

1. In the first part of the excerpt, why does the narrator value escape from his work and feel a need for occasional relief? How is this helpful to him? Support your answer with textual evidence and make annotations to explain your answer choices.

2. Analyze the format and writing style author Markus Zusak uses at the beginning of the second passage. How does the story structure affect readers? What does it help them understand? Highlight evidence from the text and make annotations to support your explanation.

3. In the second passage, how does the narrator describe the Book Thief? Which details does he include? What do these details help the reader to visualize? Highlight evidence from the text and make annotations to explain your choices.

4. What do readers learn about the Book Thief in the second passage? Who is she and where is she? What has happened to her recently? What might this foreshadow? Support your answer with textual evidence and make annotations to explain your answer choices.

5. How do Death's interactions with survivors affect him? How might his interactions with the Book Thief define and shape him as the story progresses? Highlight textual evidence and make annotations to explain your ideas.

WRITING PROMPT

How does the imagery of color work in this excerpt? Choose at least three instances of color imagery in this excerpt, and analyze what it represents and how it adds to the meaning of the passage as a whole. Your analysis should be at least 300 words long, and you should use quotes from the text in support of your assertions.

Reading & Writing
Companion

NIGHT

NON-FICTION

Elie Wiesel
1955

INTRODUCTION

studysync tv

Nobel Prize winner Elie Wiesel's autobiographical account of a Jewish teenager and his father struggling to stay alive in a World War II concentration camp delivers an impact that few readers can ever forget. The narrator describes his first night at Birkenau and its indelible physical and mental effects

"Never shall I forget those flames that consumed my faith forever."

 FIRST READ

NOTES

From Section 3

1   Never shall I forget that night, the first night in camp, that turned my life into one long night seven times sealed.

2   Never shall I forget that smoke.

3   Never shall I forget the small faces of the children whose bodies I saw transformed into smoke under a silent sky.

4   Never shall I forget those flames that consumed my faith forever.

5   Never shall I forget the **nocturnal** silence that deprived me for all eternity of the desire to live.

6   Never shall I forget those moments that murdered my God and my soul and turned my dreams to ashes.

7   Never shall I forget those things, even were I condemned to live as long as God Himself.

8   Never.

9   The barrack we had been assigned to was very long. On the roof, a few bluish skylights. I thought: This is what the **antechamber** of hell must look like. So many crazed men, so much shouting, so much brutality.

10 Dozens of inmates were there to receive us, sticks in hand, striking anywhere, anyone, without reason. The orders came:

11 "Strip! Hurry up! *Raus!* Hold on only to your belt and your shoes . . ."

12 Our clothes were to be thrown on the floor at the back of the barrack. There was a pile there already. New suits, old ones, torn overcoats, rags. For us it meant true equality: nakedness. We trembled in the cold.

13 A few SS officers wandered through the room, looking for strong men. If vigor was that appreciated, perhaps one should try to appear sturdy? My father thought the opposite. Better not to draw attention. (We later found out that he had been right. Those who were selected that day were incorporated into the Sonder-Kommando, the Kommando working in the **crematoria.** Béla Katz, the son of an important merchant of my town, had arrived in Birkenau with the first transport, one week ahead of us. When he found out that we were there, he succeeded in slipping us a note. He told us that having been chosen because of his strength, he had been forced to place his own father's body into the furnace.)

14 The blows continued to rain on us:

15 "To the barber!"

16 Belt and shoes in hand, I let myself be dragged along to the barbers. Their clippers tore out our hair, shaved every hair on our bodies. My head was buzzing; the same thought surfacing over and over: not to be separated from my father.

17 Freed from the barbers' clutches, we began to wander about the crowd, finding friends, acquaintances. Every encounter filled us with joy—yes, joy: Thank God! You are still alive!

18 Some were crying. They used whatever strength they had left to cry. Why had they let themselves be brought here? Why didn't they die in their beds? Their words were **interspersed** with sobs.

19 Suddenly someone threw his arms around me in a hug: Yehiel, the Sighet rebbe's brother. He was weeping bitterly. I thought he was crying with joy at still being alive.

20 "Don't cry, Yehiel," I said. "Don't waste your tears . . ."

21 "Not cry? We're on the threshold of death. Soon, we shall be inside . . . Do you understand? Inside. How could I not cry?"

22 I watched darkness fade through the bluish skylights in the roof. I no longer was afraid. I was overcome by fatigue.

23 The absent no longer entered our thoughts. One spoke of them—who knows what happened to them?—but their fate was not on our minds. We were

incapable of thinking. Our senses were numbed, everything was fading into a fog. We no longer clung to anything. The instincts of self-preservation, of self-defense, of pride, had all deserted us. In one terrifying moment of lucidity, I thought of us as damned souls wandering through the void, souls condemned to wander through space until the end of time, seeking **redemption,** seeking oblivion, without any hope of finding either.

24 Around five o'clock in the morning, we were expelled from the barrack. The Kapos were beating us again, but I no longer felt the pain. A glacial wind was enveloping us. We were naked, holding our shoes and belts. An order:

25 "Run!" And we ran. After a few minutes of running, a new barrack.

26 A barrel of foul-smelling liquid stood by the door. Disinfection. Everybody soaked in it. Then came a hot shower. All very fast. As we left the showers, we were chased outside. And ordered to run some more. Another barrack: the storeroom. Very long tables. Mountains of prison garb. As we ran, they threw the clothes at us: pants, jackets, shirts. . .

27 In a few seconds, we had ceased to be men. Had the situation not been so tragic, we might have laughed. We looked pretty strange! Meir Katz, a colossus, wore a child's pants, and Stern, a skinny little fellow, was floundering in a huge jacket. We immediately started to switch.

28 I glanced over at my father. How changed he looked! His eyes were veiled. I wanted to tell him something, but I didn't know what.

29 The night had passed completely. The morning star shone in the sky. I too had become a different person. The student of Talmud, the child I was, had been consumed by the flames. All that was left was a shape that resembled me. My soul had been invaded—and devoured—by a black flame.

30 So many events had taken place in just a few hours that I had completely lost all notion of time. When had we left our homes? And the ghetto? And the train? Only a week ago? One night? One single night?

31 How long had we been standing in the freezing wind? One hour? A single hour? Sixty minutes?

32 Surely it was a dream.

Excerpted from *Night* by Elie Wiesel, published by Hill and Wang.

THINK QUESTIONS

1. At the beginning of the passage, how does author Elie Wiesel say his first night at the camp affected him? How would you characterize the language he uses? Support your answer with evidence from the text.

2. What are conditions like in the camp? What details indicate these conditions? Include evidence from the text in your answer.

3. What can readers infer about Wiesel's relationship with his father? Support your answer with textual evidence.

4. Use the context clues provided in the passage to determine the meaning of **antechamber.** Write your definition of "antechamber" and tell how you arrived at it.

5. Use context to determine the meaning of the word **interspersed** as it is used in the passage. Write your definition of "interspersed" and tell how you arrived at it.

CLOSE READ

Reread the excerpt from *Night*. As you reread, complete the Focus Questions below. Then use your answers and annotations from the questions to help you complete the Writing Prompt.

FOCUS QUESTIONS

1. Explain the effect on the reader of the section that repeats the word "never." What does this section contribute to the overall mood and tone of the excerpt? Highlight evidence from the text and make annotations to explain your choices.

2. What do the actions and reactions of other inmates suggest about life in the camp? Support your answer with textual evidence and make annotations to explain your answer choices.

3. How does Elie Wiesel use paragraph and sentence structure to mirror his thinking? What effect does this have on the reader? Make annotations to explain your choices.

4. As Elie Wiesel reveals the series of events that he endured, what conclusions does he draw? Cite details from the passage to explain how Wiesel's experiences affect his thinking.

5. In what way does the experience of surviving the death camps now define Wiesel? Highlight textual evidence and make annotations to explain your choices.

WRITING PROMPT

The author keeps a mental catalog of things he "never shall forget." In an essay of at least 300 words, explore why Wiesel maintains these painful memories. Do you agree that he should keep them intact? What would he lose by forgetting them?

Please note that excerpts and passages in the StudySync® library and this workbook are intended as touchstones to generate interest in an author's work. The excerpts and passages do not substitute for the reading of entire texts, and StudySync® strongly recommends that students seek out and purchase the whole literary or informational work in order to experience it as the author intended. Links to online resellers are available in our digital library. In addition, complete works may be ordered through an authorized reseller by filling out and returning to StudySync® the order form enclosed in this workbook.

Reading & Writing Companion **361**

DOVER BEACH

POETRY
Matthew Arnold
1867

INTRODUCTION

Considered by some to be the first distinctly modern poem, the inspiration for Matthew Arnold's "Dover Beach" was likely a honeymoon trip to the English port city of Dover. Perhaps speaking to wife, Arnold writes about the beauty of nature, and notes the conflicts between science and faith.

"Ah, love, let us be true"

FIRST READ

1   The sea is calm to-night.

2   The tide is full, the moon lies fair

3   Upon the straits; on the French coast the light

4   Gleams and is gone; the cliffs of England stand;

5   Glimmering and vast, out in the **tranquil** bay.

6   Come to the window, sweet is the night-air!

7   Only, from the long line of spray

8   Where the sea meets the moon-**blanched** land,

9   Listen! you hear the grating roar

10   Of pebbles which the waves draw back, and fling,

11   At their return, up the high strand,

12   Begin, and cease, and then again begin,

13   With **tremulous cadence** slow, and bring

14   The eternal note of sadness in.

15   Sophocles long ago

16   Heard it on the Agaean, and it brought

17   Into his mind the turbid ebb and flow

18   Of human misery; we

19   Find also in the sound a thought,

20   Hearing it by this distant northern sea.

21   The Sea of Faith

22   Was once, too, at the full, and round earth's shore

23   Lay like the folds of a bright girdle furled.

24   But now I only hear

25 Its melancholy, long, withdrawing roar,

26 Retreating, to the breath

27 Of the night-wind, down the vast edges drear

28 And naked shingles of the world.

29 Ah, love, let us be true

30 To one another! for the world, which seems

31 To lie before us like a land of dreams,

32 So various, so beautiful, so new,

33 Hath really neither joy, nor love, nor light,

34 Nor **certitude,** nor peace, nor help for pain;

35 And we are here as on a darkling plain

36 Swept with confused alarms of struggle and flight,

37 Where ignorant armies clash by night.

 THINK QUESTIONS

1. What contrast in the scene of Dover Beach does the speaker's descriptions in the first stanza illustrate? What emotional effect does the scene have on the speaker? Use text evidence to support your answer.

2. The second stanza of the poem contains an allusion to Sophocles, an ancient Greek dramatist whose tragedies are still read widely today. How is this reference to Sophocles used to make a point about the human condition?

3. How does the speaker in this poem view the world, according to text evidence in the poem?

4. Use context to determine the meaning of the word **tranquil** as it is used in the first stanza of "Dover Beach." Write your definition of "tranquil" and tell how you arrived at it.

5. Use context to determine the meaning of the word **cadence** as it is used in "Dover Beach." Write your definition of "cadence" and tell how you arrived at it.

CLOSE READ

Reread the poem "Dover Beach." As you reread, complete the Focus Questions below. Then use your answers and annotations from the questions to help you complete the Writing Prompt.

FOCUS QUESTIONS

1. Explore the metaphorical significance of the ocean tides in the first two stanzas of the poem. How do words with strong connotations help develop the metaphor?

2. How do the speaker's religious beliefs influence the way he looks upon and reacts to the scene on Dover Beach?

3. Examine the denotations and connotations of the words in the final stanza of the poem and how they are used to develop the overall theme of the poem.

4. What role does the listener in the poem play? How do the speaker's interactions with this person help define his character?

5. What insight does this poem offer about how an individual's interactions with nature may help define his or her character?

WRITING PROMPT

After reading Arnold's poem about looking out on a moonlit ocean, think of a place in nature that has had a powerful effect on you. In a well-developed essay, describe that place in detail, using words with strong connotations as well as denotations. Explain what emotions it inspires in you and why, as well as what insight viewing it might offer about life, faith, the human condition, man's relationship with nature, or some other literary theme. What metaphorical significance might this place have upon deeper reflection? Compare your response to this place to the way Arnold responds to the beach in his poem, analyzing in particular how each of you uses words with strong connotations as well as denotations to set the tone and develop your theme.

Please note that excerpts and passages in the StudySync® library and this workbook are intended as touchstones to generate interest in an author's work. The excerpts and passages do not substitute for the reading of entire texts, and StudySync® strongly recommends that students seek out and purchase the whole literary or informational work in order to experience it as the author intended. Links to online resellers are available in our digital library. In addition, complete works may be ordered through an authorized reseller by filling out and returning to StudySync® the order form enclosed in this workbook.

Reading & Writing Companion

365

CATCH THE MOON

FICTION
Judith Ortiz Cofer
1995

INTRODUCTION

Hailing from a family of storytellers, Judith Ortiz Cofer is a Puerto Rican-born author of award-winning poetry, short stories, essays, and a memoir. She is also a professor of English and Creative Writing at the University of Georgia. Her poems and short stories explore cultural differences and draw upon her experiences as a Latina immigrant, and she has said, "I write in English, yet I write obsessively about my Puerto Rican experience." The selection here, "Catch the Moon," comes from *An Island Like You: Stories of the Barrio*, a book of short stories for young adults.

"Someday, son, all this will be yours..."

FIRST READ

1   Luis Cintrón sits on top of a six-foot pile of hubcaps and watches his father walk away into the steel jungle of his car junkyard. Released into his old man's custody after six months in juvenile hall—for breaking and entering—and he didn't even take anything. He did it on a dare. But the old lady with the million cats was a light sleeper, and good with her aluminum cane. He has a scar on his head to prove it.

2   Now Luis is wondering whether he should have stayed in and done his full time. Jorge Cintrón of Jorge Cintrón & Son, Auto Parts and Salvage, has decided that Luis should wash and polish every hubcap in the yard. The hill he is sitting on is only the latest couple of hundred wheel covers that have come in. Luis grunts and stands up on top of his silver mountain. He yells at no one, "Someday, son, all this will be yours," and sweeps his arms like the Pope blessing a crowd over the piles of car sandwiches and mounds of metal parts that cover this acre of land outside the city. He is the "Son" of Jorge Cintrón & Son, and so far his father has had more than one reason to wish it was plain Jorge Cintrón on the sign.

3   Luis has been getting in trouble since he started high school two years ago, mainly because of the "social group" he organized—a bunch of guys who were into harassing the local authorities. Their thing was taking something to the limit on a dare or, better still, doing something dangerous, like breaking into a house, not to steal, just to prove that they could do it. This was Luis's specialty, coming up with very complicated plans, like military strategies, and assigning the "jobs" to guys who wanted to join the Tiburones.

4   *Tiburón* means "shark," and Luis had gotten the name from watching an old movie about a Puerto Rican gang called the Sharks with his father. Luis thought it was one of the dumbest films he had ever seen. Everybody sang their lines, and the guys all pointed their toes and leaped in the air when they

were supposed to be slaughtering each other. But he liked their name, the Sharks, so he made it Spanish and had it air-painted on his black T-shirt with a killer shark under it, jaws opened wide and dripping with blood. It didn't take long for other guys in the barrio to ask about it.

5   Man, had they had a good time. The girls were interested too. Luis outsmarted everybody by calling his organization a social club and registering it at Central High. That meant they were legal, even let out of last-period class on Fridays for their "club" meetings. It was just this year, after a couple of **botched** jobs, that the teachers had started getting suspicious. The first one to go wrong was when he sent Kenny Matoa to *borrow* some "souvenirs" out of Anita Robles's locker. He got caught. It seems that Matoa had been reading Anita's diary and didn't hear her coming down the hall. Anita was supposed to be in the gym at that time but had copped out with the usual female excuse of cramps. You could hear her screams all the way to Market Street.

6   She told the principal all she knew about the Tiburones, and Luis had to talk fast to convince old Mr. Williams that the club did put on cultural activities such as the Save the Animals talent show. What Mr. Williams didn't know was that the animal that was being "saved" with the ticket sales was Luis's pet boa, which needed quite a few live mice to stay healthy and happy. They kept E. S. (which stood for "Endangered Species") in Luis's room, but she belonged to the club and it was the members' responsibility to raise the money to feed their mascot. So last year they had sponsored their first annual Save the Animals talent show, and it had been a great success. The Tiburones had come dressed as Latino Elvises and did a grand finale to "All Shook Up" that made the audience go wild. Mr. Williams had smiled while Luis talked, maybe remembering how the math teacher, Mrs. Laguna, had dragged him out in the aisle to rock-and-roll with her. Luis had gotten out of that one, but barely.

7   His father was a problem, too. He objected to the T-shirt logo, calling it disgusting and **vulgar.** Mr. Cintrón prided himself on his own neat, elegant style of dressing after work, and on his manners and large vocabulary, which he picked up by taking correspondence courses in just about everything. Luis thought it was just his way of staying busy since Luis's mother had died, almost three years ago, of cancer. He had never gotten over it.

8   All this was going through Luis's head as he slid down the hill of hubcaps. The tub full of soapy water, the can of polish, and the bag of rags had been neatly placed in front of a makeshift table made from two car seats and a piece of plywood. Luis heard a car drive up and someone honk their horn. His father emerged from inside a new red Mustang that had been totaled. He usually **dismantled** every small feature by hand before sending the vehicle into the *cementerio,* as he called the lot. Luis watched as the most beautiful girl he had ever seen climbed out of a **vintage** white Volkswagen Bug. She stood in

the sunlight in her white sundress waiting for his father, while Luis stared. She was like a smooth wood carving. Her skin was mahogany, almost black, and her arms and legs were long and thin, but curved in places so that she did not look bony and hard—more like a ballerina. And her ebony hair was braided close to her head. Luis let his breath out, feeling a little dizzy. He had forgotten to breathe. Both the girl and his father heard him. Mr. Cintrón waved him over.

9 "Luis, the señorita here has lost a wheel cover. Her car is twenty-five years old, so it will not be an easy match. Come look on this side."

10 Luis tossed a wrench he'd been holding into a toolbox like he was annoyed, just to make a point about slave labor. Then he followed his father, who knelt on the gravel and began to point out every detail of the hubcap. Luis was hardly listening. He watched the girl take a piece of paper from her handbag.

11 "Señor Cintrón, I have drawn the hubcap for you, since I will have to leave soon. My home address and telephone number are here, and also my parents' office number." She handed the paper to Mr. Cintrón, who nodded.

12 "Sí, señorita, very good. This will help my son look for it. Perhaps there is one in that stack there." He pointed to the pile of caps that Luis was supposed to wash and polish. "Yes, I'm almost certain that there is a match there. Of course, I do not know if it's near the top or the bottom. You will give us a few days, yes?"

13 Luis just stared at his father like he was crazy. But he didn't say anything because the girl was smiling at him with a funny expression on her face. Maybe she thought he had X-ray eyes like Superman, or maybe she was mocking him.

14 "Please call me Naomi, Señor Cintrón. You know my mother. She is the director of the funeral home. . . ." Mr. Cintrón seemed surprised at first; he prided himself on having a great memory. Then his friendly expression changed to one of sadness as he recalled the day of his wife's burial. Naomi did not finish her sentence. She reached over and placed her hand on Mr. Cintrón's arm for a moment. Then she said "Adiós" softly, and got in her shiny white car. She waved to them as she left, and her gold bracelets flashing in the sun nearly blinded Luis.

15 Mr. Cintrón shook his head. "How about that," he said as if to himself. "They are the Dominican owners of Ramirez Funeral Home." And, with a sigh, "She seems like such a nice young woman. Reminds me of your mother when she was her age."

16 Hearing the funeral parlor's name, Luis remembered too. The day his mother died, he had been in her room at the hospital while his father had gone for

coffee. The alarm had gone off on her monitor and nurses had come running in, pushing him outside. After that, all he recalled was the anger that had made him punch a hole in his bedroom wall. And afterward he had refused to talk to anyone at the funeral. Strange, he did see a black girl there who didn't try like the others to talk to him, but actually ignored him as she escorted family members to the viewing room and brought flowers in. Could it be that the skinny girl in a frilly white dress had been Naomi? She didn't act like she had recognized him today, though. Or maybe she thought that he was a jerk.

17 Luis grabbed the drawing from his father. The old man looked like he wanted to walk down memory lane. But Luis was in no mood to listen to the old stories about his falling in love on a tropical island. The world they'd lived in before he was born wasn't his world. No beaches and palm trees here. Only junk as far as he could see. He climbed back up his hill and studied Naomi's sketch. It had obviously been done very carefully. It was signed "Naomi Ramirez" in the lower right-hand corner. He memorized the telephone number.

18 Luis washed hubcaps all day until his hands were red and raw, but he did not come across the small silver bowl that would fit the VW. After work he took a few practice Frisbee shots across the yard before showing his father what he had accomplished: rows and rows of shiny rings drying in the sun. His father nodded and showed him the bump on his temple where one of Luis's flying saucers had gotten him. "Practice makes perfect, you know. Next time you'll probably **decapitate** me." Luis heard him struggle with the word *decapitate,* which Mr. Cintrón pronounced in syllables. Showing off his big vocabulary again, Luis thought. He looked closely at the bump, though. He felt bad about it.

19 "They look good, hijo," Mr. Cintrón made a sweeping gesture with his arms over the yard. "You know, all this will have to be classified. My dream is to have all the parts divided by year, make of car, and condition. Maybe now that you are here to help me, this will happen."

20 "Pop . . ." Luis put his hand on his father's shoulder. They were the same height and build, about five foot six and muscular. "The judge said six months of free labor for you, not life, okay?" Mr. Cintrón nodded, looking distracted. It was then that Luis suddenly noticed how gray his hair had turned—it used to be shiny black like his own—and that there were deep lines in his face. His father had turned into an old man and he hadn't even noticed.

21 "Son, you must follow the judge's instructions. Like she said, next time you get in trouble, she's going to treat you like an adult, and I think you know what that means. Hard time, no breaks."

22 "Yeah, yeah. That's what I'm doing, right? Working my hands to the bone instead of enjoying my summer. But listen, she didn't put me under house arrest, right? I'm going out tonight."

23 "Home by ten. She did say something about a curfew, Luis." Mr. Cintrón had stopped smiling and was looking upset. It had always been hard for them to talk more than a minute or two before his father got offended at something Luis said, or at his sarcastic tone. He was always doing something wrong. Luis threw the rag down on the table and went to sit in his father's ancient Buick, which was in mint condition. They drove home in silence.

24 After sitting down at the kitchen table with his father to eat a pizza they had picked up on the way home, Luis asked to borrow the car. He didn't get an answer then, just a look that meant "Don't bother me right now."

25 Before bringing up the subject again, Luis put some ice cubes in a Baggie and handed it to Mr. Cintrón, who had made the little bump on his head worse by rubbing it. It had GUILTY written on it, Luis thought.

26 "Gracias, hijo." His father placed the bag on the bump and made a face as the ice touched his skin.

27 They ate in silence for a few minutes more; then Luis decided to ask about the car again.

28 "I really need some fresh air, Pop. Can I borrow the car for a couple of hours?"

29 "You don't get enough fresh air at the yard? We're lucky that we don't have to sit in a smelly old factory all day. You know that?"

30 "Yeah, Pop. We're real lucky." Luis always felt irritated that his father was so grateful to own a junkyard, but he held his anger back and just waited to see if he'd get the keys without having to get in an argument.

31 "Where are you going?"

32 "For a ride. Not going anywhere. Just out for a while. Is that okay?"

33 His father didn't answer, just handed him a set of keys, as shiny as the day they were manufactured. His father polished everything that could be polished: doorknobs, coins, keys, spoons, knives, and forks, like he was King Midas counting his silver and gold. Luis thought his father must be really lonely to polish utensils only he used anymore. They had been picked out by his wife, though, so they were like relics. Nothing she had ever owned could be thrown away. Only now the dishes, forks, and spoons were not used to eat the yellow rice and red beans, the fried chicken, or the mouth-watering sweet

NOTES

plantains that his mother had cooked for them. They were just kept in the cabinets that his father had turned into a museum for her. Mr. Cintrón could cook as well as his wife, but he didn't have the heart to do it anymore. Luis thought that maybe if they ate together once in a while things might get better between them, but he always had something to do around dinnertime and ended up at a hamburger joint. Tonight was the first time in months they had sat down at the table together.

34   Luis took the keys. "Thanks," he said, walking out to take his shower. His father kept looking at him with those sad, patient eyes. "Okay. I'll be back by ten, and keep the ice on that egg," Luis said without looking back.

35   He had just meant to ride around his old barrio, see if any of the Tiburones were hanging out at El Building, where most of them lived. It wasn't far from the single-family home his father had bought when the business starting paying off: a house that his mother lived in for three months before she took up residence at St. Joseph's Hospital. She never came home again. These days Luis wished he still lived in that tiny apartment where there was always something to do, somebody to talk to.

36   Instead Luis found himself parked in front of the last place his mother had gone to: Ramirez Funeral Home. In the front yard was a huge oak tree that Luis remembered having climbed during the funeral to get away from people. The tree looked different now, not like a skeleton as it had then, but green with leaves. The branches reached to the second floor of the house, where the family lived.

37   For a while Luis sat in the car allowing the memories to flood back into his brain. He remembered his mother before the illness changed her. She had not been beautiful, as his father told everyone; she had been a sweet lady, not pretty but not ugly. To him, she had been the person who always told him that she was proud of him and loved him. She did that every night when she came to his bedroom door to say goodnight. As a joke he would sometimes ask her, "Proud of what? I haven't done anything." And she'd always say, "I'm just proud that you are my son." She wasn't perfect or anything. She had bad days when nothing he did could make her smile, especially after she got sick. But he never heard her say anything negative about anyone. She always blamed *el destino,* fate, for what went wrong. He missed her. He missed her so much. Suddenly a flood of tears that had been building up for almost three years started pouring from his eyes. Luis sat in his father's car, with his head on the steering wheel, and cried, "Mami, I miss you."

38   When he finally looked up, he saw that he was being watched. Sitting at a large window with a pad and a pencil on her lap was Naomi. At first Luis felt angry and embarrassed, but she wasn't laughing at him. Then she told him

with her dark eyes that it was okay to come closer. He walked to the window, and she held up the sketch pad on which she had drawn him, not crying like a baby, but sitting on top of a mountain of silver disks, holding one up over his head. He had to smile.

39 The plate-glass window was locked. It had a security bolt on it. An alarm system, he figured, so nobody would steal the princess. He asked her if he could come in. It was soundproof too. He mouthed the words slowly for her to read his lips. She wrote on the pad, "I can't let you in. My mother is not home tonight." So they looked at each other and talked through the window for a little while. Then Luis got an idea. He signed to her that he'd be back, and drove to the junkyard.

40 Luis climbed up on his mountain of hubcaps. For hours he sorted the wheel covers by make, size, and condition, stopping only to call his father and tell him where he was and what he was doing. The old man did not ask him for explanations, and Luis was grateful for that. By lamppost light, Luis worked and worked, beginning to understand a little why his father kept busy all the time. Doing something that had a beginning, a middle, and an end did something to your head. It was like the satisfaction Luis got out of planning "adventures" for his Tiburones, but there was another element involved here that had nothing to do with showing off for others. This was a treasure hunt. And he knew what he was looking for.

41 Finally, when it seemed that it was a hopeless search, when it was almost midnight and Luis's hands were cut and bruised from his work, he found it. It was the perfect match for Naomi's drawing, the moon-shaped wheel cover for her car, Cinderella's shoe. Luis jumped off the small mound of disks left under him and shouted, "Yes!" He looked around and saw neat stacks of hubcaps that he would wash the next day. He would build a display wall for his father. People would be able to come into the yard and point to whatever they wanted.

42 Luis washed the VW hubcap and polished it until he could see himself in it. He used it as a mirror as he washed his face and combed his hair. Then he drove to the Ramirez Funeral Home. It was almost pitch-black, since it was a moonless night. As quietly as possible, Luis put some gravel in his pocket and climbed the oak tree to the second floor. He knew he was in front of Naomi's window—he could see her shadow through the curtains. She was at a table, apparently writing or drawing, maybe waiting for him. Luis hung the silver disk carefully on a branch near the window, then threw the gravel at the glass. Naomi ran to the window and drew the curtains aside while Luis held on to the thick branch and waited to give her the first good thing he had given anyone in a long time.

"Catch the Moon" from *An Island Like You: Stories of the Barrio* by Judith Ortiz Cofer and published by Scholastic, Inc. Copyright (c) 1995 by Judith Ortiz Cofer. Reprinted with permission. All rights reserved.

 THINK QUESTIONS

1. What feelings do you think Luis expresses when he stands on top of the hubcaps and yells, "Someday, son, all this will be yours"? Use examples from the text and your own inferences to support your answer.

2. What personal qualities does Mr. Cintrón value, based on details in the text about his attitude and behavior? What does this teach readers about his character? Use examples from the text and your own inferences to support your answer.

3. What do you think is the significance of the title "Catch the Moon"? Use examples from the text and your inferences to support your answer.

4. Use the context to determine the meaning of the word **vulgar** as it is used in "Catch the Moon." Write your definition of "vulgar" and explain how you arrived at it.

5. Use context to determine the meaning of the word **dismantled** as it is used in "Catch the Moon." Write your definition of "dismantled" and tell how you arrived at it. Then, give a synonym for the word.

CLOSE READ

Reread the short story "Catch the Moon." As you reread, complete the Focus Questions below. Then use your answers and annotations from the questions to help you complete the Writing Prompt.

FOCUS QUESTIONS

1. What feelings and desires motivate Luis to organize and participate in the activities of the Tiburones, according to the first six paragraphs of the text?

2. Describe Luis's attitude toward and interactions with his father throughout the text and what these reveal about his character.

3. How does Luis's mother's death influence his behavior and emotions in different ways in the story?

4. What is the meaning of the title "Catch the Moon"? How does this relate to a theme of the story, according to evidence from the final two paragraphs of the text?

5. Throughout the story, how do Luis's interactions with Naomi serve to define his character?

WRITING PROMPT

How does Luis develop over the course of the story through his interaction with other characters? What do these interactions reveal about the theme of the story? Write a response to these questions. Cite evidence from the text to support your response.

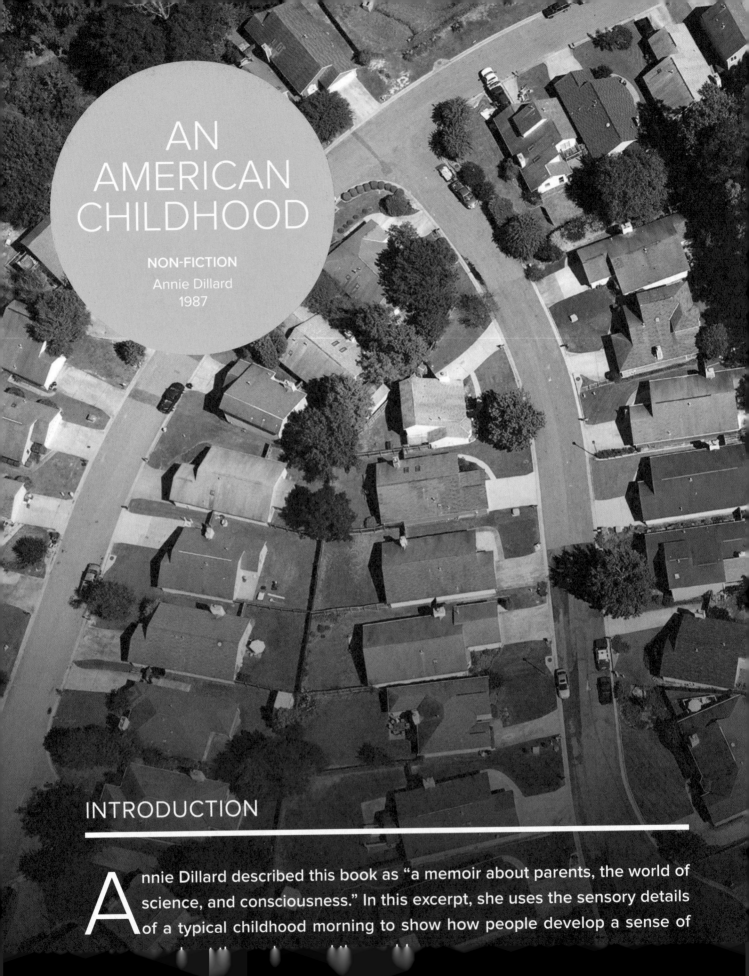

AN AMERICAN CHILDHOOD

NON-FICTION
Annie Dillard
1987

INTRODUCTION

Annie Dillard described this book as "a memoir about parents, the world of science, and consciousness." In this excerpt, she uses the sensory details of a typical childhood morning to show how people develop a sense of

"It drives you to a life of concentration, it does..."

 FIRST READ

Excerpt from Part One

1   The story starts back in 1950, when I was five.

2   Oh, the great humming silence of the empty neighborhoods in those days, the neighborhoods abandoned everywhere across continental America—the city residential areas, the new "suburbs," the towns and villages on the peopled highways, the cities, towns, and villages on the rivers, the shores, in the Rocky and Appalachian mountains, the **piedmont,** the dells, the bayous, the hills, the Great Basin, the Great Valley, the Great Plains—oh, the silence!

3   For every morning the neighborhoods emptied, and all vital activity, it seemed, set forth for parts unknown.

4   The men left in a rush: they flung on coats, they slid kisses at everybody's cheeks, they slammed house doors, they slammed car doors; they ground their cars' starters till the motors caught with a jump.

5   And the Catholic schoolchildren left in a rush. I saw them from our dining-room windows. They burst into the street buttoning their jackets; they threw dry catalpa pods at the stop sign and at each other. They hugged their brown-and-tan workbooks to them, clumped and parted, and proceeded toward St. Bede's church school almost by accident.

6   The men in their oval, empty cars drove slowly among the schoolchildren. The boys banged the cars' fenders with their hands, with their jackets' elbows, or their books. The men in cars inched among the children; they edged around corners and vanished from sight. The waving knots of children zigzagged and hollered up the street and vanished from sight. And inside all the forgotten houses in all the abandoned neighborhoods, the day of silence and waiting had begun.

NOTES

7 The war was over. People wanted to settle down, apparently, and calmly blow their way out of years of rationing. They wanted to bake sugary cakes, burn gas, go to church together, get rich, and make babies.

8 I had been born at the end of April 1945, on the day Hitler died; Roosevelt had died eighteen days before. My father had been 4-F in the war, because of a collapsing lung—despite his repeated and **chagrined** efforts to enlist. Now— five years after V-J Day—he still went out one night a week as a volunteer to the Civil Air Patrol; he searched the Pittsburgh skies for new enemy bombers. By day he worked downtown for American Standard.

9 Every woman stayed alone in her house in those days, like a coin in a safe. Amy and I lived alone with our mother most of the day. Amy was three years younger than I. Mother and Amy and I went our separate ways in peace.

10 The men had driven away and the schoolchildren had paraded out of sight. Now a self-conscious and **stricken** silence overtook the neighborhood, overtook our white corner house and myself inside. "Am I living?" In the kitchen I watched the unselfconscious trees through the screen door, until the trees' autumn branches like fins waved away the silence. I forgot myself, and sank into dim and watery oblivion.

11 A car passed. Its rush and whine jolted me from my blankness. The sound faded again and I faded again down into my hushed brain until the icebox motor kicked on and prodded me away. "You are living," the icebox motor said. "It is morning, morning, here in the kitchen, and you are in it," the icebox motor said, or the dripping faucet said, or any of the hundred other noisy things that only children can't stop hearing. Cars started, leaves rubbed, trucks' brakes whistled, sparrows peeped. Whenever it rained, the rain spattered, dripped, and ran, for the entire length of the shower, for the entire length of days-long rains, until we children were almost insane from hearing it rain because we couldn't stop hearing it rain. "Rinso white!" cried the man on the radio. "Rinso blue." The silence, like all silences, was made **poignant** and distinct by its sounds.

12 What a marvel it was that the day so often introduced itself with a firm footfall nearby. What a marvel it was that so many times a day the world, like a church bell, reminded me to recall and **contemplate** the durable fact that I was here, and had awakened once more to find myself set down in a going world.

13 In the living room the mail slot clicked open and envelopes clattered down. In the back room, where our maid, Margaret Butler, was ironing, the steam iron thumped the muffled ironing board and hissed. The walls squeaked, the pipes knocked, the screen door trembled, the furnace banged, and the radiators clanged. This was the fall the loud trucks went by. I sat mindless and eternal on the kitchen floor, stony of head and solemn, playing with my fingers.

NOTES

Time streamed in full flood beside me on the kitchen floor; time roared raging beside me down its swollen banks; and when I woke I was so startled I fell in.

14 Who could ever tire of this heart-stopping transition, of this breakthrough shift between seeing and knowing you see, between being and knowing you be? It drives you to a life of concentration, it does, a life in which effort draws you down so very deep that when you surface you twist up **exhilarated** with a yelp and a gasp.

15 Who could ever tire of this radiant transition, this surfacing to awareness and this deliberate plunging to oblivion—the theater curtain rising and falling? Who could tire of it when the sum of those moments at the edge—the conscious life we so dread losing—is all we have, the gift at the moment of opening it?

Excerpted from *An American Childhood* by Annie Dillard, published by Harper & Row.

 THINK QUESTIONS

1. What do details about five-year-old Annie's neighborhood and home suggest about her family, including their social class? Use details from the text to support your answer.

2. Why are the neighborhood and the Dillards' house so silent? How does Annie feel about this silence? Support your answer with evidence from the passage.

3. What are some of the sounds Annie hears while she plays in the kitchen, and what ultimate effect do these sounds have on her? Use details from the passage to support your answer.

4. Remembering that the Latin root *ped* means "foot" and the Latin root *mont* means "mountain," use context clues in *An American Childhood* to determine the meaning of the word **piedmont.** Write your definition of "piedmont" and explain how you arrived at it. Then look it up in the dictionary to confirm or revise your initial definition.

5. Use the context clues provided in the passage to determine the meaning of **chagrined.** Write your definition of "chagrined" and explain how you arrived at it.

Please note that excerpts and passages in the StudySync® library and this workbook are intended as touchstones to generate interest in an author's work. The excerpts and passages do not substitute for the reading of entire texts, and StudySync® strongly recommends that students seek out and purchase the whole literary or informational work in order to experience it as the author intended. Links to online resellers are available in our digital library. In addition, complete works may be ordered through an authorized reseller by filling out and returning to StudySync® the order form enclosed in this workbook.

Reading & Writing Companion   **379**

CLOSE READ

Reread the excerpt from *An American Childhood*. As you reread, complete the Focus Questions below. Then use your answers and annotations from the questions to help you complete the Writing Prompt.

FOCUS QUESTIONS

1. What purpose do the first nine paragraphs of this excerpt from Dillard's memoir serve? Analyze their significance in terms of the excerpt as a whole.

2. In paragraph 10, Annie asks herself "Am I living?" What answer does she arrive at, and how does she find it? How does this answer inform the central idea of the excerpt as a whole?

3. Where and how is the central idea of the text first introduced? How does Dillard choose and organize informational text elements to express and develop the central idea of the excerpt?

4. Paragraphs 13–15 contain an extended metaphor about Time. Identify and explain the comparison Dillard makes. What central idea in the text does Dillard express through this metaphor? How does understanding the metaphor enrich your understanding of the excerpt as a whole?

5. What impression do you have of five-year-old Annie's character? How do her interactions with other people, with objects in the house, and with her own thoughts define her? How does the adult writer Annie Dillard's use of and interaction with language, including figurative language, help to define younger Annie's character?

WRITING PROMPT

The author of the memoir *An American Childhood*, Annie Dillard, demonstrates a particularly keen awareness of sounds, finding deeper meaning in them. Think of an everyday sound or other sensory experience that you find significant. In an essay of at least 300 words, describe the sound or other sensory experience through the use of both strong sensory detail and figurative language, and explain why it has special meaning to you, such as what insight it gives you, what revelations it causes you to have, what associations it calls forth, or what symbolic significance it has in your life. Use quotations from the memoir excerpt to support your ideas and to compare Dillard's experience to your own. Be sure that your essay has a clear main idea and demonstrates an effective use of informational text elements to organize, develop, and make connections between different ideas.

THOSE WINTER SUNDAYS

POETRY
Robert Hayden
1966

INTRODUCTION

Robert Hayden was a 20th century African-American poet and essayist. Ostracized by his peers and stressed by a tumultuous home environment, Hayden turned to books at a young age. His early literary skills stayed with him, and in time Hayden was able to earn a living through the written word. His poems often balance painful experiences with hope, possibility, and a celebration of humanity. In "Those Winter Sundays," the speaker reminisces about his father.

"What did I know, what did I know...?"

FIRST READ

1   Sundays too my father got up early
2   and put his clothes on in the **blueblack** cold,
3   then with cracked hands that ached
4   from labor in the weekday weather made
5   banked fires blaze. No one ever thanked him.

6   I'd wake and hear the cold **splintering,** breaking.
7   When the rooms were warm, he'd call,
8   and slowly I would rise and dress,
9   fearing the **chronic** angers of that house,

10 Speaking **indifferently** to him,
11 who had driven out the cold
12 and polished my good shoes as well.
13 What did I know, what did I know
14 of love's **austere** and lonely offices?

"Those Winter Sundays". Copyright © 1966 by Robert Hayden, from COLLECTED POEMS OF ROBERT HAYDEN by Robert Hayden, edited by Frederick Glaysher. Copyright © 1985 by Emma Hayden. Used by permission of Liveright Publishing Corporation.

THINK QUESTIONS

1. Who is the narrator of the poem? Cite evidence from the text to support your answer.

2. Use details from the text to write two or three sentences describing the way the narrator treated his father.

3. Write two or three sentences explaining the physical and emotional living conditions in the family. Support your answer with textual evidence.

4. Use context to determine the meaning of the word **blueblack** as it is used in "Those Winter Sundays." Write your definition of "blueblack" and tell how you arrived at it.

5. Remembering that the Greek root *chron* means "time" and the suffix *-ic* means "related to," use the context clues provided in the passage to determine the meaning of **chronic.** Write your definition of "chronic" and tell how you arrived at it.

CLOSE READ

Reread the poem "Those Winter Sundays." As you reread, complete the Focus Questions below. Then use your answers and annotations from the questions to help you complete the Writing Prompt.

FOCUS QUESTIONS

1. How would you describe the character of the father? Write a brief description. Cite details from the poem that support your description, and make annotations to explain your choices.

2. What is the tone of the poem? Which words and phrases create the tone? Support your answer with textual evidence and make annotations to explain your answer choices.

3. How does the narrator allude to problems between the father and the son? Highlight textual evidence and make annotations to explain your ideas.

4. What does the narrator understand as an adult that he did not understand as a child? Support your response with evidence from the text.

5. What is the theme of the poem? Support your response with evidence from the text.

WRITING PROMPT

The Essential Question for this unit is, "How do our interactions define us?" In 300 words, describe how the narrator's interactions with his father, both as a youth and as an adult, define him. What important lessons did his upbringing ultimately teach him? Identify the poem's theme. Include details about how the tone of the poem helps to reinforce the theme.

Please note that excerpts and passages in the StudySync® library and this workbook are intended as touchstones to generate interest in an author's work. The excerpts and passages do not substitute for the reading of entire texts, and StudySync® strongly recommends that students seek out and purchase the whole literary or informational work in order to experience it as the author intended. Links to online resellers are available in our digital library. In addition, complete works may be ordered through an authorized reseller by filling out and returning to StudySync® the order form enclosed in this workbook.

Reading & Writing Companion **383**

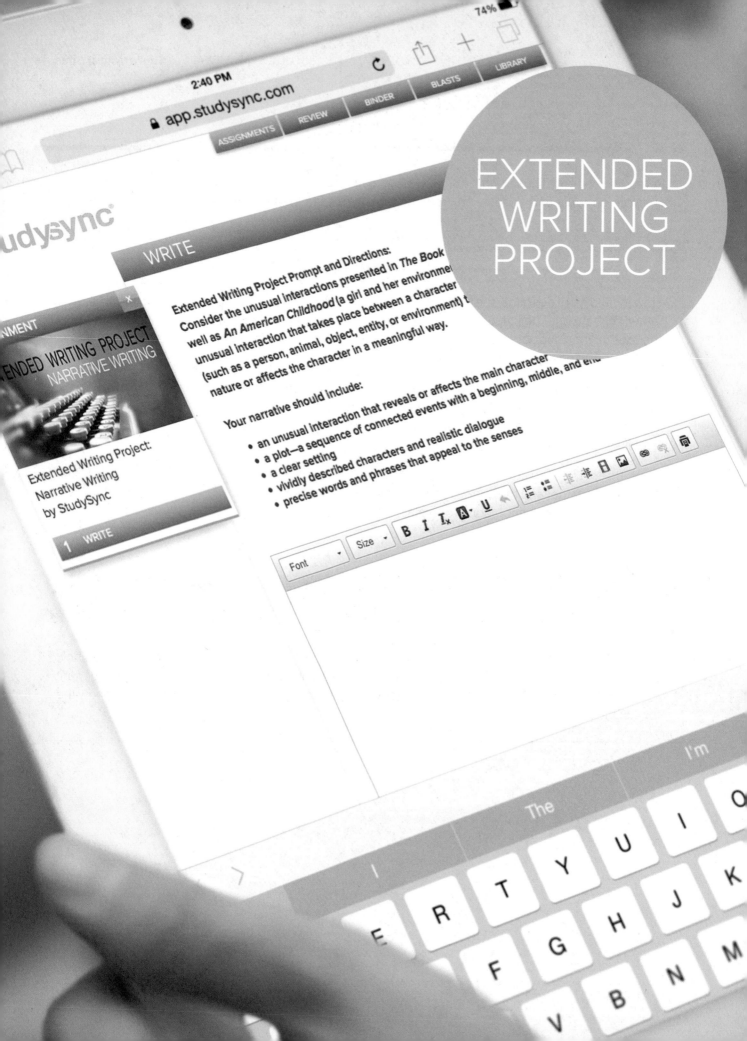

NARRATIVE WRITING

WRITING PROMPT

Consider the unusual interactions presented in *The Book Thief* (Death and a survivor) as well as *An American Childhood* (a girl and her environment). Write a narrative about an unusual interaction that takes place between a character and someone or something else (such as a person, animal, object, entity, or environment) that reveals the character's true nature or affects the character in a meaningful way.

Your narrative should include:

- an unusual interaction that reveals or affects the main character
- a plot—a sequence of connected events with a beginning, middle, and end
- a clear setting
- vividly described characters and realistic dialogue
- precise words and phrases that appeal to the senses

Narrative writing tells a story of real or imagined experiences or events. Narratives can be fiction, such as stories and poems, or non-fiction, such as memoirs and personal essays. Good narrative writing uses effective techniques, relevant descriptive details, vivid language, and well-structured event sequences to convey a story to readers. The features of narrative writing include:

- setting
- characters
- plot
- theme
- point of view

Please note that excerpts and passages in the StudySync® library and this workbook are intended as touchstones to generate interest in an author's work. The excerpts and passages do not substitute for the reading of entire texts, and StudySync® strongly recommends that students seek out and purchase the whole literary or informational work in order to experience it as the author intended. Links to online resellers are available in our digital library. In addition, complete works may be ordered through an authorized reseller by filling out and returning to StudySync® the order form enclosed in this workbook.

Reading & Writing Companion   **385**

As you continue with this extended writing project, you will receive more instruction and practice crafting each of the elements of narrative writing to create your own compelling narrative.

STUDENT MODEL

Before you get started on your narrative writing piece, begin by reading this essay that one student wrote in response to the writing prompt. As you read this student model, highlight and annotate the features of narrative writing that the student included in her essay.

Kelsey and the Poet

Kelsey was sitting on the lawn, watching the movers carry boxes out of her house, when Sharif, the mail carrier, walked up to the house at his usual time, wearing a summer uniform of blue shorts and a pale gray safari helmet.

"Sneaking out in broad daylight?" he said, smiling, as he handed her a sheaf of envelopes.

"Didn't we tell you we're moving?" she said with dismay. "I know Dad sent in a forwarding address." She began leafing through the envelopes in her hand. "I guess we'll get just as much junk mail in Oregon as in Utah, won't we?" Then she took in a sudden gasping breath, for at the sight of the return address on a greeting-card-size envelope, she became too stunned to utter words. "It's from a magazine I sent one of my poems to."

She hastily tore open the envelope and saw a two-line note with one line of handwriting under it. Under that there was a second page. The second page was a dozen short lines in big italics.

"Oh, no!" she cried out.

"They sent it back," Sharif said, understandingly.

"This is terrible. I'll never get anything published."

Sharif read Kelsey's poem over her shoulder. "May I? 'First Feelings.' I like that title. How old are you?"

"Fifteen, and this is the first manuscript I've ever sent anywhere, and I'm already a miserable failure! This is a terrible omen! I'm never going to do anything worthwhile! I'm doomed for life!"

Kelsey remembered how excited she'd been when she first mailed the poem to the magazine. She'd been positive that all she had to do was wait a couple of weeks and there'd be an answering letter—no, a thrilled, thrilling phone call—telling her that the magazine was honored to have discovered America's newest literary talent. She'd bought herself an ice cream sundae just to celebrate mailing the stupid thing!

Being fifteen is a total embarrassment, Kelsey thought, *especially when you're not a published poet yet.* She gritted her teeth at the futility of her efforts.

"I think I was seventeen when I got my first rejection," Sharif said. "I had a similar attitude, if I remember correctly."

She gave him a look of surprise. "Are you a poet too?"

"I sure am." Without warning he poured forth words about someone taking a long walk. They were beautiful, sorrowful, silken, somehow violet-colored words about not knowing what to do. They might have been written just for her.

"How can you be a poet," she asked, "when you're a mailman?"

He laughed heartily. "I write in my head as I walk my route."

Kelsey was trying to visualize herself in a safari helmet, treading along on a suburban sidewalk in solitude, but after a couple of seconds the scene of her fantasy changed to a steaming, overgrown jungle like in an old movie, where she was hacking away at the underbrush, with the howling of monkeys in the background. Then she was back in the real world—just a girl who'd gotten bad news, moaning to someone she didn't really know well.

"Have you ever published anything?" she asked Sharif.

"Now and then, in online magazines. They don't pay their writers, but their readers are primarily other poets, and so we write letters about each other's work, which makes it rewarding in other ways than money."

"Do you think you'll ever be famous?"

He laughed again, and told her that no, he probably never would be, except among a couple of hundred people—but, he added, they were people who really understood poetry.

"Well, if you'll excuse me," he said, "I have to keep going on my appointed rounds."

Kelsey glanced over her shoulder; the inside of the moving van was already half full of boxes.

"Thanks for being a great mailman," she said, shaking his hand. "And a great poet."

He shook his head, smiling to himself as if he knew something she didn't. Then he walked away.

As soon as she and her family were on the road in their little silver sedan, Kelsey began wishing she had a copy of Sharif's poem. But of course he wouldn't carry copies of his poems in his postal uniform, and even if she wanted to write to him for a copy, she didn't know his last name or address. Once they were settled in their new home, she confided in her mom about this, and Mom suggested mailing a letter to "Mail Carrier Sharif" at the zip code of their old Utah post office. The next day, Kelsey went to the nearest mailbox to send him a letter, and she envisioned herself receiving his reply and unfolding a poetic masterpiece.

She never got a reply from him, but she'd imagined it, and she knew that an active imagination was really important for a poet.

THINK QUESTIONS

1. What is the main conflict in this story? Refer to details from the text that present and develop it.

2. How does dialogue contribute to the plot and characterization in this story? Mention two or more lines of dialogue and specify what they contribute.

3. What is the crucial interaction in the story? What does it reveal about the main character? Refer to specific details from the interaction in your answer.

4. As you consider the writing prompt, which selections or other resources would you like to examine to help you create your own narrative?

5. Based on what you have read, listened to, or researched so far, how would you answer the question, *How do our interactions define us?*

Please note that excerpts and passages in the StudySync® library and this workbook are intended as touchstones to generate interest in an author's work. The excerpts and passages do not substitute for the reading of entire texts, and StudySync® strongly recommends that students seek out and purchase the whole literary or informational work in order to experience it as the author intended. Links to online resellers are available in our digital library. In addition, complete works may be ordered through an authorized reseller by filling out and returning to StudySync® the order form enclosed in this workbook.

Reading & Writing Companion **389**

SKILL:
ORGANIZE
NARRATIVE
WRITING

 DEFINE

A narrative is a story; it may be fictional or nonfictional. In either case, the basic elements of a narrative are **plot, character, setting,** and **theme.** An effective plot revolves around a **conflict,** or problem, the characters must face. It might be an **external conflict,** such as a conflict between the main character and another person or between the main character and the forces of nature. However, it might also be an **internal conflict,** or a character's struggle with something in his or her own nature, such as a debate about which of two careers to pursue. The opening part of the narrative, which introduces the setting, characters, and conflict, is called the **exposition.**

The plot develops through a **sequence of events,** each one related to the next. At times, the author may rearrange the order in which the events are narrated—such as in a **flashback,** a scene that returns to the past—but in almost all cases, the reader is able to figure out the chronological order in which the events occurred. The sequence builds to a **climax** or turning point, when the main character faces a crucial test in dealing with the problem.

Authors use a toolkit of literary techniques to tell their stories. Descriptive **details,** such as those about the setting or the characters' appearances, help readers participate imaginatively in the narrative. A key structural factor is **point of view,** or the perspective from which the story is told.

The **narrator** might be a character in the narrative (usually the main character), telling the tale in his or her own words in the **first person.** More often, the narrator is an unidentified voice telling the story from an outside perspective in the **third person,** using he or she for all the characters and I for none of them. The writer's choice of who will narrate the story affects what events and details the reader will have access to and how the reader will understand and react to the characters.

Characters are the driving force of a story. Many plots move forward through a series of interactions between characters, conveyed by action and **dialogue.** Characters often undergo a significant change by the story's end, and the change may be a strong indication of a **theme**—a main idea—that the author seeks to develop in the text. Themes are likely to be visible throughout a story, but especially at the **conclusion,** when the shape of the whole plot is complete, the main conflict is **resolved**—perhaps successfully for the main character or perhaps not—and the reader as well as the characters are left to remember and reflect on what has occurred.

IDENTIFICATION AND APPLICATION

- Characters are the heart of a narrative. Their interactions show who they are and provide the forward motion of the plot. Characters develop and change in the course of a story.

- The plot is built upon a conflict that is interesting to readers—an important problem that the main character tries to solve. The conflict may be external (the character grapples with an outside force or another person) or internal (within the character).

- Plot events are organized in a clear sequence, usually in chronological order.

- The sequence of events builds to a climax, the point at which characters are forced to take action, and finally a conclusion, in which the conflict is resolved.

- Techniques such as point of view and flashback, as well as vividly described details of setting, characters, and action, bring a narrative to life.

MODEL

The Book Thief is a nontraditional story in some ways. In the first glance at its pages, readers can see that it is not structured by standard-size paragraphs, with alternating description and dialogue, the way most works of fiction are. The structure seems free-form, as if the narrator is jotting down observations and comments as they occur to him. A close look, however, shows that *The Book Thief* contains all the tried and true elements of an enthralling narrative. The story begins as follows:

> First the **colors.**
> Then the **humans.**
> That's usually how I see things.
> Or at least, how I try.
>
> **HERE IS A SMALL FACT***

Please note that excerpts and passages in the StudySync® library and this workbook are intended as touchstones to generate interest in an author's work. The excerpts and passages do not substitute for the reading of entire texts, and StudySync® strongly recommends that students seek out and purchase the whole literary or informational work in order to experience it as the author intended. Links to online resellers are available in our digital library. In addition, complete works may be ordered through an authorized reseller by filling out and returning to StudySync® the order form enclosed in this workbook.

Reading & Writing Companion   **391**

You are going to die

I am in all truthfulness attempting to be cheerful about this whole topic. . . Just don't ask me to be nice. Nice has nothing to do with me.

At this point, the reader might be wondering, "What kind of way is that to begin a story?" But this cryptic beginning provides a lot of information about character, theme, and plot. The reader can tell from the use of the word "I" that the narrator is first-person, and that the narrating character is a strange—though as yet, unnamed—individual who thinks about deep themes such as life and death, and who has a grim sense of humor and a friendly, but also oddly threatening, tone. The setting is not specifically described, but readers know it involves colors and humans. The reader's interest is aroused, and the reader expects that as the narrative continues, answers and identities will become clear. In fact, before long, it becomes fairly clear that the narrator is none other than Death himself: "It suffices to say that at some point in time, I will be standing over you, as genially as possible. Your soul will be in my arms."

More of the setting and the exposition of the plot appears when the narrator begins to interact with other characters. The setting is given in the title of Part 2: "BESIDE THE RAILWAY LINE." The characters are described, and dialogue and details appear:

> Next to the **train line,** footprints were sunken to their shins. Trees wore blankets of ice.
>
> As you might expect, someone had died.
>
> They couldn't just leave him on the ground. For now, it wasn't such a problem, but very soon, the track ahead would be cleared and the train would need to move on.
>
> There were **two guards.**
>
> There was **one mother and her daughter.**
>
> **One corpse.**
>
> The mother, the girl, and the corpse remained stubborn and silent.
>
> "Well, what else do you want me to do?"
>
> The guards were tall and short. **The tall one always spoke first, though he was not in charge.** He looked at the smaller, rounder one. The one with the juicy red face.

Reading & Writing Companion

"Well," was the response, "we can't just leave them like this, can we?"

The tall one was losing patience. "Why not?"

In only a few words, the narrator has sketched a snowy scene by a railroad track, featuring a group of people who have specific roles with regard to each other. Two, a mother and daughter, are suffering. Two are guarding them, and the guard who is officially in charge seems weaker than the other guard. And there's a corpse. And that spooky narrator.

The dialogue is minimal, but nothing more needs to be said at this point. It is clear that terrible pain, and probably violence and injustice, are at play. The guards are unsure of how cruel or kind they are supposed to be. A corpse cannot interact, but the minds and imaginations of all the other characters are surely interacting with it in different ways. The narrator says nothing—in fact, the other characters seem unaware of his presence—but dealing with death is a powerful kind of interaction, likely to reveal the truth about the characters.

In a short space, the author of *The Book Thief* has touched on all the important narrative elements—including narrator, setting, character, plot, and conflict—and likely made readers hungry for more.

 PRACTICE

First, reread the prompt. Think about the elements of narrative writing. Then write a basic outline for your narrative about an unusual interaction that includes: how the story will be narrated (first or third-person), what type of interaction will take place, a possible conflict (driving problem of the story), the setting of the story (time of day, year, or period in history, and location—house, town, country, society, or natural surroundings), a description of at least one character (age, sex, appearance, what they think or how they feel about the conflict), and ideas about possible themes to be explored. Remember that these are ideas that can be expanded upon, eliminated, or revised as you progress in the writing process. When you are finished, trade outlines with a partner and offer each other feedback. How has your partner described each basic story element mentioned? How will each of these elements help to drive the plot of the story? Offer each other suggestions, and remember that they are most helpful when they are constructive.

PREWRITE

WRITING PROMPT

Consider the unusual interactions presented in *The Book Thief* (Death and a survivor) as well as *An American Childhood* (a girl and her environment). Write a narrative about an unusual interaction that takes place between a character and someone or something else (such as a person, animal, object, entity, or environment) that reveals the character's true nature or affects the character in a meaningful way.

Your narrative should include:

- an unusual interaction that reveals or affects the main character
- a plot—a sequence of connected events with a beginning, middle, and end
- a clear setting
- vividly described characters and realistic dialogue
- precise words and phrases that appeal to the senses

For your extended writing project, you will use the narrative writing techniques you learned to compose a narrative in which interactions between characters—or between the main character and an outside force such as nature, ideas, or history—play a central role.

Writers often take notes about story ideas before they sit down to write. Some writers list ideas about characters, plot, and other elements, and then choose the ones they think will be most entertaining for readers—and for them as writers. Others start with a beginning and an ending and then sketch out possibilities for events that could lead the characters through the plot.

Think about what you have learned so far about organizing narrative writing. What kinds of characters would you like to write about in your narrative? How would they interact? What kinds of conflict might the main character face? From which point of view should your story be told, and why?

Make a list of answers to these questions by completing the "Prewrite: Narrative Writing" chart. Record your brainstorming ideas about the characters and their interactions (with other characters or with forces or entities such as nature, ideas, or history), the conflict, and the narrator. Then look over your ideas and choose the details that create the story you want to write. Use this chart, completed by the writer of the student model narrative, to help guide your prewriting:

PREWRITE – NARRATIVE WRITING			
Characters *What characters would I like to write about?*	**Interaction** *How might these characters interact in unusual or meaningful ways?*	**Conflict** *What conflict might the main character need to address?*	**Narrator** *From which point of view should this story be told? Why?*
A teen and parent Two teenage friends A teen who is moving and someone he or she is leaving behind A brother and sister	One helps the other overcome a problem. They have a huge argument. One coaxes the other into trouble. One discovers a secret about the other.	Something bad has happened. He or she struggles to cope with it. He or she faces problems in a close relationship. He or she doesn't know whether to tell the truth or keep silent about something. He or she wants something that another isn't prepared to give.	First person, from the main character's point of view, so readers can better relate to that person's feelings. First person, from the other's character's point of view, so readers gain insight into how the main character is perceived by others. Third person, so readers can view the events from an objective perspective and form our own impressions of both characters.

SKILL:
INTRODUCTIONS

DEFINE

The **introduction** is the opening of the narrative; it sets the stage for the events to come. Because the introduction is the reader's first experience with the story, writers often include elements of **exposition**—essential information such as character, setting, and problem—in the opening paragraphs of the story. A story's introduction should capture a reader's attention and tempt the reader to move forward into the story with interest. After reading paragraph or a few paragraphs, a reader should think, "I wonder what will happen. I'd like to keep reading and discover more about these characters." A good introduction hooks a reader with precise language and sensory details that bring the reader into the world of the story.

IDENTIFICATION AND APPLICATION

- A narrative introduction should provide the reader with a sense of the story's setting.

- The introduction usually signals the story's narrative point of view, such as through the narrator's use of personal pronouns.

- Writers often introduce main characters in the opening paragraphs of a story.

- A writer may present the story's main problem, or conflict, in the introductory paragraphs, to engage the reader with the events to come.

- The opening scene of a story may contain an action that sets a sequence of events—the plot—in motion.

- Writers make precise word choices, often infusing narrative introductions with vivid sensory details that draw readers into the story.

MODEL

A skillful writer can lead the reader to imagine an entire world in the first few sentences of a story. Not all the details of that invented world and its people will be evident yet, but the reader will have been given clues. For example, here's the first paragraph of "Catch the Moon":

> **Luis Cintrón** sits on top of a six-foot pile of hubcaps and watches **his father** walk away into the steel jungle of **his car junkyard. Released into his old man's custody after six** months in **juvenile hall—for breaking and entering—and he didn't even take anything. He did it on a dare.** But **the old lady with the million cats** was a light sleeper, and good with **her aluminum cane. He has a scar on his head** to prove it.

There's an amazing amount of introductory information there, as well as descriptive details about the character that practically dare the reader not to want to know more. So far, the reader knows that:

- The main character is a young man named Luis Cintrón, who was just released from juvenile hall after six months.
- Luis committed a crime by breaking and entering on a dare, but he didn't steal anything.
- An old lady, the owner of many cats, caught him in the act and hit him with her cane, injuring his scalp.
- Luis's sentence was longer than six months, but his father got him out early by giving him a job.
- The job is at a junkyard his father owns, which is the setting of the introductory scene.
- Luis doesn't like the junkyard, and feels resentment over what's happened to him.
- The narration is third-person limited, meaning that the narrator is not Luis but reveals Luis's thoughts.

The list of things the reader knows is longer than the text that gives the information! And it doesn't even include descriptive details such as the six-foot pile of hubcaps Luis sits on.

The second paragraph of "Catch the Moon" can also be considered part of the introduction, because it continues providing exposition about the basic setup of the story.

> Now Luis is wondering whether he should have stayed in and done his full time. Jorge Cintrón of Jorge Cintrón & Son, Auto Parts and Salvage, has decided that Luis should wash and polish every hubcap in the yard.

NOTES

The hill he is sitting on is only the latest couple of hundred wheel covers that have come in. Luis grunts and stands up on top of his silver mountain. He yells at no one, "Someday, son, all this will be yours," and sweeps his arms like the Pope blessing a crowd over the piles of car sandwiches and mounds of metal parts that cover this acre of land outside the city. He is the "Son" of Jorge Cintrón & Son, and so far his father has had more than one reason to wish it was plain Jorge Cintrón on the sign.

A list of things the reader learns from that paragraph could probably go on for half a page. It adds new expository information and many details. It describes the setting of the junkyard more vividly. It clarifies that Luis's father strongly wants him to work at the junkyard and, someday, take over the business—but that Luis doesn't necessarily share his dream. It lets the reader know that the third-person-limited narrator is likely to continue showing Luis's thoughts and feelings, and not his father's.

There has been little action so far, and that's often the case with the introduction, or exposition, of a story. The important thing is that it makes the reader eager to find out what will happen next to these people.

 PRACTICE

Write an introduction for your narrative that establishes the main character, the narrative point of view, and the setting. When you are finished, trade with a partner and offer each other feedback. How precise is the language used in your partner's introduction? How well do the details help you to picture the setting and characters? What do you learn about the main character, and possibly other characters, from the introduction? What questions does the introduction raise with you that you hope the rest of the story will answer? Offer each other suggestions, and remember that they are most helpful when they are constructive.

SKILL:
NARRATIVE
TECHNIQUES AND
SEQUENCING

DEFINE

To write a story, writers use a variety of tools to develop the plot and characters, explore the setting, and engage the reader. **Narrative techniques** include dialogue, pacing, description, reflection, and the sequencing of events, which may sometimes include multiple plot lines. **Dialogue,** what the characters say to one another, is often used to develop characters and forward the action of the plot. Writers often manipulate the **pacing** of a narrative, or the speed with which events occur, to slow down or speed up the action at certain points of a story. Writers use **description** to build story details and reveal information about character, setting, and plot. Narrators and characters often engage in **reflection,** pondering the events that have occurred so far in the story. Every narrative contains a **sequence of events,** which is carefully planned and controlled by the author as the story unfolds. Longer narratives, such as novels, often contain **multiple plot lines** consisting of a main plot and one or more **subplots,** which may be connected through their characters, events, and themes.

The sequence of events in a story builds a **plot**—a chain or web or organized, related events that are introduced at the beginning, or **exposition,** gather momentum through the middle—the **rising action** and the **climax**—and come to a conclusion in the **falling action** and the **resolution.** The sequence of events in a narrative may proceed in a straight chronological line from the first event that occurs to the last event that occurs. In many cases, however, authors build detours in the sequence, most often by inserting **flashbacks.** A flashback is a scene that returns to an earlier event in the sequence. It may have taken place before the main plot sequence began. Usually, flashbacks fill in background information that helps readers understand the events of the main sequence.

The ultimate purpose of all these narrative techniques is similar: to keep readers reading.

IDENTIFICATION AND APPLICATION

- Writers plan a sequence of events that will occur in a narrative, from the story's introduction to its conclusion. The sequence may be narrated strictly from first event to last event or may include scenes out of sequence, such as flashbacks.
- Writers use pacing to control the speed at which the events of a narrative unfold or are revealed to the reader.
- Writers use dialogue and description to develop characters and advance the action of the plot.
- Reflection slows down the forward motion of the story and gives writers a chance to further develop the characters and plot.

 MODEL

In the story "Kelsey and the Poet," the student author uses narrative techniques and sequencing to develop events and characters. Look at this excerpt:

> Sharif read Kelsey's poem over her shoulder. "May I? 'First Feelings.' I like that title. How old are you?"
>
> "Fifteen, and this is the first manuscript I've ever sent anywhere, and I'm already a miserable failure! This is a terrible omen! I'm never going to do anything worthwhile! I'm doomed for life!"
>
> **Kelsey remembered how excited she'd been** when she first mailed the poem to the magazine. **She'd been positive that all she had to do was wait a couple of weeks** and there'd be an answering letter—no, a thrilled, thrilling phone call—telling her that the magazine was honored to have discovered America's newest literary talent. **She'd bought herself an ice cream sundae just to celebrate mailing the stupid thing!**
> **Being fifteen is a total embarrassment, Kelsey thought, especially when you're not a published poet yet.** She gritted her teeth at the futility of her efforts.
>
> **"I think I was seventeen when I got my first rejection,"** Sharif said **understandingly.** "I had a similar attitude, if I remember correctly."
>
> **She gave him a look of surprise. "Are you a poet too?"**

"I sure am." Without warning he poured forth words about someone taking a long walk, who was the speaker of the poem. **They were beautiful, sorrowful, silken, somehow violet-colored words about not knowing what to do.** *They might have been written just for her.*

In this exchange of dialogue, the author presents readers with many details that fill in the outlines of the two characters. Most obviously, the dialogue—the conversation between Kelsey and Sharif—helps the reader see, hear, and understand the characters in detail. Their style of speech is natural, believable, and subtly different from each other: Basically, Kelsey talks like an enthusiastic, excitable teen and Sharif talks like a sympathetic, understanding adult who probably remembers when he was more excitable himself. In addition, basic plot information is conveyed in this dialogue—namely, that Kelsey had sent a poem to a magazine and that she has just received a rejection letter. The dialogue provides the medium for the exchange between the two characters, and in this story, the events consist largely of character interaction.

Other narrative techniques in this passage bring it further to life. When Sharif reads his poem aloud, descriptions help the reader feel the impact of the words on Kelsey through vivid description: "They were beautiful, sorrowful, silken, somehow violet-colored words about not knowing what to do." Without even knowing the exact words of Sharif's poem, the reader of the story gets a sense of what they mean and even how they sound.

The most basic purpose of description in narrative is to make the reader see, hear, and feel the experiences of the story. The description of Sharif reading also has another technical purpose: it slows down the pace of the scene at a crucial point. The dialogue sections of the scene tend to be fast; Kelsey and Sharif exchange lines of banter back and forth without pausing. Sharif's reading of the poem creates a pause in the dialogue, and since the words of the poem aren't included in the dialogue, the pause is even clearer, because it's conveyed entirely in description, which takes longer to read than dialogue. This change of pace is rewarding for its own sake—who doesn't like a change now and then?—and it also makes this part of the scene feel more thoughtful or more, well, *poetic.*

Reflection also occurs when Kelsey ponders her own actions and traits: "Being fifteen is a total embarrassment, Kelsey thought, especially when you're not a published poet yet." These lines slow the narrative pace but also reveal Kelsey's character: she is dramatic and naive, but also thoughtful, self-aware, and ambitious.

In this story, reflection goes hand in hand with a shift in the sequence of events—a flashback—because the flashback is in the form of a memory of Kelsey's. The clause, "Kelsey remembered how excited she'd been" tells the reader that Kelsey is looking back into her past. The writer uses the phrases "she'd been" and "she'd bought" instead of "she was" and "she bought," thus employing grammar to signal a shift in the sequence of events.

It's important to note that narrative techniques don't always occur in isolation. More than one technique can be at work in the same sentence, or even the same phrase or word. For example, descriptions of actions, people, and places can often be found within characters' words of dialogue. A writer's job is to juggle all of the narrative elements to create a compelling story.

 PRACTICE

Write a paragraph about one of your characters to explain what his or her life has been like, and how it relates to the scene you have begun to set in your introductory paragraph. Use grammar to signal a sequence of events in your character's life. Keep in mind that the information in this writing exercise will not necessarily appear in your story unless you decide you want to incorporate it in a later stage of the writing process.

PLAN

WRITING PROMPT

Consider the unusual interactions presented in *The Book Thief* (Death and a survivor) as well as *An American Childhood* (a girl and her environment). Write a narrative about an unusual interaction that takes place between a character and someone or something else (such as a person, animal, object, entity, or environment) that reveals the character's true nature or affects the character in a meaningful way.

Your narrative should include:

- an unusual interaction that reveals or affects the main character
- a plot—a sequence of connected events with a beginning, middle, and end
- a clear setting
- vividly described characters and realistic dialogue
- precise words and phrases that appeal to the senses

Think about the elements of narrative that you studied in the Narrative Techniques and Sequencing lesson. Ask yourself the following questions to solidify your understanding: What details and events are most important in the exposition of a story? What story developments should take place during the rising action of a story? What is the purpose of a story's climax? How do writers lead readers toward a resolution of a story? What narrative techniques are the most effective?

Use the StudySync "Narrative Writing Plot Diagram" to plan a sequence of events for your narrative. Use this plot diagram, completed by the writer of the student model narrative, to help guide your planning:

Copyright © BookheadEd Learning, LLC

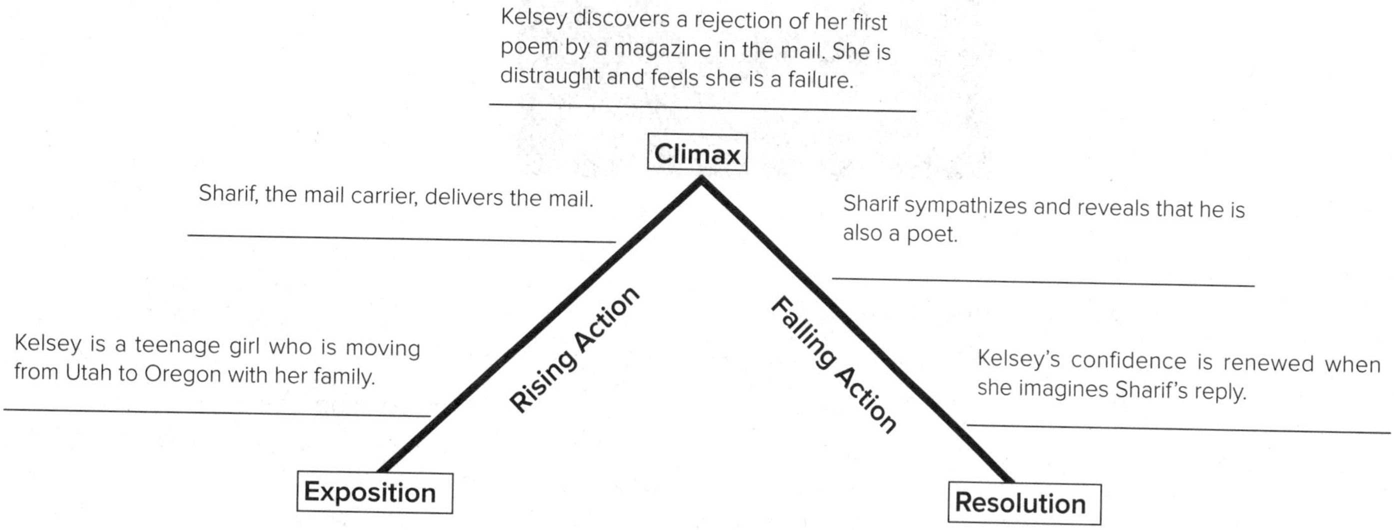

Kelsey discovers a rejection of her first poem by a magazine in the mail. She is distraught and feels she is a failure.

Climax

Sharif, the mail carrier, delivers the mail.

Sharif sympathizes and reveals that he is also a poet.

Rising Action

Falling Action

Kelsey is a teenage girl who is moving from Utah to Oregon with her family.

Kelsey's confidence is renewed when she imagines Sharif's reply.

Exposition

Resolution

SKILL: WRITING DIALOGUE

 DEFINE

Dialogue is one of the primary tools of narrative writing. Dialogue is speech between two or more characters. Dialogue is the heart of many interactions between characters, and it can also provide details in place of a descriptive narrative by illuminating a character's personality, advancing the plot, revealing details that lend insight to the driving conflict, or showcasing the setting of a narrative by using regionally or historically specific vernacular.

There are two different types of dialogue: direct and indirect. **Direct dialogue** is speech that uses a character's exact words. Direct dialogue is placed between quotation marks. Direct dialogue is the kind that is most commonly found in fiction. An example of direct dialogue would be:

"Please remember to do the laundry," Elena said.

Indirect dialogue is a second-hand report of something that was said or written, without quoting the character's exact words. Quotation marks are not used for indirect dialogue. An example of indirect dialogue would be:

Elena asked Ron to do the laundry, and Ron assured her that he would.

In dialogue between characters, it should always be clear who is speaking which lines. Speech tags such as *she said, he replied, she demanded,* and *he shouted* identify the speakers and, sometimes, their tone of voice. If the identity of the speaker is completely clear, such as if two characters have been exchanging one line at a time during a long conversation, then speech tags are sometimes omitted. Correct punctuation is important when writing dialogue.

IDENTIFICATION AND APPLICATION

Though every writer's style can differ, there are a few basic guidelines to follow when using **direct dialogue** in your narrative:

- Use open (") and closed (") quotation marks to indicate the words that are spoken by the characters.

- Always begin a new paragraph when the speaker changes.

- Make sure the reader knows who is saying what.

- When writing an interaction between characters, the author can use phrases other than simply "he said", "she said", or "they said." Depending on the nature or emotion of character's quotation, it can be followed by stronger verbs, adjectives, or adverbs. However, when in doubt, "said" and "asked" are the most reliable choices.

- Use correct punctuation marks and capitalization.

Use **indirect dialogue** without quotation marks

- when the exact words spoken are not important enough to the narrative to be showcased, but the occurrence and details of the conversation are important for the reader to know.

- when a character is describing or paraphrasing an interaction he or she had.

Writers can use both direct and indirect dialogue to develop characters by revealing the characters' opinions, reactions, emotions, experiences, personalities, and even appearances through

- what the characters say (direct or indirect speech.)

- how the characters say it (their speech patterns; the vocabulary and level of language they use.)

- the way the characters say it (usually following the quote; such as *said happily* or *yelled angrily.*)

- the characters' body language as they are speaking (such as *said, smiling.*)

- the characters' actions as they are speaking (such as *responded, twirling a lock of her hair.*)

- the characters' thoughts as they are speaking (such as, *"I'd rather not go there," he said, reflecting that he'd absolutely refuse to go there under any circumstances.*)

MODEL

Read the following passage of dialogue from "Kelsey and the Poet" to see how the author uses direct dialogue:

> "Oh, no!" she cried out.
>
> "They sent it back," Sharif said, understandingly.
>
> "This is terrible. I'll never get anything published."
>
> Sharif read Kelsey's poem over her shoulder. "May I? 'First Feelings.' I like that title. How old are you?"
>
> "Fifteen, and this is the first manuscript I've ever sent anywhere, and I'm already a miserable failure! This is a terrible omen! I'm never going to do anything worthwhile! I'm doomed for life!"

In this conversation, Kelsey and Sharif tell each other a good deal of information about themselves—which means that they tell the reader, too. In addition, their way of speaking helps characterize them. For instance, Kelsey's overwrought emotional exclamations show that she is a sensitive teenager, and her vocabulary shows her intelligence.

This excerpt also shows that the author has followed the technical guidelines for direct dialogue. She has set off the direct speech of each character with open quotation marks. She also

- places the closed quotation marks outside the end punctuation of the quote, while the rest of the sentence has its own end punctuation.
- begins a new paragraph when the speaker changes.
- makes sure the reader knows who is saying what ("she cried out," "Sharif said understandingly").

Now let's look at a second excerpt to see how the author uses indirect dialogue:

> He laughed again, and told her that no, he probably never would be, except among a couple of hundred people—but, he added, they were people who really understood poetry.

Within this passage, the author uses indirect dialogue to give the reader more information about Sharif, through the process of Sharif providing Kelsey

Reading & Writing Companion

with that information. Although the author could have invented direct dialogue for the same purpose, she decided that indirect dialogue works better in this particular passage. It makes Sharif's response "sound" quieter and more thoughtful; this way, it's easier for the reader to tell that the prospect of never becoming well-known makes him sad but also resigned. The use of indirect dialogue in the passage above creates a subtle change of mood, making it somewhat subdued compared to the direct dialogue. At the same time, the description, "He laughed again," implies that Sharif has made his peace with the realities of life.

In short, indirect dialogue can help enhance the process of characterization as well as convey important information about events. Although not apparent in this excerpt, indirect dialogue can also be an exciting technique if

- a character interprets another character's intent or emotions, putting a "spin" on what he or she said.
- we as readers witness the original conversation, and then, through a character's paraphrasing of the conversation, discover that the character is lying about it to serve his or her own purpose.

Through the use of dialogue in "Kelsey and the Poet," we as readers learn not only about the subject being discussed, but who the characters are: how they sound, how they feel, how they interact with people, and a considerable amount about their lives. Dialogue performs many jobs within a narrative—sometimes, several jobs at once.

 PRACTICE

Write a scene for your narrative in which two or more characters engage in both direct and indirect dialogue. When you are finished, trade with a partner and offer each other feedback. Has the writer followed the technical guidelines for direct dialogue? Do you see areas where the indirect dialogue can be improved? How does the dialogue help develop character? Does the dialogue reveal information about the plot? Offer each other suggestions, and remember that they are most helpful when they are constructive.

NOTES

SKILL:
CONCLUSIONS

DEFINE

A narrative **conclusion** is the story's end. It reflects on what has occurred during the narrative—what the characters have experienced and observed, what problems they have faced, and in what state they now find themselves after the **resolution** (or lack thereof) of these problems. In **fiction** narratives, the conclusion brings the plot to an end: the main **conflict** has been dealt with, the **climax** has been lived through, and a resolution has been arrived at. In **nonfiction** narratives, such as **memoir,** the conclusion often represents the opening of a new stage of life or a new understanding on the part of the author. The conclusion may point toward or hint at the characters' future without actually describing it, for the future is another story, which the writer may or may not ever write. At the conclusion, the main character might reflect on what has occurred and on the changes that have occurred within him or her. Or a different character might **reflect** based on observations of the main character. Or a **third-person narrator** might reflect on the events or give hints about what impact they have had. In most stories, the main character has been **transformed,** or changed, in a significant way. The conclusion is the place where such a transformation is most strongly revealed or suggested to the reader. After the **falling action,** the resolution settles the situation down into a calmer state, allowing the reader to form a lasting impression of the people, events, and **themes.** The author's hope is that the reader will carry that impression around for a long time after closing the story's final pages.

IDENTIFICATION AND APPLICATION

- A narrative conclusion includes the final actions and events in the story.
- Especially in fiction and often in nonfiction narratives, the conclusion presents a resolution of the conflict that the main character faced.
- Conclusions often focus on a final interaction between characters who have faced the main problem in the narrative.

- Authors often use descriptive details to elicit an emotional response from the reader upon a narrative's conclusion.

- A narrative conclusion often conveys the author's theme, or central idea, either through explicit statements or through a scene that allows the reader to infer the theme.

- The conclusion is the natural place for a final reflection by the narrator or main character, such as on the characters' lives and transformations and on the ideas the story has developed.

- A strong narrative conclusion leaves the reader with a lasting impression of the narrative that enhances the reader's memory of the work.

 MODEL

In Annie Dillard's memoir *An American Childhood*, the author describes what it looked and felt like to be a child growing up in the 1950s United States in the aftermath of World War II. Dillard's poetic, sensitive observations run all throughout the memoir, but in this excerpt, the conclusion brings them to a fine point of greater understanding—not only about the author's childhood, but about what it means to be alive, to be a person who observes and thinks and feels.

A text does not usually come with a note saying "The conclusion begins here," but in this excerpt the sentence beginning, "What a marvel it was," signals that the narrator is turning from descriptions of specific scenes to more general reflections:

> **What a marvel it was** that the day so often introduced itself with a firm footfall nearby. What a marvel it was that so many times a day the world, like a church bell, reminded me **to recall and contemplate the durable fact that I was here,** and had awakened once more **to find myself set down in a going world.**

This paragraph is not just about the sounds and events on the street where Dillard grew up. It is about the whole world. Most conclusions do not get that deep! But it is an example of how conclusions can move from the specifics of a storyline to larger concerns—to what Dillard calls "the sum of those moments" that have gone before. And that is realistic, because our experiences do sometimes cause us to think beyond what has immediately happened.

Dillard's conclusion returns to specific description in the next paragraph, but the final two paragraphs are pure reflection:

Please note that excerpts and passages in the StudySync® library and this workbook are intended as touchstones to generate interest in an author's work. The excerpts and passages do not substitute for the reading of entire texts, and StudySync® strongly recommends that students seek out and purchase the whole literary or informational work in order to experience it as the author intended. Links to online resellers are available in our digital library. In addition, complete works may be ordered through an authorized reseller by filling out and returning to StudySync® the order form enclosed in this workbook.

Reading & Writing Companion   **411**

Who could ever tire of this heart-stopping transition, of **this breakthrough shift between seeing and knowing you see, between being and knowing you be? It drives you to a life of concentration,** it does, a life in which effort draws you down so very deep that when you surface you twist up exhilarated with a yelp and a gasp.

Who could ever tire of **this radiant transition, this surfacing to awareness** and this deliberate plunging to oblivion—the theater curtain rising and falling? Who could tire of it when **the sum of those moments** at the edge—the conscious life we so dread losing—is all we have, the gift at the moment of opening it?

In addition to presenting a profound observation, this passage strengthens the characterization of the author/main character, Annie Dillard, as someone with a vast imagination and highly individual thought processes, certainly as an adult and even to some extent as a child. The passage resolves the character's emotional conflict about her existence. She asks, "Am I living?" and receives a resounding affirmative from her environment. It also expresses the adult writer's reflection upon the deep significance of those intense, solitary moments as child. This conclusion also gives further proof of what the reader has noticed all along—that Dillard is a very fine stylist in prose, really a kind of prose poet, who consistently devises unpredictable figurative comparisons ("the world, like a church bell"), original descriptive wordings ("you twist up exhilarated"), even distortions of grammar ("between being and knowing you be") to convey profound insights about the experience of being alive.

This conclusion leaves a lasting impression.

 PRACTICE

Plan and draft a conclusion to the narrative you have been prewriting and planning for this unit's extended writing assignment. Consider what you have learned from this lesson about how to use your conclusion to wrap up the plot and the characters' conflicts or interactions. Try to make your conclusion insightful and memorable. Practice using strong verbs, concrete nouns, and varied, interesting sentence structures. When you are finished, trade with a partner and offer each other feedback. Does this conclusion draft give you confidence that the writer's story will have an effective ending with a decisive resolution? Does the narrative leave you with a lasting impression, perhaps through an intriguing or insightful final thought? What do you wish this conclusion had more of, or less of? Offer suggestions, and remember that they are most helpful when they are constructive.

DRAFT

WRITING PROMPT

Consider the unusual interactions presented in *The Book Thief* (Death and a survivor) as well as *An American Childhood* (a girl and her environment). Write a narrative about an unusual interaction that takes place between a character and someone or something else (such as a person, animal, object, entity, or environment) that reveals the character's true nature or affects the character in a meaningful way.

Your narrative should include:

- an unusual interaction that reveals or affects the main character
- a plot—a sequence of connected events with a beginning, middle, and end
- a clear setting
- vividly described characters and realistic dialogue
- precise words and phrases that appeal to the senses

You have already made progress toward writing your narrative. You have planned your story and thought about how writers use event sequences, point of view, dialogue, descriptive details, and pacing to bring a narrative to life. You have drafted your introductory paragraphs and a passage containing dialogue, and you have practiced writing a strong and effective conclusion. You have also considered how your story would connect with its audience and serve its intended purpose. Now it is time to write a full draft of your narrative.

Use your prewriting graphic organizer, plot diagram, practice drafts, and other prewriting materials to help you as you write. Remember that the in the rising action of a narrative, writers introduce characters, setting, and conflict and begin to develop characters and plot. The rising action leads to the story's climax, the turning point in the story, where the most exciting action takes place. The falling action of a story occurs after the climax and leads to the resolution of the conflict and the story's conclusion. Keep readers in mind as you write, and aim to keep your audience interested.

When drafting, ask yourself these questions:

- What would be the most interesting and effective narrative point of view for this particular story?
- What can I do to improve my introduction so that readers understand expository information early in my story?
- How can I use dialogue to reveal character and advance the plot?
- How can I use pacing to make my story an engaging reading experience?
- What details can I improve and expand on to make events, characters, and settings clearer?
- How will I resolve the story's conflict in a way that is satisfying and memorable?

Before you submit your draft, read it over carefully. You want to be sure that you have responded to all aspects of the prompt.

TRANSITIONS

sync•skills
Writing

SKILL:
TRANSITIONS

 DEFINE

Transitions clarify the relationship of words and ideas. The use of transition words, clauses, and phrases helps readers understand and follow the structure of a narrative. Writers use time-order words and phrases and clauses (for example, *first, the following day,* and *soon after*) to transition from one event to the next. Transitions can also signal a change in the setting, or where a story takes place. Spatial transitions such as *on top of, behind, near,* and *to the left* help describe the settings of actions and the spatial relationships of objects or people. Transitional phrases such as *but, in addition, on the other hand,* and *as a result,* when they appear at the beginning of a paragraph, show how ideas are related to those in the previous paragraph.

 IDENTIFICATION AND APPLICATION

- Transitions act like bridges between sentences or paragraphs.
- Narrative writers use transitions to signal shifts in time or setting.
- Transitions help writers to convey sequence of events in a story.
- Writers can also use transitions to show the relationships among character experiences and story events.

 MODEL

This excerpt from *The Book Thief* contains transitions that help the reader understand the setting and sequence of events. Read the passages to identify the transitions the author used:

> As for me, I had **already** made the most elementary of mistakes. I can't explain to you the severity of my self-disappointment. **Originally,** I'd done everything right.

Please note that excerpts and passages in the StudySync® library and this workbook are intended as touchstones to generate interest in an author's work. The excerpts and passages do not substitute for the reading of entire texts, and StudySync® strongly recommends that students seek out and purchase the whole literary or informational work in order to experience it as the author intended. Links to online resellers are available in our digital library. In addition, complete works may be ordered through an authorized reseller by filling out and returning to StudySync® the order form enclosed in this workbook.

Reading & Writing
Companion

415

I studied the blinding, white-snow sky who stood at the window of the moving train. I practically inhaled it, **but still,** I wavered. I buckled—I became interested. In the girl. Curiosity got the better of me, and I resigned myself to stay as long as my schedule allowed, and I watched.

Twenty-three minutes later, when the train was stopped, I climbed **out** with them.

A small soul was in my arms.

I stood a little **to the right.**

In the first paragraph from this excerpt, the author uses the **time word** "already" as a **transition** to show that he is about to say something about what happened previously. This transition word indicates a change in the narrative sequence—a brief **flashback.** The word "originally," in the same paragraph, also serves as a transition showing that the narrator is casting a glance backward in time, at something that had happened earlier. Two paragraphs later, the phrase "Twenty-three minutes later" is a transition that moves the action forward in time. In fact, with that phrase, the sequence of events has jumped forward into the next scene, in which the train stops and the characters climb out. The narrator does not communicate anything about what happens during those twenty-three minutes. The transition enables the story to advance without going into unnecessary specifics and reinforces the idea that Death is doing something very out of the ordinary by remaining with a particular group of humans for so long.

The word "out" in "I climbed out with them" is a **spatial transition** helping the reader visualize how the characters move from the setting of the train to the next setting, the platform. Another spatial transition is "to the right," which places the narrator physically in a specific spot.

There is also **a transition of idea relationships** in the passage: "but still." That phrase presents a **contrast** between the idea that comes before it and the idea that comes after it. The narrator "practically inhaled" the sky—he was enthralled by the scenery—but then his interested wavered and focused on the girl, something he regretted.

Whether they are about time, place, or ideas, transitions are **signals** that help the reader see where the narrative is going.

PRACTICE

Write one body paragraph for your narrative that uses transition words, clauses, and/or phrases. When you are finished, trade with a partner and offer each other feedback. How effective are the transitions in indicating the passing of time? How well do the transitions show relationships among character interactions and story events? Offer each other constructive, respectful suggestions for revision.

Please note that excerpts and passages in the StudySync® library and this workbook are intended as touchstones to generate interest in an author's work. The excerpts and passages do not substitute for the reading of entire texts, and StudySync® strongly recommends that students seek out and purchase the whole literary or informational work in order to experience it as the author intended. Links to online resellers are available in our digital library. In addition, complete works may be ordered through an authorized reseller by filling out and returning to StudySync® the order form enclosed in this workbook.

Reading & Writing Companion **417**

EXTENDED WRITING PROJECT
REVISE

REVISE

WRITING PROMPT

Consider the unusual interactions presented in *The Book Thief* (Death and a survivor) as well as *An American Childhood* (a girl and her environment). Write a narrative about an unusual interaction that takes place between a character and someone or something else (such as a person, animal, object, entity, or environment) that reveals the character's true nature or affects the character in a meaningful way.

Your narrative should include:

- an unusual interaction that reveals or affects the main character
- a plot—a sequence of connected events with a beginning, middle, and end
- a clear setting
- vividly described characters and realistic dialogue
- precise words and phrases that appeal to the senses

You have written a draft of your narrative and received feedback from your classmates about how to improve it. Now you will revise your draft.

Here are some recommendations to help you revise:

- Review the suggestions made by your peers.
- Examine the introduction of your narrative.
  - › Do your introductory paragraphs contain expository information about your characters and setting?
  - › Does your story's introduction help the reader identify and visualize the setting?

> Have you introduced the conflict in the introductory paragraphs of your narrative?
> Does your introduction contain details that will interest readers?

- Evaluate the sequencing of events in your narrative.
  > Do the events in your narrative follow a logical order?
  > Have you used transition words to signal shifts in time or setting?
  > Does the sequence of events help build and develop the plot, including the main conflict?
  > Does the sequence of events focus on interactions between the main character and other people, ideas, or forces?

- Examine the prose you have used to tell your story.
  > Have you included descriptive details that help readers visualize the characters, setting, and events?
  > Are your descriptive words and phrases precise, vivid, concrete, and clear?
  > Do your transitions show the relationships among character experiences and story events?

- Look at the dialogue in your story.
  > Do your characters address one another in direct dialogue?
  > Does the dialogue reveal the characters' traits?
  > Does the dialogue help build the conflict and advance the plot?
  > Have you followed the technical guidelines for writing direct and indirect dialogue?
  > Is it clear to readers who is speaking during dialogue passages?

- Evaluate the conclusion of your story.
  > Does the conclusion present a satisfying, sensible resolution of the conflict?
  > Have you crafted a conclusion that will leave the reader with a lasting impression of your story?
  > Will your conclusion trigger an emotional response in readers?

Use these questions to help you evaluate your narrative to determine areas that should be strengthened or improved. Then revise those areas.

EXTENDED WRITING PROJECT
EDIT, PROOFREAD, AND PUBLISH

EDIT, PROOFREAD, AND PUBLISH

WRITING PROMPT

Consider the unusual interactions presented in *The Book Thief* (Death and a survivor) as well as *An American Childhood* (a girl and her environment). Write a narrative about an unusual interaction that takes place between a character and someone or something else (such as a person, animal, object, entity, or environment) that reveals the character's true nature or affects the character in a meaningful way.

Your narrative should include:

- an unusual interaction that reveals or affects the main character
- a plot—a sequence of connected events with a beginning, middle, and end
- a clear setting
- vividly described characters and realistic dialogue
- precise words and phrases that appeal to the senses

You have revised your story and received input from your peers on that revision. Now it is time to edit and proofread your work to produce a final version. This is also your last chance to correct details before submitting your narrative. Have you included all the valuable suggestions from your peers? Ask yourself: Have I included precise details described in vivid, concrete language? Does each character's dialogue sound realistic? Are there any last-minute word changes that I can make to help the reader see and hear the characters and events? What more can I do to make my story readable?

When you are satisfied with your work, move on to proofread it for errors.

- Have you formatted and punctuated dialogue correctly?
- Have you spelled all words correctly?
- Have you used noun suffixes correctly?
- Do your sentences and paragraphs flow smoothly?

Once you have made all your corrections and given your story a title, you are ready to submit and publish your work. You can distribute your writing to family and friends, post it on your blog, or submit it to a literary magazine or contest.

Powered by BookheadEd Learning, LLC

Text Fulfillment Through StudySync

If you are interested in specific titles, please fill out the form below and we will check availability through our partners.

ORDER DETAILS

Date:

TITLE	AUTHOR	Paperback/ Hardcover	Specific Edition *If Applicable*	Quantity

SHIPPING INFORMATION

Contact:

Title:

School/District:

Address Line 1:

Address Line 2:

Zip or Postal Code:

Phone:

Mobile:

Email:

BILLING INFORMATION   ☐ *SAME AS SHIPPING*

Contact:

Title:

School/District:

Address Line 1:

Address Line 2:

Zip or Postal Code:

Phone:

Mobile:

Email:

PAYMENT INFORMATION

☐ CREDIT CARD

Name on Card:

Card Number: Expiration Date: Security Code:

☐ PO

Purchase Order Number:

StudySync Text Fulfillment, BookheadEd Learning, LLC
610 Daniel Young Drive | Sonoma, CA 95476